D1711403

OXFORD CLASSICAL MONOGRAPHS

*Published under the supervision of a Committee of the
Faculty of Literae Humaniores in the University of Oxford*

The aim of the Oxford Classical Monographs series (which replaces the Oxford Classical and Philosophical Monographs) is to publish books based on the best theses on Greek and Latin literature, ancient history, and ancient philosophy examined by the Faculty Board of Literae Humaniores

THE FRAGMENTS OF TIMOTHEUS OF MILETUS

EDITED WITH
AN INTRODUCTION AND COMMENTARY BY

J. H. HORDERN

OXFORD
UNIVERSITY PRESS

PREFACE

WHEN I was a graduate student at Oxford, the statement that I was working on Timotheus was invariably greeted by my fellow graduates with a somewhat bewildered look. More recently I have seen the same response from my students in Dublin, and even from some more senior scholars. If this book brings his name and work greater attention, then I shall be satisfied.

Timotheus is doubtless a difficult author. An acquaintance of mine described the task of reading the *Persae* as 'unpleasantly philological', and it must be admitted that on many occasions I have myself been baffled by the poet's meaning. But I do not think this should discourage us from reading what remains of his work. He was an important poet in antiquity, and, now that so little work of this type survives, should be even more so for us. In the numerous cases where we cannot really be sure what Timotheus wrote or meant, I have simply tried to explain the possible solutions to the problem. This means that I do not necessarily commit myself to any particular interpretation, even when I supply a suggestion of my own. The commentary is heavily concerned with textual and linguistic matters. I hope, however, that the reader looking for enlightenment on more literary matters will also find something to interest him. Timotheus clearly has much to tell us about the Greeks' attitude to Asia, and about their reconstruction of the past. But he also has much to tell us about Greek poetry at an important stage in its history for which we have little other evidence. The text on the whole attempts to be conservative. I have based my text for the book-fragments on Page's, whose numeration I have decided to retain for convenience of reference. The edition of the papyrus of *Persae* is completely new, as is the apparatus. It has not always been possible to produce a text free from obscurities: with an author as complex as Timotheus one is reluctant to introduce too many uncertain conjectures or supplements.

The book began life as a D.Phil. thesis, written in the three years between 1995 and 1998. My greatest debt is owed to my supervisor, Martin West, whose scholarly perspicacity and superb knowledge of Greek have aided me at every turn. Dirk Obbink provided invaluable papyrological advice and support. I examined the papyrus in Berlin in Easter 1997, with financial assistance from the Craven Committee, and am grateful for the help afforded me there by Dr Günther Poethke. Chris Collard read a draft of the thesis in 1997, and made several useful comments. My examiners, James Diggle and Peter Parsons, saved me from many errors and misapprehensions. James Diggle, in particular, provided me with six densely typed pages of notes after the viva—'not', he said, 'for the thesis, but for the book'. I would like to thank him for his confidence. The difficult process of transformation from thesis to book was overseen by Gregory Hutchinson, who made many new suggestions and devoted to the work much invaluable care and attention. Particular thanks go to the Press's copy-editor, Dr Leofranc Holford-Strevens, who pulled the book into shape in the final stages, imposed order on still-unruly sections (thus making it, I hope, a little more readable), and whose perceptive questioning caused me to revise my opinions on a number of issues even at so late a stage. Without their assistance the book would be much worse than it is, but needless to say all errors and faults are entirely my own. Further thanks go to Corpus Christi College, Oxford, where I spent three pleasant years with the aid of a Commonwealth Scholarship, and to the Fellows, especially Ewen Bowie and Stephen Harrison, who asked me to organize a seminar series where I first presented my views on the *Cyclops*. Richard Janko kindly allowed me to see his unpublished text of Philodemus' *On Poetry* (Oxford, 2000), which contains a new fragment included here with his permission. Sections of the text have appeared in two previous articles, 'Two Notes on Greek Dithyrambic Poetry', *CQ*[2] 48 (1998), 289–91, and 'Observations on the *Persae* of Timotheus', *CQ*[2] 49 (1999), 433–8; I am grateful to Oxford University Press for permission to republish these here. A Research Fellowship at University College, Dublin, provided time to complete the work of revision. Finally, I would like to thank David Mackie and Ian Repath for their support and friendship both on and off the cricket field, and my parents, whose generosity enabled me to live in a style well beyond a student's usual means.

J.H.

CONTENTS

REFERENCES AND ABBREVIATIONS

THE following list not only records all general works cited frequently in the text, but also attempts to give a complete bibliography on Timotheus, apart from a few short notices of Wilamowitz's *editio princeps* of *Persae* that add nothing new. I therefore note several works not cited in the book, but to whose existence it seems worth calling the reader's attention.

ABV	J. D. Beazley, *Attic Black-Figure Vase-Painters* (Oxford, 1956)
Ageno¹	F. Ageno, 'Note a Timoteo', *Studi della scuola papirologica*, 3 (1920), 86–110
Ageno²	—— 'Nuove note a Timoteo', *Aegyptus*, 1 (1920), 269–96
Alexiou	M. Alexiou, *The Ritual Lament in Greek Tradition* (Cambridge, 1974)
Amado Rodruíguez	Mª. T. Amado Rodríguez, 'Las distintas interpretaciones de μακραυχενόπολους (Timoteo, «Persas», 89–90)', in *Actas del VII Congreso Español de Estudios Clásicos* (Madrid, 1989), 95–100
von Arnim	H. von Arnim (ed.), *Stoicorum veterum fragmenta* (Leipzig, 1903–24)
Aron	K. Aron, *Beiträge zu den Persern des Timotheos* (diss. Erlangen; Greifswald, 1920)
*ARV*²	J. D. Beazley, *Attic Red-Figure Vase-Painters*, 3 vols. (Oxford, 1963²)
Barker	A. Barker, *Greek Musical Writings*, 2 vols. (Cambridge, 1984–9)
Bassett	S. E. Bassett, 'The Place and Date of the First Performance of the *Persians* of Timotheus', *CP* 26 (1931), 153–65
Bechtel	F. Bechtel, *Die griechischen Dialekte*, 3 vols. (Berlin, 1921–4)
Bélis	A. Bélis, *Corpus des Inscriptions de*

Delphes, iii: *Les Hymnes à Apollon* (Paris, 1992)

Bélis, '*Ajax*'   A. Bélis, 'Un *Ajax* et deux Timothée', *REG* 111 (1998), 74–100

Bergk   T. Bergk, *Poetae Lyrici Graeci* (Leipzig, 1882⁴)

Bippart   G. Bippart, *Philoxeni, Timothei, Telestis dithyrambographorum reliquiae* (Leipzig, 1843)

Blass¹   F. Blass, review of Wilamowitz, *GGA* 8 (1903), 653–70

Blass²   —— review of Wilamowitz, *APF* 3 (1906), 268–75

Bowra   C. M. Bowra, 'Varia Lyrica', *Mnem.*³ 1 (1934), 179–80

Borchardt   L. Borchardt, 'Ausgrabungen der Deutschen Orient-Gesellschaft bei Abusir im Winter 1901/2', *Mitt. d. Deut. Orient-Gesellschaft*, 14 (1902), 1–59

Brussich, 'Artemide'   G. F. Brussich, 'L'inno ad Artemide di Timoteo', *QUCC* 34 (1990), 25–38

Brussich, 'Lingua'   —— 'La lingua di Timoteo', *QTLCG* 1 (1970), 51–80

Brussich, rec.   —— review of Janssen, *Sileno*, 15 (1989), 327–31

Buck   C. D. Buck, *The Greek Dialects* (Chicago, 1955²)

Burkert   W. Burkert, *Greek Religion* (Oxford, 1985)

CA   *Collectanea Alexandrina*, ed. J. U. Powell (Oxford, 1925)

Campbell   D. A. Campbell, *Greek Lyric Poetry*, v (Cambridge, Mass., and London, 1993)

Casson   L. Casson, *Ships and Seamanship in the Ancient World* (Baltimore and London, 1995²)

CEG   *Carmina epigraphica Graeca*, ed. P. A. Hansen, 2 vols. (Berlin and New York, 1983–9)

Chantraine   P. Chantraine, *Dictionnaire étymologique de la langue grecque* (Paris, 1968)

Chantraine, *Formation*   P Chantraine, *La Formation des noms en grec ancien* (Paris, 1968²)

Chantraine, *Grammaire*   ——*Grammaire homérique*, 2 vols. (Paris, 1942–53)

Colvin   S. C. Colvin, *Dialect in Aristophanes* (Oxford, 1999)

Conomis   N. C. Conomis, "Κριτικά σταχυολογήματα", *Hellenika*, 38 (1987), 140–1

Craik   E. Craik (ed.), *'Owls to Athens': Essays on Classical Subjects for Sir Kenneth Dover* (Oxford, 1990)

Cricca (1984)   E. Cricca, 'Note ai «Persiani» di Timoteo (fr. 15P) I', *GFF* 7 (1984), 105–9

Cricca (1985)   —— 'Note ai «Persiani» di Timoteo (fr. 15P) II', *GFF* 8 (1985), 9–14

Croiset   M. Croiset, 'Observations sur les *Perses* de Timothée de Milet', *REG* 16 (1904), 323–48

Crönert   W. Crönert, 'De Elpenore Timothei', *SO* 14 (1935), 126–33

Dale   A. M. Dale, *The Lyric Metres of Greek Drama* (Cambridge, 1968²)

Danielsson   O. A. Danielsson, 'Zu den Persern des Timotheos', 'Weiteres zu den Persern des Timotheos', *Eranos*, 5 (1903), 1–39, 98–128

Del Grande   C. Del Grande, *Ditirambografi: Testimonianze e frammenti* (Naples, 1947)

Del Grande, 'Timoteo'   —— 'Timoteo, «Persiani»', vss. 99–101', in *Filologia minore* (Milan and Naples, 1956), 187–94

Denniston   J. D. Denniston, *The Greek Particles* (Oxford, 1954²)

DGE   E. Schwyzer (ed.), *Dialectorum Graecarum exempla epigraphica potiora*, rev. P. Cauer (Leipzig, 1923²)

Diehl   E. Diehl, *Anthologia lyrica Graeca*, ii (Leipzig, 1925¹, 1942²)

Diggle, *Euripidea*   J. Diggle, *Euripidea* (Oxford, 1994)

Diggle, *Studies*   ——*Studies on the Text of Euripides* (Oxford, 1981)

DK   H. Diels and W. Kranz (eds.), *Die Fragmente der Vorsokratiker* (Berlin, 1961¹⁰)

Düring	I. Düring, 'Studies in Musical Terminology in Fifth Century Literature', *Eranos*, 43 (1945), 176–97
Ebeling	H. L. Ebeling, 'The *Persians* of Timotheus', *AJP* 46 (1925), 317–31
Edmonds	J. M. Edmonds, *Lyra Graeca*, iii (Cambridge, Mass., and London, 1940²)
Edmonds, 'Notes'	—— 'Some Notes on the *Persians* of Timotheus', *PCPS* 130 (1925), 4–17
Ellingham	C. J. Ellingham, 'Timotheus's *Persae*', in J. U. Powell and E. A. Barber (eds.), *New Chapters in Greek Literature* (Oxford, 1921), 59–65
Farnell	L. R. Farnell, *Cults of the Greek States*, 5 vols. (Oxford, 1896–1909)
Farnell, *GLP*	G. S. Farnell, *Greek Lyric Poetry* (London, 1891)
FGE	D. L. Page, *Further Greek Epigrams* (Cambridge, 1981)
FGrH	F. Jacoby *et al.* (eds.), *Die Fragmente der griechischen Historiker* (Berlin and Leiden, 1923–)
FHG	C. and T. Müller (eds.), *Fragmenta historicorum Graecorum* (Paris, 1853–70)
Fraccaroli	G. Fraccaroli, 'Note critiche ai *Persiani* di Timoteo', *RFIC* 39 (1911), 223–36
Fraenkel, *Kl. Beitr.*	Eduard Fraenkel, *Kleine Beiträge zur klassischen Philologie*, 2 vols. (Rome, 1964)
Fraenkel, *Nomina Agentis*	Ernst Fraenkel, *Geschichte der griechischen Nomina Agentis auf -τήρ, -τωρ, -της (-τ-)* (Strasburg, 1910–12)
Friedrich	J. Friedrich, 'Das Attische im Munde von Ausländern in Aristophanes', *Philol.* 75 (1918), 274–303
Frisk	H. Frisk, *Griechisches etymologisches Wörterbuch*, 3 vols. (Heidelberg, 1960–72)
Führer	R. Führer, *Formproblem-Untersuchungen zu den Reden in der frühgriechischen Lyrik* (Munich, 1967)

Fuochi	M. Fuochi, review of Wilamowitz, *AeR* (1903), 56–8
Gargiulo (1996)	T. Gargiulo, 'Mare e vino nei *Persiani*: una congettura a Timoteo, fr. 791, 61–62 Page', *QUCC* 54 (1996), 73–81
Gargiulo (1997)	—— 'Timoteo, *Persiani* 70–71 P.', *Lexis*, 15 (1997), 163–7
Gildersleeve	B. Gildersleeve, review of Wilamowitz, *AJP* 24 (1903), 222–36
GMAW	E. G. Turner and P. J. Parsons, *Greek Manuscripts of the Ancient World* (*BICS* Suppl. 46; London, 1987²)
Gomperz	T. Gomperz, 'Skylla in der aristotelischen Poetik und die Kunstform des Dithyrambos', *Jahrb. f. klass. Philol.* 133 (1886), 771–5
Gould, 'Hiketeia'	J. Gould, 'Hiketeia', *JHS* 93 (1973), 74–103 = *Myth, Ritual, Memory, and Exchange* (Oxford, 2001), 22–74
GP	*The Garland of Philip*, ed. A. S. F. Gow and D. L. Page, 2 vols. (Cambridge, 1968)
Groeneboom	P. Groeneboom, 'Varia', *Mnem.*² 44 (1916), 319
Gurlitt	L. Gurlitt, 'Der Dichter Timotheos und sein Gedicht zum Ehren der Opis zu Ephesos', *Philol.* 19 (1906), 382–7
Hall, *Barbarian*	E. Hall, *Inventing the Barbarian* (Oxford, 1989)
Hall, 'Drowning'	—— 'Drowning by Nomes: The Greeks, Swimming and Timotheus' *Persians*', in H. A. Kahn (ed.), *The Birth of the European Identity: The Europe–Asia Contrast in Greek Thought 490–322 BC* (Nottingham, 1993), 44–80
Hansen (1984)	O. Hansen, 'On the Place and Date of the First Performance of Timotheus' *Persae*', *Philol.* 128 (1984), 135–8
Hansen (1990)	—— 'The So-Called Prayer to the Fates and Timotheus' *Persians*', *RhM*² 133 (1990), 190–2
Hartung	I. A. Hartung, 'Über den Dithyrambos', *Philol.* 1 (1846), 395–420

HE	*Hellenistic Epigrams*, ed. A. S. F. Gow and D. L. Page, 2 vols. (Cambridge, 1965)
Headlam	W. Headlam, 'Various Conjectures II', *JPh* 21 (1892), 84–5
Herington	J. Herington, *Poetry into Drama: Early Tragedy and the Greek Poetic Tradition* (Berkeley and Los Angeles, 1985)
Hertel	A. Hertel, *Timotheos, Perserne: Den græske Nomospoesi* (Copenhagen, 1907) [non vidi]
van Herwerden	H. van Herwerden, 'Timotheos. *Perser* 105', *BpW* 28 (1903), 896
Herzfeld	E. Herzfeld, *The Persian Empire: Studies in the Geography and Ethnicity of the Ancient Near East* (Wiesbaden, 1968)
Hiller	E. Hiller, s.v. 'Timotheos', *Bursians Jb* 26 (1881), 134–5
Hiller–Crusius	—— and O. Crusius, *Anthologia Lyrica* (Leipzig, 1897)
Hordern, '*Cyclops*'	J. H. Hordern, 'The *Cyclops* of Philoxenus', *CQ*[2] 49 (1999), 445–55
Hordern, 'Notes'	—— 'Two Notes on Greek Dithyrambic Poetry', *CQ*[2] 48 (1998), 289–91
Hordern, 'Observations'	—— 'Some Observations on the *Persae* of Timotheus', CQ[2] 49 (1999), 433–8
ICS	O. Masson, *Les Inscriptions chypriotes syllabiques* (Paris, 1983)
IEG	*Iambi et elegi Graeci*, ed. M. L. West, 2 vols. (Oxford, 1989–92[2])
Immisch	O. Immisch, review of Wilamowitz, *Neue Jbb. für klass. Alt.* 61 (1903), 65–6
Inama	V. Inama, review of Wilamowitz, *RIL* 36 (1903), 626–49
Janssen	T. H. Janssen, *Timotheus, Persae* (Amsterdam, 1984)
Janssen, *Commentaar*	——*De 'Perzen' van Timotheus: Inleiding en commentaar* (diss. Utrecht, 1976)
Jurenka	H. Jurenka, review of Wilamowitz, *ZÖG* 54 (1903), 577–87

K.–A.	R. Kassel and C. Austin, *Poetae comici Graeci* (Berlin and New York, 1984–)
Kaibel	G. Kaibel, *Comicorum Graecorum fragmenta*, i (Berlin, 1899, rev. K. Latte, 1958)
Keil	B. Keil, 'Zu den Persern des Timotheos', *Hermes* 48 (1913), 99–140
Kenyon	F. G. Kenyon, review of Wilamowitz, *EHR* 18 (1903), 762–4
Korzeniewski	D. Korzeniewski, 'Die Binnenresponsion in den Persern des Timotheos', *Philol.* 118 (1974), 22–39
Kovacs	D. Kovacs, *Euripidea* (Leiden, 1992)
Kühner–Blass	R. Kühner and F. Blass, *Ausführliche Grammatik der griechischen Sprache*, 2 vols. (Hanover, 1890–2³)
Kühner–Gerth	—— and B. Gerth, *Ausführliche Grammatik der griechischen Sprache*, 2 vols. (Hanover, 1898–1904³)
Kukula (1904)	R. C. Kukula, 'Die angebliche Jahrtausendfeier des Dianatempels von Ephesos', *ZÖG* 55 (1904), 1–8
Kukula (1905)	—— 'Brände des ephesischen Artemisions', *Jh. des öst. arch. Inst.* 8 (1905), 23–32
van Leeuwen	J. van Leeuwen, 'Ad Timothei Persarum carminis lyrici fragmentum nuper repertum', *Mnem.*² 31 (1903), 337–40
Levi	L. Levi, 'Intorno a Timoteo', *RSA* 9 (1904–5), 54–68
LIMC	J. Boardman *et al.* (eds.), *Lexicon iconographicum mythologiae classicae*, 18 vols. (Zurich, 1981–99)
Longman	T. Longman, 'Timotheus, *Persae* 162', *CR*² 4 (1954), 208–9
LSJ	H. G. Liddell and R. Scott, *A Greek–English Lexicon*, rev. H. Stuart Jones and R. McKenzie, with revised Supplement (Oxford, 1996⁹)
Maas	P. Maas, s.v. 'Timotheos', *RE* viA, cols. 1331–7
Marzi	G. Marzi, 'Il «decreto» degli Spartiani

<table>
<tr><td></td><td>contro Timoteo', in B. Gentili and R. Pretagostini (eds.), La musica in Grecia (Rome and Bari, 1988), 264–72</td></tr>
<tr><td>Mayser–Schmoll</td><td>E. Mayser and H. Schmoll, Grammatik der griechischen Papyri aus der Ptolemäerzeit (Berlin, 1970²–)</td></tr>
<tr><td>Mazon</td><td>P. Mazon, 'Les Perses', RPh 27 (1903), 209–14</td></tr>
<tr><td>Meineke</td><td>A. Meineke, 'Kritische Bemerkungen I. Zu Timotheus dem Lyriker', Philol. 12 (1858), 368–9</td></tr>
<tr><td>Melber</td><td>J. Melber, 'Der neuaufgefundene kitharodische Nomos des Timotheos von Milet, "Die Perser"', Bayerisches Gymnasium, 5/6 (1903), 419–27 [non vidi]</td></tr>
<tr><td>van Minnen</td><td>P. van Minnen, 'The Performance and Readership of the Persai of Timotheus', APF 43 (1997), 246–60</td></tr>
<tr><td>ML</td><td>R. Meiggs and D. Lewis, A Selection of Greek Historical Inscriptions to the End of the Fifth Century BC (Oxford, 1988)</td></tr>
<tr><td>Morrison–Williams</td><td>J. Morrison and R. Williams, Greek Oared Ships (Cambridge, 1968)</td></tr>
<tr><td>N²</td><td>A. Nauck (ed.), Tragicorum Graecorum fragmenta (Leipzig, 1889²)</td></tr>
<tr><td>Nieddu</td><td>G. F. Nieddu, 'Parola e metro nella sphragis dei Persiani di Timoteo (PMG fr. 971.202–236)', in Pretagostini ii. 521–9</td></tr>
<tr><td>Paduano</td><td>G. Paduano, 'Una versione poetica dei Persiani di Timoteo', in Pretagostini ii. 531–6</td></tr>
<tr><td>Para</td><td>J. D. Beazley, Paralipomena: Additions to ABV and ARV² (Oxford, 1971)</td></tr>
<tr><td>Parker, Miasma</td><td>R. Parker, Miasma: Pollution and Purification in Early Greek Religion (Oxford, 1983)</td></tr>
<tr><td>Parker, Religion</td><td>——Athenian Religion: A History (Oxford, 1996)</td></tr>
<tr><td>Parker, Songs</td><td>L. P. E. Parker, The Songs of Aristophanes (Oxford, 1997)</td></tr>
</table>

PEG	A. Bernabé (ed.), *Poetarum epicorum Graecorum testimonia et fragmenta, Pars I* (Leipzig, 1987)
PGB	W. Schubart (ed.), *Papyri Graecae Berolinenses* (Berlin, 1911)
Pickard-Cambridge	A. W. Pickard-Cambridge, *Dithyramb, Tragedy and Comedy* (Oxford, 1927)
Pickard-Cambridge²	—— *Dithyramb, Tragedy, and Comedy*, rev. T. B. L. Webster (Oxford, 1962²)
Pickard-Cambridge, *Festivals*	—— *The Dramatic Festivals of Athens*, rev. J. Gould and D. M. Lewis (Oxford, 1968²)
PMG	D. L. Page (ed.), *Poetae melici Graeci* (Oxford, 1962)
PMGF	M. Davies (ed.), *Poetarum melicorum Graecorum fragmenta*, i (Oxford, 1991)
Pretagostini	R. Pretagostini (ed.), *Tradizione e innovazione nella cultura greca da Omero all'età ellenistica: Scritti in onore di Bruno Gentili*, 3 vols. (Rome, 1993)
Pritchett	W. K. Pritchett, *The Greek State at War*, 5 vols. (Berkeley, 1971–91)
Privitera (1952)	G. A. Privitera, 'Timoteo, *Persiani*, vv. 102–104', *Maia*, 5 (1952), 82–4
Privitera (1953)	—— 'Due passi dei *Persiani* di Timoteo', *Maia*, 6 (1953), 214–19
Pulleyn	S. Pulleyn, *Prayer in Greek Religion* (Oxford, 1997)
Reinach	T. Reinach, 'Les *Perses* de Timothée', *REG* 16 (1903), 62–83
Rijksbaron	A. Rijksbaron, *The Syntax and Semantics of the Verb in Classical Greek: An Introduction* (Amsterdam, 1984)
Risch	E. Risch, *Wortbildung der homerischen Sprache* (Berlin and New York, 1974²)
Saija	A. Saija, 'Interpretazione metriche', *Analecta papyrologica*, 4 (1992), 29–32
Schmidt	M. Schmidt, *Diatribe in dithyrambum poetarumque dithyrambicorum reliquias* (Berlin, 1845)
Schönewolf	H. Schönewolf, *Der jungattische Dithyrambos* (diss. Giessen, 1938)

Schoofs	S. Schoofs, *La vie de Timothée de Milet* (diss. Lüttrich, 1934/5)
Schroeder	O. Schroeder, review of Wilamowitz, *BpW* 23 (1903), 897–906
Schwyzer	E. Schwyzer, *Griechische Grammatik*, 3 vols. (Munich, 1939–53)
Seaford, 'Hyporchema'	R. Seaford, 'The "Hyporchema" of Pratinas', *Maia*, 29/30 (1978/9), 81–94
Seeliger	K. Seeliger, review of Aron, *BpW* 40 (1920), 913–16
Seider	R. Seider, *Paläographie der griechischen Papyri*, 2 vols. (Stuttgart, 1967–70)
Setti	G. Setti, review of Wilamowitz, *RSA* 7 (1903), 590–4
SH	H. Lloyd-Jones and P. J. Parsons, *Supplementum Hellenisticum* (Berlin and New York, 1983)
Sitzler (1897)	J. Sitzler, s.v. 'Timotheos', *Bursians Jb* 92 (1897), 138
Sitzler (1903)	—— review of Wilamowitz, *NPhR* 18 (1903), 409–13
Sitzler (1907)	—— s.v. 'Timotheos', *Bursians Jb* 133 (1907), 245–58
Sitzler (1919)	—— s.v. 'Timotheos', *Bursians Jb* 178 (1919), 99–101
Sitzler (1922)	—— review of Aron, *Bursians Jb* 191 (1922), 62
SLG	D. L. Page (ed.), *Supplementum Lyricis Graecis* (Oxford, 1974)
Smyth	H. W. Smyth, *Greek Melic Poets* (London, 1904)
Snodgrass	A. M. Snodgrass, *Arms and Armour of the Greeks* (London, 1967)
Stanford	W. B. Stanford, 'Marginalia', *Hermathena*, 97 (1963), 107–9
Strazulla	V. Strazulla, *I Persiani di Eschilo ed il nomo di Timoteo* (Messina, 1904)
Stevens	P. T. Stevens, *Colloquial Expressions in Euripides* (Hermes Einzelschr. 38; Wiesbaden, 1976)
Sudhaus	S. Sudhaus, 'Zu den Persern des Timotheos', *RhM²* 58 (1903), 481–99
Susemihl	F. Susemihl, 'Timotheos von Milet bei

	Aristot. *Poet.* 2', *RhM²* 35 (1880), 486–8
Sutton	D. F. Sutton, *Dithyrambographi Graeci* (Hildesheim, 1989)
Taccone	A. Taccone, *Antologia della melica greca* (Turin, 1904), 237–47
Threatte	L. Threatte, *The Grammar of Attic Inscriptions*, 2 vols. (Berlin and New York, 1980–98)
Thumb–Kiekers	A. Thumb and E. Kiekers, *Handbuch der griechischen Dialekte*, i (Heidelberg, 1932)
Thumb–Scherer	A. Thumb and A. Scherer, *Handbuch der griechischen Dialekte*, ii (Heidelberg, 1959)
TrGF	B. Snell, R. Kannicht, and S. Radt, *Tragicorum Graecorum fragmenta* (Göttingen, 1971–)
Tropea	G. Tropea, 'Ancora su Timoteo', *RSA* 7 (1903), 595–601
Wærn	I. Wærn, *ΓΗΣ ΟΣΤΕΑ: The Kenning in Pre-Christian Greek Poetry* (Uppsala, 1951)
Watzinger	C. Watzinger, *Griechische Holzsarkophage aus der Zeit Alexanders des Großen* (Leipzig, 1905)
West, 'Analyses'	M. L. West, 'Metrical Analyses: Timotheus and others', *ZPE* 45 (1982), 1–13
West, *Metre*	—— *Greek Metre* (Oxford, 1982)
West, *Music*	—— *Ancient Greek Music* (Oxford, 1992)
West, 'Stesichorus'	—— 'Stesichorus', *CQ²* 21 (1971), 302–14
West, *Stud. Aesch.*	—— *Studies in Aeschylus* (Stuttgart, 1990)
West, *Studies*	—— *Studies in Greek Elegy and Iambus* (Berlin and New York, 1974)
Wilamowitz	U. von Wilamowitz–Moellendorff, *Timotheos, Die Perser* (Leipzig, 1903)
Wilamowitz, *Lichtdruck*	—— *Der Timotheos-Papyrus (Lichtdruck-Ausgabe)* (Leipzig, 1903)
Wilamowitz, 'Perser'	—— 'Die Perser des Timotheos', *Mitt.*

	d. Deut. Orient-Gesellschaft, 14 (1902), 51–9
Wilamowitz, *Textgesch.*	—— *Die Textgeschichte der griechischen Lyriker* (Berlin, 1900)
Wilamowitz, *Verkskunst*	—— *Griechische Verskunst* (Berlin, 1921²)
Zimmermann	B. Zimmermann, *Dithyrambos: Geschichte einer Gattung* (Göttingen, 1992)

Other abbreviations are as in LSJ and *APh*, or easily identifiable. The numbering of fragments follows *PMG* and *PMGF* for melic poets; *IEG* for elegy and iambus; E. Lobel and D. L. Page, *Poetarum Lesbiorum Fragmenta* (Oxford, 1955) for the Lesbians; *TrGF* for the tragedians, with the exception of Euripides, who is cited according to Nauck (N²); Kassel and Austin (K.–A.) for comedy, but Kaibel for Epicharmus and Sophron.

References to Simonides are to *PMG* unless otherwise indicated (fr. eleg. = *IEG*). Epic fragments are cited from *PEG* (Bernabé). Epigrams are cited from *GP* and *HE* where possible. Pindar and Bacchylides are cited from the most recent Teubner editions: B. Snell and H. Maehler, *Pindarus*, 2 vols. (Leipzig, 1987–9) and *Bacchylides* (Leipzig, 1992). Callimachus is cited after Pfeiffer (Oxford, 1949–53), Satyrus' *Life of Euripides* after Kovacs.

Old Persian inscriptions are mainly cited after R. G. Kent, *Old Persian: Grammar, Texts, Lexicon* (New Haven, 1953²); the Behistun inscription after R. Schmitt, *The Bisitun Inscriptions of Darius the Great* (London, 1991).

Timotheus' *Persae* is abbreviated as *P.*; other fragments are given according to the numeration in *PMG*.

INTRODUCTION

THIS book gathers together the not inconsiderable remains of one of the most important and interesting figures in the history of Greek lyric poetry, Timotheus of Miletus. Timotheus was a controversial figure in his own time, and enjoyed various fortunes in antiquity until his texts vanish from the surviving record in about the fourth or fifth century AD.

The rediscovery of a large papyrus fragment of his poem describing the battle of Salamis, the *Persae*, may not have helped his case. Despite a reasonable amount of immediate scholarly interest in the papyrus, his style was almost universally deplored. In a letter to Eduard Schwartz, Ulrich von Wilamowitz-Moellendorff, the first editor, confessed his boredom with Timotheus already in 1903, the year his edition was published: 'für jetzt ist mir der Kerl langweilig und ich möchte ihn vergessen'.[1] Even with this fragment of the *Persae*, the remains of his poetry, when gathered together, look scant indeed. Of eighteen or nineteen citharodic songs we have only the half of one, and perhaps one or two scraps of others; of his eighteen dithyrambs not even one quotation firmly ascribed, and a couple of testimonia; of the many hymns, encomia, and other works only a few lines, if that. However, this is perhaps not as little as it may seem. The works of other important poets of the time, Phrynis, Philoxenus of Cythera, Telestes, Licymnius, survive in an even worse state, though all the available evidence suggests a reasonable level of popularity not just for Timotheus, but for his contemporaries, well into the imperial period, even though

---

[1] *The Preserved Letters of Ulrich von Wilamowitz-Moellendorff to Eduard Schwartz*, ed. W. M. Calder III and R. L. Fowler (Munich, 1986), no. 13. In a letter to Paul Wendland in 1902, Wilamowitz had not unfairly described the task of editing Timotheus as 'monstrously hard' ('ungeheuer schwer').

they never acquired classic status in Alexandria. Isolated testimonia point to the continued performance of their works, sometimes accompanied by new music, at least into the third century AD.

Timotheus played an important part in the musical developments which occurred in the late fifth and early fourth century. These were largely bound up with dithyrambic and citharodic poetry, though influences apparently filtered through to tragic and comic music. In later periods the *avant-garde* of this period was considered a coherent 'school', the 'New Music', and we hear occasionally of other musicians opposed to them and their innovations. This picture of the late fifth century may not be entirely correct: it is not clear, for instance, how coherent a group these musicians felt themselves to be. They are closely associated by the comic poet Pherecrates, for instance, but Timotheus himself seems to criticize Phrynis for his musical modulations. The 'New Music' could well be to some extent an invention of later scholarship. Certainly, later writers sometimes seem keen to connect the important poets in any way possible: the *Suda* improbably makes Philoxenus of Cythera a slave, bought and educated by the earlier lyric poet Melanippides of Melos. Much of their activity seems to have been carried out in Athens, which no doubt had the power and cultural influence to attract the best poets to its festivals, but we also find them courting patronage from wealthy tyrants and kings. Most of them, indeed, seem to have been non-Athenians. Their influence on later lyric is hard to judge in the absence of much material, but there is clear evidence that they had some impact on Hellenistic poetry. Indeed, many features that we now regard as characteristic of the Hellenistic period may have been foreshadowed in the lyric of the late fifth and fourth centuries. Timotheus and his contemporaries were undoubtedly important poets. It is regrettable that so little of what they wrote has survived, but this means that what little we have is even more important. Aristotle's remark, that without Timotheus we should be without much lyric poetry (*Metaph.* a 1. 993^{b}15), may still be in some senses true.

I. TIMOTHEUS OF MILETUS

A. Life[2]

If the Parian Marble can be relied upon, Timotheus was born in Miletus in about the middle of the fifth century. The damaged text (Ep. 76 p. 19 Jacoby) gives a date for his death at the age of 90 between the archonship of Cephisodorus in 366/5 and the accession of Philip II of Macedon in 357/6. On this evidence, his birth should be placed between 456/5 and 447/6. Although the accuracy of the Parian Marble is open to some doubt, its statement broadly agrees with the testimony of Diodorus (D.S. 15. 46. 6) that Timotheus was in his prime in 398, at the same time as the dithyrambographers Philoxenus of Cythera, Telestes of Selinus, and Polyidus.[3] The *Suda* (τ 620) places his death at the age of 97: this figure, like the Parian Marble's 90, is not above suspicion given the appearance in this age of other near-centenarians such as Simonides (over 90 [Lucian], *Macr.* 27; 90 Parian Marble; 89 *Suda*), Sophocles, and Isocrates.

Miletus in the mid-fifth century was still a relatively important city. It had gained strength and influence in the seventh century under the tyrant Thrasybulus, and in the sixth century was amongst the most powerful Greek cities in Asia Minor, apparently also on good terms with its non-Greek neighbours. Later, Miletus played a pivotal role in the Ionian Revolt under the tyrant Aristagoras, but after Aristagoras' defeat near Ephesus and his flight to Thrace, the city was besieged and subsequently sacked (494 BC; the occasion inspired Phrynichus' *Sack of Miletus*). The harbour was destroyed and never rebuilt; the people were killed or enslaved, though the city was repopulated after the Persian Wars. Despite some evidence for a close connection with Athens as a member of the Delian League,[4] it joined

[2] The testimonia relating to Timotheus' life are collected in the Loeb editions by Edmonds and, albeit somewhat less fully, Campbell.

[3] Philoxenus of Cythera: d. 380/79 (*Marm. Par* Ep. 69); Telestes: victorious in Athens in 402/1 (Ep. 65); Polyidus: victorious in Athens between 399/8 and 380/79 (Ep 68).

[4] Its aristocracy claimed descent from the kings of Athens, and was supported by Athens in a dispute with Samos in 441 BC.

the revolts of Athenian allies in 412, and although Athens regained control, Miletus finally fell again under Persian jurisdiction after the end of the Peloponnesian War. Timotheus seems to have spent a considerable amount of time in Athens, as did most of the well-known dithyrambic poets of the day, attracted no doubt by the high level of cultural activity. He is sometimes connected with Euripides, whose interest in the new musical trends is observable in his later lyrics, and is said to have written the tragedian's epitaph (*Vit. Eur.* 17–18, p. 4 Kovacs = *FGE* pp. 307–8), though the ascription is extremely doubtful. He was certainly well enough known in Athens to have been satirized in the list of dithyrambic abusers of Music in Pherecrates' *Cheiron.* He boasts of a victory over Phrynis, the most prominent citharodic poet of the previous generation, who is said to have won the first Panathenaic prize for citharody in 446/5,[5] and who may still have been alive in 423 when Aristophanes mentioned him at *Nub.* 969 ff. From Timotheus' tone, it may be assumed that the victory occurred relatively early in his career. Philotas, a pupil of Polyidus, later boasted in turn of a victory over Timotheus (Athen. 8. 352 B); although the date is uncertain, it was presumably later in Timotheus' career rather than earlier. As we have seen, Polyidus' floruit is put by Diodorus in 398 BC; according to Ps.-Plutarch (*Mus.* 21. 1138 B) he was a major proponent of a musical school apparently opposed to the developments of the New Music.

Plutarch recounts an anecdote connecting him with the Macedonian king Archelaus. Timotheus, singing for Archelaus, is said to have alluded (πολλάκις: on numerous occasions? Or perhaps as a refrain?) to his parsimony with the words 'You commend earth-born silver'; to this Archelaus once responded, 'But you demand it' (fr. 801). This story is of doubtful authenticity: the line may well have been taken out of context, and the narrative invented around it, as so often with ancient biographical material. Certainly it is hard

⁵ Σ Ar. *Nub.* 971a (p. 187 Holwerda), reading with Meier ἐπὶ Καλλι⟨μάχ⟩ου ἄρχοντος, rather than Καλλίου as given in the MSS (see J. A. Davison, *JHS* 78 (1958), 40–1 = *From Archilochus to Pindar* (London, 1968), 60–1), which would refer to 457/6, 412/11, or 406/5.

to imagine a context in which the line could have been used explicitly of Archelaus. Stephanus of Byzantium records a tradition that Timotheus died in Macedonia, and quotes his epitaph (pp. 452–3 Meineke): θνήιϲκει δ' ἐν Μακεδονίαι. ἐπιγέγραπται δ' αὐτῶι τόδε· πάτρα Μίλητος τίκτει Μούϲαιϲι ποθεινὸν | Τιμόθεον κιθάραϲ δεξιὸν ἡνίοχον (FGE anon. 124a). This 'epitaph' is more probably a late epigram.[6] Nevertheless, a connection with Macedon is not at all unlikely. Archelaus, and his successors after him, made concerted efforts to attract well-known poets from other parts of Greece, and to make Macedonia a centre of Panhellenic culture. Euripides and Agathon notoriously spent time there; the dithyrambic poet Melanippides of Melos the younger visited the court of Perdiccas, who died c.413; and Choerilus of Samos received a stipend from Archelaus.[7] The *Suda* (τ 620) connects both Euripides and Timotheus with the reign of Philip II (357–336): ἦν δὲ (Τιμόθεος) ἐπὶ τῶν Εὐριπίδου χρόνων τοῦ τραγικοῦ, καθ' οὓς καὶ Φίλιππος ὁ Μακεδὼν ἐβαϲίλευεν. Although it is technically possible that Timotheus died after Philip's accession, the statement as a whole is clearly inaccurate. Reinesius, and at first Rohde, argued that the statement was the result of a confusion with Timotheus of Thebes; Rohde later revised this view and suggested that Philip had been confused with Archelaus, with whom both poets might more plausibly be connected.[8] Perhaps Timotheus' presence in Macedon may also have been motivated by the troubled relationship between Athens and Miletus in the later fifth century, or

---

[6] Cf. the various other epigrams from the Hellenistic period or later purporting to be the epitaphs of famous poets: e.g Archilochus: Theocr. *AP* 7. 664 (*HE* 3434 ff.); Alcman: Leon. Tarent. *AP* 7. 19 (*HE* 2321 ff.), Antip. Thess. *AP* 7. 18 (*GP* 135–40); Stesichorus: Antip. Thess. *AP* 7. 75 (*GP* 483–6); Sappho: Antip. Sid. *AP* 7. 14 (*HE* 236 ff.), Tullius Laur. *AP* 7. 17 (*GP* 3909–16), Antip. Thess. *AP* 7. 15 (*GP* 481–2); Anacreon: Antip. Sid. *AP* 7. 27 (*HE* 260 ff); Aeschylus: Antip. Thess. *AP* 7. 39 (*GP* 141–4) etc.

[7] Melanippides: *Suda* μ 454, 455, Choerilus: Theopomp. *FGrH* 115 F 236 We might also compare Philoxenus of Cythera's residence at the court of Dionysius I of Syracuse (D.S 15. 6, *Suda* φ 397, *PMG* 816, etc.), or Arion's stay at the court of Periander.

[8] E. Rohde, *RhM*² 33 (1878), 192 n. 1; *RhM*² 34 (1879), 574 = *Kl Schr.* 1. 148, 378. Chares (*FGrH* 125 F 4) knows of a Timotheus as a piper in Philip's retinue, and it is possible that Timotheus of Thebes is meant; see also the discussion of *PMG* 840 below, pp. 74–5.

by the subsequent Persian dominion there. There is little anecdotal evidence to associate him with his home town. The *Suda* gives his father's name as Thersander, Philopolis, or Neomusus; the first name is also given by Alexander Aetolus. Philopolis and Neomusus are probably comic patronymics, although Bippart suggested that they may have been the paternal names of Timotheus of Thebes and Timotheus the comic poet.[9] However, Neomusus is not attested as a Greek personal name, and is readily understood as a joke about Timotheus' musical innovations and the pride he took in them. Such comic genealogies were by no means uncommon: we might compare that provided for Cinesias by Plato Comicus (fr. 200 K.–A.), who describes him as the son of Oeagrus (Kock) or Diagoras (Kaibel)[10] and Pleurisy. Other possible examples are not so obviously comic in origin, but Arion is named in the *Suda* (α 3886) as the son of Cycleus, clearly a reference to his importance as the reputed inventor of the dithyramb (cf. the phrase κύκλιος χορός). A similar joke can be seen in the name Μύρμηξ, used, according to the *Suda* (φ 393), for Philoxenus of Cythera, and referring to the meandering modulations of his music; the New Music was regularly compared to 'ant-runs' by the comic poets.[11] The *Suda* (ι 487) says that Ion of Chios was the son of Orthomenes, but was nicknamed the son of Xuthus, after the mythical Ion; this joke could also have been originally made in comedy (cf. Ar. *Pax* 832 ff.).

Philopolis, by contrast, is well attested as a Greek name in Euboea, Rhodes, Teos, and Attica itself, although all the evidence dates to the fourth century or later,[12] and possibly

---

[9] Bippart 57–8.

[10] Codd. have Εὐαγόρου. Oeagrus was the father of Orpheus, appropriately for a poet. Diagoras was a well-known atheist, and Cinesias appears to have had his own reputation for impiety (cf. Ar. *Ra.* 366; Lysias fr. 53 Thalheim). His father was actually Meles; cf. Pl. *Gorg.* 501 E–502 A

[11] Cf. Ar. *Thesm.* 100 for the μύρμηκος ἀτραπούς of Agathon; Pherecr. 155. 23 K.–A. for the ἐκτραπέλους μυρμηκιάς of Timotheus; also Ar. *Nub.* 971 τὰς κατὰ Φρῦνιν ταύτας τὰς δυσκολοκάμπτους (sc. καμπάς).

[12] J. K. Davies, *Athenian Propertied Families 600–300 BC* (Oxford, 1971), 467–8, gives evidence for a Philopolis in Athens in the 4th c. (cf. *IG* ii². 1499, 12658, 12967). P. M. Fraser and E. Matthews, *A Lexicon of Greek Personal Names*, i (Oxford, 1987), list a Philopolis from Euboea in the 3rd c. (c.262 BC), two from Rhodes (one from c.236 BC, the other from the 2nd c. BC) and one from Tenos (3rd c. BC).

in this case confusion arose in later biography between two people called Timotheus and the names of their fathers. However, Philopolis may have been the name of a real individual in fifth- or fourth-century Athens, totally unconnected with Timotheus of Miletus, though for some reason associated with him by a comedian's witticism (as perhaps with Diagoras and Cinesias in Plato's genealogy). Perhaps the word had overtones in the context of Miletus' revolt in 412; the sobriquet may, for instance, have indicated that Timotheus remained loyal to Athens.

The other main anecdotal material about Timotheus links him with Sparta, and with hostile treatment at the hands of the Spartan ephors at one of the musical festivals there. This tradition may have been developed to explain his statements about the Spartans at the end of *Persae*, and have no historical basis.[13] Timotheus is supposed to have used a lyre with more than the standard seven strings, and as a result incurred the censure of the authorities. The story later seems to have become a stock literary anecdote, and Plutarch tells it of both Phrynis (*Agis* 10. 799 F–800 A; *Apophth. Lac.* 220 C) and Terpander (*Inst. Lac.* 17. 238 C), in addition to Timotheus.

The earliest source for this anecdote dates to the second century BC: the grammarian Artemon of Cassandrea (*FHG* iv. 342), whose note is preserved at Athen. 14. 636 E, relates that Timotheus, when performing at Sparta, used a *magadis*, traditionally regarded as an instrument somewhat like a harp or lyre, but having an exceptionally large number of strings.[14] When the ephors objected and threatened to remove the offending strings, he is said to have pointed at a nearby statuette of Apollo, shown playing an instrument with the same number of strings. Cicero (*Leg.* 2. 39) is familiar with a version apparently close to this one, though in his account Timotheus is convicted. At least by the second century AD a traveller could see Timotheus' lyre hanging in the market-place in Sparta, where it was supposedly exhibited after his conviction (Paus. 3. 12. 10). Of

---

[13] For the phenomenon, cf. M. Lefkowitz, *The Lives of the Greek Poets* (London, 1981), *passim*.

[14] This sense of *magadis* may be a late development; see West, *Music*, 72–3.

course, the lyre which Pausanias saw is unlikely to have been Timotheus'. Plutarch (*Agis* and *Apophth. Lac.*, locc. citt.) relates versions in which one of the Ephors at the Carneian games simply asked Timotheus from which end of the lyre he should remove the superfluous strings. Particularly interesting in this connection is the forged Laconian Decree against Timotheus preserved at Boethius, *Mus.* 1. 1 (p. 182 Friedlein).[15] This purports to be the official decree censuring Timotheus for the use of more than seven strings at the festival of Eleusinian Demeter,[16] and for corrupting the young men by teaching them his *Semele*. The Decree not only appears to contain a reminiscence of Timotheus' own phrasing at the end of *Persae* (cf. *P.* 212 n.), but is apparently modelled on the decree against

[15] The Decree (re-edited by Calvin Bower in his translation, *Fundamentals of Music* (New Haven, 1989), 4–5) almost consistently rhotacizes final sigma, which was not a feature of classical or Hellenistic Laconian. It appears, irregularly applied, only in a few texts of the 2nd c. AD, though its origin and the exact date at which it became a feature of Laconian are unknown; it is probably an independent development, although the same feature is attested at an earlier date for Elean (Buck 56; Bechtel iii. 329–30; Thumb–Kiekers 91, 243). Its survival in Tsakonian, the modern Greek descendant of Laconian, indicates that it must have been adopted generally by the dialect at some point, perhaps well after the end of the literary record (O. Charalambakis, *Lakonikai Spoudai*, 10 (1990), 463–82). However, the archaeological record indicates that Laconian was supplanted as an inscriptional language by the West Greek koine by the end of the 2nd c. BC, and its revival in a few inscriptions of the 2nd c. AD reflects an antiquarian revival of the type which finds parallels elsewhere in the Greek world at the time (e.g. the Lesbian poems of Balbilla). If the text of the Decree dates to this period, Boethius is likely to have taken it from the 2nd-c. AD treatise on music by Nicomachus, on which he is known to have been heavily dependent. Whether Boethius' treatise is essentially a translation or paraphrase of this work, or whether his debt was somewhat less, is still debated: see U. Pizzani, *Sacris Erudiri*, 16 (1965), 5–164, esp. 160–2, C. Bower, *Vivarium*, 16 (1978), 1–45; also H. Chadwick, *Boethius: The Consolations of Music, Logic, Theology and Philosophy* (Oxford, 1981), 84–101.

[16] The Spartan Eleusinium was situated at Kalyvia, about 2 km west of Amyclae, and although competitions in honour of the goddess are attested from the 5th c. BC (*DGE* 12), there is no evidence that contests, either musical or athletic, were ever actually held at the sanctuary; see S. Walker, in A. Cameron and S. Walker (eds.), *The Greek Renaissance in the Roman Empire* (*BICS* Suppl. 55; London, 1989), 131; J. M. Cook, *ABSA* 45 (1950), 261–81. At Eleusis itself games were celebrated, independently of the Mysteries, in biennial and quadrennial sequences in the classical period (R. M. Simms, *GRBS* 16 (1975), 269–79). Spawforth affirms that no contests are known for the Spartan festival for Demeter (in P. Cartledge and A. Spawforth (eds.), *Hellenistic and Roman Sparta* (London and New York, 1989), 194), but Hesychius (ε 2026) also mentions an agonistic festival for Sparta ('Ελευcίνια· ἀγὼν θυμελικὸc ἀγόμενοc Δήμητρι παρὰ Λάκωcιν).

Socrates, which Favorinus (ap. D.L. 2. 40)[17] claimed was preserved in the Metroon in Athens.[18] Socrates is accused of rejecting the traditional civic gods and εἰcαγούμενοc καινὰ δαιμόνια; Timotheus of rejecting playing on seven strings (διὰ τᾶν ἑπτὰ χορδᾶν κιθάριξιν ἀποcτρεφόμενορ) and introducing a multiplicity of notes (πολυφωνίαν εἰcάγων). Socrates thereby corrupts the young (τοὺc νέουc διαφθείρων); Timotheus λυμαίνεται τὰρ ἀκοὰρ τῶν νέων.

B. The Poems

(i) The oeuvre

Two lists of Timotheus' works survive in ancient sources:

1. Steph. Byz. (pp. 452–3 Meineke): ἐποίηcε νόμων κιθαρωιδικῶν βίβλουc ὀκτωκαίδεκα εἰc ἐπῶν ὀκτακιcχιλίων τὸν ἀριθμόν, καὶ προνόμια ἄλλων χιλίων (Salmasius: χίλια codd.).
2. Suda, τ 620 (iv. 556–7 Adler): . . . γράψαc δι' ἐπῶν νόμουc μουcικοὺc ιθ', προοίμια λς', Ἄρτεμιν, διαcκευὰc η', ἐγκώμια, Πέρcαc {ἢ: del. Bernhardy}, Ναύπλιον, Φινεΐδαc, Λαέρτην, διθυράμβουc ιη', ὕμνουc κα', καὶ ἄλλα τινά.

Rohde plausibly conjectured that the source for both the *Suda* (here immediately dependent on Hesychius of Miletus) and Stephanus was ultimately Philo of Byblos' περὶ πόλεων καὶ οὓc ἑκάcτη αὐτῶν ἐνδόξουc ἤνεγκεν, written in the second century AD.[19] A full list, probably similar to or identical with that in the *Suda*, would have stood in Philo's text; Stephanus, when he came to transcribe it, may only have mentioned the citharodic νόμοι, the most famous of Timotheus' works. Consequently, it is likely that we should equate Stephanus' eighteen books of nomes with the *Suda*'s nineteen nomes (perhaps Stephanus' ὀκτωκαίδεκα was influenced by the following ὀκτακιcχιλίων; but the actual number of nomes is unknown).[20] A nome that took up an entire book would not be excessively long: the roll containing *Persae* seems to have held no other poems. In both authors ἐπῶν may seem to imply hexameters; the *Suda*, for instance,

---

[17] Fr. 51 Mensching = fr. 34 Barigazzi.
[18] Burnett on Pl. *Apol.* 24 B 8. Cf. also Xen. *Mem.* 1. 1; Pl. *Apol.* 24 B 8–10.
[19] E. Rohde, *RhM*² 34 (1879), 561 ff., 572 = *Kl. Schr* i. 365 ff., 376.
[20] So e.g. Smyth 463.

always uses δι' ἐπῶν of hexametrical verse, including elegiacs. This would be unlikely given Timotheus' reputation for polymetric astrophic verse, and thus what we have (especially considering Stephanus' ungrammatical εἰς ἐπῶν) is presumably a corrupted version of Philo's text.[21]

The προνόμια mentioned by Stephanus are presumably equivalent, at least in theory, to the Suda's προοίμια; these were introductory compositions, which were originally independent of particular poems, both in the case of epic, and apparently in that of citharodic poetry.[22] The sense to be given to διασκευαί is unclear; Wilamowitz regarded them as 'Überarbeitungen alter Nomen', which would suit the use of διασκευή to describe a new edition or recension of a work (cf. e.g. Ep. Aristeas 310, Athen. 3. 110 b). We could perhaps imagine them to be versions of traditional pieces of music such as auletes produced of the Pythikos Nomos.[23] Few of the other genres of poetry recorded by the Suda are represented in the fragments. Eighteen dithyrambs are mentioned, and are well represented in the fragments; fr. 803 might be from a hymn, and fr. 800 perhaps from a paean.

We have the names of eleven of Timotheus' poems. Some of these are certainly dithyrambs. The Ajax was performed by the aulete Timotheus of Thebes in the later fourth century, and Elpenor by a boys' chorus in 318 BC. The Birthpangs of Semele was also most probably a dithyramb, since Dio Chrysostom mentions its being performed by an aulete. Alcaeus of Messene refers to the piper Dorotheus' performing a work of the same name. The Laconian Decree in Boethius says of Timotheus τὰρ γὰρ Cεμέλαρ ὠδῖναρ οὐκ

---

[21] ἔπος may denote a line of verse, e.g. Hdt. 4. 29, [Pl.] Min. 319 D, Isoc. 12. 136, etc.; a spoken line in a play, Ar. Ra. 862, 956. It can even be used for counting lines in a prose work (although the more prosaic cτίχος is favoured in such cases): see Dover on Ar. Ra. 358; C. Wendel, Die griechisch-römische Buchbeschreibung verglichen mit der des vorderen Orients (Halle, 1949), 34, 38–40.
[22] For the sense of προνόμιον, cf. Pollux 4. 53, and especially the apparent equation of the two terms at Jul. Or. 2. 56 D ὥсπερ ἦν ἄξιον τὸν ἐκ τοιούτων προοιμίων καὶ προνομίων ἀρξάμενον, and see further on fr. 788. The set of prooimia for epic was traditionally ascribed to Homer (the Homeric Hymns), and that for citharody to Terpander. See West, 'Stesichorus', 308–9. It is not unusual for these to be listed separately; cf. e.g. Suda a 3886 (of Arion) ἔγραψε δὲ ἄιcματα· προοίμια εἰς ἔπη β'.
[23] Cf. West, Music, 212–14.

ἔνδικα τὼρ νέωρ διδάκκε, where διδάκκε stands for common Greek ἐδίδαϲκε, the usual verb for teaching a work to a chorus. The parallel to the charge against Socrates may have influenced the phrasing here, and we cannot be certain that the author of the Decree knew that the *Semele* was a choral work. Plato (*Rep.* 3. 395 DE) refers to the musical mimesis of a woman in labour, but it is not clear in the context what sort of poetry he is discussing (tragedy and comedy are mentioned at *Rep.* 3. 395 AB). Finally, Aristotle, who in his *Poetics* (26. 1461^{b}30) mentions pipers 'dragging the chorus-leader about if they are playing the *Scylla*', guarantees that the *Scylla* was also dithyrambic.

By contrast the *Artemis* and *Persae* were certainly monodic, the latter definitely a nome, and reported to have been performed at the Nemean games in 205 BC by the citharode Pylades of Megalopolis. Alexander Aetolus and Plutarch state that the *Artemis* was sung by Timotheus in performances at Ephesus and Athens respectively, but it is uncertain whether this means that we should regard it as a nome, since other forms of lyric, such as hymns, could also be monodic. However, it may be significant that both the *Suda* and Plutarch give it a name, Ἄρτεμιϲ, rather than a description, e.g. ὕμνοϲ εἰϲ Ἄρτεμιν. Less certainly we might include the *Nauplius* and *Niobe* among the monodic fragments. Suetonius (*Nero* 39. 3) records that Nero performed a monodic *Nauplius*, possibly Timotheus' poem. Citharodic *Nauplioi* are mentioned by two epigrammatists (Crinagoras, *AP* 9. 429; Lucillius, *AP* 11. 185). Wilamowitz asserted that the *Nauplius* was a dithyramb, since its critic Dorion was an aulete, and doubted whether Timotheus' music would still have been available in the first century AD.[24] The evidence for the survival of the original music is certainly not strong, but it is unreasonable to suppose that Dorion could not have criticized music belonging to a genre other than the one he practised. Suetonius (*Nero* 21. 2) also knows of a monodic *Niobe* performed by Nero in a contest at Rome. Wilamowitz argued that the death-scene, analogous to that in Euripides' *Alcestis*, would be more easily dealt with in a nome than in a

---

[24] Wilamowitz 80 n. 2.

dithyramb, but there are no real grounds for thinking this.[25] The genre of the *Cyclops* remains uncertain.[26] Nothing is known of the *Laertes* or the *Phineidae*. Some MSS of the *Etymologicum Magnum* have Ὀδυccείαc δ′ or the equivalent written after the quotation from Timotheus at 630. 30 (fr. 799). According to Gaisford, P (Paris. gr. 2654 = N: 1273 AD) has the full text; M (Marcianus gr. 530: xiii s.) has simply oᵟ; while D (Bodleian, D'Orville X 1.1,2 = O), based on a thirteenth-century exemplar, has oᵟ᾿ δ′.[27] On the strength of these readings several scholars have suggested that the four poems on Odyssean themes, the *Elpenor*, *Cyclops*, *Laertes*, and *Scylla*, should be grouped together to form an 'Odyssey' in four books.[28] Two of these poems were definitely dithyrambic, the *Scylla* and *Elpenor*, but there is no firm evidence for the genre of the other two. Dithyrambic cycles of poems are not otherwise attested,[29] but in the mid-second century BC Menecles of Teos composed a citharodic cycle of narrative poems on Cretan legend and history: ἀλλὰ καὶ ἐπεδείξατο Μενεκλῆc μετὰ κιθάραc τά τε Τιμοθέου καὶ Πολυίδου καὶ τῶν ἁμῶν παλαιῶν ποιητᾶν καλῶc καὶ πρεπόντωc εἰc(ή)νεγκε δὲ κύκλον ἱcτορημένον ὑπὲρ Κρήταc κα[ὶ τ]ῶν ἐν [Κρή]ται γεγονότων θεῶν τε καὶ ἡρώων, [ποι]ηcάμενο[c τ]ὰν cυναγωγὰν ἐκ πολλῶν ποιητᾶ[ν] καὶ ἱcτοριαγράφων (*Inscrip. Cret.* i. 280–1). Such cycles may have been associated with the dithyrambic poets of the late fifth century, whose work, including that of Timotheus, was obviously known to Menecles, but κύκλοc in such a context could refer to no more than a collection of otherwise

[25] Wilamowitz 81 n. 1
[26] See the discussion in the commentary, and my 'Cyclops', 445–55.
[27] Cf. R. Reitzenstein, *Geschichte der griechischen Etymologika* (Leipzig, 1897), 212 ff. Both MSS (A and B) of the *Et. Gen.* omit the words.
[28] So e.g. O. Waser, *Skylla und Charybdis in der Literatur und Kunst der Griechen und Römer* (Zürich, 1894), 66–8; Sitzler (1897); Del Grande 90–9. Bergk oddly appears to think that the marginalia are referring to Homer (*sed potius dithyrambi nomen latet*), and gives the dithyramb the name Ὀδυccεύc; he goes on to comment: 'ceterum Ὀδυccεύc fortasse non diversum fuit a *Cyclope*', but such a view hardly accounts for the reference to 'book 4' Bippart (72–3) ascribes the fragment to the *Cyclops*, but does not give a reason for doing so.
[29] The only apparent parallel might be Simonides' *Deliaka*, perhaps a collection of dithyrambs composed for the festival at Delos, but there is no evidence that these were connected thematically: the only one whose name we know is the *Memnon* (fr. 531). The collection may have been the result of later editorial activity.

unrelated poems on the same general theme, as in the case of the Epic Cycle. Furthermore, even if accepted as evidence for citharodic cycles, this does not establish that dithyrambic cycles also existed. The *Cyclops* and *Elpenor* were both performed separately in the fourth century, and a better alternative would be to believe that the organization of these four poems into a group, if such an arrangement ever existed, was the result of later compilation.

We can obtain from this a general overview of the type of theme which Timotheus tended to choose for his poems. Most of the titles suggest narratives, predominantly mythological. The *Persae* is his only known poem on a historical subject, but of course the Persian wars had already been 'mythologized' in tragedies by Phrynichus and Aeschylus. We cannot tell, however, in what way these narrative themes were developed. In the *Persae* there is a clear division of the poem into speeches and third-person narrative, and although there are sometimes transitional verses between these two elements, these are never gnomic statements or generalizations as in Pindar's epinicians. In this concentration on simple narrative Timotheus shows closer similarities to his fellow citharode Stesichorus, who only rarely indulges in gnomic utterance (e.g. frr. 244, 245, though both without a context; they may be from speeches within poems).

There are clearly a number of poems connected with epic or tragedy, but the precise influence of either genre is generally difficult to ascertain; both may have played some part in the development of any particular poem. Stories about the Trojan War are a favourite source of material (*Aias, Elpenor, Cyclops, Nauplius, Scylla*); in the case of the *Cyclops* in particular there is no suggestion of tragic influence, but close linguistic parallels between fr. 780 and several passages in the *Odyssey*. We may again compare the material favoured by Stesichorus, whose *Helen, Wooden Horse, Sack of Troy* (probably the same poem), *Nostoi*, and *Oresteia* all dealt with the Trojan War or its aftermath. A citharodic preference for poems on the same basic material is attested by Stesichorus' other poems (e.g. the Heracles group: *Geryoneis, Cycnus, Cerberus*), and by Menecles' Cretan cycle. The most immediate influence on the *Persae*

seems to have been Aeschylus' play of the same name. If we
had more fragments of the other named works, a better
assessment could no doubt be made.

(ii) Dating

Considerable energy has been wasted in attempts to identify
dates for two of the poems, the *Artemis* and the *Persae*. In
both cases there is simply too little reliable information to
reach a convincing conclusion.

(a) *Artemis* (fr. 778)

Macrobius, probably on the authority of Alexander Aetolus,
from whom he subsequently quotes, claims that the *Artemis*
was commissioned by the Ephesians for the rededication of
the temple of Artemis, which was destroyed by the arson of
Herostratus in 356 (cf. Cic. *De div* 1. 47, *De nat. deor.* 2. 69;
Plu. *Alex.* 3. 665 E). Since 356 is an impossibly late date for
the composition of the *Artemis*, we might believe that
Alexander should be referring to the dedication after its
completion in 430, but at this early stage Timotheus is
unlikely to have acquired a reputation as great as that
ascribed to him by Alexander and Macrobius.

Wilamowitz believed that Alexander's statement arose
from some confusion, perhaps with the aulete Timotheus
of Thebes, while Kukula suggested that the temple may
have been partially destroyed by fire in the early fourth
century.[30] Some late authorities record that there was a fire
in 398 (Hier. *Chron.* 2. 10, p. 118 Helm–Treu; Syncellus,
p. 311. 1 Mosshammer), but the authority for this statement
is unknown. It may simply be the result of confusion about
the date of Herostratus' arson, though there is nothing *prima
facie* impossible about Kukula's theory.[31] 398 is the year
given by Diodorus as Timotheus' floruit; Plutarch (*De
superstit.* 10. 170 A, *De aud. poet.* 4. 22 A) has him performing
the *Artemis* in Athens in the presence of Cinesias, though
there is no guarantee that this anecdote is true. The latter

---

[30] Wilamowitz 10; Kukula (1905).
[31] There is no archaeological evidence for such a partial destruction, but we
should not necessarily find any, especially if the damage was relatively minor. For
the archaeological evidence, see A. Bammer, *Das Heiligtum der Artemis von Ephesos*
(Graz, 1984), 74–83.

was alive at least until 393, when he moved a motion in the Council that a compliment be paid to Dionysius I and his brothers and brother-in-law (*IG* ii². 18).[32] In the same year he is mentioned by Aristophanes at *Eccl.* 330.[33]

(b) *Persae* (frr. 788–91)

The date of the *Persae* has been the subject of considerable debate; opinions have ranged from 419 to 399–396 (Ol. 95). At any rate it was roughly the middle period of Timotheus' life, given ἰcήβαν at *P.* 214);[34] a *terminus ante quem* is possibly provided by the context of fr. 790 (if Plutarch's account is reliable), which is said to have become a common saying in Asia Minor in 395, at which stage the poem was presumably relatively well known. However, this would not indicate whether the poem had just been composed or whether it had already become something of a classic.

Wilamowitz noted the absence of any reference to Athens in this poem, and stated that this would only be possible after the events of 412, when Miletus rebelled from Athenian hegemony, and hardly likely before the end of the war.[35] Nevertheless, it is hard to imagine a poem on Salamis in which Athenians were not at least implicitly present, and there is some indication that the first part of the poem may have had a different emphasis from the second. Their absence from the extant section proves nothing. Equally ambiguous is Timotheus' statement about the Spartans. Wilamowitz took μέγαc ἀγεμών (207) to be a complimentary acknowledgement of Sparta's hegemony over Greece after 404. By contrast, Bassett suggested 412 as a probable *terminus ante quem* as the year in which Sparta made a treaty with Persia (Thuc. 8. 18), largely in the hope of receiving Persian financial assistance (cf. Thuc. 8. 37).[36] But the correct interpretation of the lines about the

[32] See M. N Tod, *Greek Historical Inscriptions* (Oxford, 1948), ii. 24–6 no 108
[33] For the date of the play, see R. G. Ussher, edn , pp. xx–xxv.
[34] So Maas and Ebeling respectively. For a fairly complete list of the various suggestions, see Hansen (1984). Levi (54–68) suggested 407; Keil (137 n. 1) names 405 as the *terminus post quem*, without any clear reason.
[35] Wilamowitz 61.
[36] In this connection Bassett also places some importance on the reference to Persian gold in fr. 790 He proceeds to argue for a close connection between the *Persae* and the Phrygian's aria in Euripides' *Orestes* (produced in 408) The

Spartans is hardly clear, and need not in any case refer so closely to political affairs. Bassett also cites Satyrus' anecdote that the proem to the poem was written by Euripides, in order to prevent Timotheus from committing suicide out of depression at the reception of his work.[37] This unconvincing story is hardly a trustworthy piece of evidence. The biographies of Greek poets from later periods are often largely fabrications based on the comedians and on quotations from the poets themselves,[38] and allegations in comedy that tragedians were not responsible for their own work are not uncommon, especially in the case of Euripides.[39] Some such joke could be the source for Satyrus' story. Hansen's suggestion that the poem was written to celebrate the victory of the Athenian fleet at Cyzicus in the spring of 410 is entirely conjectural.[40]

In fact, whether treated as an affirmation of Athenian superiority and national pride, or as presenting a Panhellenic ideal in order to affirm the cause of Greek unity, the poem could easily be fitted into a date either before or after the end of the war.

The location of the first performance has also generated

parallels which Bassett adduces are, however, either negligible or absurd, and in any case similarity of theme or treatment would not indicate whether the *Persae* depends on *Orestes*, or vice versa, and certainly would not guarantee that the one was roughly contemporary with the other.

[37] Satyrus, *Vit. Eur.* p. 26 Kovacs; cf. Plu. *An sen* 23. 795 D.

[38] See M R. Lefkowitz, *The Lives of the Greek Poets* (London, 1981), esp. 88–104 on Euripides' *Vita*, which, however, does not know Satyrus' story about Euripides and Timotheus.

[39] For instance, Iophon and Sophocles (Ar. *Ra.* 73–9 with Dover); Euripides and Cephisophon (Ar. *Ra.* 944, 1407–9, 1415 with Σ); Euripides and Iophon or Timocrates of Argos (said to have written his lyrics at *Vit. Eur.* 5 Kovacs); Euripides and Mnesilochus or Socrates (ibid.).

[40] See Hansen (1984) His belief that the complex structure of the poem indicates that it could not have been first performed at an ordinary festival is completely without support. Increased complexity appears to be a general feature of late 5th-c. lyric, and there is no reason to believe that the *Persae* is at all unusual. His view that it may have been performed at the Munichia (a festival of Artemis on 16 Munichion) is perhaps more felicitous, if the battle of Salamis was celebrated annually at the festival; cf. Plu. *De glor. Athen.* 7. 349 F τὴν δ' ἕκτην ἐπὶ δέκα τοῦ Μουνυχιῶνος Ἀρτέμιδι καθιέρωσαν, ἐν ἧι τοῖς Ἕλλησι περὶ Cαλαμῖνα νικῶσιν ἐπελάμψεν ἡ θεὸς πανσέληνος, *Lys.* 15. 1 and see L. Deubner, *Attische Feste* (Berlin, 1932), 204. Parker, *Religion*, 187 n. 124, however, believes that Plutarch's account is ahistorical, and even if there was a celebration in later times it may not yet have been customary in the late 5th c.

considerable discussion. Arguing again from the absence of
any reference to Athens and the improbability of a Spartan
context, Wilamowitz suggested the Panionion at Mycale,
though later revised his view on the very reasonable grounds
that the Panionion was not celebrated in the fifth century,
and instead proposed that the location of the first performance was Miletus.[41] Other suggestions follow the same line
of argument.[42] Such speculations are largely inconclusive;
Zenobius mentions the poem's success in Athens (2. 47),
and implies that this was its first performance, but that is no
path to certainty either.

II. GENRE

A. The Dithyramb

(i) Nature

In its earliest form the dithyramb was a type of impromptu
komastic song involving a chorus and an *exarchon* (Archil.
fr. 120). The *exarchon* probably improvised a simple solo
part, which was joined with a formulaic and well-known
refrain. In early times it was connected with the cult of
Dionysus, but there is evidence for performances at non-
Dionysiac festivals from at least the fifth century. It is not
my purpose here to trace the development of the dithyramb
from this early stage through to the classical period. Suffice
to say that it appears to have been established as a literary
genre at some stage late in the sixth century, and about the
time of Pindar may have altered its form from a processional
to a circular chorus.[43] At earlier periods there may in any
case have been some variation in form from state to state.
Herodotus 1. 23 perhaps implies that the semi-mythical
Arion performed dithyrambs to cithara-music, though this
passage is notionally set in the sixth century. However, by
the end of the sixth century in Athens, and apparently

[41] Wilamowitz 62–3; *Sitzb. Preuß. Akad.* 1906, 38–57 = *Kl. Schr.* v/1. 128–51.
[42] Patras or Pellene: Croiset 325–7; somewhere in Ionia: Reinach 67, 76 n. 2;
Ephesus (the Ephesia): Aron 37, 40 ff.
[43] Pickard-Cambridge² 9–31. The transformation of the dithyramb from a
processional to circular chorus is argued convincingly by A. D'Angour, *CQ²* 47
(1997), 331–51.

elsewhere in the Greek world, it was a choral song performed by a circular chorus and always accompanied by the
aulos.

Little connection with the cult of Dionysus can be identified in the extant fragments from the fifth century. Plato
(*Rep.* 3. 394 C) associates the dithyramb instead with heroic
narrative. He divides poetry into two main types: that in
which the story is presented διὰ μιμήσεως, including especially comedy and tragedy, and that in which it is presented
δι' ἀπαγγελίας, especially the dithyramb. The distinction
here is clearly between a form in which third-person narrative is dominant and a form in which the action is presented
by actors playing different roles. In the Hellenistic period a
controversy between Aristarchus and Callimachus over the
genre of Bacchylides' *Cassandra* (Ba. 23) suggests a similar
view. A second-century papyrus commentary on Bacchylides (P. Oxy. 2368 col. i) records that Aristarchus believed
the poem to be a dithyramb διὰ τὸ παρειλῆ[φθαι ἐν α]ὑτῆι τὰ
περὶ Κασ[cάνδρας. This obviously implies a belief, perhaps
derived from Plato, that dithyrambs involved narratives.
Callimachus, by contrast, regarded the poem as a paean
because it included the ritual cry ἰή. A similar debate, over
the paeans of the Locrian poet Xenocritus or Xenocrates, is
preserved in Ps.-Plutarch (*Mus.* 10. 1134 c). Some ancient
scholars believed these to be dithyrambic because they
included heroic themes; Xenocritus may in fact have been
a citharode.[44] The view that dithyrambs of the fifth century
and later were mainly heroic narratives broadly agrees with
what we know of Bacchylides' poetry,[45] and with the titles of
and testimonia to the poetry of the late classical period.

Zimmermann has recently argued for a stronger link
between the late classical dithyramb and the cult of Dionysus. He calls particular attention to the emphasis on wine in
Melanippides (frr. 760, 761)[46] and Timotheus (fr. 780), and
to the story of the invention of the aulos in Melanippides
(fr. 758) and Telestes (fr. 805). However, the references to

[44] See Pickard-Cambridge[2] 10–11.
[45] Even in the clearest case of Dionysus' appearing in Bacchylides' dithyrambs
(Ba. 19), he only surfaces at the end of the poem (ll. 49–51) and not in a central role.
[46] There is no evidence to support Hartung's view that these two fragments
belong to the same poem, an *Oeneus*.

wine are unlikely to have had any particular significance beyond their immediate narrative context. The description of Athena's discovery of the aulos in Telestes can hardly have formed an integral part of the *Argo*, and may have been an introduction analogous to that at Pi. *Dith.* 2.[47] The main subject of the poem does not seem to be connected in any way with Dionysus or his cult. Similarly, although the Great Mother is mentioned by Telestes in association with the Phrygian *harmonia* (fr. 810), there is nothing to connect this fragment with a Dionysiac poem. The place of the fragment in the work of which it was part is unknown; the poem may not even have been dithyrambic. Seaford argued that the topos of musical invention, particularly prominent in the fragments of Telestes, was a feature of Dionysiac poetry and ritual.[48] But the topos is hardly restricted to dithyrambic poetry, or other forms of verse traditionally connected with Dionysus.[49]

It is not in doubt that the dithyramb *could* deal with Dionysiac subjects. At least one fragment of Melanippides was addressed to the god (fr. 762), [50] and Timotheus' *Semele* clearly dealt with the story of his birth. Licymnius may have mentioned Dionysus in an erotic context.[51] If Philoxenus wrote a Κωμαστής, as Berglein conjectured, it may also have dealt with Dionysus: κωμαστής is an epithet of the god at Ar. *Nub.* 606.[52] A late papyrus commentary, in which the names

---

[47] Athenaeus (14. 616 F) says that Telestes was here 'taking up the cudgels against' (ἀντικορυccόμενος) Melanippides, whose *Marsyas* (fr. 758) dealt with the same subject. But the Marsyas story appears to have been a frequent subject in the plastic arts in the late fifth century (see A. Weis, *LIMC* vi/1. 366–78), and Telestes may simply have been responding to a popular motif.

[48] R. Seaford, 'On the Origins of Satyric Drama', *Maia*, 28 (1976), 216–19, and n. on E *Cyc.* 464–5.

[49] e.g. Pi. *O.* 13, fr. 140b; see West, *Music*, 344–5. The large number of fragments of Telestes' work collected in Athen. 14 (frr. 805–6, 808, 810) all deal with musical inventions. Athenaeus may easily have relied for these quotations on an earlier handbook. Elsewhere he shows no knowledge of Telestes (whom he otherwise mentions only at 11 501 F–502 A in a quotation from Theopompus, fr. 4 K.–A) The only other source for Telestes is Philodemus, *De piet.* 2 (frr. 807, 812).   [50] See my 'Notes', 289–90.

[51] Licymn. fr. 768 (ap. Athen. 13. 603 D), from a dithyramb: Ἀργύννου φηcìν ἐρώμενον Ὑμέναιον γενέcθαι. But Argynnus, whom Athenaeus says Agamemnon loved, is an improbable lover for a god, better here therefore is Wilamowitz's Διονύcου (*Kl. Schr.* iv. 613–14).

[52] On the basis of *Suda* α 2657. Ἀντιγενίδης, Cατύρου, Θηβαῖος μουcικòς, αὐλωιδòς

of Melanippides, Philoxenus, and perhaps Telestes are mentioned, quotes an invocation of Dionysus at the advent of spring (*PMG* adesp. 929(*b*)), but none of the other seven fragments quoted refers to the god.[53] Another papyrus, perhaps containing fragments of Aristoxenus' *Elementa Rhythmica*, contains a number of quotations which are described as dithyrambic by Campbell.[54] But the author does not explicitly say that they are, and only two of them actually mention Dionysus. The language of these fragments is in any case simple and strongly traditional; they may be from cult hymns which bear little relation to the narrative literary dithyrambs of the classical period.[55] These few instances hardly illustrate a close relationship between the dithyramb and Dionysus cult in the fifth century. Dionysus could no doubt be addressed in dithyrambs, or be made the subject of one; but there is no reason to believe that all dithyrambs had to have something to do with Dionysus.

Of greater interest is the apparent connection between the narrative dithyramb of the fifth century and Hellenistic poetry. There is some evidence to suggest that the later dithyramb paves the way for pastoral lyric, if we may compare Philoxenus' *Cyclops* or *Galatea*, and the poems of

Φιλοξένου· οὗτος ὑποδήμασι Μιλησίοις πρῶτος ἐχρήσατο καὶ κροκωτὸν ἐν τῶι Κωμαστῆι περιεβάλλετο ἱμάτιον· ἔγραψε μέλη. The word could also simply mean 'reveller'.

[53] P. Vindob. Gr. 19996ab (1 BC/1 AD). Crönert ascribed *PMG* adesp. 929(*f*) to Timotheus, but though some phrases are vaguely suggestive (e.g. νύμφαν φοινι-κοπ[τέρ]υγα), there are no real grounds for the ascription. Frr. (*g*) and (*h*) may belong together, since both describe the effects of Hypnos. Licymnius wrote of Hypnos' love for Endymion (fr. 777).

[54] P. Oxy. 2687; L. Pearson, *Aristoxenus. Elementa Rhythmica* (Oxford, 1990), 36–44. Five of the poetic fragments were published by Page as *PMG* adesp. 926 (P. Oxy. 9); P. Oxy 2687 provides two more. Campbell published all seven fragments as lyr. adesp. 926(*a*)–(*g*); I use his numeration here.

[55] In fr. (*a*) the scene described could be the dancing of the initiated in the afterlife rather than any worldly Bacchic chorus: ἔνθα δὴ ποικίλων ἀνθέων ἄμβροτοι λ(ε)ίμακες | βαθύςκιον παρ' ἄλcος ἁβροπαρθένους | εὐιώτας χορους ἀγκάλαις δέχονται. For the motif of the holy meadow in the afterlife, cf. Pi. fr. 129 S.–M. φοινικορόδοις ⟨δ'⟩ ἐνὶ λειμώνεccι, Ar. Ra. 449; one of the gold leaves from Thurii (A4) λειμῶνάς τε ἱερους καὶ ἄλcεα Φερcεφονείας; D.S. 1. 96. 5, perhaps depending on Hecataeus (*FGrH* 264 F 25) τὰc δὲ τῶν ἀcεβῶν ἐν ''Αιδου τιμωρίαc καὶ τοὺc τῶν εὐcεβῶν λειμῶναc . . . παρειcαγαγεῖν μιμηcάμενον τὰ γινόμενα περὶ τὰc ταφὰc τὰc κατ' Αἴγυπτον . . . τοῦ δ' Ὀρφέωc τοῦτο καταδείξαντοc κτλ.; Orph. fr. 222; Pl. Gorg. 524 A, Rep. 616 B; Plu. fr. 178 Sandbach; AP 7. 189. 3–4; Orph. H. 18. 1–2. Fr. (*b*), ὅcτιc εὐθυμίηι καὶ χοροῖc ἥδεται (of an initiate?), could belong to the same poem.

Stesichorus II of Himera, to whom should probably be attributed not merely a *Cyclops*, but the *Daphnis, Calyce,* and *Rhadine* included among the spuria for Stesichorus I (frr. 277–9).[56] Philoxenus was certainly a model for Theocritus (*Idylls* 6, 11). The interest in pastoral may be extended to Polyidus of Selymbria, who is said to have made Atlas a shepherd in his poem on the Perseus myth (fr. 837). Melanippides told the story of Linus (fr. 766), though in what context is uncertain, and may have presaged the more humorous qualities of Hellenistic poetry in his ridicule of pipe-playing in the *Marysas* (fr. 758). Licymnius shows some interest in divine love affairs with mortals (frr. 768, 768A ap. Phld. *De piet.* P. Herc. 243 VI 12–18, 771), as well as in human love stories (fr. 772), with which we could perhaps compare the light-hearted interest in erotic matters found in Hellenistic epigram and elsewhere. His account of the story of Nanis was taken up in part by Hermesianax.[57]

(ii) Performance

There are a number of ancient terms used to describe dithyrambic performance. διθύραμβος is common, as are words for a dithyrambic poet derived from it, such as διθυραμβοποιός and διθυραμβοδιδάσκαλος (Ar. *Pax* 829). The form διθυραμβογράφος is not attested earlier than Tzetzes. Characteristic of the fifth century seems to be the phrase κύκλιος χορός, perhaps used to distinguish the dithyramb, which danced in a circle, from the tragic chorus, which danced in a rectangular formation. Again, there are occasional derived forms, such as κυκλιοδιδάσκαλος of Cinesias at Ar. *Av.* 1403. It is also dithyrambs to which, especially in agonistic contexts, the phrases χορὸς παίδων and χορὸς ἀνδρῶν seem to refer.

How long or how detailed the narratives were is unknown. Bacchylides' dithyrambs vary in length. The longest, poem 17, has 132 lines, but may not actually be a dithyramb.

---

[56] See M. L. West, *CQ²* 20 (1970), 206; H. J. Rose, *CQ* 26 (1932), 89 ff. L. Lehnus, *SCO* 24 (1974), 191 ff., argues in favour of Stesichorus I.

[57] Cf. Parthenius, *Erot. Path.* 22; see J. L. Lightfoot, *Parthenius of Nicaea* (Oxford, 1999), pp. 348–9, and for Parthenius' sources ibid. 504–5.

There is little evidence that the basic conditions of performance changed significantly over the course of the fifth century, although it is possible that by the late fourth century
soloists had been introduced as performances became more
professional and in the hands of the τεχνῖται (cf. [Arist.]
Probl. 19. 15).[58]

The amount of poetry produced must have been enor-
mous. Probably only the best of it was preserved into the
Hellenistic period. Some poems may not have survived
much more than a single performance. At Athens the City
Dionysia alone, for which dithyrambic choruses were first
established in 509/8, required twenty dithyrambs each year,
as each of the ten tribes seems to have produced both a
men's and a boys' chorus (cf. Σ Aeschin. 1. 10; *IG* ii². 2318.
22–4).[59] The cost of a performance could be high: the
speaker of Lysias 21 (§156) spent 5,000 drachmai on a
dithyrambic chorus for the City Dionysia (including the
cost of a tripod for the victor), as opposed to 2,000 drachmai
on a chorus for the Thargelia and 300 on one for the Lesser
Panathenaea. At the Thargelia only ten choruses competed,
five men's and five boys' ([Arist.] *Ath. Pol.* 56. 3), one for
every two tribes.[60] The διδάσκαλος was chosen by lot (Anti-
phon 6. 11–13). Performances remained in the hands of the
tribes throughout the fourth century; in the second half of
the century they acquired from the archon the right to
appoint choregoi ([Arist.], loc. cit.).

The differences between the arrangements at the City
Dionysia and the Thargelia should make us wary of assuming anything about conditions at less well-documented festivals. In fifth-century Athens the standard number of
chorus-members was fifty, but this number may also have
varied from festival to festival, and at rural competitions, in

[58] The arguments of recent scholars (D. F. Sutton, *QUCC*² 13 (1983), 37–43;
Zimmermann 127–8; West, *Music*, 365–6), that the *Cyclops* of Philoxenus of
Cythera (frr. 815–24) was quasi-dramatic, seem to me to be unsupported by the
evidence. See my '*Cyclops*', 445–55.

[59] There may have been some revivals, but there is no evidence for them until
the end of the 4th c.; see below, pp. 25, 74–5

[60] Cf. *IG* i³. 965, where the choregia of Cleisthenes son of Autocrates for the
Erechtheid and Aegeid tribes is commemorated; the chorus was taught by
Cedeides, who is mentioned at Ar. *Nub.* 984–5 as an old-fashioned poet (see
Dover on 985).

particular, it may have been hard to raise fifty singers for each chorus. Professional choruses after the fourth century may also have had fewer than fifty members.[61]

Dithyrambic performances are attested at a large number of other festivals both in Attica and in wider Greece. Most of the famous dithyrambic poets of the fifth century, with the exception of the much-abused Cinesias,[62] were non-Athenians, although several were certainly based at Athens. They probably began their careers at less prestigious local festivals. Their status in Athens is uncertain. We know of several non-Athenian tragedians, such as Pratinas of Phlius and his son Aristias, Neophron of Sicyon, Achaeus of Eretria, Spintharus of Heraclea, Hippias of Elea, and Ion of Chios, most of whom were perhaps metics.[63] The position of the dithyrambic poets may not have been significantly different, although they were probably obliged to spend more time travelling for work outside Attica. In Athens, apart from the City Dionysia and the Thargelia, we also have evidence for performances, first in the third century, at the Lenaea. The late date at which these performances were instituted implies that dithyrambic poetry retained a great deal of popularity well into the Hellenistic period, although few composers of this period are known. The genre is relatively unattested in Alexandria, and dithyrambic poets may by that stage have been largely restricted to their local communities. If so, there may have been less concern to record their texts and names. It is also intriguing that the inscription attesting the presence of dithyrambs at the Lenaea (IG ii². 3779 Νικοκλῆc . . . Λήναια διθυράμβωι) details the victories of a famous citharode, Nicocles of Taras (cf. Paus. 1. 37. 2). Although, as we have seen, in the archaic period dithyrambs were sometimes performed to the cithara, this was certainly not the case throughout the classical period, and it is possible that this 'dithyramb' was far removed from its

[61] Pickard-Cambridge 79–80.
[62] Cf. e.g. Pherecr. 155 K.–A., Plu. De glor. Athen. 5. 348 B. The remark at Σ Ar. Ra. 152–3, that he was a Theban, is an odd error, perhaps due to an association of the dithyramb with the aulos and the aulos with Thebes, which was renowned for auletes.
[63] See M. L. West, BICS 32 (1985), 72–3.

classical roots. Alternatively Nicocles may have composed dithyrambs as well as citharodic poetry, as did Timotheus and, no doubt, many other poets.[64] There is an isolated reference to performances at the Lesser Panathenaea (Lysias 21. 1–2).

Outside Athens itself dithyrambic performances are also found at the Poseidonia in the Piraeus, where they were added only in the late fourth century ([Plu.] *X orat. vit.* 7. 842 A), at Eleusis (*IG* ii². 1186), at Salamis in the early fourth century (*IG* ii². 3091), and possibly at Acharnae (*IG* ii². 3092). The last of these mentions Dicaeogenes, a tragic and dithyrambic poet of the mid-fourth century, but whether the reference in the inscription is to dithyrambs or tragedies is unclear (see also *TrGF* 52 T 2). The same inscription refers to a victory by a certain Ariphron, perhaps Ariphron of Sicyon, who is known to have been active in the early fourth century; numerous copies of his paean to Hygieia (fr. 813) are extant. It is not otherwise attested that he wrote dithyrambs. Ps.-Plutarch tells us that at the Poseidonia a minimum of three choruses competed; choregoi were appointed, but responsibility for the cost was often shared between two individuals (*synchoregia*). It seems improbable that the choruses were organized tribally. Again, although we cannot always take the date at which dithyramb is first attested at a festival to indicate the date at which it was first introduced, it is likely that the amount of evidence pointing to fourth-century performances reflects a high level of public interest in the genre at that time. Ps.-Plutarch also mentions the value of the prizes: the victor received 10 mnai, second place 8 mnai, and third place 6 mnai.[65]

---

[64] See also Pickard-Cambridge, *Festivals*, 42. For the tenuous evidence, still sometimes cited, for dithyrambic contests at the Anthesteria, see Pickard-Cambridge² 37–8; id , *Festivals*, 16–17.

[65] These are considerable sums. An inscription from the 2nd c. AD (*SEG* 38. 1462B) lists prizes at a provincial festival at Oenoanda in Asia Minor: tragedians receive 250 denarii for first place, and 125 for second. Citharodes receive 300 and 150 for first and second place. Comedians are in third place, with 200 denarii for first prize and 100 for second. Pipers for dithyrambic choruses receive even less: 125 for first, and 75 for second place. Another inscription of similar date, from Aphrodisias (*CIG* 2758) awards in one year to dithyrambic pipers 350 denarii, to tragedians 500, to comedians 400, and to citharodes 500. The same inscription

Outside Attica there is good evidence for performances at Delos at least as early as the Peisistratid period, when the island came under partial Athenian authority, and at Delphi. Simonides may have written a number of poems for performance on Delos, the *Deliaka*, of which one had the title *Memnon* (fr. 539). Dithyrambic contests continued well into the fourth century.[66] A series of archon-lists with entries recording victors in the Delian festivals provides evidence for men's and boys' choruses performing at both the Apollonia and Dionysia in Delos from about 286 to 172 (*IG* xi/2. 105–33).[67] At Delphi the performances were associated with Apollo's three-month absence during his yearly winter visit to the Hyperboreans (Plu. *De Ei ap. Delph.* 9. 389 c); they may also have been established for the Soteria in the third century (*SIG*³ 424).[68] In the Hellenistic period there was a proliferation of new agonistic festivals, and many of these must have included dithyrambic performances, like the Lenaea in Athens. There was some revival of old dithyrambs, but no doubt new pieces were also composed. Little of this material, however, has survived.[69]

B. The Nome[70]

(i) Nature

The word νόμος was adopted at an early stage to refer to musical compositions, but originally seems to have lacked any more precise meaning than 'melody'. At a later stage it

records higher awards for later festivals. For citharodic and other prizes in the 4th c. BC, see below, p. 32–3.

[66] See Parker, *Religion*, 149–51, 222–3.

[67] See Pickard-Cambridge² 3.

[68] On the latter point, see id., *Festivals*, 283–4. The Soteria were only established in the 3rd c., probably in order to commemorate the defeat of the Gauls' attack on Delphi in 279; see A. Cameron, *Callimachus and his Critics* (Princeton, 1995), 281–2. Again, the presence of dithyramb at the festival points to the genre's continuing popularity.

[69] For the preponderance of agonistic festivals in the Hellenistic period and later, and the evidence for new poetry, see ibid. 44–53.

[70] See in general H. Grieser, *Nomos: Ein Beitrag zur griechischen Musikgeschichte* (Heidelberg, 1937), *passim*; W. Vetter, *RE* xvii. 840–3; E. Laroche, *Histoire de la racine NEM- en grec ancien* (Paris, 1949), 166–71; T. J. Fleming, *CJ* 72 (1976/7), 222–33; Barker i. 249–55; West, *Music*, 215–17.

came to be used of compositions of a traditional or fixed
nature, especially for the aulodic and auletic nomes which
formed part of particular rituals or festival contests.[71]
Aulodic nomes consisted of pipe music accompanied by
singing; auletic nomes were unaccompanied. It was presumably through this connection that a citharodic composition came to be called νόμος κιθαρωιδικός, which, in turn, was
by the fifth century regularly abbreviated as νόμος, at least in
Athens. It is in this sense that we find the word defined in
the *Suda* (ν 478): νόμος· ὁ κιθαρωιδικὸς τρόπος τῆς μελωιδίας,
ἁρμονίαν ἔχων τακτὴν (G: ταύτην cett.) καὶ ῥυθμὸν ὡρισμένον,
and it is with this sense that we are concerned here.

For most Greeks the history of the nome began with
Terpander, but its prehistory goes back well into the
Mycenaean period and beyond. The Mycenaeans appear
to have taken the lyre from the Minoans: West calls
attention to a fresco found at Pylos depicting a lyre-player,
and to the discovery in the royal tomb at Attic Menidi of the
fragments of two ivory-faced lyres; these indicate that lyre-
playing was an important aspect of court life.[72] This is, of
course, presupposed by Homer. Phemius, the *aoidos* of *Od.*
1. 153–5, 325–7, sings an epic *nostos* to the accompaniment
of his cithara, and his Phaeacian counterpart, Demodocus,
sings two poems, one at *Od.* 8. 73–82 on a quarrel between
Odysseus and Achilles, the other at *Od.* 8. 266–369 on the
love of Ares and Aphrodite. The latter is accompanied by a
dancing, but not singing, chorus. The presence of a chorus
is particularly intriguing. Later citharodes always sang as
soloists, a development attributed by Proclus to the Cretan
citharode Chrysothemis (*Chrest.* ap. Phot. *Bibl.* 320[b]1). It is
unlikely that there was a stage when silent choruses always
accompanied singing to the lyre, but Stesichorus, if a
citharode, may still have been singing to the accompaniment
of a dancing chorus in the first half of the sixth century.[73]
Ps.-Plutarch (*Mus.* 8. 1134 AB) claims that the early sixth-
century aulode Sacadas of Argos composed an aulodic nome

---

[71] See Barker I. 249–55; West, 'Stesichorus', 309–11; id., *Music*, 215–17.
[72] West, *Music*, 237.
[73] Id., 'Stesichorus', 302–14; but see F. D'Alfonso, *Stesicoro e la performance*
(Rome, 1994) for arguments against this view.

(the *trimeles nomos*) for choral performance. But Clement of
Alexandria's statement (*Strom.* 1. 133), that Timotheus
introduced choruses into his nomes, is likely to be based
on a late scholarly confusion.

There is also substantial evidence for the singing of
hexameters, epic and other, to lyre accompaniment.[74] Terpander is said by Heraclides (fr. 157 Wehrli ap. [Plu.] *Mus.*
3. 1132 C) to have set to music his own and Homer's
hexameters and to have sung them in festival competitions.
Hexametric hymns were still being sung, though not necessarily to the cithara, in Epidauros in the third century AD.[75]
Aristophanes' Euripides alleges (*Ra.* 1281–2) that Aeschylus
has borrowed his tragic lyrics from the citharodic nome.
This might be expected to give us some idea of what these
early poems looked like, but the ensuing parody (1284–95)
points merely to the use of a lyre as accompaniment.[76] The
similarity may reside simply in Aeschylus' use of 'dactylic
rhythms of an epic cast', and Aristophanes may not have had
any close musical resemblance in mind.[77] Other early
examples are unfortunately lacking.

The invention of the nome was almost universally
ascribed to Terpander (Pl. *Ion* 533 B; [Plu.] *Mus.* 4. 1132
D).[78] Heraclides (fr. 157 Wehrli) says that he was the first to
provide names for the citharodic nomes. A list of names is
given by Ps.-Plutarch (Boeotian, Aeolian, Trochaic, Oxys,
Cepion, Terpandrean, and Tetraoidios), and Pollux 4. 65
provides a similar catalogue, which, however, includes an
eighth (the *orthios nomos*).[79] These names appear to describe
not individual compositions, but traditional melodic structures to which hexametrical, or at least predominantly
dactylic poetry, could be sung. They may well have been

[74] See M. L. West, *JHS* 101 (1981), 113–29.

[75] Id., *ZPE* 63 (1986), 39–46

[76] But see Fleming (n. 70) for an ingenious, if unconvincing, approach. Smyth
proposes that the lyric dialogue between Cassandra and the chorus at A. *Ag.*
1072 ff could represent 'the spirit of the old nome' (p. lxvi), a suggestion
completely without foundation

[77] West, *Music*, 352

[78] There are indications of alternative traditions: [Plu.] *Mus.* 5. 1133 B mentions
some of the early nomes as being the work of Philammon of Delphi. Timotheus
himself (*P.* 222–8) associates its early history with Orpheus.

[79] Cf. also *Suda* μ 1279; ν 458; ο 575.

used by early citharodes, but Terpander himself is a more or less legendary figure. He was credited with the development of the seven-stringed lyre, which would have allowed an increased musical range (Plin. *NH* 7. 204; [Plu.] *Mus.* 30. 1141 C); it is suspicious that seven nomes are associated with his name in Ps.-Plutarch's list. Early, semi-mythical figures in Greek literary history are usually, and without much reliability, credited with most of the major developments of their art.[80] Other names for the nome are also attested: Stesichorus is said to have used the *harmateios nomos*, which was equated with the nome of Athena and was in the Phrygian mode and enharmonic genus.[81] For Pollux' division of the Terpandrean nome into seven parts (again suspicious), see pp. 124–5.

How much information was conveyed by these terms is unknown. They do not seem to describe the contents of a poem in any way, and we do not know quite what is meant when, for instance, Herodotus says (1. 23) that Arion sang the *orthios nomos* before leaping into the sea to save himself from pirates. One of the fragments (erroneously?) ascribed to Terpander is described as the beginning of the prelude to the *orthios*, *Boiotos*, or *Aiolos nomos* (*PMG* 697 = fr. 2 Gostoli): ἀμφί μοι αὖτε ἄναχθ' ἑκατηβόλον ἀιδέτω ⟨ἁ⟩ φρήν. For Terpander's hexameter preludes, which presumably played for citharodic performance the role played by the Homeric hymns for rhapsody, see [Plu.] *Mus.* 4. 1132 D, 6. 1133 C.

Proclus claims that the nome was written in honour of Apollo, just as the dithyramb was written in honour of Dionysus (*Chrest.* ap. Phot. *Bibl.* 320ᵃ33).[82] Both the paeanic invocation to Apollo at the end of Timotheus' *Persae* and the 'Terpandrean' prelude to the *orthios nomos* may support this statement. However, there is no indication

---

[80] See A. Gostoli, *Terpander* (Rome, 1990), pp. xvi–xxviii, xxxix–xliii, West, *Music*, 330; also A. Kleingünther, Πρῶτος εὑρετής: *Untersuchungen zur Geschichte einer Fragestellung* (*Philol.* Supplbd. 26; Leipzig, 1933), *passim*, for the development in the latter part of the 5th c. of the πρῶτος εὑρετής motif.

[81] West, *Music*, 339.

[82] Proclus makes the impossible assertion that the name derived from Apollo's title 'Nomios'. Other dubious derivations of νόμος abounded in antiquity: cf. also Pl. *Lg.* 3. 799 C, [Arist.] *Probl.* 19. 28.

that Apollo was always involved. Most nomes may have
ended with a hymnic section of some sort, but the god
invoked presumably varied depending on the context of
performance. Proclus' statement that the nome developed
from the paean also casts doubt on the truth of his account.
There is no other indication in the ancient testimonia that
the nome and the paean were at all related, and both poetic
forms continued to exist side by side well into the later
period. We may better regard Proclus' highly artificial
scheme as the result of a later scholarly desire for excessively
neat classifications, though Apollo was early established as
the citharode's particular patron.

Ps.-Plutarch (*Mus.* 6. 1133 b) says that citharody showed
little development between the virtually mythological period
dealt with in these sources and the late fifth century. This
may simply be due to a paucity of materials available by his
day. At any rate, it is unlikely that the fixed musical forms
employed in the early period were still being used for sung
nomes by the time of Phrynis. Those melodic schemes were
presumably designed for predominantly dactylic poetry;
once non-dactylic cola were introduced, they would no
longer be suitable, and this development may lie behind
the charge that Phrynis and his successors introduced
modulations of genus and mode.[83]

By the time of Timotheus, the nome was apparently still a
predominantly narrative genre, and may well have been of
about the same length,[84] but musically and metrically it was
remarkably different from its early form. It permitted variation of mode and genus within the same work, and
presumably involved musical extravagances such as those
parodied at Ar. *Ra.* 1309–63 (of Euripidean lyric). It was
now astrophic; the statement at [Arist.] *Probl.* 19. 5 that
most nomoi were astrophic should be taken to refer to the
later fifth century at the earliest. A similar development
occurred in the dithyramb, and we can also compare some

---

[83] See in general West, *Music*, 360–1.

[84] Smyth conjectures that the nomes of Timotheus 'would seem on an average to
have been slightly shorter than the shortest books of the *Iliad* or *Odyssey*' (p. lxvii),
which seems plausible in the light of the *Persae*, and may well hold true for the
earlier period.

passages of tragic lyric. Presumably more traces of the
contemporary nome could be clearly seen in some of
Euripides' later lyrics if more evidence were available to
us. The essential aspects of Timotheus' contribution will
appear in the course of the following pages. Here it is
sufficient to note that he also is associated with an increase
in the number of strings on the lyre, with astrophic verse,
and with the use of modulations between genus and mode
(Dion. Hal. *Comp.* 19. 131–2).

(ii) Performance

Most citharodic performances took place in a theatre, and
citharodes adopted at an apparently early date a formal
costume for competition. Herodotus simply mentions
Arion's citharodic ϲκευή,[85] but later descriptions, and vase
depictions, of citharodic costume are more elaborate and
precise.[86] The first-century BC Auctor ad Herennium (4.
60) describes an ill-educated rich man, who is likened to a bad
citharode dressed in a gold-embroidered robe with a purple
cloak into which various colours are woven, wearing a
golden crown bright with gems, and holding a highly ornate
lyre inlaid with gold and ivory: his voice, of course, is harsh
and unpleasant. Ovid, *Met.* 11. 165–70, depicts Apollo,
competing with Pan, dressed in a purple robe, garlanded
with bay-leaves, and carrying in his left hand a lyre inlaid
with gems and Indian ivory; his right hand holds the
plectrum.[87] Similarly Lucian's citharode, a figure of fun
called Euangelus of Taras, wears a purple robe and carries a
golden, gem-encrusted lyre. When called on to sing (at the
Pythian games) he breaks the strings and his voice is terrible
(*Adv. indoc.* 9–11). A less gaudily dressed singer easily
defeats him.

Some sources may refer to dancing or some other type of
movement on the part of the citharode. This subject has

[85] Cf. Herington 16.
[86] Further references in West, *Music*, 55 n. 24.
[87] The image of Apollo here probably owes much to Scopas' statue, set up in the god's Augustan temple on the Palatine (see Bömer on the passage), although, as noted, he is frequently represented in this attitude. See W. Lambrinudakis *et al.* in *LIMC* ii/1. 199–213. Depictions of citharodes are often similar to those of Apollo: see J. D. Beazley, *JHS* 42 (1922), 70–98; R. R. Holloway, *Archaeology*, 19 (1966), 112–19.

been discussed at some length by Herington, but the evidence is in fact rather limited. The Auct. Her. says that the bad citharode may sing badly and move his body in an ugly fashion, and an earlier source, Phillis of Delos (ap. Athen. 1. 21 F), refers to the marching and dancing movements of early citharodes: Herington believed that such dancing movements may have formed a part of the performance of ll. 196–201 of Timotheus' *Persae*.[88] He also cites vase depictions of citharodes, which give the impression of physical movement, though it is unclear whether such movement need amount to much more than an attempt on the citharode's part to keep time.[89]

One of the most prestigious festivals associated with citharodic contests was the Carneia, the Spartan festival of Apollo, which according to the local historian Sosibius (4th/ 3rd c. BC: *FGrH* 595 F 3) was founded in the twenty-sixth Olympiad (676–672 BC). Hellanicus of Lesbos, in his *Carneian Victors* (*FGrH* 4 F 85a), said Terpander was the first victor in citharody there. This is doubtful in view of Terpander's uncertain historical status. The statement could be based on records fabricated at a later date to emphasize the festival's high antiquity, though Hellanicus, as a Lesbian himself, may well have had a personal interest in putting forward the claims of a Lesbian poet. But it is also worth noting that the Lesbians had long been associated with citharody, and that at least according to Ps.-Plutarch (*Mus.* 6. 1133 C, perhaps also based on Hellanicus) there was an unbroken line of Lesbian victors at the Carneia until Pericleitus of Lesbos (said to be earlier than Hipponax), who was the last.

There is also evidence for early citharodic contests at the Pythian festival at Delphi (Paus. 10. 7. 2–8), and it is likely that official victor-lists, beginning in 586 BC when auletic and citharistic contests were added to the existing citharodic competition, still survived in the second century AD and were available to Pausanias. Performances presumably went back well into the prehistoric period. Terpander is said by Ps.-Plutarch (*Mus.* 4. 1132 E) to have won four victories there, and it is at least possible that records, perhaps

[88] Herington 158   [89] Ibid. 17

fragmentary, from before 586 were preserved in Ps.-
Plutarch's (here unidentified) source. Pausanias (10. 7.
2–3) says that at the same festival one Eleuther won a victory
by performing a song (ᾠδή) not of his own composition, but
it is unclear whether this refers to hexameters or to lyric (the
context suggests hexameters; Pausanias has just mentioned
Orpheus, Homer, and Hesiod). There were also performances at the Panathenaea, though
it is not clear when they were introduced. An early sixth-
century Panathenaic vase of the school of Exekias (*ABV*
139. 12) depicts a man playing a cithara, but he may be a
citharist rather than a citharode. However, they were
certainly established by the mid-fifth century: a scholion
to Ar. *Nub.* 969–71 records Phrynis' first victory at the
Panathenaea in 446/5.[90] Nevertheless, despite the paucity of
evidence, musical competitions were probably in place
much earlier. The Panathenaea was reorganized in about
566, but it is not until later that it became an important
cosmopolitan festival, and we should not necessarily expect
much firm evidence for the early period. In the first half of
the fourth century five prizes were awarded for citharody at
the Panathenaic games (*IG* ii². 2311 = *SIG* 1055); we do not
know how many singers competed. Evidence from other
festivals indicates that three prizes were usual.[91] The fourth-
century inscription for the Eretrian festival of Artemis also
gives an indication of the importance of the citharodic
contests. Citharodic victors received 200, 150, and 100
drachmai for first, second, and third prize respectively,
which may be contrasted with the prizes for citharists
(110, 70, and 55 drachmai) and rhapsodes (120, 30, and 20
drachmai); parodists[92] are at the lower end of the scale, with

[90] See J. A. Davison, *From Archilochus to Pindar* (London, 1968), 61–2 = *JHS*
78 (1958), 40–1.

[91] Cf. *IG* xii/9. 189: Eretria, mid-4th c. Lucian, *Adv. indoc.* 9, mentions two
other citharodes competing against Euangelus at the Pythian games; whether this
number was usual is unknown, nor does he state whether three prizes were
awarded.

[92] A slightly obscure category: Matron and Sopater are usually named as
παρῳδοί. Aristotle claims that Hegemon of Thasos originated the genre (*Poet.* 2.
1448ᵃ12–13). They probably wrote burlesques of epic and other styles of poetry.
Archestratus may also belong in this group. See S. D. Olson and A. Sens,
Archestratus of Gela (Oxford, 2000), pp. xxxi–xxxvi.

50 and 10 drachmai for first and second prize respectively. With these prizes for what was presumably a relatively minor local festival we may compare the evidence for Panathenaic prizes. The fourth-century inscription mentioned above records that first prize was a silver crown worth 1,000 drachmai and 500 drachmai in cash; the other prizes were worth 700, 600, 400, and 300 drachmai respectively. The two aulodic prizes at the same festival were worth 300 and 100 drachmai, and the most valuable citharistic prize was 500 drachmai; the details for auletes are not extant.[93] Performances at the Panathenaea took place in Themistocles' Odeion, built at some stage in the 470s; before that they had probably been sung in the theatre. The theatre presumably continued to be the place of performance at other festivals: Pylades, singing Timotheus' *Persae* at the Nemean games in 205 BC, is said to have sung in the theatre. At some stage performances were also added to the Pythian and Isthmian games, at least by the early third century, when they are mentioned in the inscription (*IG* ii². 3779) which details the victories of the citharode Nicocles of Taras (above, p. 23). The Isthmian victory is said to have been the first, but unfortunately the exact date of the text is unknown.

As with the dithyramb, we find remarkably few references in the literary record to citharodic composition after the fourth century, although performances certainly continued; they are probably attested for Nero at Rome in the first century AD, and definitely in Greek festivals until the third. Nicocles refers to victories in royal festivals in Macedonia and Alexandria, and Alexander is known to have taken citharodes with him on his Asian campaign: two performed at his wedding in Susa (Chares, *FGrH* 125 F 4).

III. MUSIC AND STYLE

A. Music

There were important developments in the history of music in the late fifth century, particularly in the fields of the

[93] See Davison, op. cit. 56–7 = *JHS* 78 (1958), 37–8.

dithyramb and the citharodic nome. Similar developments can be identified to some extent in tragedy, particularly in the cases of Agathon and Euripides, and occasionally in comedy. However, the most significant innovations appear to have been made by the dithyrambographers and citharodes. In a fragment of Pherecrates' *Cheiron* (fr. 155 K.–A.), Music herself is brought on stage to complain to Justice about her rough treatment at the hands of various poets. The ruffians mentioned are Melanippides, who started the whole thing off, Cinesias, Phrynis, and Timotheus.[94] This is not an isolated passage in comedy, which likes to mock striking novelty. Cinesias was the subject of an entire play by Strattis (frr. 14–20 K.–A.), and his style was ridiculed by Aristophanes at *Av.* 1372–1409. Aristophanes also mentioned him in his *Gerytades* (fr. 156 K.–A.) as the dithyrambic representative in the underworld, together with Sannyrion for comedy and Meletus for tragedy. Similarly, Aristophanes alludes to Phrynis' musical modulations at *Nub.* 969 ff., where a scholion remarks that he was accused of changing the ancient character of song and making music effeminate. Aristophanes also parodied Philoxenus of Cythera's *Cyclops* or *Galatea* at *Plu.* 290 ff.; the emphasis seems to be on mocking peculiar musical effects, as well as on elements in the portrayal of the Cyclops.[95]

   The precise details of the musical developments are difficult to recover, and are not our main concern here.[96] Broadly, however, the poets of the 'New Music' broke away from the formalism of the old musical categories. The literary historian Dionysius of Halicarnassus refers to the use of modulations between *harmoniai* (Dorian, Phrygian, and Lydian) and genera (enharmonic, chromatic, and diatonic) in the same song.[97] Aristotle (*Pol.* 8. 1342^{b}7–12)

---

[94] The latter part of the text is corrupt, but the reference to Philoxenus at [Plu.] *Mus.* 30. 1142 A 4–6 is clearly an interpolation, probably of a marginal note.

[95] Much of the focus is musical; contrast the comic treatment of tragedy. See K. J. Dover's discussion in his commentary on Ar. *Ra.*, pp. 24–37; C. Kugelmeier, *Reflexe früher und zeitgenössischer Lyrik in der alten attischen Komödie* (Stuttgart and Leipzig, 1996), 195–305.

[96] See the discussions by Barker i. 93–8; West, *Music*, 356–7.

[97] Dion. Hal. *Comp.* 19. 131–2 (vi. 85–6 Radermacher) Plu. *Quaest. Conviv.* 3. 1. 1. 645 DE tells us that Agathon was the first to use the chromatic genus in tragedy; it was particularly associated with the citharodic nome, and was regarded

comments that Philoxenus tried to compose his dithyrambic *Mysians* (fr. 826) in the Dorian *harmonia*, but failed and fell back into the Phrygian, which was natural to the dithyramb. This is unlikely to be strictly true; like Dionysius, Aristotle is probably talking about deliberate modulations; the twists and turns in Ionian style criticized by Timotheus (fr. 802. 3 τὸν ἰωνοκάμπταν) may include changes of *harmonia*, for Pherecrates' *Music* mentions Cinesias' use of 'exharmonic' modulations (ἐξαρμονίους καμπάς) within strophes; Phrynis seems to be accused of similar wrongs. Timotheus is also said to have used exharmonic variations.[98]

Dionysius ascribes this development to poets 'of the school of' Timotheus, Philoxenus, and Telestes (οἱ . . . κατὰ Φιλόξενον καὶ Τιμόθεον καὶ Τελέστην). Other poets were associated with earlier changes. Pherecrates connects Melanippides with an increase in the number of strings (fr. 155. 5), though this is a standard charge against innovative poets,[99] and nothing more specific is clearly alleged against him. However, Aristotle (*Rhet.* 3. 9. 1409[b]27) states that he was the first to abandon strophic structure, which could be the meaning of Pherecrates' claim that he made Music 'looser' (χαλαρωτέραν . . . (με) ἐποίησε).[100] But criticisms were not merely directed at musical innovation. Both Philoxenus and Cinesias seem to be parodied as much for their style, and 'dithyrambic' language was frequently the subject of mockery.

---

as more difficult (and thus more suited to performance by a highly trained professional).

[98] The Laconian Decree in Boethius preserves the charge that Timotheus composed his poems in the chromatic genus instead of the enharmonic. This reflects the same critical tradition, but has little independent factual value.

[99] Cf. e.g. Pl. *Rep.* 3 399 C; [Plu.] *Mus.* 12 1135 C.

[100] According to [Plu] *Mus.* 15. 1136 C, Aristoxenus (fr. 80 Wehrli) said that the mythical aulete Olympus was the first to use the Lydian mode when playing the lament for the Python, but εἰcὶν δ᾽ οἳ Μελανιππίδην τούτου τοῦ μέλους ἄρξαι φαςίν. It is not clear whether the lament or the Lydian mode is meant, and in either case the report is improbable.

B. Style

'In the *Persae* of Timotheus we possess an example of Greek
Melic poetry popularised, and degraded in the process . . .
the diction is monstrous. There is a profusion of unwieldy
metaphor . . . The only admirer of such a style can be the
philologist.' So Ellingham in 1921 (60, 63–4). The judgement of modern scholarship has weighed heavily on
Timotheus.[101] Ancient writers appear to have differed.
Timotheus clearly stands out as unusual in classical
literature, although there are similarities to the other fragments of late fifth-century lyric, and to some of the elements
of Euripides' later monodies and choral odes. Ps.-Plutarch
characterizes the diction of his nomes as dithyrambic (*Mus.*
4. 1132 DE), and there is evidence that the style of the
dithyramb was regarded in the late classical period as
linguistically florid and even occasionally meaningless.
The parody of Cinesias' lyrics in Aristophanes (*Av.* 1372–
1409), together with the scholiast's remarks, are good
examples of this view.[102] By contrast, Agathon's song in
Thesmophoriazusae (101–29) and the few fragments of his
work are, despite his connections with the new music,
linguistically unremarkable. Analogous trends can perhaps
be seen in contemporary Greek prose. Schönewolf compared the ornate, alliterative style of the rhetorician Gorgias
of Leontini, and although Gorgias shows little interest in the
obscure compounds of the *Persae*, he appears to share with
Timotheus an interest in alliteration and rhyme.[103]

(i) Vocabulary

Despite Timotheus' reputation for innovation, his phraseology and vocabulary are in fact at times highly traditional.
Occasionally this seems to be motivated by his subject. The
paeanic content of fr. 800, for instance, is accompanied by

[101] For more appreciative comments in recent times, see Herington 151–60;
West, *Music*, 361–4.
[102] Σ *Av.* 1392 πλείϲτη γὰρ αὐτῶν ἡ λέξιϲ τοιαύτη ὁ δὲ νοῦϲ ἐλάχιϲτοϲ, ὡϲ ἡ παροιμία
καὶ διθυράμβων νοῦν ἔχειϲ ἐλάττονα; Σ *Av.* 1385 παίζει δὲ πρὸϲ τὰ ἐπίθετα τῶν
διθυραμβοποιῶν καὶ πρὸϲ τὸ κοῦφον αὐτῶν.
[103] Schönewolf 45–8. Gorgias has only one extended compound (B 15 πτωχο-
μουϲοκόλακεϲ); cf. K. J. Dover, *The Evolution of Greek Prose Style* (Oxford, 1997),
112. For Gorgias' influence, see ibid. 136–7.

the use of standard or formulaic language. Elsewhere we find no such explanation. He seems to have been influenced particularly by elements of tragic vocabulary, particularly by that of Aeschylus and Euripides: however, the preponderance of Aeschylean material in the surviving fragments may simply be due to the tragedian's influence on *Persae*. It is harder to identify clear reminiscences of lyric or iambic material, and, most surprisingly, there is little influence from epic. Nevertheless, where Homeric phraseology appears to have been important, we usually find that formulae have been slightly altered so as to achieve genuine novelty. Several linguistic features appear closer to the Hellenistic than to the classical age, as does occasionally his use of individual words; this characteristic is less surprising if we regard late classical lyric as the obvious bridge between the two periods.

There is also a large neologistic element to Timotheus' vocabulary, although given the fragmentary nature of our sources, it is sometimes difficult to be sure whether a hapax legomenon is a genuine neologism or simply an ancient rarity. There is also some evidence for an interest in technical language. The descriptions of naval matters seem to show some technical features (cf. on *P.* 10, 12, 15, etc.), and that of the drowning man at 60–71 may owe something to the medical terminology of the late fifth century, when the Hippocratic corpus was largely in the process of formation. Varying degrees of influence from medical terminology have been discerned in tragic and prose works of the same period (see commentary for details), but the language of the Hippocratic corpus may itself depend in part on earlier didactic poetry.[104] There is little concern with the technicalities of musical description: the concluding section, although it deals with the subject in an extended fashion, shows only occasional elements of jargon. Similarly Telestes, although he shows great interest in describing musical instruments (pipes: frr. 805–6; lyre: fr. 808; pektis: fr. 810)

---

[104] Cf. D. R. Langslow, 'The Language of Poetry and the Language of Science: The Latin Poets and 'Medical Latin', in J. N. Adams and R. G. Mayer (eds.), *Aspects of the Language of Latin Poets* (PBA 93; London, 1999), 183–225; *Medical Latin in the Roman Empire* (Oxford, 2000), esp. 26 ff.

and modes (Lydian/Dorian: fr. 806; Phrygian: fr. 810), uses
little technical jargon. Of course, neither Timotheus nor
Telestes was writing for an audience composed of fellow
musicians, and in any case Athenaeus shows little interest in
technical musicological details.[105] There is some evidence in
the Celaenaean's speech (*P.* 150–61) for an awareness of how
Greek may have been spoken by an Asiatic; as a citizen of
Miletus, Timotheus would clearly be more familiar than, for
instance, an Athenian with the kinds of error such barbarians were likely to make.

(ii) Mimesis

One of the strongest trends often associated with late classical lyric, both choral and monodic, is an increasing interest
in musical imitation. Plato (*Rep.* 3. 397 A; cf. *Lg.* 2. 669 B–
670 A) criticizes the tendency in contemporary music to
imitate the sounds of 'thunder, and the noises of winds and
hail and axes and pulleys, and the voices of *salpinges* and
auloi and *syringes* and instruments of every kind, and even
the sounds of sheep and birds . . .'.[106] This should clearly be
associated with the New Music, and thus with Timotheus:
Stratonicus attacks the birth-cries of Semele (fr. 792) and
Dorion the representation of a storm in *Nauplius* (fr. 785).[107]
For instrumental music this mimetic element appears to
have been traditional, if we can compare the descriptions of
the *Pythikos Nomos*, which depicted musically the battle
between Apollo and the serpent at Delphi, and of the
Polykephalos Nomos, which at one point imitated the hissing
of the Gorgon Euryale.[108] This sort of musical mimesis
probably occurred in both the dithyramb and the nome;
the narrative of the Persian fleet's destruction in Timotheus'

---

[105] See A. Barker, 'Athenaeus on Music', in D. Braund and J. Wilkins (eds.),
Athenaeus and his World (Exeter, 2000), 434–44

[106] Barker i. 128. We might perhaps adduce the Frog chorus of Ar. *Ra.* 209–67
and the Hoopoe's song at Ar. *Av.* 227–62 (see Dunbar's comments on the passage
for connections with the dithyrambic style).

[107] Dorion was an aulete who seems to have been opposed to the New Music.
See West, *Music*, 369 and n. 54, and cf. Theopomp. *FGrH* 115 F 236, [Plu.] *Mus.*
21. 1138 A (Aristoxenus), Athen. 8. 337 C–338 A.

[108] The *Pythikos nomos* is discussed by Pollux 4. 84, Strabo 9. 3. 10; for the
polykephalos nomos, cf. Pi. *P.* 12 with *Σ*; see also West, *Music*, 12–14.

Persae would also be ideal for a display of the sort of musical mimesis described by Plato. The interest in musical mimesis occasionally may have extended itself to other elements of performance. The Celaenaean's speech (*P.* 150–61) is an evident example, but it is possible that the other speeches, although not linguistically distinguished, were differentiated from each other in delivery.

(iii) Periphrasis and Metaphor

Obscure and riddling circumlocutions are particularly noticeable in Timotheus. They were regarded as typical of his style in antiquity, and the comic poets of the fourth century found them an apt subject for ridicule or parody; cf. Timoth. frr. 797, 798; Antiphan. fr. 55 K.–A.[109] Seaford has argued that periphrasis of this sort was typical of dithyramb in general and suggested a connection with the religious language of Dionysiac cult.[110] However, there is little evidence that periphrases in dithyrambic poetry relate in any particular way to Dionysiac subjects, even in the earlier period. Pindar makes some use of periphrasis in his dithyrambs, but no more than in the epinicia and it is not clearly restricted to Dionysiac subjects.[111] Nor is periphrasis typical of Bacchylides' dithyrambic style. It is therefore better to regard the device as a standard poetic trope in classical and archaic poetry, and to refrain from seeking its origins in cultic language.[112]

---

[109] Antiphanes does not specifically refer to Timotheus, but the similarities between this passage and Timoth. fr. 780 are notable (see comm).

[110] Seaford, 'Hyporchema', 88. The only ancient evidence (which he ignores) to support this hypothesis is a scholion on Philostr. *vit. Apollon.* 1. 17: διθυραμβώδη· cυνθέτοιc ὀνόμαcι cεμνυνομένην καὶ ἐκτοπωτάτοιc πλάcμαcι ποικιλλομένην· τοιοῦτοι γὰρ οἱ διθύραμβοι, ἅτε Διονυcίων τελετῶν ἀφωρμημένοι (quoted by Pickard-Cambridge 67), but this is clearly of little independent value. P. Gurôb 1, a fragment of syncretistic Orphic–Dionysiac ritual of the 3rd c. BC, shows no interest in periphrastic language: see *ZPE* 129 (2000), 131–40.

[111] See R Hamilton, *HSCP* 93 (1990), 211–22, on the style of Pindar's dithyrambs; he concludes (216) that periphrasis is more a feature of 'late poetry . . . or the description of Dionysiac ritual . than of dithyramb *per se*'.

[112] Periphrastic language is particularly common in Lycophron's *Alexandra* (e.g. 21 παρθενοκτόνον Θέτιν = the Hellespont, 32 πεύκαιcιν οὐλαμηφόροιc = ships); there, however, the connection with the riddling style of oracular speech is made explicit (Lycophr. 3–12). For the occasional use of periphrasis in Euripides, see Breitenbach 201.

Timotheus forms his periphrases in a variety of ways. The type substantive (sometimes with a qualifying adjective) + genitive substantive is commonest (e.g. fr. 780. 4 αἷμα Βακχίου 'wine', 5 νεορρύτοιcιν δακρύοιcι Νυμφᾶν 'water', P. 37–9, 90–1, 91–3, fr. 797, etc.), but occasionally a periphrasis is simply expressed by an adjective combined with a substantive, as in fr. 798 πυρικτίτωι cτέγαι. Both types are attested elsewhere in Greek literature,[113] and the phenomenon of periphrasis is hardly restricted to any particular date or group of authors. Timotheus' usage nevertheless stands out, because he never gives the basic word in apposition to the periphrasis.[114] It also stands out because of the boldness of some of the resulting imagery, even to the point of obscurity: the meanings to be given to the μαρμαροφεγγεῖc παῖδεc of P. 92–3 and the sense of ὀρφανὸν μαχᾶν at 142 have been endlessly debated.[115]

Periphrastic language is a particularly common feature of Old Norse verse, though it also features in early Icelandic prose texts such as some of the sagas. Several modern writers, most notably Wærn in her ΓΗΣ ΟΣΤΕΑ, have therefore adopted the Old Norse term 'kenning' (pl. kenningar) to denote the wider poetic phenomenon of periphrasis. Snorri Sturluson, the great medieval Icelandic scholar, distinguished three types of kenning, simple, double, and extended, depending on the number of terms involved, in his commentary on his own virtuoso poem, Háttatal.[116] Thus, he says, fleinbrak 'clash of spears' for 'battle' is a simple kenning, whence fleinbraks fúrr 'fire of the clash of spears' for 'sword' is a double kenning. It may be

---

[113] See esp. Breitenbach 196–202 on Euripidean periphrasis; there are, however, no instances shared by the two poets (unless TrGF adesp. 244 ὀρείοιc ποcί is by Euripides, but there is little to support such a hypothesis).

[114] Almost none of Pindar's periphrases is appositional. Wærn 51 lists only five examples: O. 3. 20, 11. 2, P. 1. 6, 19, I. 6. 50. However, as she herself appears to note on p. 49, it is not the case that at O. 3. 20 ἑcπέραc ὀμφαλόν is in apposition to Μήνα, and it is doubtful whether the phrase αἰετόc . . . ἀρχὸc οἰωνῶν at P. 1. 6, and in the accusative at I. 6. 50, is genuinely periphrastic. About half the instances in Aeschylus are appositional.

[115] On metaphor in general in Greek poetry see M. S. Silk, Interaction in Poetic Imagery (Cambridge, 1974), 27–56.

[116] Snorri Sturluson, Edda: Háttatal, ed. Anthony Faulkes (Oxford, 1991), 5. Snorri's description here is slightly at odds with that in his later account of peotic conventions, Skáldskaparmál, ch. 54.

doubted to what extent Greek instances are quite comparable with this. Though in terms of formation there appears little difference, and some examples are common to both literatures (such as the Homeric ἕρκος ὀδόντων = Norse *tanngarðr*, which indeed is common in prose), there is no suggestion that Greek poetry ever developed a formal periphrastic vocabulary as Icelandic and to a lesser extent other early Germanic languages (e.g. Old English poetry) did.[117] It therefore seems preferable to restrict the word 'kenning' to discussions of the Germanic phenomenon.

(iv) Compound Words

Aristotle (*Poet.* 22. 1459ᵃ8) notes that compound words are characteristic of the dithyramb, a view largely borne out by the number of neologistic, and sometimes obscure, nominal compounds in Timotheus, and in Aristophanes' elaborate parody of Cinesias' lyric.[118] Possibly Aristotle was particularly referring to the dithyrambic diction of contemporary poetry. The dithyrambs of Pindar and Bacchylides certainly contain a number of new and old compounds, but such forms are also found abundantly in the epinician odes. The large number of neologistic compounds in Euripidean lyric is perhaps due to dithyrambic influence at this time.[119]

Of course, not all Timotheus' compounds are new, and the compound is a standard feature of Greek poetry of all genres. Furthermore, very few of the neologisms defy analysis according to conventional understanding of IE compounds. What is remarkable, of course, is the sheer number of compounds used over a short period, and the startling imagery which often results.

---

[117] For a good discussion, see E. O. G Turville-Petre, *Scaldic Verse* (Oxford, 1976), pp. xlv–lix.

[118] e.g. Ar. *Av.* 1385 ἀεροδονήτους, νιφοβόλους (otherwise only at 952, E. *Ph.* 206), 1390, 1402 πτεροδόνητα, 1394 αἰθεροδρόμων, ταναοδείρων; cf. further Arist. *Rhet.* 3. 3. 1406ᵇ1, Pl. *Crat.* 409 c, Ar. *Pax* 827–31, *Nub.* 332–9 and later Demetr. *Eloc.* 91 (*PMG* adesp. 962), who cites the phrases θεοτεράτους πλάνας and ἄστρων δορίπυρον στρατόν as examples of compounds in the dithyrambic manner (τὰ διθυραμβικῶς συγκείμενα) and *PMG* adesp. 963 Πλούτων μελανοπτερύγων, Hor. *Od.* 4. 2. 10–12.

[119] For compounds in Euripides, see Breitenbach 61–103. Most of Euripides' new compounds are of well-recognized types, and provide few difficulties in interpretation. They tend to be restricted to lyric passages.

(v) Parataxis

The monotonously paratactic style seems peculiar to Timotheus; there is nothing quite like it even in similar types of lyric (e.g. late Euripides, [Arion], etc.). Clauses tend to follow at very short intervals, almost invariably linked by δέ. There is a certain amount of subordination, but generally in the form of temporal rather than relative clauses, which are almost unattested. In part this speeds up the course of the narrative; by contrast, the syntax of the speeches in the *Persae* is slightly more complex than that in the narrative, though subordination is still rare. Much of the work of subordinate clauses usually introduced by relative pronouns or particles is therefore achieved in Timotheus, as in classical Sanskrit, by the frequent use of compound phrases.

(vi) Repetition

The Greek ear appears to have been remarkably insensitive to the effect of casual repetitions of the same word or root at various intervals.[120] This insensitivity is particularly noticeable in *Persae*, where we find the following examples: 8/13/ 14 -φερ-, 32/35 ναΐοιc, νάϊοc, 34/36 -μιγ-?, 101/102 [γ]όωι, γοηταί, 119/129 δυcέκφευκτον, 140/144 ἄγοι, ἄγεν (or ἆγεν), 145/146 πλεκ-, 162/163 -πορον. Similar repetitions feature in the hymn to Poseidon attributed to Arion (939. 18/19 ἁλιπ-, 13/17/19 πορ- with 15 φορ-).

In some cases, however, repetitions are clearly intentional; for instance the 'etymological' repetitions of roots and sounds in Melanippides and Licymnius can only be deliberate (Melanipp. 759 ἄχε᾽ εἶcιν [Bergk : ἀχεοῖcι codd.] προχέων Ἀχέρων, 761 οἶνον Οἰνέωc, Licymnius fr. 770(b) Ἀχέρων ἄχεα πορθμεύει βροτοῖcιν). Equally contrived seems Telestes fr. 805(a). 1 cοφὸν cοφάν,[121] as also the phrase ἄλλοc δ᾽ ἄλλαν κλαγγὰν ἱείc at fr. 808. 1. Occasionally a particular effect is also observable in Timotheus. At *P.* 76 and 129 the anadiplosis of ἐμόc seems comparable to the extremely frequent anadiplosis in late Euripidean lyric; the homoiote-

---

[120] See J. Jackson, *Marginalia Scaenica* (Oxford, 1955), 220–2, for some cases from Attic drama.
[121] cοφὰν cοφόν transp. Bergk, Wilamowitz, unnecessarily.

leuton in fr. 778(*b*), where all four epithets end in -άδα, must also be considered. Particularly noticeable is the sequence of sounds at *P*. 82 ff., where we find repeated both -ματι and -ρευγόμενος, as well as a marked alliteration of initial β and the assonance ἄχναν ~ ἄλμαν. The repetitions in the Celaenaean's speech at 150–61 are evidently intended to reproduce the inadequacies of oriental Greek (see commentary).

IV. LANGUAGE[122]

A. Dialect

A precise account of Timotheus' dialectal peculiarities is complicated by the available evidence. Like most choral lyric poets he employed a poetic dialect with some Doric elements. The papyrus of *Persae*, however, shows a mixture of forms, fluctuating between Doric long α and the η found in Attic (in most positions) and Ionic (throughout).[123] For instance, the nominative singular of the *a*-stem is usually formed in -α/-ας, but there are occasional instances of endings in -ης. In the accusative singular the texts usually have -ην, sometimes -αν. The extent to which this is due to scribal error is uncertain, though some evidence suggests that the scribe may have been an Ionian (below, pp. 68–9). The quotation fragments, where scribal normalization is certainly to be suspected, show similar variation. However, in the papyrus texts of Bacchylides we also find a mixture of Doric and non-Doric forms; Ionic influence is there not in doubt, but there is little apparent reason why Bacchylides (or the scribe) should have preferred semi-Ionic εἰρήνα over εἰράνα. Other features also suggest Ionic influence, such as θυι- against Attic θυ- at *P*. 65 (see n.). Timotheus' own practice cannot be recovered with any confidence. Other

---

[122] See also Wilamowitz 38 ff.; Brussich, 'Lingua'

[123] See G. Björck, *Das Alpha impurum und die tragische Kunstsprache* (Uppsala, 1950), for the standard discussion of this phenomenon in Attic tragedy. B. Hutzfeldt, *Das Bild der Perser in der griechischen Dichtung des 5. vorchristlichen Jahrhunderts* (Wiesbaden, 1999), 180, claims that Ionicisms and 'Homericisms' occur mainly in the speeches of the 'Mysians' (as he calls them) and the Celaenaean. This is not borne out by the evidence.

than the occasional use of original long α, the texts provide little evidence for much Doric influence. Homericisms are comparatively rare, though epic -οιο in the genitive singular of the o-stem is well attested, and the augment frequently omitted. The fragments attributed to Terpander are too exiguous and unreliable for a judgement about his language to be made, but Stesichorus, if a citharode, could suggest that 'choral Doric' was traditional for the nome.

I have refrained from 'normalizing' the text, and in the following discussion cite the forms as preserved in the papyrus and medieval MSS.

B. *Phonology*

(i) Original long α

As in Attic, original long α is always preserved after ε, ι, ρ. It is also generally retained in a nominal stem (e.g. *P*. 8 πλαγά, 32 νάϊοις, 41 ἀμερο-, 128 Μᾶτερ etc., fr. 803. 2 cελάναc), but there are a few cases where η is found (e.g. *P*. 45 νηcιώτας, 102 γοηταί, 180 ἤλικ᾽, 193 cκηνάc).

(ii) Contraction

As would be expected, the historically early contraction of ε + ε (> ει) is attested regularly in verbal forms (e.g. *P*. 45 ἔ]πλει, 50 κάλει, 64 ἐχεῖτ᾽). We find contraction of εο to Attic ου at *P*. 128 ἱκνοῦμαι; but contraction is not marked orthographically at 104 ἐπανεκα[λ]έοντ᾽, where the metre appears to indicate it (as also at 200, where -κτύπεον is probably ∪ –). At 89 οο is contracted to ου. We may also adduce 70 †μιμούμενοc, which, although clearly corrupt, at least suggests a contracted form in the original. The combination εω is never contracted, but may be subject to synizesis.

C. *Morphology*

(i) Nouns

(a) *a*-stems

The nominative singular is almost always formed in -α/-αc (e.g. *P*. 31 cμαραγδοχαίταc, 138 θοινά, 170 οἰμωγά), although we find δεcπότηc at *P*. 116 and Πέρcηc at *P*. 86. In the accusative generally -ην is written (except after ε, ι, ρ), but

we may note *P.* 84 ἄχναν, 180 ἤβαν, 238 τάνδε. In some cases
an accusative in -ην alternates with a dative singular -αι (e.g.
P. 114 στέγην against fr. 798 στέγαι cj., *P.* 163, 174 φυγήν, 120
καταφυγήν against 86 φυγᾶι). In the dative singular -αι is the
regular form (e.g. *P.* 34 κρ]αυγᾶι, 66 δόξαι, 147 φωνᾶ⟨ι⟩, 86
φυγᾶι). The genitive singular is almost always -ας, but there
are two exceptions: *P.* 95 λιποπνόης (the Doric form πνοά is
rare, but occurs in contemporary lyric at e.g. E. *Or.* 145,
Ariphr. fr. 813. 7 ἀμπνοά, who regularly uses the Doric form
of the *a*-stem) and 144 κόμης. The genitive plural is always
-ᾶν (e.g. fr. 780. 5 Νυμφᾶν, *P.* 141 Κελαινᾶν, 142 μαχᾶν).

The Doric forms are standard for the other dithyrambographers, in all the cases, though there are some
gaps in the evidence. Melanippides has e.g. fr. 757. 1 μομφάν
(cj. Lloyd-Jones : μορφάν cod.), 2 τὰν ὀργὰν (cj. West : τὰν
αὐτάν cod. : τὰν ἀλκάν Lloyd-Jones), 758. 2 ἱερᾶς, 759. 1
γαίας, 760. 4 ὀμφάν, 762. 2 ψυχᾶς, etc.; Telestes shows -ας at
fr. 805(*b*). 3 τέχνας, (*c*). 1 ςεμνᾶς, and the genitive plural
ἀγλαᾶν (χειρῶν) at fr. 805(*c*). 3, χορδᾶν at fr. 808. 3. Nowhere
are there Ionic forms comparable to those in the MSS of
Timotheus.

(b) *o*-stems

There are no irregularities in the declension of *o*-stems. As
might be expected, the genitive singular alternates freely
between epic -οιο (e.g. *P.* 41, 111, fr. 803. 2) and later -ου (*P.*
195, fr. 804). Only -ου is found in Melanippides (frr. 760. 2,
762. 2), but the evidence is hardly substantial; Telestes has
only -οιο at fr. 805(*a*). 5 εὐηράτοιο. Ariphron's paean has one
case of -ου (fr. 813. 3). Pindar and Bacchylides usually
employ forms in -οιο for metrical reasons; while Simonides
provides too few examples for a firm conclusion, there are
more instances of -ου than -οιο in his lyric fragments,
whereas in the elegiac fragments, where the metre has a
dactylic basis, -οιο is predictably common.[124]

(c) Dative plural

In the text as printed there are 8 cases of -οιςι(ν) against 14
cases of -οις, and only 2 cases of -αιςι(ν) against 9 of -αις. We

---

[124] O. Poltera, *Le langage de Simonide* (Berne, 1997), 514–16.

may conclude that although the short form of the dative plural of both the *a*- and *o*-stem was the more usual, the longer form was readily admitted.

A similar picture emerges from the fragments of the other dithyrambic poets, although the evidence is necessarily rather scant. Melanippides has three examples of the dative plural, two of which use the short form (fr. 757. 3 -οις, 4 -αις against 759. 1 -οισι). Licymnius provides slightly more information: there are six datives plural, and again only one (fr. 770(*b*) -οισιν) has the longer form. By contrast, he has three cases of -αις (frr. 770(*a*) twice, 771. 2) and two of -οις (frr. 771. 2, 3). Telestes only preserves forms in -οις (frr. 805(*b*). 3, 806. 3, 4, 810. 1, 4 twice); there are no examples of the *a*-stem. Ariphron too lacks any *a*-stem datives plural, but has three dative plural *o*-stems in -οις (fr. 813. 4, 5, 9) against two examples of -οισι (fr. 813. 1, 6), all in the same poem. Philoxenus has one case of -αις (fr. 822), one of -οις (fr. 822), again both in the same fragment, while in [Arion] we find an equal distribution of -οις (*PMG* adesp. 939. 4, 15) and -οισι (6, 15), but again no examples of the *a*-stem.[125]

(ii) Verbs

(a) The augment

The augment is frequently found with the imperfect and the aorist indicative: fr. 780. 3 (twice), 790A, *P*. 6, 9, 13, 15, 17, 19 cj., 23, 25, 29, 32, 34, 37, 45 cj., 61, 64, 65, 84, 92, 96, 97, 104, 105, 139, 146, 163 (aor.), 165, 174 (aor.), 198, 199, 222 (aor.). However, we also find numerous unaugmented forms: fr. 780. 1, *P*. 50, 61 cj., 68, 88, 90, 144, 166, 168, 169, 171, 176, 226 (aor.), 228.

Forms without the syllabic augment are common in tragic lyric and occasionally appear in messenger speeches, where they are probably due to the influence of epic narrative. Interestingly, the *Persae* furnishes the majority of Aeschylean examples (310, 313, 376, 416, 458, 490, 506; twice also in choruses: 656, 915). This may suggest deliberate imita-

---

[125] In Attic prose forms in -οισι become less frequent after the middle of the 5th c.: see K. J. Dover, *The Evolution of Greek Prose Style* (Oxford, 1997), 80, 86.

tion of this feature by Timotheus, but numerous examples of unaugmented forms are also found in Euripides.[126]

(b) Tmesis

Only two possible cases of tmesis can be identified, both with postpositives: *P*. 23 ἐν δ' ἔπιπτε, 180 κατὰ μὲν ἥλικ' ὠλέϲαθ' (see n.). There are no certain examples in the other dithyrambic fragments of the period, but tmesis is very frequent in Euripidean and earlier lyric (e.g. Pindar).[127] Though common in Herodotus tmesis is generally rare in classical Attic prose, where it was probably regarded as a poetic use. However, it is unlikely that the dithyrambic poets were affected by the constraints of 'conventional' speech in this matter. The evidence is simply too scant to judge the matter accurately. For the force of περί at *P*. 134, see n.

(iii) Word-formation

(a) Preverbs

Timotheus shows a certain fondness for both existing and apparently innovative formations with two preverbs: fr. 781 εἰϲαναβήϲει, ὑπεραμπέχοντ', *P*. 61 ἐπειϲέπιπτον, 105 ἐπανεκαλέοντ', 231 ἐξανατέλλει (cf. also the adjectival formation δυϲέκφευκτον at 119, 129). The second preverb often seems to add little to the sense, and the formations may be employed largely in order to achieve a particularly sonorous and high poetic effect. Such forms are well attested in epic, which also occasionally shows formations with three preverbs.[128]

(b) Compounds[129]

Most of Timotheus' compounds are readily comprehensible, and find parallels in the compound formations of other late classical (and earlier) poets. Many forms are

[126] See A. Sideras, *Aeschylus Homericus* (Göttingen, 1971), 258–9; Page on E. *Med.* 1141; Diggle, *Studies*, 65–6. For the epic material, see Chantraine, *Grammaire*, i. 479–84
[127] Breitenbach 266–7, Kuhner–Gerth i. 530–8.
[128] Chantraine, *Grammaire*, ii. 144–5.
[129] For the dithyrambographers' interest in compounds, cf. Σ Pl. *Phdr.* 267 B: ὁ Λικύμνιος . . . διήιρει τὰ ὀνόματα εἰϲ κύρια, ϲύνθετα, ἀδελφά, ἐπίθετα καὶ εἰϲ ἄλλα τινά.

48   LANGUAGE

shared only with Euripides, occasionally also with later
poets who are clearly borrowing from these earlier authors.
It is often not clear whether Euripides or Timotheus should
be regarded as the originator of any given form.
Many of Timotheus' compounds pertain to a type of
which a familiar example is the Homeric epithet of Apollo,
ἀργυρότοξοϲ 'with/possessing a silver bow'. They consist of
two elements, of which the second in some sense 'belongs' to
the main noun, while the first further qualifies the second.
Thus, in ϲμαραγδοχαίταϲ . . . πόντοϲ the hair 'belongs' to the
sea, and is further described as being 'of emerald'. Such
compounds are known by the Sanskrit term *bahuvrīhi*, or
more familiarly as possessive compounds, although the
relation is not always one of possession: The second element
is regularly substantival, while the first may be either a
substantive or an adjective, often a numeral. Both adjectival
and substantival formations of the same word are possible;
cf. the alternation of χαλκο- and χαλκεο- in Homer, where the
adjectival formation may have been introduced for metrical
reasons,[130] and also Philox. fr. 821 χρυϲεοβόϲτρυχε[131] against
[Arion], *PMG* adesp. 939. 2 χρυϲοτρίαινε.
In the following examples the first term is a numeral, and
indicates the number of items described by the second term:
P. 12 πολυκρότο[?], 141 πολυβότων 'with many herds', 230
ἑνδεκακρουμάτοιϲ 'with eleven notes', 232 πολύυμνον 'with
many songs', 235 δυωδεκατειχέοϲ 'with twelve walls'.
Adjectival first terms appear in 29 τανυπτέροιϲι 'having
long wings', 115 τελεόπορον, 202 χρυϲεοκίθαριν 'with a golden
cithara', 221 ποικιλόμουϲον 'possessing variegated music'.
In the case of substantival first terms, the first noun
usually describes a material of which the second is made:
fr. 790A χαλκεμβόλοιϲ 'with bronze rams', *P.* 30 χαλκόκραϲι
'with bronze heads', 31 ϲμαραγδοχαίταϲ 'emerald-haired', 38
μαρμαροπ[τύχ]οιϲ 'with shining folds', 106 δενδροέθειραι 'tree-
tressed', 127 χρυϲοπλόκαμε 'golden-haired', 143 ϲιδαρόκωποϲ
'with an iron sword'.

---

[130] See Risch 183.
[131] Bergk unnecessarily suggests χρυϲο- here; χρυϲεοβόϲτρυχον is otherwise found
only at E. *Ph.* 191, and there are at least three other Euripidean hapax legomena
formed in χρυϲεο- in the later lyrics (Mastronarde on E. *Ph.* 176).

There are two instances of possessive compounds formed with three terms: *P*. 123 μελαμπεταλοχίτωνα 'with a robe of black leaves', 219 λιγυμακροφώνων 'with shrill, loud voices'. A second category is the verbal compound, which also usually consists of two elements. One of these will be either a verbal stem or a verbal noun. The other has a close connection to the verbal element, such as direct/indirect object or agent, and tends to be either a substantive or adjective. Thus, in λαιμοτόμωι (*P*. 130) the second term is a verbal noun derived from the verb τέμνω and the first term functions here as the object of the verbal element, hence 'throat-cutting'. In Ἰλιοπόρος the second term is a verbal noun from πορεύω, and the first is its indirect object, 'conveying to Ilium'. In most examples of this type Timotheus places the verbal element in second position (e.g. 132 ναυσιφθόροι 'destroying ships', 138 ὠμοβρῶσι 'eating flesh', fr. 799 μυελοτρεφῆ?, fr. 802. 3 ἰωνοκάμπταν 'twisting Ionian melodies', see n.). There are only two examples where the verbal part appears as the first term: *P*. 9 ῥηξ[ίκωπ]ος 'oar-breaking' and 95 λιποπνόης(?) 'deprivation of air' (but cf. Philox. fr. 832 ἀρκεσίγυιον 'limb-helping'[132]). In ῥηξ[ίκωπ]ος the first term is from ῥήγνυμι (stem ῥηγ-). The verbal element -σι-, which produces the form ῥηξι- (i.e. ῥηγ-σι-), derives from an original -τ- (as in e.g. βωτιάνειρα), of uncertain origin. However, the form in -σι- resembles the stem of the sigmatic aorist, and may have been regarded as such in the fifth century (cf. e.g. *IT* 451 παυσίπονος, *Andr*. 129 δεξίμηλος, *Ph*. 664 ὀλεσίθηρ for the type in Euripides). More rarely the substantival term in a verbal compound can have an instrumental or locative force: *P*. 15 λι[νο]ζώσ-τους, 22 ἀγκυλένδετ[ο]ς, 74 λινοδέτωι, 79 οἰστρομανές, fr. 801 γηγένεταν. Compare Telest. fr. 805(*a*). 4 χειροκτύπωι 'clapping with the hands'.[133] In these cases the substantival

---

[132] 'Limb-strengthening', according to LSJ, but cf. the subst. ἄρκεσις at S. *OC* 73 (only here in literary texts) and ἀρκέω 'help' at e.g. *Od*. 16. 261, S. *Ai*. 824, and thus 'helping the limbs' (with the -σι- usual for verbs and -γυιος understood as an object). Cf also ἀρκ]εσίβουλ[ος 'availing in command' (LSJ), cj. by Hunt at Cercidas fr. 16. 4 Lomiento (Rome, 1993), and the late adjectival formation ἀρκέσιμος.

[133] The reading is disputed: χοροιτύπωι Jacobs (cf. Pi. fr. 156 S.–M. ὁ ζαμενὴς δ' ὁ χοροιτύπος, | ὃν Μαλέας ὄρος ἔθρεψε, Ναΐδος ἀκοίτας | Σιληνός, where 'the Silenus' may refer to Marsyas, cf. fr. 157 S –M.), χοροκτύπωι (improbably) Meineke, Bergk.

element is formed from the simple stem; occasionally a dative stem is attested. This seems to be the case at *P.* 77 ὀριγόνοιcιν, where the form ὀρι- is not strictly dative (although locative in meaning), but may have been regarded as a possible alternative to ὄρει- by Timotheus (see n.).[134] Clearer examples are fr. 798 πυρικτίτωι 'made in/by fire', and fr. 789 δοριμάχου 'fighting with the spear'. In γονυπετής 'falling to one's knees' (*P.* 176) the sense of the substantive is presumably 'directive' in some way.

There are a number of cases where the first term apparently functions adverbially. Some of these are simply adverbs in their own right: *P.* 162 παλίμπορον 'travelling backwards', 173 παλινπόρευτον, 182 ὀπιccoπόρευτον, 201 ὑψι-κρότοιc, 206 εὐγενέταc 'well-born'.

There are three instances of three-term verbal compounds: *P.* 89 μακραυχενόπλουc, 132 κατακυμοτακεῖc (for the unparalleled formation, see n.), 216 μουcοπαλαιολύμαc.

A third category is the co-ordinative compound, in which each term qualifies the main noun. For instance, at *P.* 99 γυμνοπαγεῖc both γυμνο- 'naked' and -παγεῖc 'frozen' qualify the pronoun, and the full meaning of the compound is 'naked and frozen'. Occasionally this category is described by the Sanskrit term 'dvandva'. In Sanskrit, however, adjectives are only compounded to form dvandvas comparatively rarely. Another example may be *P.* 25 cτερεοπαγῆ, and perhaps *P.* 81 κλυcιδρομάδοc (see n.). The compound ὀξυπαρανδήτωι at *P.* 65a is in fact a two-term compound, and should be understood to mean 'shrill and distorted' (ὀξυ-παρανδήτωι). *P.* 79 παλαιομίcημα, in which the first element is adjectival and the second a substantive, is simply equivalent to the phrase παλαιὸν μίcημα.

D. Syntax

(i) The article

In the *Persae* the article usually has a pronominal sense, and occurs in the first position in a sentence or clause (fr. 790A,

---

[134] Risch argues that the passive sense given to -γονοc is a Greek innovation; traditionally such forms were active in meaning, cf. κουροτρόφοc vs. later ὀρεcίτροφοc and see Risch 196–8. The latter type may originally have been possessive, 'having one's birth in the mountains'. See Barrett on E. *Hipp.* 677–9 for the view that this range of meanings is inherent in Greek compound adjectives.

SYNTAX 51

P. 4, 14, 16, 18, 28 cj., 98, 145, 162, 191, 196, 216). There are two apparent exceptions: 173–4 ὁ δέ . . . Βαςιλεύς, 206–7 ὁ γάρ μ' εὐγενέτας κτλ. The separation of the article from the noun is, in the first case, particularly violent, and should be taken as analogous to the epic construction at e.g. *Il.* 1. 488–9 αὐτὰρ ὁ μήνιε νηυςὶ παρήμενος ὠκυπόροιcι | διογενὴς Πηλῆος υἱός, πόδας ὠκὺς Ἀχιλλεύς. Here the pronoun that is the subject of μήνιε is merely clarified by the addition of the name, and there is no suggestion that it is functioning as an article. At *P.* 225 ἐπὶ τῶι, the sense is also pronominal, 'after him'.

This evidence is somewhat balanced by the book-fragments, where the definite article is much commoner (frr. 781, 796. 1, 3, 4, 800. 1, 801, 802. 3). It is not clear what effect the article has in these instances; they do not appear formally different from many cases in the *Persae* where the article is happily omitted. The masculine nominative plural is οἱ; contrast τοί in Melanippides (fr. 760. 3, 4) and Telestes (fr. 810. 4), where, in all three cases, it is used pronominally. Melanippides also has τὰν ὀργάν (fr. 757. 2), ἁ . . . Ἀθάνα (fr. 758. 1), τὤργαν' (fr. 758. 2), τὰς . . . ψυχὰς (fr. 762. 2), but Telestes shows a reluctance to use the article.[135] Two instances are found in Philoxenus of Cythera (822, 832 cj.), two in Ariphron (813. 2, 4); however, the extant material is too scant for these data to have any independent value. Forms of ὅδε are found with some frequency in the concluding personal statement in *Persae* (*P.* 215 τῶνδε, 238 τάνδε, 240 τῶιδε), where the force may almost be deictic, but not in the narrative section even in speeches.

(ii) Tenses

The imperfect is standard in narrative, although we find a few cases of the aorist in temporal clauses (*P.* 163, 174) and also at the conclusion (198 ἐκελάδηcαν), where it has the

---

[135] At Telest. fr. 805(a). 1 †ὄν† coφὸν coφὰν λαβοῦcαν οὐκ ἐπέλπομαι νόωι | δρυμοῖc ὀρείοιc ὄργανον | δίαν Ἀθάναν δυcόφθαλμον αἶcχοc ἐκφοβηθεῖcαν αὖθιc χερῶν ἐκβαλεῖν | νυμφαγενεῖ χειροκτύπωι φηρὶ Μαρcύαι κλέοc, where Page conjectures τάν (ἕν Schweig-häuser : ἦν Stephanus : ἄν Meineke), read perhaps οὐ (emphatic as at *Od.* 3. 27–8 οὐ γὰρ ὀίω | οὔ cε θεῶν ἀέκητι γενέcθαι), or -)ον.

effect of marking the end of the narrative. This use of the imperfect is no doubt intended to add to the generic nature of the scenes described in the *Persae*, but also adds to the vividness of the details (see e.g. Barrett on E. *Hipp.* 907–8, 1180, 1209). This should be contrasted with the narrative passages in e.g. Aeschylus, where the aorist is standard for single events (Fraenkel on A. *Ag.* 407), though the present tense may be used for vivid descriptions (Fraenkel on *Ag.* 1383). In Pindar and Bacchylides we also find the expected aorist for single events and the imperfect or equivalent (but not the historic present) for generalized clauses. Timotheus uses the aorist a few times in the closing section (*P.* 222, 226, 228), where it describes simple factual events. In the speeches, as might be expected, a wider range of forms is found.

(iii) Prepositions

Most prepositions are attested, though often the force of a preposition is expressed through a preverb followed by the appropriate case. The instrumental or agentive dative regularly stands alone (e.g. *P.* 16–17, 19–20, 23, 44, 32–3, 96, 107, etc.). Timotheus admits both εἰς (*P.* 63, 174) and ἐς (*P.* 188), and it may be only coincidence that the two instances of εἰς precede a consonant while the one case of ἐς precedes a vowel. On περί at *P.* 134, see n.

(iv) Subordinating conjunctions

εἰ is found (in conjunction with μέν and δέ) with the optative at *P.* 7, 11.

ἐπεί is found with three senses: 'when' (with the indicative, *P.* 64, 162), 'whenever' (with the optative, *P.* 140), 'since' (with the future indicative, *P.* 129).

ὅτε, followed by an optative, 'whenever' is conjectured at *P.* 60; elsewhere it is only attested with an indicative and means 'when' (frr. 802. 1, 804).

ὡς 'when' (with indicative) is found at *P.* 173.

εὖτε is supplemented by Page at *P.* 14, and conjectured for codd. ὅτε by Wilamowitz at fr. 802. 1. Neither suggestion is adopted here.

(v) Particles

ἀλλά: normally inceptive (*P.* 7, 189, 202, 237), rather than adversative; the Celaenaean has ἀλλὰ κάθω 'but I stay (put)' at *P.* 156, where the particle has the stronger, and perhaps more prosaic, adversative sense.

γάρ: restricted to speeches (*P.* 108, 110, 116, 134) and 'personal statements' (*P.* 206, fr. 796), which may be regarded as direct addresses to the audience. It may have been regarded as more conversational or informal. γάρ may occur in narrative at Philox. fr. 829 αὐτοὶ γὰρ διὰ Παρνασσοῦ | χρυσορόφων Νυμφέων εἴcω | θαλάμων, but the context is uncertain; the lines may be from an address (e.g. the Cyclops to Galatea?) within narrative. On γάρ at *P.* 108, see n.

δέ: the standard connective between clauses, but only rarely found in association with μέν (fr. 780, *P.* 7/11, 164/166, 180/182, 190/191). At *P.* 164–6 the real contrast expressed is not between the two words immediately preceding the particles (αὐτίκα . . . δρύπτετο), but between the verbs. αὐτίκα has perhaps been 'fronted' to respond to ἐπεί in the preceding clause. At fr. 780 μέν merely establishes the potential for opposition with δέ in the next clause, and is not a true connective (see n.).

καί: twice emphatic (*P.* 72, 152), but there is one clear instance of τε . . . καί at *P.* 99 ff. The sense of καί at *P.* 150, in the Celaenaean's speech, is probably connective.

μέν: see δέ.

τε: common as a connective between verbs and nouns within a clause (*P.* 26, 48, 67, 80, 125, 179, 210, etc.). For τε . . . καί, s.v. καί.

τοι: once only, at *P.* 40 (see n.), but οὔτοι at fr. 781.

This list of particles broadly agrees with those that are commonest in Melanippides and in later fifth- and fourth-century dithyramb. Melanippides has the standard (adversative) ἀλλά (fr. 757. 3), γάρ (fr. 757. 1), δέ (*passim*), μέν (fr. 758. 1), and τε (*passim*), and in addition the collocation δή . . . μὲν οὖν (fr. 760. 3). Such collocations are generally rare in late fifth-century dithyramb. In later lyric the following particles are found: ἀλλά (Telest. fr. 805(*b*). 1, where it answers the rhetorical question at the end of fr. (a);[136] Philox. fr. 819), γάρ (Melanipp. fr. 763; Telest. fr. 805(a). 5, where it appears in direct address to the audience;[137] Ariphr. fr. 813. 3; Philox. fr. 829. 1), δέ (Telest. frr. 808. 1, 810. 4; Ariphr. fr. 813. 2, 10; [Arion], *PMG* adesp. 939. 4), καί (Ariphr. fr. 813. 9; Telest. fr. 805(a). 6), τε (Philox. fr. 820). In epigraphic poetry to the end of the fifth century the commonest particles are ἀλλά, γάρ, δέ, καί, μέν, and τε (see *CEG* i, index s.v.). In inscriptions after the end of the fifth century the same particles predominate; we find only occasional instances of e.g. ἄρα, δή, γε (*CEG* ii, index s.v.). In the *Deipnon* attributed by Page to Philoxenus of Leucas (*PMG* 836)[138] τε, καί, and δέ are all common, ἀλλά and μέν occur twice each, at (b). 7, 24 and 11, 40 respectively, as does δή at (b). 34, (e). 1; τοί, γε, and the rare combination δέ τε occur once each, respectively at (c). 3, (b). 19, (e). 4.[139]

A brief examination of late Euripidean lyric (especially Electra's monody and the Phrygian's aria in *Or.* 960 ff., 1369 ff., and the monodies of Jocasta and Antigone in *Ph.* 301 ff., 1485 ff.) shows relatively frequent use of ἀλλά, γάρ, μέν, δέ, καί, and τε, but little else.

This evidence should be contrasted with the rich list of particles found, for example, in Pindar. Apart from the common ones already mentioned, we find in addition μάν, δή, ἄρα, ἀτάρ, τοι, ἤτοι, and γε.[140] Bacchylides also has a slightly wider range of particles, including e.g. ἄρα, γε, δή,

---

[136] For this usage see Denniston 7–9.

[137] τί γάρ νιν εὐηράτοιο κάλλεος ὀξὺς ἔρως ἔτειρεν | ἆι παρθενίαν ἄγαμον καὶ ἄπαιδ' ἀπένειμε Κλωθώ; The opening of fr. (a) is in the first person (οὐκ ἐπέλπομαι) and amounts to a personal statement by Telestes.

[138] Athenaeus firmly ascribes this, a lengthy account of an elaborate banquet, to the Leucadian at 1. 5 B, and goes on to tell a comical story also attributed to the Cytherian (1. 5 F), elsewhere (4. 146 F), he expresses doubt as to the authorship (Φιλόξενος δ' ὁ Κυθήριος ἐν τῶι ἐπικαλουμένωι Δείπνωι, εἴπερ τούτου καὶ ὁ κωμωιδιοποιὸς Πλάτων ἐν τῶι Φάνωι ἐμνήσθη [fr. 189 K.–A.] καὶ μὴ τοῦ Λευκαδίου Φιλοξένου). But at 15. 685 D and 11. 487 A he ascribes it to 'Philoxenus the dithyrambic poet' (which can only mean the Cytherian, even though the poem is not a dithyramb), and in two other places (11. 467 D, 14. 642 F) he gives it explicitly to Philoxenus of Cythera. Given Athenaeus' own confusion we can form no firm judgement, but there is no real reason to deny the poem to the Cytherian. Cf. E. Degani, 'Filosseno di Leucade e Platone Comico (fr. 189 K.–A.)', *Eikasmos*, 9 (1998), 81–100.

[139] For this combination, see Denniston 529.

[140] For a list and detailed discussion, see P. Hummel, *La Syntaxe de Pindare* (Paris, 1993), 378–412.

τοι. This may again suggest that there was a decline in particle-use in lyric towards the end of the fifth and into the fourth centuries.[141]

(vi) Asyndeton

There are only a few cases of unexpected asyndeton; normally its presence can be accounted for stylistically, as at e.g. frr. 778(*b*), 790, *P.* 107, and the extensive asyndeton in the Celaenaean's speech at *P.* 150–61 (see nn.). The asyndeta at *P.* 167 and fr. 796. 3 (perhaps emphatic) are less easily explained.

V. METRE AND PROSODY

A. Metre

The main evidence for Timotheus' metrical practice is the *Persae*, though more information, especially about metres not represented in that poem, can be acquired from an examination of the book fragments. The *Persae* is written mainly in astrophic iambo-trochaics; cretics and dochmiacs are freely allowed as variants for iambo-trochaic elements, together with the expected admission of lekythia and ithyphallics. The iambo-trochaic sections are occasionally interrupted by passages in which aeolic metra predominate. Dactylo-anapaestic cola can be found in both environments. The final section of the poem (202–40) is composed almost entirely of aeolic metra, predominantly glyconic and pherecratean.

The most noticeable feature of the *Persae* is the absence of strophes and strophic responsion. Probably all Timotheus' poems were composed in this style. Hephaestion says as much of his citharodic nomes (*Poem.* iii(3) pp. 64–5 Consbruch), and there is no particular reason to suppose that he would have written strophically in his dithyrambs. Nevertheless Korzeniewski implausibly argued for an elaborate system of 'internal responsion' in *Persae*, based on the

---

[141] Emphatic particles become less common in Hellenistic prose, although connectives are no less common than they are in the classical period. Whether this is because they were felt to be too colloquial, or for some other reason, is unclear. See J Blomqvist, *Greek Particles in Hellenistic Prose* (Lund, 1969), 132 ff.

number of of cola in each section rather than on exact
metrical responsion.[142] For instance, in the concluding
hymn ll. 202–5 are said to respond with ll. 237–40, both
having four cola and roughly analogous content; ll. 206–12 ~
221–8, both having seven cola; and ll. 213–20 ~ 229–36,
both having eight cola. However, not only should ll. 237–40
actually be analysed as five cola ($hi \mid hi \mid hag^{..} \mid 2\ sp \mid tl^{..} \mid\mid$),
and 221–8 as eight cola, but it is in any case unclear that
metra of significantly different lengths can be said to
respond in any meaningful way,[143] and the resulting system
of imperfect responsions, admitted explicitly by Korzeniewski in his analysis of the body of the poem (e.g.
ll. 161–8 ~ 186–201, though the first passage has 15 metra
and the second only 10), itself discredits the position.

The other notable characteristic of *Persae* is the polymetric rhythm. This type of polymetric composition seems
to become more common in the latter part of the fifth
century, and can be found in a number of Euripides'
monodies and sung dialogues, especially in the later plays.
Jocasta's astrophic monody at *Ph.* 301–54 is a fairly simple
polymetric mix of dochmiac and iambic rhythms, with a
dactylic close (350–4). More complex are Antigone's solo
lyrics in the same play (1485–1581), which begins with a
sequence of dactylic metra (1485–1507), but turns into a
medley of aeolic and ionic/choriambic metres (1508–29).
Dochmiacs begin to intrude at 1533, and the song closes
with the predominantly dactylic metre with which it
opened. In the *Orestes*, the Phrygian's long aria, in five
parts (1369–1502), shows an even more complex metrical
scheme. The first part of the song (1369–74) begins with D^2,
and continues in syncopated iambo-trochaic dimeters, ending in ithyphallics. The second section (1381–92) also begins
D, before a sequence of dochmiacs, with occasional iambic
segmentation. The third (1395–9) is mainly in lyric anapaests; the fourth (1400–7) mixes dochmiacs and iambic
metra with a sequence of anapaests. The last part of the song

---

[142] Korzeniewski *passim*; the idea was first proposed in his *Griechische Metrik*
(Darmstadt, 1968), 182–5.
[143] Cf. Parker, *Songs*, 21. 'In polymetric lyric, metron-counting becomes
altogether questionable. In what sense can metra so different in length as the
anapaest and the dactyl be treated as equivalent?'

(1408–15) reverts to iambo-trochaic rhythms, but ends with a dochmiac.

In the same play, the song at *Or.* 960–1012 begins with a traditionally structured responding iambo-trochaic strophe and antistrophe (960–70 = 971–80), probably sung by the chorus, but Electra's epode is metrically freer and shows some similarities to the Phrygian's monody, with which it may have had musical connections (see Willink ad loc.). In the *Ion*, Creusa's astrophic monody (859 ff.) consists mainly of anapaests and paroemiacs, with occasional iambs; this recalls the rhythms of the epode in Ion's song at 112–83. Both may owe something to the metrical innovations of the new music. Closer to Timotheus is the astrophic Recognition Duet between Helen and Menelaus in the *Helen* (625–97), another late play, a mixture of trimeters and related metres (e.g. dochmiacs, bacchiacs, etc.). Similar lyric dialogues in Euripides share this characteristic; cf. e.g. the Recognition Duets at *IT* 827–99, *Ion* 1439–1509, *Hyps.* fr. 64. 70–111. In the last of these we find predominantly iambic metra (iambs, cretics etc.), with occasional dochmiacs and dactylic rhythms (including anapaests).

The polymetric style was certainly sufficiently recognizable as characteristic of Euripidean tragic lyric to be parodied by Aristophanes at *Ra.* 1331–63. However, it also features in some of Sophocles' later plays. Thus, in the *Philoctetes* a long lyric dialogue between the chorus and Philoctetes (1081–1168) in responding strophes is followed by a long epode that begins in iambics, but turns into ionics at 1175. At 1186 Sophocles introduces anapaests and aeolic metra (glyconics and anaclastic glyconics), with some dactylic elements, which predominate from 1196 to 1207. The final section of the song (1208–17) is a medley of aeolics, iambics, dactyls, and dactylo-epitrite, ending with a penthemimer. At S. *OC* 207–53 we find a similarly polymetric epode following a responding lyric dialogue between Oedipus and the chorus.

But polymetry was not limited to tragedy. The Hoopoe's astrophic song at *Av.* 229–59 is a virtuoso piece, mixing iambo-trochaic metres with dochmiacs, dactylo-epitrite, and ionics. Parker sees the influence of birdsong, and suggests possible influence from Alcman. But with its mimetic qualities and perhaps unusual dance-steps,[144] it may also have been intended to recall directly, though not parody, contemporary dithyrambic music (see Dunbar ad loc.). Outside drama the most extensive example is perhaps [Arion], *PMG* adesp. 939.[145]

(i) Iambo-trochaic

Timotheus shows a strong preference for short anceps in both iambic and trochaic metra (*c*.70% of instances for both), a preference shared by Aeschylus, which surprisingly seems to indicate a certain metrical conservatism.[146] However, this may well be deliberate in the context of *Persae*. Anceps is never resolved, which was probably usual in lyric of the period; Aristophanes has only five examples (*Ach.* 1040, *Nub.* 812, *Pax* 947, *Lys.* 345, *Thesm.* 680).[147] But both principes freely admit resolution, perhaps with a slight preference for resolution of the first princeps in the case of iambic metra. Syncopated iambic metra are also readily admitted. The first princeps of the cretic may be resolved; although a metron of the resulting type ⏑⏑⏑- might be analysed as a resolved bacchiac, its status as a resolved cretic is guaranteed by the absence of other resolved forms of the bacchiac.

Ithyphallics are common iambo-trochaic variants at period-end (*P.* 13; 14; 61; 85; 149; 155; 161), as they are in late Euripides: cf. E. *Ph.* 1581, *Or.* 963 ~ 974, 965 ~ 976, 984, 988, 1374. Resolution of the first (⏑⏑⏑-⏑--) or, more commonly, of the third syllable (-⏑⏑⏑⏑--) is admitted. The absence of resolution of the second princeps of the cretic indicates that the sequence should be here regarded as a separate metron rather than a simple combination of a cretic and a baccheus. There are occasional instances of resolution elsewhere in the metron. The sequence -⏑⏑ -⏑-- is also a common way to end a period (*P.* 10; 185;

---

[144] Dale, *CR²* 9 (1959), 199–200 = *Coll. Pap.* 135–6.
[145] For a metrical analysis, together with a discussion of some of the poem's textual problems, see West, 'Analyses', 5–9.
[146] See West, *Metre*, 100.
[147] Parker, *Songs*, 33.

201), and may be analysed as either a choriamb + a baccheus or an aristophanean. The molossus is occasionally admitted, as also sometimes in tragic iambic lyric (e.g. at E. *Ph.* 321 in Jocasta's monody, and in Ion's monody at E. *Ion* 125–7 ~ 141–3).

Word-end between two short metra produced by resolution ('split resolution') is generally avoided, as in dramatic iambo-trochaic lyric.[148]

(ii) Aeolic

Timotheus uses glyconics, pherecrateans, ibyceans, occasional hipponacteans and isolated anaclastic forms of the hagesichorean and telesillean. Glyconic cola ($\circ\circ - \cup\cup - \cup -$) show a tendency towards $--$ in the aeolic base, though both $- \cup$ and $\cup -$ are possible:

$--$ *P.* 134, 138, 207, 221, 223, 225, 227, 230, 232, 234
$- \cup$ *P.* 137, 216, 229
$\cup -$ *P.* 191, 204, 206, 209, 213, 219

Euripidean glyconics also show a preference for double long in the aeolic base; of his 312 glyconic pairs about half are of this form. Aeschylus, by contrast, shows a slight preference for bases with the form $\cup -$ or $- \cup$.[149] A similar preference for double long in the aeolic base is observable in pherecrateans:

$--$ *P.* 136, 186, 203, 212, 215, 217, 218, 220, 228, 233, fr. 796. 1
$- \cup$ *P.* 181, 192, 205, 222, 224 cj., 236
$\cup -$ *P.* 128, 208, 210

In the hipponacteans at *P.* 236, 238 both positions are again long; at 237 the same colon takes the form $- \cup\cup - \cup\cup - \cup --$, where the second long position in the aeolic base has been resolved. At 235 the anaclastic hipponactean takes the form $--- \cup - \cup\cup --$. Timotheus appears to allow resolution in the base in glyconics at *P.* 198, 211, both of which have the form $\cup\cup\cup - \cup\cup - \cup -$ and in the anaclastic glyconic at 180 $\cup\cup\cup - \cup - \cup\cup -$. In tragedy $\cup\cup\cup$ in the base of glyconics is restricted almost entirely to Euripides; Sophocles has two pairs of glyconics where $\cup\cup\cup - \cup\cup - \cup -$ respond, and one pair

---

[148] See L. P. E. Parker, *CQ²* 18 (1968), 241–69.
[149] See K. Itsumi, *CQ²* 34 (1984), 67.

where ∪∪∪ in the base responds with – –.[150] Resolution is not permitted elsewhere in aeolic metra, though common enough in Euripidean glyconics, especially in the forms o o – ∪∪∪∪∪ – and o o – ∪∪∪ – ∪∪∪, and occasionally attested for Sophocles.[151]

(iii) Ionics

Ionics are found in two fragments (fr. 796. 3–5, 801), and perhaps should be compared with the ionics in the parody of Cinesias' lyrics at Ar. *Av.* 1372–1409.[152] Possibly they were felt to be typically associated with the New Music, and free ionics have also been traditionally identified as the basic metre of Agathon's song at Ar. *Thesm.* 101–29.[153] However, Parker has recently rejected this analysis and identifies the song as consisting of a number of essentially aeolic cola with some limited ionic admixture (e.g. at 101, 108, 122?).[154]

B. Prosody

(i) Correption

There are only three final diphthongs followed by vowels in the *Persae*, all correpted: 130, 137 (both αι), 132 (οι). Within words correption seems less regularly applied. It may have influenced the scribal form παλεο- at *P.* 79 if this is not simply an error. At *P.* 197 Παιᾶν' may but need not exhibit correption of the first syllable; Παιάν at 205 and fr. 800. 4 requires two longs. There is no firm instance of correption of other diphthongs (e.g. ευ, υι), or of long vowels (e.g. η, ω). Correption seems to be required at Telestes fr. 805(a). 6 καὶ ἄπαιδ', (c). 2 αἰολοπτέρυγον (cj.), but not at frr. 805(b). 1 ματαιολόγων, 806. 3 αἰολομόρφοις (cj.). We find correption of οι at Melanipp. fr. 762. 1 μοι ὤ.

(ii) Stop + liquid

The problem of alternative analyses also applies to the question of stop + liquid combinations. However, it seems that where the combination occurs at the beginning of a

[150] Itsumi, *CQ²* 34 (1984), 67.   [151] Ibid. 77–8.
[152] Analysis in Parker, *Songs*, 340–5, and Dunbar, edn. ad loc.
[153] See J. W. White, *The Verse of Greek Comedy* (London, 1912), 189–91.
[154] Parker, *Songs*, 398–405.

word it is not usually treated as syllable-closing. This can be assumed in all cases in Timotheus (fr. 790A, *P.* 4, 8, 18, 27, 63, 78, 81, 85, 123, 148, 150, 166, 185, 195, 196, 228), and is the rule for poetry of the period (e.g. Melanipp. fr. 762.1; Licymnius frr. 769. 1, 770; Telestes frr. 806. 2, 808. 5; Ariphron fr. 813. 1, 5). At Melanipp. fr. 760. 2 τὸ πρίν, the combination is best treated as syllable-closing (*D²*–). This is also usual in tragic lyric, though in Attic speech such instances are normally syllable-releasing.[155] If we read cταλά[γμαcι ‿–‿– at 33, period-end must be assumed; but we might instead read cταλά[γμαcιν. A short-vowelled open syllable ending the first term of a nominal compound also regularly counts as short before stop + liquid; *P.* 12 πολυκρότουc, 24 αἰθεροδρόμοc cj., 30 χαλκόκραcι, 41 ἀμερο-δρόμοιο,[156] 89 (probably) -αυχενόπλουc, 127 χρυcοπλόκαμε, 138 ὠμοβρῶcι, 201 ὑψικρότοιc, 230 ἐνδεκακρουμάτοιc. This broad rule may explain 39 Ἀμφιτρίταc, which is also treated in this way at [Arion], *PMG* adesp. 939. 11. At 170 πολυ⟨γ᾽λώccωι⟩ cj. we should not expect γλ to be syllable-releasing. Verbal compounds are less regular; cf. *P.* 24 διακραδαίνων, 145 περιπλεκείc (cf. Telestes fr. 806. 4 ἀμφιπλέκων) against 209 ἐπιφ᾽λέγων.

At *P.* 84 ἄχναν, the combination -χν- could be regarded as either syllable-releasing or -closing without changing the metre (a lekythion of the form –‿–‿–‿‿ against one of the form –‿–––‿‿), but it is definitely syllable-releasing at 149 ἐξιχνεύων (ith.), and at Telestes fr. 805(*b*). 3 τέχναc, and is likely to have been usually so. The phonetically similar combination -κν- is twice treated as syllable-releasing (128 ἱκνοῦμαι, 222 ἐτέκνωcεν). Other combinations can be treated in either way: we have *P.* 89 (probably) μακ᾽ραυχενόπλουc and 219 λιγυμακ᾽ροφώνων against 206 μακραίων; fr. 780. 5 δακ᾽ρύοιcι and 139 κατεδάκ᾽ρυον against 100 δακρυ- (cf. Licymnius fr. 770 δακρύων; Melanipp. fr. 757. 5 ἱερόδακ᾽ρυν);

---

[155] West, *Metre*, 17; Barrett on E. *Hipp.* 760 Parker, *Songs*, 92–3 cites only two instances from Aristophanes, one of which (*Vesp.* 1232–3) is a quotation from Alcaeus, while the analysis of the other (*Nub.* 513 ὅτι π᾽ροήκων) is uncertain (see also Dover ad loc.).

[156] West, 'Analyses', 1, analyses this as ἀμεροδ᾽ρόμοιο, but this seems unlikely in view of the parallels, and the metre is subject to an alternative analysis (see n.).

135 ἄγριος against 184 ἀγ'ρίωι;[157] *P.* 199 cύμμετροι and 229 μέτροιc against fr. 780. 3 μέτ'ρ'. These, and the other instances, cannot be reduced to any sort of coherent system. At *P.* 61 ἄφρει the first syllable is long by nature because of the temporal augment (contrast ἀφρῶι at fr. 780. 2).

(iii) Zeta

Wilamowitz believed that ζ at 190 ζεύγνυτε did not make position.[158] This is extremely improbable, since, with the exception of the Homeric Ζάκυνθος, Ζέλεια, the earliest instance where ζ fails to make position is Theocr. 29. 20, by whose time the pronunciation of zeta had shifted from /sd/ to initial /z/, medial /zz/. There is no evidence for this sound change before the latter half of the fourth century, and it is unlikely to feature in Timotheus.[159]

(iv) Movable nu

Generally movable nu is only used to avoid hiatus (*P.* 23, 29, 65, 77 (twice), 88, 95, 96, 138, 222, and perhaps at *P.* 4), but it occasionally makes position (fr. 780. 3, 4, *P.* 44, 88, 144 cj.).

VI. THE PAPYRUS

A. The Archaeological Context

The Timotheus papyrus was found in 1902 by a German archaeological team led by Ludwig Borchardt, which was excavating a Greek necropolis at Abusir (ancient Busiris) north-west of Memphis. The main site excavated was the temple associated with the pyramid of Ne-woser-reʿ, an Egyptian king of the Fifth Dynasty (*c.*2500 BC). Archaeological evidence suggests that the temple was probably in use throughout the Middle Kingdom period (first quarter of second millennium BC), but by the New Kingdom (second half of the second millennium BC) the site had diminished in importance.[160] Borchardt also identified a large number of

---

[157] The analysis in the case is especially ambiguous: see the commentary.
[158] Wilamowitz 39.   [159] See Threatte i. 547–9; West, 'Analyses', 4.
[160] Borchardt 28, 42.

sarcophagi dating to a much later period (certainly after 700),[161] and, to the north of the temple site, between two of the monumental graves of the Middle Kingdom, a smaller group of Greek graves.

The Memphite Greek community dated from at least the sixth century, although archaeological evidence for Greek finds begins as early as the late seventh, perhaps as the result of trade.[162] The community continued to exist into the third century and Hellenistic times, and seems to have retained its Greek identity even under Persian rule. The Abusir site was probably the main Greek cemetery; the Ionian and Carian communities also had their own living quarters, located just to the north of the city proper.[163] The main Memphite necropolis, both in the Persian and Ptolemaic periods, was at nearby Saqqara, to the west of the city.[164]

The majority of Greek graves excavated in the necropolis contained wooden sarcophagi in the form of chests with gabled lids, a type also attested in the Milesian colonies on the northern Black Sea coast, generally dated to the time of Alexander the Great or slightly earlier, and also familiar from Athenian clay and stone sarcophagi.[165] The bodies were mummified, but naturally, not chemically as were Egyptian corpses. Greek pottery finds from the site range in date from the archaic to the classical age, but there is no evidence from after the middle of the fourth century; none of the coins portrayed Alexander, as we might have expected from perhaps the middle of his reign and certainly later. This suggests that the cemetery ceased to be used by Egyptian Greeks in Ptolemaic times, and thus probably that the Timotheus papyrus was deposited there at the

---

[161] Ibid. 44–5.

[162] Hdt. 2. 154 mentions a mercenary settlement, consisting of both Ionian Greeks and Carians, established under Amasis (570–528 BC) See further M. M. Austin, *Greece and Egypt in the Archaic Age* (Cambridge, 1970), 20–2; D. J. Thompson, *Memphis under the Ptolemies* (Princeton, 1988), 17.

[163] Thompson, op. cit. 17, 83–5.

[164] Ibid. 31.

[165] See Watzinger 32 ff., and for the Athenian sarcophagi, D. C. Kurtz and J. Boardman, *Greek Burial Customs* (London, 1971), 267–72. Wooden sarcophagi tend not to be preserved in Greek soil. Borchardt (46) concluded from the presence of ventilation holes in these sarcophagi that they were not intended for burial, and thus that they may have been imported.

time of Alexander the Great at the latest, and possibly
somewhat earlier.[166]

The papyrus itself was found on the ground to the north
of a wooden anthropoid sarcophagus dating to the period of
the Middle Kingdom.[167] It is not clear, especially given the
discovery of grave-goods actually inside the coffin,[168] that
the two finds should necessarily be closely linked, although
this has been the academic consensus in the past. The
western desert was also a site for waste-disposal, and the
papyrus may well have been casually discarded, or simply
lost.

The site-report records that a number of additional items
were found together with the papyrus near the sarcophagus.[169] These are listed together in a pre-war manuscript
catalogue of the Staatliche Museen zu Berlin (cat. no. 16214)
as follows: remains of an iron scraper, remains of a sponge,
remains of a leather bag, wooden object.[170] According to

[166] Watzinger 8–15.

[167] Photographs in Borchardt 47; Wilamowitz, *Lichtdruck* 5, 12. I am indebted
to Herr Prieser of the Staatliche Museen zu Berlin—Preußischer Kulturbesitz for
the opportunity to examine the sarcophagus, which is not on general display. It is
not particularly elaborate; it has eyes painted on in black paint, but is otherwise
undecorated. Given its Middle Kingdom date, it has been commonly suggested
that the coffin had been found at some stage and sold for reuse, although the
reasons for this, when traditional Greek coffins were clearly readily available, are
obscure. A nearby grave contained only the lid of a similar anthropoid sarcophagus,
dated by Borchardt (44–5) to *c*.580 BC, without the matching chest, which bears the
name of Abhem the son of Qert, an Asiatic immigrant who took the name Hophra
in Egypt; Borchart sees a connection with the early 6th-c. Egyptian king Hophra.
Such old, reused coffins might represent a cheaper form of burial, but it is not
immediately obvious that these are paupers' graves; Borchart (45) argues that the
Abusir Greeks belonged to the propertied classes. Nor is it clear that reusing old
coffins was a particularly widespread phenomenon among the Egyptian Greeks,
although the practice is attested elsewhere at Abusir. There is, however, evidence
for the reuse of archaic coffins in classical Corinth (see D. C. Kurtz and
J. Boardman, op. cit. 192). At any rate the practice should not be taken to reflect
any significant degree of Egyptianization among the Abusir community.

[168] These were found inside the bindings of the mummy itself. By and large they
are items belonging to everyday life (make-up case, spoon, etc.). Two bronze items
were identified by Watzinger (7) as pens, but though bronze pens are attested
elsewhere in the Greek world (cf. W. E. H. Cockle, *BICS* 30 (1983), 150), there is
no real indication that these are writing implements.

[169] Borchardt 47.

[170] I cite the descriptions of the Berlin catalogue here, and for the finds inside the
coffin, with the kind permission of Herr Prieser (n. 167). I have been unable to
examine any of these finds myself, as their exact location in Berlin is unknown to
the curators.

Borchardt, the piece of iron, together with a piece of turned wood which may have belonged with it, was found on top of the sarcophagus. The exact significance of these items has been the subject of some debate. As Wilamowitz noted, although the presence of a sponge might suggest that the man was a scribe, this hypothesis seems to be excluded by the absence of any further writing-materials such as pen or ink-jar;[171] sponges were also used in preparing corpses for burial.

In conclusion, there is little reason to connect the papyrus with the dead man. There is no evidence that he was a scribe. The papyrus does not appear to have been a performance text like the Elephantine scolia, and there is no indication that the supposed owner was a singer or musician of any sort.[172] The presence of other grave-goods inside the sarcophagus suggests that the position of the papyrus is merely a matter of coincidence. We do not know why it lay where it did, but we cannot discount the possibility that it was simply lost by accident.[173]

B. Description

The papyrus (P. Berol. 9875) consists of six irregular columns of writing. The irregularity of line-length within a column is presumably a reflection of the early date of the papyrus, but may also reflect the scribe's feeling that lyric poetry should be written κατὰ cτίχον, though the text is clearly non-colometric. Column-width is regular in the Derveni papyrus, as also in the contemporary epigraphic

---

[171] Wilamowitz 4. Sponges were used by scribes to erase mistakes; see *GMAW* 6–7.

[172] For the Elephantine scolia (P. Berol. 13270) as performance texts, see F. Ferrari, *SCO* 38 (1989), 181 ff. and the brief discussion in A. Cameron, *Callimachus and his Critics* (Princeton, 1995), 74–5 We might also contrast the (as yet unpublished) 5th-c. BC papyrus found, together with a bronze pen, the remains of a tortoise-shell lyre, and two white-ground lekythoi, in a tomb in Attica on the road between Athens and Sounion. It seems clear that this was the tomb of a singer; for this information, see W. E. H. Cockle, *BICS* 38 (1983), 147.

[173] P van Minnen has recently argued that the Panhellenism of the poem was an important part of its popularity in the Greek world outside Athens, and perhaps especially to the Hellenomemphites at a time when the Persians, having lost control of Egypt, were trying to re-establish their political authority Memphis finally surrendered in 343, remarkably close to the time when the owner of the papyrus was buried. But the evidence casts serious doubt on this theory.

texts on which the papyrus scripts are modelled; early lyric texts, however, tend to be less regular. The scribe generally attempts to end a line at the end of a word, but occasionally words are split across lines. This could be due to inaccurate calculation of the space available. Furthermore, on several occasions he incorrectly judges the amount of space required between columns, with the result that some of the longer lines project across the intercolumnium. The left-hand side of the column is generally more regular, but, as we might expect, drifts to the left further down the column (Maas's Law). There are few diacritical marks, although paragraphoi are found indicating the end of speeches on column iv, and the end of the narrative on column v. In the latter case it is used in conjunction with what appears to be a primitive (or stylized) coronis. In column vi a paragraphos indicates the end of the poem. In each of these cases the divisions are also marked by leaving the rest of the line blank after the last word of the preceding section; the lemmata in the Derveni papyrus are marked in the same way. We might compare the inscriptional use of the paragraphos in the text of Limenius' Delphic paean (*CA* 149–59) to separate the concluding prayer from the rest of the poem.[174] No paragraphoi are observable in columns i–iii, but the left-hand margins of i–ii, and the bottom left of column iii, are badly damaged. There is no subscription, as might be expected, at least in later texts, so that if the roll contained a title, this must have stood at the beginning (see below, p. 73). *Scriptio plena* is used as a rule, but there are nevertheless a number of instances where the spelling reflects elision, although it is never marked. Phonetic assimilations are usually written, even across words. Corrections, in the same hand as the main text, and occasional expunction marks, are found sporadically.

The script is largely bilinear, although omicron, delta, zeta, theta, and omega are written somewhat smaller than

---

[174] In the Derveni papyrus paragraphoi are normally used to indicate a quotation or (accompanied by a dash) to mark the end of a period. However, this is not entirely regular; Obbink notes that there is 'at least one irrationally placed *paragraphos*'. See D. Obbink, in A. Laks and G. Most (eds.), *Studies on the Derveni Papyrus* (Oxford, 1997), 44–5, and M. S. Funghi, ibid. 26.

the other letters and hang from the upper line.[175] The style is generally described as 'epigraphic', and attempts to imitate the regularity of monumental inscriptions. There is a fairly consistent, if not always successful, attempt to make each letter occupy an approximately equivalent space on the papyrus in an effort to reproduce the stoichedon style of early inscriptions, and both these features can be observed in the similarly early Derveni papyrus.[176] The epigraphic influence is most evident in the square epsilon, the angular phi, and in the forms of tau and theta. Theta is written as a circle with a point, rather than a crossbar, and tau is formed with only a short horizontal stroke. The omega is described by Roberts as 'transitional', and is more cursive than that found in the Derveni papyrus.

The 'broken sigma', written in four movements, disappears, except in deliberately archaizing scripts, by the end of the fourth century, but can still be observed in the Order of Peucestas (c.331–321).[177] In later papyri it is replaced by lunate sigma. Mu is written in four movements, as sometimes in the Derveni papyrus, where a form written in three movements is also found; this way of writing mu is again generally restricted to the fourth century, but occasionally attested in the third. Zeta is made with an upper and a lower stroke, and a dot central, xi with three unconnected cross-strokes. In the Derveni papyrus, as in Grenfell's tragic fragment,[178] xi is already written either with a vertical line or a simple dot between each pair of bars. The form of pi, made in three strokes, with a shortened right-hand vertical, is not seen again after the first half of the third century.

This evidence suggests strongly that we should date the text to about the third or second quarter of the fourth

---

[175] A full collection of plates is to be found in Wilamowitz, *Lichtdruck*; individual plates are published in Seider ii. 37 no. 2; C. H. Roberts, *Greek Literary Hands 350 B.C.–A.D. 400* (Oxford, 1955), no. 1; *PGB* no. 1.

[176] *GMAW* no. 51; Seider i. 35–56 no. 1.

[177] P. Saqqara inv. 71/2 GP 9 (*GMAW*, no. 88); cf. also the tragic fragment (*TrGF* adesp. 625) published by Grenfell, *Greek Papyri*, ii (Oxford, 1897), no. 1a, originally ascribed to the 3rd c. BC, but almost certainly to be dated to the 4th. The omega and square epsilon are similar to those in the Timotheus papyrus, but the three horizontal bars of xi are now connected by a vertical line, which is a later form of the letter (although still epigraphic).

[178] See previous n.

century, before the death of Alexander in 323. It is certainly earlier than the Elephantine marriage-contract (311/10)[179] or the Elephantine scolia (which have a *terminus ante quem* of 284/3),[180] and probably also pre-dates the Order of Peucestas. It may be earlier than the Derveni papyrus, although it is unclear to what extent scripts varied in different areas. Since the Derveni text is the only secure example of a manuscript written outside Egypt at this period, it is uncertain how exact a comparison can be made. The similarities between the Timotheus and Derveni papyri may indicate that there was no significant divergence in scripts between Egypt and Greece in the fourth century, although of course the provenance of the Timotheus papyrus is uncertain. It may have been imported into Egypt.[181] Alternatively, similarities between the Derveni papyrus and the other early texts might indicate little more than the fact that they all have a common Macedonian origin. But we cannot use such a hypothesis to suggest that the Timotheus scribe had Macedonian connections.

Wilamowitz in fact argued that the scribe of the papyrus must have been an Ionian, since iota adscript, though regularly written after omega except at 240 τωδε, tends to be omitted after alpha (e.g. 66 φωνα, 133 βορεα, 227–8 Αντιcca); he took this to indicate that while iota adscript stood in the scribe's exemplar, the scribe himself was not in the habit of pronouncing it after a final alpha. This usage, he claimed, would have been impossible in a fourth-century Attic text but agrees with the practice of Ionic inscriptions of the same period. There are almost no instances of a for αι in Attic inscriptions before 300 BC, and even in the Ptolemaic papyri αι is rarely replaced by a, and is regularly preserved in the dative singular. Ionian inscriptions show highly irregular retention of iota adscript after alpha. Similarly, -χιτωνα

---

[179] Seider i. 33–4 no. 1; *PGB* no. 2. The Marriage Contract has a slightly more slanted script and lunate sigma, but epigraphic omega and square epsilon, and a rough bilinearity reminiscent of the Timotheus papyrus. Omicron is again written slightly smaller than the rest of the letters.

[180] Seider ii. 38–9 no. 3; *PGB* no. 3. The scolia should probably be dated to c.300 BC; the script has slightly more rounded capitals and lunate sigma, but epigraphic omega is the same as in the Timotheus papyrus.

[181] Cf. E. Crisci, *Papyrologica Florentina*, 27 (1996), 7–30.

appears as -κιτωνα (124), possibly reflecting Ionian κιθών vs. Attic χιτών.[182] This argument has a certain amount of strength, although we cannot be entirely certain about the skill of the scribe, and the linguistic conditions of pre-Ptolemaic Egypt. It is possible that iota adscript ceased to be pronounced or written well before it was lost in Athens, and that with the peculiar mixture of communities in Egypt we should not ascribe the practice to a particular national group. However, even if Wilamowitz's argument is accepted, it does not follow from this that the papyrus was imported from Ionia; there were certainly Ionians living in Egypt in the pre-Ptolemaic period, and there is no reason to suppose that the papyrus could not have been produced locally.

When discovered, the papyrus, originally a complete roll, was cut open, and each column is now separate from the others. This means that the columns are of an irregular shape; I therefore do not give exact measurements which tell us nothing about the appearance of the ancient text. However, I have tried to indicate where possible the length of the longest line, and the minimum intercolumnium allowed. Each column of writing is 18.5 cm high, but varies in the number of lines allowed because of the variation in the space left between lines. According to Borchardt, the unrolled papyrus measured 1.11 m in length.[183] When it was initially unrolled, a series of photographs were taken of each column, which preserve some information about the positioning of, and relationship between, fragments, which is not apparent from their present condition. These photographs, published in Wilamowitz's *Lichtdruck-Ausgabe* of 1903, are therefore still of use in reconstructing the text.

(i) Column i

A variety of scattered fragments, some more extensive and legible than others. The position of the larger fragments can be determined to some extent, either because they were removed from the back of column ii, or because their

---

[182] Wilamowitz 10; see also Kühner–Blass i. 183–5; Buck 35; Threatte i. 358 ff., and for the papyrological evidence Mayser–Schmoll i/1. 96–7.
[183] Borchardt 47.

margins are preserved. There are nine main fragments, and many smaller, unplaced ones, some of which contain little more than an isolated letter or illegible traces of ink. Most of these I have not thought worth transcribing.

Fragment 1. Two separate pieces (1a) 3 × 1.2 cm,[184] first with a left-hand margin of 0.5 cm. and traces of an upper margin; (1b) 4.8 × 1.7 cm, with an upper margin of 0.5 cm. They were still joined when photographed in Abusir.[185] The left-hand side of fr. 1a is remarkably straight, and does not appear to have frayed edges like the other external edges of the columns. Wilamowitz suggests that it was deliberately cut from the preceding column, and thus that what we have here is only the last part of the original roll.[186] It is therefore uncertain how much of the poem is missing, but it should be noted that all the quotation-fragments belong to this earlier section and that it must have been long enough to include the *prooimion* and the preparations for battle, as well as several (at least two) speeches. In later times a standard roll appears to have had twenty sheets, with an average length of 340 cm, but since these figures can vary from roll to roll, and do not necessarily reflect earlier practice, it is impossible to calculate the poem's probable length on this basis.[187]

Fragment 2 (3.1 × 2.4 cm). Separated on unrolling from fr. 4/5, and thus to be placed on the upper edge of the column, although its exact position is uncertain and there is no trace of a margin. Wilamowitz did not transcribe the fragment, but placed it c.5 letters away from fr. 1. 4.

Fragment 3. Also belonging to the top half of column, perhaps somewhere in the centre (so Wilamowitz). At discovery the fragment consisted of one piece, but there are now three separate pieces: (3a) 1.6 × 1.2 cm, (3b) 1.5 × 1.5 cm, (3c) 2 × 2.5 cm.

Fragment 4. Two separate pieces, the first (4a: 7 × 2.8 cm) with an upper margin of 0.4 cm, the second (fr. 4b:

---

[184] Dimensions are given as height × width.

[185] Wilamowitz 10.

[186] Ibid. 3.

[187] See T. C. Skeat, *ZPE* 45 (1982), 169–75. Bassett (157 n. 2) ignores the fact that the first section of the roll is missing, and incorrectly attempts to calculate the length of the poem on the basis of two rolls, the first approximately equivalent to the extant six columns. So also Korzeniewski and Campbell.

5.3 × 2.2 cm) with an upper margin of 0.5 cm and a right
margin of varying size (max. 0.9 cm at lines 2, 6). Fr. 4a was
removed from column ii, and its position can thus be
determined with some clarity: it belongs shortly before
fr. 4b on the upper part of the page. The space between
the two pieces varies from 2 to 3 cm. Lines 8 and 9 of 4b
appear to be empty, but could be stripped.

Fragment 5 (1.7 × 2.3 cm). Below fr. 2, perhaps separated
by about six lines (Wilamowitz 12).

Fragment 6 (2.4 × 2.2 cm). From the lower half of the
column, about four letters from the left-hand side (Wilamowitz 12). The fragment was not transcribed in the *editio
princeps*.

Fragment 7. Two separate, but closely connected, pieces,
the first of which (7a: 2.5 × 2.1 cm) was not transcribed by
Wilamowitz, but which shows traces of five (not four) lines.
Fr. 7b (2.7 × 2.5 cm) appears to be torn at the second line,
and the two sections should perhaps be brought closer
together.

Fragment 8: The first three lines transcribed by
Wilamowitz are no longer attached, but are preserved in
the original photographs taken at Abusir. The fragment now
measures 3 × 3.1 cm.

Fragment 9: Three separate fragments from the right-
hand side of the column. Fr. 9a (13 lines; 7 × 3 cm) preserves
a margin of varying size; according to Wilamowitz, it should
be placed about 3 lines distant from the bottom of fr. 4.
Fr. 9b: 2.5 × 1 cm. Fr. 9c (3 lines; 3 × 2.5 cm) gives a lower
margin of 1 cm (and perhaps a right margin of *c*.1 cm in the
first line).

Fragment 10: 2.9 × 1.4 cm. Of uncertain position; it is the
largest of the unplaced fragments.

Of the remaining unplaced fragments most are illegible or
preserve at most a single letter. They are therefore of little
use in reconstructing the text of column i, and I have not
deemed most of them worth transcribing. They were neither
transcribed nor numbered in the *editio princeps*. I have given
the text of fr. 17 (1.3 × 1.3 cm) and fr. 20 (1.3 × 1.1 cm), as
these are among the larger fragments, although neither is of
much help in reconstructing the text.

(ii) Column ii

Four separate fragments, with many serious lacunae. The longest line is 25.5 cm, but there are a number of much shorter lines. The left-hand intercolumnium is regularly 1 cm, and the lower margin measures 1.2 cm. The upper margin is not preserved. There are twenty-nine lines. There are some marginalia on the right upper corner, of uncertain significance, but they appear to be written in the same hand as the main text, although slightly more cursive.

(iii) Column iii

Twenty-six lines. Relatively well preserved, although there is some damage along the bottom edge and in the lower third of the column. The upper margin also shows evidence of damage, but was at least 0.4 cm wide. At the widest point the column is 24 cm wide, although this line juts into column iv. The intercolumnium is thus variable, but is in places quite wide.

(iv) Column iv

Twenty-six lines. This column was on display and not available for collation or detailed examination. Although one line of column iii breaks into the regular line of the left-hand margin, it is clear that a wide intercolumnium was generally allowed for. I was unable to calculate the width of the column at its widest point, but at times, especially in the lower part of the column, the writing almost abuts the line-beginnings of column v. Both upper and lower margins are preserved.

(v) Column v

Twenty-six lines. Again a fairly regular left-hand margin, with significant variation in line-length, and with an upper margin (slightly damaged) of 0.5 cm, and a lower margin of c.1.3 cm. The most interesting thing about this column is the coronis in the left intercolumnium denoting the end of the narrative and the beginning of the sphragis. The way the column has been cut is particularly instructive. It appears that the scribe left enough space at the end of column iv to fit the coronis into the intercolumnium, but that immediately after the point where this stands, he began writing longer lines, so that they almost adjoin the beginnings of column v. We may conclude from this that his exemplar may also have had a coronis, or that even if it did not it cannot have looked significantly different from our copy. There is no other way the scribe can have been sure of where the coronis had to be placed. This may also explain his tendency to vary line-lengths so greatly.

(vi) Column vi

The last column, with only four lines of writing, and a maximum line-length of 15.5 cm. There is a large margin of 4.5 cm on the right-hand side; after the final paragraphos the rest of the papyrus is left blank. One marked peculiarity is the absence of an end-title, such as appear to have been almost standard in papyrus rolls in later periods. Some later texts also have titles at the beginning of the roll; in larger collections of works, such as the London Bacchylides, they are sometimes written in the intercolumnium. It is possible that in pre-Alexandrian papyri the title was only written on the outside of the roll.[188]

VII. TIMOTHEUS IN ANTIQUITY

The fourth-century papyrus preserves the main extant fragment of Timotheus' work. Otherwise we rely for our knowledge on quotations by other authors, but the variety of sources provides a good deal of evidence for the transmission of the poems in antiquity. It must be assumed that texts of his poems were in circulation during his life, and were subject to performance by other citharodes or by dithyrambic choruses under someone else's supervision. For instance, not all the Greeks who quoted fr. 790 in Asia Minor in 390 could have been at the first performance of the *Persae*. We should probably imagine individual works circulating in the form of single papyrus rolls like that of the *Persae*, but it is possible that his works were collected into a corpus either during his lifetime or shortly after his death.

---

[188] So R. P. Oliver, *TAPA* 82 (1951), 241 ff.

There was no Alexandrian edition of the dithyrambic poets, nor were they part of the Alexandrian canon. The reason for this is perhaps that they were still being performed well into the Hellenistic period and possibly after. Whereas Euripides' works were both edited and still performed in the third century and later, the canon of lyric poets seems to have consisted of those ancient poets whose work survived the classical period primarily, or only, in book form.[189] There were, naturally, book-texts of the later lyric poets available already in the fourth century: Alexander the Great, whilst on campaign in Asia, sent for copies of the dithyrambs of Philoxenus and Telestes as part of his reading matter (Plu. *Alex.* 8. 668 D).

Lucian, *Harmon.* 1 mentions a performance of the *Ajax* in Athens by Timotheus of Thebes, probably early in his career, although the exact date is uncertain (πρῶτον ἐλθὼν οἴκοθεν . . .).[190] He won a prize for the performance. The *Elpenor* was revived in Athens by the piper Pantaleon of Sicyon together with a boys' chorus in 320/19 (*IG* ii². 3055); the date is confirmed by the inscription, which mentions the archonship of Neaechmus,[191] and which states that the performance took place, and won the prize, at the Dionysia. Philoxenus of Cythera's *Cyclops*, together with two other Cyclops dithyrambs, was allegedly presented in the presence of Philip of Macedon shortly before the siege of Methone (at which Philip reportedly lost an eye) in 354:[192]

τὰ μ(ὲν) γ(ὰρ) περὶ τῶν αὐλητ(ῶν) ὁμολογεῖται κ(αὶ) παρὰ Μαρςύαι (*FGrH* 135–6 F 17), διότι cυντελοῦντι μουcικοὺc ἀγῶναc αὐτῶι μικρὸν ἐπάνω τῆc cυμφορ(ᾶc) κ(ατὰ) δαίμονα cυνέβη τὸν Κύκλωπα πάνταc αὐλῆcαι, Ἀντιγενείδην μ(ὲν) τὸν Φιλοξένου, Χρυcόγονον δ(ὲ) τὸν

---

[189] See Wilamowitz, *Textgesch.* 7, 17.

[190] The precise dates of Timotheus of Thebes are uncertain: he is mentioned by Diphilus (fr. 78 K.–A.), and may have performed before Philip of Macedon in 354 (see n. 193). Chares says a Timotheus played at Alexander's wedding in Susa in 324 (*FGrH* 125 F 4). Bélis, '*Ajax*', makes much of these dates, and suggests that the *Ajax* may have been written for Timotheus of Thebes, and that Lucian is referring to a performance before the death of Timotheus of Miletus: possible, but tenuous.

[191] See U. Köhler, *Ath. Mitt.* 10 (1885), 231–6.

[192] For the date of the siege of Methone, see J. Buckler, *Philip II and the Sacred War* (*Mnem.* Suppl. 109; Leiden, 1989), 181–5.

[Cτ]ηcιχόρου, Τιμόθεον δ(ὲ) τὸν Οἰνιάδου (Didym. in [Dem.] xii. 55–62, pp. 45–6 Pearson–Stevens = *PMG* adesp. 840).[193]

The reliability of this convenient anecdote may be doubted.[194] There were presumably other revivals, especially perhaps at rural festivals which might not have been wealthy enough to commission new compositions by famous poets.

Aristotle was clearly familiar with Timotheus' poetry, and appears to have seen a performance of the *Scylla*, if Timotheus' poem is meant at *Poet.* 26. 1461[b]30. He also mentions the *Cyclops* (2. 1448[a]11). Elsewhere in the *Poetics* and the *Rhetoric* Aristotle quotes Timotheus without ascription (Timoth. fr. 797). Antiphanes, who produced his first play in 385, cites the same phrase in his *Caeneus* (fr. 110 K.–A.), and attributes it explicitly to Timotheus; the date of the *Caeneus* is uncertain, though it may have been produced in Timotheus' lifetime. Together with another comic quotation at Anaxandr. fr. 6 K.–A., this suggests a certain amount of familiarity with Timotheus' work on the part of the average Athenian, as we should of course expect. Probably what stuck in the average person's mind were particularly the strong compounds and bizarre periphrases. Similarly, Antiphanes, in his *Traumatias* (fr. 205 K.–A. = *PMG* 832) quotes Philoxenus' neologism ἀρκεcίγυιον, and Theopompus refers to Telestes' use of ἄκατον 'boat' as a word for 'cup' (fr. 4 K.–A. = *PMG* 811). Antiphanes seems on the whole to have been rather fond of the dithyrambographers as a

[193] Foucart emended the last phrase to read Οἰνιάδην δ(ὲ) τὸν Τιμοθέου, which, if correct, would indicate a performance of the *Cyclops* shortly after Timotheus' death. Oeniades is known as a piper from an inscription dating to 384/3 (*IG* ii². 3064), but is not otherwise mentioned as a composer. It is possible that he was still performing thirty years after this victory, as we have no idea of his age at the time, or we might even think of a reference to his son, who could have been called by the same name. Families of musicians are not unknown: Oeniades' father was the famous aulete Pronomus, who also composed a processional hymn to Delos (*PMG* 767: cf. Athen. 14. 631 E). However, it is equally likely that he, or another poet/musician of the same name, composed a dithyrambic *Cyclops*, and that the piper was another Timotheus, perhaps Timotheus of Thebes.

[194] A. S. Riginos, *JHS* 114 (1994), 105–11, has recently suggested that 'Cyclops' may have been an epithet applied to Philip during his life, and that the story about the pipers developed out of this nickname. N. G. L. Hammond, by contrast, believes that the details 'are likely to be right'; see *A History of Macedonia* (Oxford, 1979), ii. 257 n. 2.

subject for humour: a character in the *Tritagonistes* (fr. 207 K.–A.) indulged in (comically?) high praise of Philoxenus.

Aristoxenus (fr. 76 Wehrli) says that a contemporary of his, the otherwise unknown Telesias of Thebes, learnt by heart the works of Timotheus and Philoxenus when he was seduced by the elaborate music of the theatre (ὑπὸ τῆς cκηνικῆς τε καὶ ποικίλης μουcικῆς), after a sound education in the style of Pindar and other older lyric poets. However, when he came to compose himself, he found that, because of his excellent education, he could only compose in the Pindaric style. This anecdote may point to a certain high-brow disapproval of Timotheus' poetry in the latter part of the fourth century.

The apparently high level of interest in the dithy-rambographers continued at least into the second century BC. Alexander Aetolus mentions a tradition that Timotheus performed the *Artemis* at the rededication of the Temple at Ephesus after its destruction; the difficulties of this passage are discussed in some detail elsewhere (see above, pp. 14–15, and commentary on fr. 778), but it should at least be noted that Alexander seems to have known Timotheus' work and to have had access to some sort of biographical tradition (even if perhaps sightly inaccurate). Similarly bookish may be the reference to the *Cyclops* at Chrysippus, π. ἀποφατ. 10 (Timoth. fr. 781), where it is unclear whether Chrysippus actually knew the poem, or merely took the quotation and the reference from an earlier rhetorical textbook. But firm evidence for actual performance comes from Plutarch (*Philopoem.* 11. 362 CD) and Pausanias (8. 50. 3), both of whom report that the citharode Pylades of Megalopolis gave a performance of the *Persae* at the Nemean games in 205. It is not stated in either source what music the nome was performed to, or whether the original music still survived. It is possible that it did, having been transmitted essentially by continued performance rather than by the comparatively rare musically annotated texts with which we are familiar. Finally, Machon, in an anecdote about the gluttony of Philoxenus of Cythera, refers to Timotheus' *Niobe*, with the detail that Charon appeared as a character. Philoxenus seems to have been a particular favourite of the Hellenistic

poets: apart from his influence on Theocritus (*Id.* 6, 11), he
is mentioned by Hermesianax (fr. 7. 69 ff. Powell). Hermesianax also seems to have borrowed the story of Nanis from
Licymnius (fr. 6 Powell).
In the second century itself we find a Cretan inscription
(*Inscrip. Creticae*, i. 66, no. 11 + i. 280, no. 1 = *DGE* 190)
set up to honour Menecles, a Tean ambassador to Crete,
who is said to have often performed to the cithara the songs
of Timotheus, Polyidus, and certain unnamed ancient
Cnossian poets, ὡc προcῆκεν ἀνδρὶ πεπαιδευμένωι. *Inscrip.
Creticae*, i. 280–2, no. 2 (from Prianos), gives a slightly
different text, but the same sense. It is interesting that
Menecles also composed his own poems on Cretan legend
and history. Polybius records, as a matter for praise, that
the poems of Timotheus and Philoxenus were part of the
school curriculum in Arcadia in the second century BC (4.
20. 8–9):

ταῦτα γὰρ πᾶcίν ἐcτι γνώριμα καὶ cυνήθη διότι cχεδὸν παρὰ μόνοιc
Ἀρκάcι πρῶτον μὲν οἱ παῖδεc ἐκ νηπίων ἄιδειν ἐθίζονται κατὰ νόμουc
τοὺc ὕμνουc καὶ παιᾶναc οἷc ἕκαcτοι κατὰ τὰ πάτρια τοὺc ἐπιχωρίουc
ἥρωαc καὶ θεοὺc ὑμνοῦcι· μετὰ δὲ ταῦτα τοὺc Φιλοξένου καὶ Τιμοθέου
νόμουc μανθάνοντεc . . .

After the second century BC there is a slight gap in the
evidence, though how seriously this is to be viewed is
debatable. Dionysius of Halicarnassus (*Comp.* 19. 131–2)
appears to be aware of the differences between early archaic
lyric, classical lyric (Pindar), and the 'new dithyrambic'
poetry, and mentions Philoxenus, Timotheus, and Telestes.
He reveals some knowledge of their musical and metrical
innovations, but could owe this knowledge to earlier musical
treatises, such as that of Heraclides Ponticus. There is no
further reference to Timotheus' works which can be dated
to this period, and no testimony which would indicate
whether they were still being performed or not. Clearly
the texts survived, but the original music, possibly transmitted in an unbroken line from the early fourth century,
may have been lost at this stage, if Timotheus' works ceased
to be part of the citharodic repertoire. Two of his poems

may have been sung by Nero; we do not know to what music.[195]

In the second century AD there is firm evidence that the poems were performed to modern music. However, we do not know whether this was because the original music had been lost. A certain C. Aelius Themison records in an inscription that he was honoured by the Milesians for setting the works of Timotheus, as well as those of Sophocles and Euripides, to his own music:[196]

ἡ βουλὴ καὶ ὁ δῆμος | Μειλησίων Γ. Αἴλιον | Θεμίcωνα Θεοδότου υ(ἱὸν) | νεικήcαντα Ἴcθμια | Νέμεα κοινὸν ε' | καὶ τοὺς λοιποὺς ἀγῶ|νας πθ' μόνον καὶ | πρῶτον Εὐρειπίδην | Cοφοκλέα καὶ Τειμόθεον | ἑαυτῶ(ι) μελοποιήcαντα | Ψ(ηφίcματι) Β(ουλῆc) (SEG 11. 52c p. 215)

This presumably, but not certainly, refers to Timotheus the citharode rather than to the fourth-century tragedian of the same name (cf. IG ii². 3091 = DID B 5 Snell TrGF, dated to c.380), whose plays are hardly likely to have survived into the second century AD.[197] It may be significant that Themison was so successful at Miletus. Broneer suggests that Themison's 'accomplishment may have consisted in borrowing themes from the works of the three playwrights for the composition of lyric poetry which he set to his own music'. But it seems more probable that, as Latte suggests, he in fact borrowed the words, which he then set to his own music. In the third century, Aurelius Hierocles won a victory at the Great Didymeia, in which he defeated the 'Timotheasts and Hegesiasts' (Inscrip. Didym. no. 181. 5 ἡ βουλὴ καὶ ὁ δῆμος ἐτείμηcαν Αὐρήλιον Ἱεροκλέα νεικήcαντα τὰ Μεγάλα Διδύμεια τειμο[θε]αcτὰc καὶ ἡγηcια[c]τὰc κτλ.).[198] This presumably describes citharodes and orators in the style of Timotheus and Hegesias[199] respectively, though it is not clear whether these so-called 'Timotheasts' were merely stylistic imitators or were actually singing poems by

[195] Cf. above, p. 11.
[196] K. Latte, Eranos, 52 (1954), 125–7 = Kl. Schr. 590–2.
[197] O. Broneer, Hesperia, 22 (1953), 192–3, confuses the two; he mentions the 'dramas of Timotheus', but also refers to his Milesian origin and his musical innovations.
[198] A. Rehm, Didyma, ii: Die Inschriften (Berlin, 1958). See also K. Latte, Eranos, 53 (1955), 75–6 = Kl. Schr. 593–4; West, Music, 382.
[199] For Hegesias, see E. Norden, Die antike Kunstprosa (Stuttgart, 1958⁵), i. 134.

Timotheus (perhaps to their own music like Themison at Miletus in the second century). Compare also Sophocles' paean for Asclepius (PMG 737(b)), which was revived in Athens $c.$174/5 AD, and survives in inscriptional form from that date.[200] Ariphron of Sicyon's famous paean to Health (fr. 813) survives in an Athenian inscription from about 200 AD (IG ii². 4533).

Several passages are quoted by Athenaeus and Plutarch, but there is little later literary evidence. With our few fragments it is, of course, difficult to detect influences or reminiscences of his work, but *Persae*, for instance, does not seem to have had much effect on Latin or Greek poetry at any time. Much the same applies to the other dithyrambographers. However, if their work was not regarded as 'classical' by the Alexandrians and their successors, this relative anonymity is not surprising. After the third century AD Timotheus' works, with the exception of one or two isolated quotations in the grammarians, sinks into obscurity. Few lexicographical texts show any knowledge of the dithyrambic poets in general, despite the complexity and abstruseness of the lexicon. This may be due either to ignorance of his work, or its lack of classic status. Porphyry (ap. Stob. 1. 49. 61) cites an isolated line, along with fragments of Melanippides (fr. 759) and Licymnius (fr. 77), which may suggest that these passages were found together in an earlier treatise. Macrobius quotes fr. 800, but may have relied on Apollodorus, whom he has just quoted ($FGrH$ 244 F 95), for the material; at *Sat.* 5. 22. 4 (Timoth. fr. 778a) he shows no independent knowledge of Timotheus. The ninth-century *Etymologium Genuinum* quotes 'Origen' on the length of the second syllable of ὀρίγανον (fr. 799), where the name may be an error for that of the fifth-century grammarian Orus.[201]

How long Timotheus' poetry survived after the third century AD is thus unknown, though Hierocles' victory over the Timotheasts at Didyma may reflect a decrease in popularity. Possibly, however, his work did not long outlive the transfer of Greek literature from roll to codex.[202]

---

[200] Cf. J. H. Oliver, *Hesperia*, 5 (1936), 109 ff.   [201] Campbell 117 n. 1.
[202] For this phenomenon, see L. D Reynolds and N G. Wilson, *Scribes and Scholars* (Oxford, 1991³), 32.

SIGLA

Signa papyro edendae adhibita

Π	papyrus
a̦	littera incerta
.	litterae deperditae vestigia
[ ]	textus papyri periit
ʼ ʼ	inseruit librarius
⟨ ⟩	inserendum
⟦ ⟧	delevit librarius
{ }	delendum
†	corruptum
ac	ante correcturam
pc	post correcturam
‖	finis columnae

Nominum compendia

Dan.	O. A. Danielsson
Edm.	J. M. Edmonds
JD	J. Diggle (per litt.)
GOH	G. O. Hutchinson (per litt.)
MLW	M. L. West (per litt.)
Wil.	U. von Wilamowitz-Moellendorff

TIMOΘEOY TOY MIΛHCIOY TA CΩIZOMENA

AIAC EMMANHC

777 Lucian. *Harmonides* 1 (iii. 375 Macleod)
(Timotheum Thebanum adloquitur Harmonides poeta) . . . ὥσπερ ὅτε καὶ
cύ, ὦ Τιμόθεε, τὸ πρῶτον ἐλθὼν οἴκοθεν ἐκ Βοιωτίας ὑπηύλησας τῆι Πανδιονίδι
καὶ ἐνίκησας ἐν τῶι Αἴαντι τῶι ἐμμανεῖ, τοῦ ὁμωνύμου coι ποιήσαντος τὸ μέλος,
οὐδεὶς ἦν ὃς ἠγνόει τοὔνομα, Τιμόθεον ἐκ Θηβῶν.

2 ὑπηύλησας ΓΕ: ἐπ- Γ^c

APTEMIC

778 (a) *Suda* s.v. Τιμόθεος, iv. 556 Adler γράψας . . . Ἄρτεμιν
Macrob. *Sat.* 5. 22. 4–5 (i. 342–3 Willis)
Alexander Aetolus, poeta egregius, in libro qui inscribitur Musae refert
quanto studio populus Ephesius dedicato templo Dianae curauerit
praemiis propositis ut qui tunc erant poetae ingeniosissimi in deam
carmina diuersa componerent. in his uersibus Opis non comes Dianae
sed Diana ipsa uocata est. loquitur autem ut dixi de populo Ephesio (fr. 4,
p. 92 Magnelli),

> ἀλλ᾽ ὅ γε πευθόμενος πάγχυ Γραικοῖcι μέλεcθαι
> Τιμόθεον κιθάρης ἴδμονα καὶ μελέων
> υἱὸν Θερcάνδρου ⟨κλυ⟩τὸν ἤινεcεν ἀνέρα cίγλων
> χρυcείων †ερην δὴ τότε χιλιάδα†
> ὑμνῆcαι ταχέων Ὦπιν βλήτειραν ὀϊcτῶν
> ἥ τ᾽ ἐπὶ Κεγχρείωι τίμιον οἶκον ἔχει

et mox

> μηδὲ θεῆc προλίπηι Λητωίδος ἀκλέα ἔργα.

Alexandri v. 3 ⟨κλυ⟩τὸν Schneidewin   4 ερην NP: ἱερὴν vulg : ιερων cod.
Camer.: αἴρων Wil.: ἱερῶν Diels: χρείων Kukula: ⟨προφ⟩έρων JD   δὴ τότε P:
ανθοντε N   χειλιαδα P: χιωλαιαλα N: fort. χιλιάδος: Gronovium secutus Meineke
ἱερῆι χιλιάδι comprobauit, idem postea ἱερὴν χιλιάδα   5 ταχέων ⟨τ᾽⟩ Meineke,
Bergk: ταχειων P

(b) Plu. *De superstit.* 10. 170 A (i. 350 Paton–Wegehaupt)
τοῦ Τιμοθέου τὴν Ἄρτεμιν ᾄδοντος ἐν Ἀθήναις καὶ λέγοντος

> θυιάδα φοιβάδα μαινάδα λυccάδα

Κινηcίας ὁ μελοποιὸς ἐκ τῶν θεατῶν ἀναcτάc· τοιαύτη coι, εἶπε, θυγάτηρ γένοιτο.

Plu. *De aud. poet.* 4. 22 A (i. 43 Paton–Wegehaupt) Τιμοθέωι μὲν γὰρ ᾄδοντι

82   ΤΙΜΟΘΕΟΥ

τὴν Ἄρτεμιν ἐν τῶι θεάτρωι "μαινάδα θυάδα φοιβάδα λυσσάδα", Κινησίας εὐθὺς
ἀντεφώνησε "τοιαύτη σοι θυγάτηρ γένοιτο".

ΕΛΠΗΝΩΡ

779   *CIA* 1246 (*IG* ii². 3055)
Νι[κ]ί[α]ς Νι[κ]οδήμου Ξυ[π]εταίων ἀνέθηκε νικήσας χορηγῶν Κεκροπίδι
παίδων·
[Πα]νταλέων Σικυώνιο[ς] ηὔλει, ἆισμα Ἐλπήνωρ Τιμοθέου, Νέ[αιχ]μ[ο]ς ἦρχεν
(320/19 BC).

ΚΥΚΛΩΨ

780   Athen. 11. 465 C (iii. 13 Kaibel)
Τιμόθεος δ᾽ ἐν Κύκλωπι·
    ἔγχευε δ᾽ ἓν μὲν δέπας κίσσινον μελαίνας
    σταγόνος ἀμβρότας ἀφρῶι βρυάζον,
    εἴκοσιν δὲ μέτρ᾽ ἀνέχευ᾽, ἀνέμισγε
    δ᾽ αἷμα Βακχίου νεορρύτοισιν
5   δακρύοισι Νυμφᾶν.
Eust. *Od.* 1631. 61 (ex Athen. epit.) ὡς δηλοῖ φασι καὶ Τιμόθεος ἐν τῶι κατ᾽
αὐτὸν Κύκλωπι παραφράσας οὕτως· ἓν μὲν δέπας κίσσινον μελαίνας σταγόνος
ἀμβρότας ἀφρῶι βρυάζον, εἴκοσι δ᾽ ὕδατος μέτρ᾽ ἔχευεν.

1 Bergk: ἔχευεν A   3 ἐνέχευ᾽ Kaibel: ἀνέχευαν A: ἐνέχευεν E   3–4 ἀνέμισγε
δ᾽ αἷμα Grotefend: ἔμισγε διαμα A: ἀνέμισγε δ᾽ ἆμα E   4 βακχεῖα E   νεωρυτως
A: νεορρύτοις E: -οισιν Page (-οισι iam Wil.)   5 δακρύουσι A: -οισι E sec.
Peppink (sed -ουσι sec. Kaibel): corr. C (teste Schweigh.)   νυμφᾶν A: πηγᾶν E

781   Chrysipp. π. ἀποφατ. 10 (ii. 54–5 von Arnim)
εἰ Κύκλωψ ὁ τοῦ Τιμοθέου πρός τινα οὕτως ἀπεφήνατο·
    οὗτοι τόν γ᾽ ὑπεραμπέχοντ᾽ οὐρανὸν εἰσαναβήσει.
bis eadem refert Chrysippus

782   Arist. *Poet.* 2. 1448ᵃ9 (p. 5 Kassel)
καὶ γὰρ ἐν ὀρχήσει καὶ αὐλήσει καὶ κιθαρίσει ἔστι γενέσθαι ταύτας τὰς ἀνομ-
οιότητας· καὶ [τὸ] περὶ τοὺς λόγους δὲ καὶ τὴν ψιλομετρίαν, οἷον Ὅμηρος μὲν
βελτίους, Κλεοφῶν δὲ ὁμοίους, Ἡγήμων δὲ ὁ Θάσιος ⟨ὁ⟩ τὰς παρωιδίας ποιήσας
πρῶτος καὶ Νικοχάρης ὁ τὴν Δειλιάδα χείρους· ὁμοίως δὲ καὶ περὶ τοὺς
διθυράμβους καὶ περὶ τοὺς νόμους, ὥσπερ †γᾶς Κύκλωπας Τιμόθεος καὶ
Φιλόξενος μιμήσαιτο ἄν τις. ἐν αὐτῆι δὲ τῆι διαφορᾶι καὶ ἡ τραγωιδία πρὸς τὴν
κωμωιδίαν διέστηκεν· ἡ μὲν γὰρ χείρους, ἡ δὲ βελτίους μιμεῖσθαι βούλεται τῶν
νῦν.

4 ὥσπερ | γᾶς κυκλωπᾶς A (Paris. 1741): ὡς πέργας 'καὶ' κύκλωπας Parisinus 2038:

ὡc πέρcαc καὶ κύκλωπαc cod. Robortelli: *sicut kyklopas* Lat. (Moerbeke, 1278) cf. Ar *sicut adsimulat aliquis et imitatur sic Cyclopas* Tim. *et Phil.* (trans. Tkatsch) γᾶc: Οἰνώπαc vel Οἰνωνᾶc susp. Holland: γὰρ Vahlen (ed. *Poet.* 1885³): ⟨Πέρcαc Τιμόθεοc καὶ Ἀρ⟩γᾶc, Κύκλωπαc κτλ. Susemihl: ὥcπερ ⟨θεοὺc Ἀρ⟩γᾶc vel sim. Vahlen (ed. 1874²; Ἀργᾶc iam Castelvetro): Γα⟨λατείαc ἐρῶντα⟩c Κύκλωπαc Musso

783   Aristonicus in Σ A Hom. *Il.* 9. 219b (ii. 446 Erbse)
       ὅτι θῦcαι οὐ cφάξαι ⟨ὡc⟩ ὁ Τιμόθεοc ὑπέλαβεν καὶ Φιλόξενοc ὁμοίωc τῆι ἡμετέραι cυνηθείαι, ἀλλὰ θυμιᾶcαι.

       ⟨ὡc⟩ Lehrs

ΛΑΕΡΤΗϹ

784   Suda s.v. Τιμόθεοc, iv. 556 Adler γράψαc . . . Λαέρτην

ΝΑΥΠΛΙΟϹ

785   (a) Suda s.v. Τιμόθεοc, iv. 556 Adler γράψαc . . . Πέρcαc {ῆ} Ναύπλιον

       (b) Hegesandros (FHG iv. 416) ap. Athen. 8. 338 A (ii. 242 Kaibel) ὁ αὐτὸc Δωρίων καταγελῶν τοῦ ἐν τῶι Τιμοθέου Ναυπλίωι χειμῶνοc ἔφαcκεν ἐν κακκάβαι ζεούcαι μείζονα ἑωρακέναι χειμῶνα.

       Ναυπλίωι Casaubon: Ναυτίλωι codd.

ΝΙΟΒΗ

786   Machon fr. 9. 81 ss. Gow (ap. Athen. 8. 341 C)
                                                         ἀλλ' ἔπει
       ὁ Τιμοθέου Χάρων cχολάζειν οὐκ ἐᾶι,
       οὐκ τῆc Νιόβηc, χωρεῖν δὲ πορθμίδ' ἀναβοᾶι,
       καλεῖ δὲ μοῖρα νύχιος, ἧc κλύειν χρεών . . .
       etiam huc spectare coni. Nauck (trag. adesp. 520 N²), Bergk (PLG⁴ p. 621), Teletem ap. Stob. 3. 1. 98 (iii. 46 Wachsmuth–Hense) ὥcπερ ἐκ cυμποcίου ἀπαλλάττομαι οὐδὲν δυcχεραίνων, οὕτω καὶ ἐκ τοῦ βίου, ὅταν {ἡ} ὥρα ἦι, ἔμβα πορθμίδοc ἔρυμα. Cf. O. Hense, *Teletis Reliquiae* (Tubingae, 1909²), p. 16. 4. Sunt qui versiculum alicui tragico, fortasse Euripidi, tribuant (*TrGF* adesp. 520); proverbium suspicatur Fuentes González ad loc. Teletis.

       Machonis v. 3 πορθμίδ' Casaubon, Meineke: πορθμὸν AC, Gow

787   D. L. 7. 28 (i. 462–3 Marcovich)
       ἐτελεύτα δὴ οὕτωc (ὁ Ζήνων)· ἐκ τῆc cχολῆc ἀπιὼν προcέπταιcε καὶ τὸν δάκτυλον περιέρρηξε· παίcαc δὲ τὴν γῆν τῆι χειρί, φηcὶ τὸ ἐκ τῆc Νιόβηc

84 ΤΙΜΟΘΕΟΥ

ἔρχομαι· τί μ' αὔεις;
καὶ παραχρῆμα ἐτελεύτησεν ἀποπνίξας ἑαυτόν.

Stob. ecl. 3. 7. 44 (iii. 321 Wachsmuth–Hense) Ζήνων ὡς ἤδη γέρων ὢν πταίσας κατέπεσεν "ἔρχομαι" εἶπε, "τί με αὔεις;", καὶ εἰσελθὼν ἑαυτὸν ἐξήγαγεν, unde etiam Gnomolog. Paris. (= Florileg. cod. Par. 1168) 302 sec. Wil.; Suda, s.v. αὔεις (i. 411 Adler) αὔεις· φωνεῖς, λαλεῖς. Ζήνων γὰρ ὁ Κιτιεὺς ἐκ τῆς σχολῆς ἀπιὼν προσέπταισε καὶ τὸν δάκτυλον περιέρρηξε. πταίσας δὲ τὴν γῆν τῆι χειρί φησι τὸ ἐκ τῆς Νιόβης· "ἔρχομαι, τί μ' αὔεις;" καὶ παραχρῆμα ἐτελεύτησεν ἀποπνίξας ἑαυτόν; D.L. 7. 31 (i. 464 Marcovich) εἴπομεν ὡς ἐτελεύτα ὁ Ζήνων καὶ ἡμεῖς ἐν τῆι Παμμέτρωι τοῦτον τὸν τρόπον (AP 7. 118)· "τὸν Κιτιᾶ Ζήνωνα θανεῖν λόγος ὡς ὑπὸ γήρως | πολλὰ καμὼν ἐλύθη μένων ἄσιτος· | οἱ δ' ὅτι προσκόψας ποτ' ἔφη χερὶ γαῖαν ἀλοίσας | ἔρχομαι αὐτόματος· τί δὴ καλεῖς με;"; [Lucian.] Macrob. 19 (i. 78 Macleod) ὅν (sc. Ζήνωνα) φασιν εἰσερχομένον εἰς τὴν ἐκκλησίαν καὶ προσπταίσαντα ἀναφθέγξασθαι, "τί με βοᾶις;" καὶ ὑποστρέψαντα οἴκαδε καὶ ἀποσχόμενον τροφῆς τελευτῆσαι τὸν βίον.

Tim. trib. Nauck

ΠΕΡΣΑΙ

788 Plu. Vit. Philopoem. 11. 362 CD (ii. 2. 14 Ziegler)
Πυλάδην τὸν κιθαρωιδὸν ἄιδοντα τοὺς Τιμοθέου Πέρσας ἐνάρξασθαι·
κλεινὸν ἐλευθερίας τεύχων μέγαν Ἑλλάδι κόσμον.
ἅμα δὲ τῆι λαμπρότητι τῆς φωνῆς τοῦ περὶ τὴν ποίησιν ὄγκου συμπρέψαντος, ἐπίβλεψιν γενέσθαι τοῦ θεάτρου παντοχόθεν εἰς τὸν Φιλοποίμενα καὶ κρότον μετὰ χαρᾶς, τῶν Ἑλλήνων τὸ παλαιὸν ἀξίωμα ταῖς ἐλπίσιν ἀναλαμβανόντων καὶ τοῦ τότε φρονήματος ἔγγιστα τῶι θαρρεῖν γινομένων.

Paus. 8. 50. 3 ἄιδοντος Τιμοθέου νόμον τοῦ Μιλησίου Πέρσας καὶ καταρξαμένου τῆς ὠιδῆς, κλεινὸν ἐλευθερίας τεύχων μέγαν Ἑλλάδι κόσμον κτλ.

789 Plu. De aud. poet. 11. 32 D (i. 65 Paton–Wegehaupt–Pohlenz) ἀφ' ὧν (Il. 16. 422 et 13. 121) καὶ Τιμόθεος ὁρμηθεὶς οὐ κακῶς ἐν τοῖς Πέρσαις τοὺς Ἕλληνας παρεκάλει·
σέβεσθ' αἰδῶ συνεργὸν ἀρετᾶς δοριμάχου.
Plu. De fort. Rom. 11. 323 E οἷς πολλὴν τόλμαν καὶ ἀνδρείαν αἰδῶ τε συνεργὸν ἀρετᾶς δοριμάχου, ὥς φησι Τιμόθεος, τίς οὐκ ἂν ὁμολογήσειεν; αἰδῶ συνεργὸν aud. codd.: αιδω τε cυν. fort. cod. ΣFmgl: πρὸς cυν. rell. (προσενεργῶν Z¹)

790 Plu. Vit. Agesil. 14. 603 D (iii. 2. 210 Ziegler)
πολλοῖς ἐπήιει τὰ τοῦ Τιμοθέου λέγειν·
Ἄρης τύραννος· χρυσὸν Ἑλλὰς οὐ δέδοικε.
Plu. Demetr. 42. 910 DE Ἄρης μὲν γὰρ τύραννος, ὥς φησι Τιμόθεος κτλ.; Zenob. Athous 2. 47 (Miller, Mélanges, p. 363) Ἄρης τύραννος· τοῦτο τὸ κομμάτιον ἐκ τῶν Τιμοθέου Περσῶν, ὃ διὰ τὴν ἐπὶ τῆι ὠιδῆι εὐημερίαν Ἀθήνησιν ἐπιπολάσαν εἰς παροιμίαν περιέστη. μέμνηται ταύτης Μένανδρος ἐν Θαΐδι (Men.

fr. 189 Körte); et cf. Hsch. a 7174 Ἄρης τύραννος· παροιμία, *Suda*, a 3858
Ἄρης τύραννος· ἐπὶ τῶν μετὰ βίας τι διαπραττομένων, Macar. *Cent.* 2. 39
(*Paroem. Gr.* ii. 147), eadem.

τύραννον *Ages.* cod. Y   δ' Ἑλλὰc codd.: δ' del. *G. S.* Farnell: Ἑλλὰc δ' οὐ Bergk

790A Dion. Hal. *Comp.* 15. 110 (vi. 72 Usener–Radermacher) = fr. 1027(*f*) Page
ἓν ἔτι λείπεται τρισυλλάβων ῥυθμῶν γένος, ὃ συνέστηκεν ἐκ δύο μακρῶν καὶ
βραχείας, τρία δὲ ποιεῖ σχήματα· μέσης μὲν γὰρ γινομένης τῆς βραχείας, ἄκρων δὲ
τῶν μακρῶν, κρητικός τε λέγεται καὶ ἔστιν οὐκ ἀγεννής· ὑπόδειγμα δὲ αὐτοῦ
τοιοῦτον·

> οἱ δ' ἐπείγοντο πλωταῖc ἀπήναιcι χαλκεμβόλοιc.

Tim. *Pers.* dederunt Usener, Diehl, Wil. (*Verskunst* 333 n.), Edm.

791 P. Berol. 9875
col. i
fr. 1 + fr. 4

```
       c.[.]ιον[                        ]χα[ . . . .]ιπο
       ρ[.]καθα[                        ] . .()[. . . .]ν
       ν[υ]μφα.[                        ]ναιαν.[ . . .]ντεc
       επ[ε]υκυκλ[                      ].ουροθωι[. . . .].οcαλλα[
  5    επ[ε]υθυφ[                        ]cκοι[ ]πι[. . . .]υγαc
       cυ.[.]ὸρομ[                       ]αιcεωνεπ[. . . . . .]δε
       [. .]δοκ[                         ]ξοδοιcμ[. . .]ιοπω[
             ]ω[                         ]υθυγε[        ]
                                         ]αμ[.]κ[        ].
 10                                      ]υcτρọ[
                                         ]παλιμμ[
                                         ]μουcα[

 fr. 2                      ]η[
                            ]αν[.]ọ[
                            ]π ρ ρι.[
                            ]αυπε[
      5                  ]β[
                         ].[

 fr. 3                      ]c[
                            ]δε[
                            ]οιχ[
                         ].. [
      5                  ].ηị.[
                         ].ιcι[
                         ] ὀc'cου[
```

        ]λν.[
        ]υανακ[
10].επιπα[
        ]πορο[

fr. 5   ] [..].[
        ]   [
        ]ικομα[.].[

fr. 6   ]ν...[
        ]αραξει[
        ].[.].[
        ].θ[]ο[
   5]...[

fr. 7   ]..[
        ]. και.[
        ]...ι..[
        ]ο...τ[
   5].[.].χ[
        ]πλοιςκλ[
        ]ιςειρες[
        ]πιφοβαι[
        ] εοξυ[

fr. 8   ]..ερ[
        ]ιαοντε[
        ]φουσι.υς[
        ].υρεκ[
   5]αρουκοιλ[
        ]λὶ́νοιοδ[
        ]ιςεπαλ[
        ]γυιαελ[

fr. 9   ].[
        ]ρρ[
        ]α[
        ] (+ 1.4 cm.)
   5].ες [
        ]ιαδιοπλ[
        ]αζον (+ 0.9 cm.)
        ]ιοςκολιο[

10]αϲειχον[
]οα̣ (+ 2.7 cm.)
]κατε.[
]υ̣ (+ 0.7 cm.)
]ϲ[
]π̣οϲ[
15]ιυ[
]εα̣[
]..ι[
]φαγ[
]ϲμα.[

fr. 10]αζε[
]ανο̣[
] ηειγ[
]δ̣ερηϲ[
5]λλαγ[
]ευι̣[

fr. 17]ιονα[
]ιχο[
].[

fr. 20]τ ε΄..[
]ρ.[

coll. ii–vi

[.].[ ].[....]υν̣τ[ ]ν̣[.]ν̣[.....]υν [ἐμ]βόλ[οιϲ]ι γειτ[..]ϲ[..]υ[
.....]αντιαιι̣[...]πρ.[..]ν ἐχάρα[ξ]α̣ν π.ι δὲ γε[..]λογχο[..
..] ἀμφέθ[ε]ντ᾿ ὀδόντων ϲτον[.]χ
    αἱ δ[ὲ] κυρτοῖ[ϲι] κραϲὶν[
5   ......]μεναι [χε]ῖ-
ραϲ παρέϲυρον ἐλα[τίνα]ϲ·
†αδλ† εἰ μὲν [ἐ]νθένδ[.....]ι-
ϲτοϲ ἐπ[ιφ]έροιτο πλαγά

omnia suppl. et corr. ed. primus praeter ea quae notantur
Coll. ii–vi 1 c]ὺν [ἐμ]βόλ[οιϲ]ι Wil.: -βολ[αῖϲ]ι Janssen   γείτ[ονε]ϲ Wil.. γειτ[νιῶ]ϲι
JD   2 ἐνεχάρα[ξ]αν Wil.   fort. πο ι vel πρ ι: πο[ϲ]ὶ δὲ γε[ιϲό]λογχο[ν
ὄγκωμα Wil. (γε[ιϲό]λογχον Diels): πο[τ]ὶ δὲ γε[ιϲό]λογχ[ον (vel πεντελογχον) ἔρκοϲ]
Dan.: πο[ϲ]ὶ δὲ γ[εῖϲα] λογχο[ειδέων Sitzler   in marg : χιων [   ]ε|
τωνηρακλειαϲ   3 ϲτον[α]χ⟨ᾶι·⟩ possis (vel ϲτόν[υ]χ⟨εϲ ⟩, ϲτον[υ]χαί iam
Reinach)   5 ἀμφεϲτεμ]μέναι Wil.: ἀνθωρμη]μέναι vel ἐπειγό]μεναι Sitzler
7 ἀλλ᾿ εἰ Wil.: αδλει vel αδαει Π   [ἀπρόϲο]ιϲτοϲ Page: [ἀπροφάϲ]ιϲτοϲ Wil

ῥηξ[....]ος, πάντες [ἄμ'] ἀνέ-
10 πι[πτον] ἐκεῖσε να[ῦ]ται·
εἰ δ' ἀντίτοιχος ἀκτ[..
.]ος[.]ξειεμ [πο]λυκρότο̣[υς
..]ς̣ιμο̣υ̣ς πεύκας, πάλιν ἐφέροντο·
αἱ δὲ̣ [...(.)]α̣ι̣.η γυῖα [δ]ιαφέρουσα[ι
15 πλ]ευρὰς λιν̣[ο]ζώςτους ἔφαινον, τὰς μ[ὲν......]ις
σκηπ[τοῖς] ἐ̓πεμβάλλ[ο]ντες ἀνε-
[χ]αίτιζον, αἱ δὲ πρα[..
.........]ας ἀπηγλαϊ-
20 ςμένα[ι] ςιδα[ρ]ῶι κράνει·
ἴςος δὲ πυρὶ δαμ[....
...]ν̣ ἀγκυλένδετ[ο]ς μεθίετο
χερςίν, ἐν δ' ἔπιπτε γυίοις
αἰθε[........]ωμα διακρα[ι][δ]αίνων·
25 ςτερεοπαγῆ δ' ἐφέρετο φόνι-
α [.......].α̣[.]τα τε περίβολα πυρὶ φλεγόμεν' ἐν ἀποτομάςι
βουδο[........]βίοτο̣ς
ἐθύετ' ἀδιν̣[ὸ]ς ὑπὸ τανυπτέ-
30 ροιςι χαλκόκραςι νευρε[.......(.)]
ςμαραγδοχαίτας δὲ πόν-
τος ἄλοκα ναΐοις ἐφοι-
νίςςετο ςταλά[γμαςι,
κρ]αυγᾶι βοὰ δὲ [ςυ]μμι[γ]ὴς κατεῖχεν·
35 ὁμοῦ δ[ὲ] νάϊος ςτρατὸς
βάρβαρος ἄμμι[.....(.)]

9 ῥηξί[κωπ]ος Page: -[ζυγος] Wil. [ἄμ'] ἀνε- MLW: [ἐπ]ανε- Dan. 10 et
-πι[τνον] possis ἐκεισε να[ῦ]ται Dan. 11 ἀκτ[ὰ Page: ἀκτ[ὶς Wil.
12 μῆχ]ος [ἄ]ξειεμ Page: πρ]ος[άι]ξ. Wil. 12–13 -κρότο[υ πρὸς] ςιμόν Dan.:
-κρότο[ιο πλώ]ςιμον Page (-)ςιμον legit Schubart, ap. Wil. p. 14) 14 fort. δ'
[ἀκρ]αινῆ: δ' ε[ὔτ' ἀν]αιδῆ Page 16 τ[ὰς μὲν μολυβδίνο]ις possis: τ[ὰς μέν, αἰόλας
ὕβρει]ς Page 17 ςκηπτ[οῖς Edm.: ςκηπτ[οὺς] Janssen: ςκηπτ[ῶν Page
18–19 e.g. πρα[νεῖς ἔδυνον καθ' ἄλμ]ας (πρα[νέες Page: πρα[νές Wil.) vel ἔδυνον
κορύμβ]ας 21 δαμ[αςίφως Wil.: δαμ[αςτάς Page 22 ἄκω]ν Jurenka:
Ἄρη]ς Wil. 24 αἰθε[ροφόρητον ς]ῶμα Wil.: αἰθε[ροφόρητος ς]ῶμα Janssen,
sed melius αἰθε[ροδρόμος: αἰθέ[ρια δούρατ'] ὠμὰ διακρ. vel ὠμάδια κρ. Page
26 λίθια πιςς]ά[ν]τά Edm. (πιςς]ά[εν]τά iam Wil.) 27 -τομεςι Π: corr.
Wil. 28 βουδό[ροις Wil. (-οις Page): βούδορα Janssen: fort. βουδό[νοις(ι)
τῶν δὲ] Page: ἰοῖς δὲ] GOH: ὄφεςι δὲ] Wil. 30 e.g. νευρε[πεντάτοις vel -ρύςτοις
Wil.: fort. -ςιν εὑρε[-? 32 δαίοις van Leeuwen 33 ςταλά[γμαςι Dan.:
-[γμοῖς Wil. 34 πα]μμι[γ]ὴς Diehl 36 ἄμμι[γα αὖτις] Wil.

ἀντεφέρετ᾽ ἐ[π᾽ ἰχ]θυ[ο]-
cτεφέcι μαρμαροπ[τύχ]οιc
κόλποιcιν [Ἀμφι'τρί]ταc.

40 ἔνθα τοι τ[ιc...]πέδιοc
ἀνὴρ ἀμεροδρό-
μοιο χώραc ἄναξ [...
...]μβρίαν α.[..
ποcί τε χ]ερcίν τε παί-
45 ω[ν ἔ]πλει νηcιώ-
ταc [......]c θεινομε[
...] διεξόδουc μ[...]ν
ἰcόρροπά τε παλευό[
] ηλ[.......]ων
50 κάλει θ[...]cιον θεὸν
πατέρα τ[
...].νο[..]φι[......].κεπ[.]. [..........]λαccων.[
....]αcπ[..]τε[.....]μεγαν[.]ον[.........]α περcαν[
..].εφαc[.].ρ.[.....]αντεχειαι[.......]νιν κελαι.[
55 ..]βλυδωπιρον[......]c κατεccφραγ[......].cτα
..]πεπα[.]ολλ[.....].υτεκ.τοc[.....].νωτου
..]ε διαπαλεύων[....]που βάcιμου[...]ν δίοδον
.]εcμ[.]c [ἄπ]ειροc[.....]φι ναίοιc τρυ[...]λιχθειc
.........]υλακ[...]φον[.]ζευμα.[   ]· ||
60 ὅ]τε δὲ τᾶι λείποιεν αὖραι,
τᾶι δ᾽ ἐπειcέπιπτον, ἄφ-
ρει δ᾽ ἀβακχίωτοc ὄμβροc,
εἰc δὲ τρόφιμον ἄγγοc
ἐχεῖτ᾽· ἐπεὶ δ᾽ ἀμβόλιμοc ἄλ-
65 μα cτόματοc ὑπερέθυιεν,

37 ἰχ]θυ[ο]- suppl. Dan.: ἰχ]θυ[c]- Wil   38 van Leeuwen: -π[έπλ]οιc Dan..
-π[τέρ]οιc Wil.   40 Φρυγιο]πέδ. Wil.: ἀμετρο]πέδ. Page: Πέρcηc] Sitzler:
Ἑρμο]πέδ. Edm.: εὐρο]πέδ MLW: fort. ὑγρο]πέδιοc?   42 ποcί τε Page
42–3 πλάκ᾽] ὀμβρίαν ἀρ[ῶν cκέλεcι χ]ερcίν Wil.: δυcο]μβρίαν tempt. Page: ἐc
μεc]ημβρίαν ἄκ[ωποc Jurenka   44 suppl. Page   46 ποντίαι]c Page:
ἀνέμοι]c Wil.   46–7 θεινόμε[νοc ἄταιc vel sim. Page:]cτεινομε[possis
47 ἀλίαc δ]ιεξ. Diehl: πελαγίαc δ]ιεξ. Keil, Sitzler   μ[ατεύω]ν Wil.: μ[ετρῶ]ν
MLW   48 τ᾽ ἐπαλευό[μενοc Diehl. τε παλευο[ν Wil.· cαλε{υ}ο[- vel
παλε{υ}ο[- possis   50 θ[αλάc]cιον Wil.   51 πατέρα τ[ε Δία] ex. grat.
GOH   55 ἀμ]βλὺ δ᾽ ὠχρὸν Wil.   κατεccφραγ[ιcμέν]οc Wil.   58 δ]εcμ[ὸ]c
Wil.   ἀμ]φὶ ναίοιc τρύ[φεcιν ἑ]λιχθείc Dan. (ἐ)λιχθείc iam Wil.)
61 ἐπειcέπιπτεν Wil.   61–2 ἄφρει δ᾽ Dan.: αφρωι[c]δε| Π· ἀφρῶι δ᾽ ⟨ὕ⟩ Page:
ἀφρώδηc Wil.: ἄφριζε(ν) Sitzler: ἀφρῶι δὲ ⟨περιέζεcεν⟩ Sudhaus: ἀφρῶι δ᾽ ἔ⟨ζε᾽⟩
Gargiulo   62 ἀβαχχ- Π

65a ὀξυπαραυδήτωι
  φωνᾶ⟨ι⟩ παρακόπωι
  τε δόξαι φρενῶν
  κατακορὴς ἀπείλει
  γόμφους ἐμπρίων
70 †μιμούμενος λυμεώ-
  νι cώματος θαλάc⟨c⟩αι·
  "ἤδη θραcεῖα καὶ πάροc
  λάβρον αὐχέν' ἔcχεc ἐμ
  πέδαι καταζευχθεῖcα λινοδέτωι τεόν·
75 νῦν δέ c' ἀναταράξει
  ἐμὸc ἄναξ ἐμὸc
  πεύκαιcιν ὀριγόνοιcιν, ἐγκλήιcει δὲ πεδία πλόϊμα νο{μ}μάcι ναύταιc,
  οἰcτρομανὲc παλαιομί-
80 cημ' ἄπιcτον τ' ἀγκάλι-
  cμα κλυcιδρομάδοc αὔραc".
  φάτ' ἄ⟨c⟩θματι
  cτρευγόμενοc, βλοcυρὰν
  δ' ἐξέβαλλ' ἄχναν ἐπανε-
85 ρευγόμενοc cτόματι βρύχιον ἅλμαν.
  φυγᾶι δὲ πάλιν ἵετο Πέρ-
  cηc cτρατὸc βάρβαροc ἐπιcπέρχων·
  ἄλλα δ' ἄλλαν θραῦεν cύρτιc
  μακραυχενόπλουc,
90 χειρῶν δ' ἔγβαλλον ὀρείουc πόδαc ναόc, cτόματοc
  δ' ἐξήλλοντο μαρμαροφεγγεῖc παῖδεc cυγκρουόμενοι·
  κατάcτεροc δὲ πόντοc ἐγ
95 λιποπνόηc λιπ[ ]cτερέcιν
  ἐγάργαιρε cώμαcιν,
  ἐβρίθοντο δ' ἀϊόνεc.

69 γόμφουc Sitzler: γόμφοιc Π (-οιc⟨ιν⟩ coni. Page)   70 μιcουμένωι Croiset: θυμούμενοc van Leeuwen: βριμούμενοc Dan. (βριμώμ- Inama): μιγνύμενοc Janssen: μύλου μένοc MLW: λαιμοῦ μένοc Keil: δινούμενοc C. Collard (per litt.)   71 θαλάc⟨c⟩αι Wil.: θα⟦θ⟧λαcαc (λ ex θ facto) Π: θαλάccαc Dan.   λυμεῶνα . . θάλαccαν Sudhaus: λυμεῶνα . . . θαλάccαc Gargiulo   75 ἀνταράξει coni. Sitzler   77 ἐπ⟨ι⟩κλ. Dan.   78 νομάcι ναύταιc Dan., Sitzler: νομμαcιναυγαιc Π: νομάcιν αὐγαῖc Wil.   79 παλεο- Π   84 ἐξέβαλλ' West: εξεβαλλεν Π   87 βάρβαροc del. Wil.: Πέρcηc del. Edm.   94 κατάcτεγοc van Herwerden   95 ψυχ[ο]- Wil.: αὐγ[ο]- Page: alii alia

οἱ δ' ἐπ' ἀκταῖc ἐνάλοιc
ἥμενοι γυμνοπαγεῖc
ἀϋτᾶι τε καὶ δακρυ-
100   cταγεῖ [γ]όωι
cτερνοκτύποι γοηταὶ
θρηνώδει κατείχοντ' ὀδυρμῶι·
ἄμα δὲ [γᾶν] πατρίαν ἐπανεκα[λ]έοντ'·
105   "ἰὼ Μύcιαι
δενδροέθειραι πτυχαί,
[ῥύ]cαcθέ μ' ἐνθένδε· νῦν ἀήταιc
φερόμεθ'· οὐ γὰρ ἔτι ποτ' ἀμὸν
[cῶ]μα δέξεται [πόλ]ιc.
110   κ[ ] εγ γὰρ χερὶ ναε[.] νυμφαιογόνον
110a   [ ]ιον ἄντρον ο[.....]αιαcτακαπε[...]ονειτεο
       βαθύ[τ]ερον πόντοιο χ[άcμ]α·
       ἄπεχε μάχιμο[ν
       α[.] πλόϊμον ελλαν.
       εἴ[θε μ]ὴ cτέγην ἔδειμε
115   [.]η [ ]τελεοπορον ἐμὸc
       [δ]εcπότηc· οὐ γὰρ ἄ[ν Τμ]ῶλον οὐδ'
       ἄcτυ Λύδιον [λι]πὼν Cάρδεων
       ἦλθον ["Ε]λλαν' ἀπέρξων Ἄρ[η·
       νῦν] δὲ πᾶι τιc δυcέκφευκ[τ]ον εὔ-
120   ρηι || γλυκεῖαν μόρου καταφυγήν;
       Ἰλιοπόροc κακῶν λυαί-
       α μόνα γένοιτ' ἄν, εἰ
       δυνα{c}τὰ πρὸc μελαμ-
       πεταλοχίτωνα Ματρὸc οὐρείαc
125   δεcπόcυνα γόνατα πεcεῖν
       εὐωλένουc τε χεῖραc ἀμφιβάλλων
       †λιccων χρυcοπλόκαμε

99 ημενο[ν] Πᵃᶜ: ημενοιγ Πᵖᶜ   101 [γ]όωι Wil.: [ῥ]όωι Keil
102 -νοκτύπωι Π   γοηταὶ: βοητᾶι Edm.   104 [γᾶν] Wil.: [γαῖαν] Sitzler
108 φερο⟨ί⟩μεθ' Dan., Sudhaus   109 cῶ]μα Wil.   [πόλ]ιc Dan.: [κόν]ιc
Wil.   110 κ[ῦρ]εγ γὰρ Wil: κ[εῖ]θεγ γὰρ Dan.: κ[αὶ] ἐν γὰρ possi
110–110a χερὶ πα[λ]ε[ο]νυμφα{ιο}γόνον [ἄβατ]ον ἄντρον Wil.   111 χ[άcμ]α
Dan.· τ[έρμ]α Wil.: τ[έλμ]α MLW   112 suppl. Dan.   113 δ]ά[ιον] πλ.
Sitzler   114 suppl. Dan.   115 [δ]ῆτ[α] τελεόπορον MLW:
[τ]ηλ[ε]τελεοπορον Wil.: [τ]ηλ[ε] τελεόπορον Page   118 Wil.: ελλανατερξων Π:
Ἑλλανά τ' ἔρξων Dan.   121 Ἰδαιόπορος Keil: Ἰλίου πόρος Edm.   λυαία : λύcιc
GOH   123 δυνα{c}τά ⟨τῶι⟩ vel δύναιτό ⟨τιc⟩ Page: δυνα{c}τά ⟨μοι⟩
Janssen   124 -πεταλακιτωνα Π   126–7 αμφεβαλλωνλιccων Π: ἀμφέβαλλον·

θεὰ Μᾶτερ ἱκνοῦμαι
ἐμὸν ἐμὸν αἰῶνα δυσέκφευκτον, ἐπεί

130 μ' αὐτίκα λαιμοτόμωι τις ἀποίσεται ἐνθάδε
μήστορι σιδάρωι
ἢ κατακυμοτακεῖς ναυσιφθόροι αὖραι
νυκτιπαγεῖ βορέα⟨ι⟩ 'δ'ια⟨ρ⟩-
ραίσονται· περὶ γὰρ κλύδων

135 ἄγριος ἀνέρρηξεν ἄπαγ
γυίων εἶδος ὑφαντόν·
ἔνθα κείσομαι οἰκτρός, ὀρ-
_νίθων ἔθνεσιν ὠμοβρῶσι θοίνα".
τοιάδ' ὀδυρόμενοι κατεδάκρυον.

140 ἐπεὶ δέ τις λαβὼν ἄγοι
πολυβότων Κελαινᾶν
οἰκήτορ' ὀρφανὸν μαχᾶν
σιδαρόκωπος Ἕλλαν,
ἄγεγ κόμης ἐπισπάσας,

145 ὁ δ' ἀμφὶ γόνασι περιπλεκεὶς
ἐλίσσετ', Ἑλλάδ' ἐμπλέκων
Ἀσιάδι φωνᾶι διάτορον
σφραγῖδα θραύων στόματος,
Ἰάονα γλῶσσαν ἐξιχνεύων·

150 "†ἐγω μοι σοι† κῶς καὶ τί πρᾶγμα;
αὖτις οὐδάμ' ἔλθω·
καὶ νῦν ἐμὸς δεσπότης
δεῦρό μ' ἐνθάδ' ἥξει·
τὰ λοιπὰ δ' οὐκέτι, πάτερ,

155 οὐκέτι μαχές' αὖτις ἐνθ⟨ά⟩δ' ἔρχω
ἀλλὰ κάθω.
ἐγώ σοι μὴ δεῦρ', ἐγὼ
κεῖσε παρὰ Σάρδι, παρὰ Σοῦς',
Ἀγβάτανα ναίων·

λῦσον Wil. (ἐλέησον Dan.): -ον· ⟨ἄλλα⟩ σῶσον Sitzler²: ἀμφιβάλλων λίσσειν vel -βάλλειν
(et Sitzler¹) λίσσων vel -βάλλοι Dan.: -βάλλων λίσς⟨οιτο· λῦς⟩ον Page: λισς⟨οίμαν· . . .
ἀπάλλαξ⟩ον et lacunam indicavit West: -βάλλων λίς⟨σεσθαί σε, μάκαρα, νῦν δυναίμαν
ἐρύσασθαι δισ⟩σῶν κτλ. Sudhaus
129 ἀγῶνα coni. West   131 μήστωρι tempt. Diggle   132 -ταχεῖς coni.
Dan.   136 ἔρκος Sudhaus   142 ὀρφανόν: fort. ὄρχαμον?   μαχᾶν: μάχας
GOH   144 ἄγεγ Diels: ἄγει Π: ἄγοι Dan.   146 ελλαδι Π
150 επω vel εγω Π· ἔπω Longman: ἔπω Page: ἐγῶιμι Gildersleeve: ἔποιμι Stanford:
ἔπωμαι Janssen   153 ἦξε coni. Wil.   155 μάχες⟨θ⟩' coni. Wil.   ἔρχω
Πᵖᶜ: εχχω Πᵃᶜ   157 μὴ Wil.: μεν Π

160 Ἄρτιμιc ἐμὸc μέγαc θεόc
  παρ' Ἔφεcον φυλάξει".
οἵ δ' ἐπεὶ παλίμπορον φυ-
  γὴν ἔθεντο ταχύπορον,
αὐτίκα μὲν ἀμφιcτόμουc ἄ-
165   κονταc ἐχ χερῶν ἔρ{ρ}ιπτον,
δρύπτετο δὲ πρόcωπ' ὄνυξι.
Περcίδα cτολὴν περὶ cτέρ-
  νοιc ἔρεικον εὐϋφῆ,
cύντονοc δ' ἁρμόζετ' Ἀcιὰc
170 οἰμωγὰ †πολυcτόνωι.
κτύπει δὲ πᾶcα Βαcιλέωc πανήγυριc
φόβωι τὸ μέλλον εἰcορώμενοι πάθοc.
ὁ δὲ παλινπόρευτον ὡc ||
  ἐc ἐῖδε{ν} Βαcιλεὺc εἰc φυγὴν
175 ὁρμῶντα παμμιγῆ cτρατόν,
γονυπετὴc ἄικιζε cῶμα,
φάτο δὲ κυμαίνων τύχαιc{ιν}·
  "ἰὼ καταcκαφαὶ δόμων
cείριαί τε νᾶεc Ἑλλανίδεc, αἳ
180 κατὰ μὲν ἥλικ' ὠλέcαθ' ἥ-
  βαν νέων πολύανδρον·
νᾶεc δ' οὐκ{ι} ὀπιccοπόρευ-
  τόν ⟨νιν⟩ ἄξουcιμ, πυρὸc
δ' αἰθαλόεμ μένοc ἀγρίωι
185 cώματι φ'λ'έξει{c}, cτονόεντα δ' ἄλγη
ἔcται Περcίδι χώραι·
  ⟨ἰ⟩ὼ βαρεῖα cυμφορά,
ἅ μ' ἐc Ἑλλάδ' ἤγαγεc·
ἀλλ' ἴτε, μηκέτι μέλλετε,
190 ζεύγνυτε μὲν τετρά⟨ορ⟩ον ἵππων ὄχημ', οἵ δ' ἀνάριθμον ὄλβον φορεῖτ' ἐπ' ἀπήναc·
πίμπρατε δὲ cκηνάc,

165 ἐχ χερῶν Πᵖᶜ: εχιερων Πᵃᶜ   166 πρόcωπ' ὄνυξι Sitzler, Blass: προcωπονονυξι Π: πρόcωπον ὄνυχι Wil.: -ον ὄνυξι Diehl   167 Περcίδα ⟨δέ⟩ Sitzler: ⟨καὶ⟩ Περcίδα Sudhaus   170 πολυ⟨γλώccωι⟩ cτόνωι coni. Page: πολυcτόνωι ⟨γόωι⟩ GOH   174 ἐc ἐιδε{ν} Πᵖᶜ (c ex ι factum): ειδεν Πᵃᶜ   177 τύχαιc Maas   181 ναῶν Mazon: νεῶν tempt. Page   182–3 MLW: post νᾶεc δὲ lacunam indicavit Wil.: οὖ νι⟨ν⟩ van Minnen: ⟨μ' ἀπ⟩άξουcιμ Page ὀπιccο-· ὀπιcθο- possis   186–7 χώραι· ἰὼ Page: χωραιω Π: χώραι· ὦ Wil.

195 μηδέ τις ἡμετέρου γένοιτ'
 ὄνησις αὐτοῖσι πλούτου".
 οἳ δὲ τροπαῖα στησάμενοι Διός
 ἁγνότατον τέμενος, Παιᾶν'
 ἐκελάδησαν ἰήϊον
200 ἄνακτα, σύμμετροι δ' ἐπε-
 κτύπεον ποδῶν
 ὑψικρότοις χορείαις.
 ἀλλ' ὦ χρυσεοκίθαριν ἀέ-
 ξων Μοῦσαν νεοτευχῆ,
 ἐμοῖς ἔλθ' ἐπίκουρος ὕ-
205 μνοις{ιν} ἰήϊε Παιάν·
 ὁ γάρ μ' εὐγενέτας μακραίων Σπάρτας μέγας ἁγεμὼν
 βρύων ἄνθεσιν ἥβας
 δονεῖ λαὸς ἐπιφλέγων
210 ἐλᾶι τ' αἴθοπι μώμωι,
 ὅτι παλαιοτέραν νέοις
 ὕμνοις Μοῦσαν ἀτιμῶ·
 ἐγὼ δ' οὔτε νέον τιν' οὔτε γεραὸν οὔτ' ἰσήβαν
215 εἴργω τῶνδ' ἑκὰ⟨ς⟩ ὕμνων·
 τοὺς {ο}δὲ μουσοπαλαιολύμας, τούτους δ' ἀπερύκω,
 λωβητῆρας ἀοιδᾶν,
 κηρύκων λιγυμακροφώ-
220 νων τείνοντας ἰυγ{γ}άς.
 πρῶτος ποικιλόμουσον Ὀρ-
 φεὺς †υν† ἐτέκνωσεν
 υἱὸς Καλλιόπα⟨ς ‿ –
 †πιεριασενι†·
225 Τέρπανδρος δ' ἐπὶ τῶι δέκα
 ζεῦξε Μοῦσαν ἐν ὠιδαῖς·

196 ⟨καὶ⟩ Διὸς GOH: ⟨ἐς⟩ Διὸς Holford-Strevens 197 ἁγνότατον ⟨τε⟩ Janssen
τέμενος ⟨κάτα⟩ Blass 202 χρυσο- coni. Wil. 215 δεκαδυμνων Π
221–2-μουσον Ὀρφεύς Wil.: μουσοσορινς Π 222 ⟨χέλ⟩υν Wil.: ⟨λύρ⟩αν Jurenka:
⟨τέχν⟩ην GOH 223 καλλιοπα| Π: Καλλιόπα⟨ς⟩ Wil. 224 περιασενι:
Πιερίας ἔπι Wil.: Πιερία⟨ι⟩ς ἔνι Dan.· lacunam indicavit Page (⟨‿ ‿ – | – ‿⟩
Πιερίαθεν), suppl. MLW ex. grat. ⟨κόρας Διὸς⟩: ⟨κόλποισι⟩ Πιερίας ἔνι van Minnen:
Πιερίαι ἔνι Janssen 225–6 Wil.: τερπανδροσαεπιτωιδεκατευξε Π ἐπὶ τῶιδε
κατηῦξε Aron

Λέςβος δ' Αἰολία ν⟨ιν⟩ Ἀν-
τίccαι γείνατο κλεινόν·
νῦν δὲ Τιμόθεος μέτροις
230   ῥυθμοῖς τ' ἐνδεκακρουμάτοις
κίθαριν ἐξανατέλλει,
θηςαυρὸν πολύυμνον οἴ-
ξας Μουςᾶν θαλαμευτό⟦c⟧ν·
Μίλητος δὲ πόλις νιν ἁ
235   θρέψας' ἁ || δυωδεκατειχέος
λαοῦ πρωτέος ἐξ Ἀχαιῶν.
ἀλλ' ἑκαταβόλε Πύθι' ἀγνὰν
ἔλθοις τάνδε πόλιν cὺν ὄλβωι,
πέμπων ἀπήμονι λαῶι
240   __τῶ⟨ι⟩δ' εἰρήναν θάλλουcαν εὐνομίαι.

227–8 Wil.: λεcβοcδαιολιανανττιccαγειν- Π: Λεcβὶc δ' Αἰολία⟨ι⟩ ν⟨ιν⟩ Ἄντιccα κτλ.
Maas   235 θρέψαcα δυωδεκα- Blass   δωδεκα- GOH   236 πρώτευc⟨εν⟩
Croiset   240 εὐνομίαι Wil.: ευνομιαν Π   θάλλουcάν ⟨τ'⟩ εὐνομίαν Dan ; εὐνομίαν
⟨τ' ἀδελφάν⟩ ex. grat. GOH

CEMEΛHC ΩΔIC

792   Athen. 8. 352 A (ii. 271 Kaibel)
ἐπακούcαc δὲ τῆc Ὠδῖνοc τῆc Τιμοθέου, εἰ δ' ἐργολάβον, ἔφη (ὁ Cτρατόνικοc),
ἔτικτεν καὶ μὴ θεόν, ποίαc ἂν ἠφίει φωνάc;
Alcaeus Messenius, AP 16. 7. 2–3 (HE 55–6) Δωρόθεοc γοερὸυc ἔπνεε
Δαρδανίδαc | καὶ Cεμέλαc ὠδῖνα κεραύνιον; Dio Chrys. 78. 32 (ii. 216 von
Arnim), ὥcπερ αὐλοῦντα τὴν τῆc Cεμέληc ὠδῖνα; Boeth. Inst. mus. 1. 1
(pp. 182 ss. Friedlein) διεcκεύαcατο (ὁ Τιμόθεοc) . . . τὰν τᾶρ Cεμέλαρ
ὠδῖνα (οδυναρ codd.).

CKYΛΛA

793   Arist. Poet. 15. 1454[a]28 (p. 24 Kassel)
ἔcτιν δὲ παράδειγμα . . . τοῦ δὲ ἀπρεποῦc καὶ μὴ ἁρμόττοντοc ὅ τε θρῆνος
Ὀδυccέωc ἐν τῆι Cκύλληι . . .
Arist. Poet. 26. 1461[b]30 (p. 47 Kassel) πολλὴν κίνηcιν κινοῦνται, οἷον οἱ
φαῦλοι αὐληταὶ κυλιόμενοι ἂν δίcκον δέηι μιμεῖcθαι καὶ ἕλκοντεc τὸν κορυφαῖον ἂν
Cκύλλαν αὐλῶcιν; T. Gomperz, Mittheil. Samm. Pap. Erz. Rainer, 1
(1887), 84 ss., H. Oellacher, Études de papyrologie, 4 (1938), 135 ss. εἰcὶν
δέ τινεc οἳ ὃν μὲν προτίθενται οὐ μειμοῦνται {δέ}, ἄλλον δὲ καὶ τοῦτον καλῶc, [οὗ
τ]υγχάνομεν ἔχοντεc ([εἰ τ]υγχάνοιεν ἐνέχοντεc Gomperz) ἔννοιαν καὶ παράδειγμα παρ' ἡμεῖν αὐτοῖc, ὥcπερ καὶ Τειμόθεοc ἐν τῶι θρήνωι τοῦ Ὀδυccέωc εἰ

96 ΤΙΜΟΘΕΟΥ

μέν τινα μειμεῖται καὶ τὸ ὅμοιόν τινι οἶδεν ἀλλ[ὰ] τῶι Ὀδυccεῖ [(ἀλλ' ο[ὖ] τῶι
Ὀδ Gomperz)

Fr. 794 Page ut alienum abieci; vide pp. 250–1.

ΦΙΝΕΙΔΑΙ

795 Suda s.v. Τιμόθεος, iv. 557 Adler γράψας ... Φινείδας

INCERTI LOCI

796 Athen. 3. 122 CD (i. 279 Kaibel)
εἰ οὖν κἀγώ τι ἥμαρτον, ὦ καλλίcτων ὀνομάτων καὶ ῥημάτων θηρευτά, μὴ
χαλέπαινε· κατὰ γὰρ τὸν Μιλήcιον Τιμόθεον τὸν ποιητήν·
οὐκ ἄιδω τὰ παλαιά,
καινὰ γὰρ ἀμὰ κρείccω·
νέος ὁ Ζεὺς βαcιλεύει,
τὸ πάλαι δ' ἦν Κρόνος ἄρχων·
5   ἀπίτω Μοῦcα παλαιά.
Eust. Od. 1422. 50 (ex Ath. epit.) καὶ Τιμόθεος δέ φαcιν ὁ Μιλήcιος γράφει
οὕτως· οὐκ ἀείδω κτλ.

1 ἄιδω G. S. Farnell: ἀείδω codd.: τὰ παλαί' οὐκέτ' ἀείδω vel τὰ παλαιὰ δ' οὐκ ἀείδω
Headlam   2 καινὰ γὰρ CE: καὶ ταγὰρ ἅμα A (ἅμα om. CE, Eust.): τὰ γὰρ ἀμὰ
Wilamowitz: καινὰ γὰρ μάλα Bergk: et μάλα γὰρ τὰ καινά κρ. vel τὰ γὰρ ἀμὰ κάρτα
Headlam: καινὰ γὰρ ἄιcματα Schneidewin   3 νέον Conomis   4 τὸ
παλαιὸν CE, Eust., corr. Meineke   5 ἀπείτω A, corr. CE, Eust.

797 Athen. 10. 433 C (ii. 442 Kaibel)
οὐκ ἂν ἁμάρτοι δέ τις καὶ τὸ ποτήριον αὐτοῦ (sc. τοῦ Νέcτορος) λέγων φιάλην
Ἄρεως κατὰ τὸν Ἀντιφάνους Καινέα, ἐν ὧι λέγεται οὕτως (110 K.–A.)·
εἶτ' ἤδη δὸς
φιάλην Ἄρεως
κατὰ Τιμόθεον ξυcτόν τε βέλος.
Athen. 11. 502 B Ἀναξανδρίδης δὲ φιάλας Ἄρεος καλεῖ τὰ ποτήρια ταῦτα;
Arist. Poet. 21. 1457^b22 λέγω δὲ οἷον ὁμοίως ἔχει φιάλη πρὸς Διόνυcον καὶ
ἀcπὶς πρὸς Ἄρη· ἐρεῖ τοίνυν τὴν φιάλην ἀcπίδα Διονύcου καὶ τὴν ἀcπίδα φιάλην
Ἄρεως; Arist. Rhet. 3. 4. 1407^a16 οἷον εἰ ἡ φιάλη ἀcπὶς Διονύcου, καὶ τὴν
ἀcπίδα ἁρμόττει λέγεcθαι φιάλην Ἄρεως; Arist. Rhet. 3. 11. 1412^b35 (Mel.
adesp. 951) εἰcὶν δὲ καὶ αἱ εἰκόνες, ὥσπερ εἴρηται καὶ ἐν τοῖς ἄνω, αἱ
εὐδοκιμοῦcαι τρόπον τινὰ μεταφοραί· ἀεὶ γὰρ ἐκ δυοῖν λέγοντα, ὥσπερ ἡ ἀνάλογον
μεταφορά, οἷον ἡ ἀcπίς, φαμέν, ἐcτὶ φιάλη Ἄρεως, καὶ τόξον φόρμιγξ ἄχορδος.

Koppiers: φιάλην τὸ ὅπλον Ἄρεως codd. (τὸ ὅπλον glossema, ut vid.)

798 Athen. 10. 455 F (ii. 490–1 Kaibel)
Ἀναξανδρίδης Αἴςχραι (fr. 6 K.–A.)·

> ἀρτίως διηρτάμηκε καὶ τὰ μὲν διανεκῆ
> cώματoc μέρη δαμάζετ'·
>   ἐν πυρικτίτωι cτέγαι
> Τιμόθεος ἔφη ποτ', ἄνδρες, τὴν χύτραν οἶμαι λέγων.

Kock: ἐν πυρικτίτοιcι γᾶc AEC, Kassel–Austin (η sup. a scriptum ɪn A): περικτίτοιcι γαῖc Dobree cτέγηι van Herwerden

799 *Et. Gen.* A, B (p. 227 Miller, *Mélanges*) = *Et. Mag.* 630. 40 + cod. Paris. 2720 ap. *Anec. Par.* Cramer iv. 12. 25
ὀρίγανον· . . . ὥc φηcιν Ὠριγένης, εὕρηται ἐν cυcτολῆι ἡ ρι cυλλαβή, ὡc παρὰ Τιμοθέωι τῶι κιθαρωιδῶι, οἷον·

>   τεταμένον ὀρίγανα διὰ μυελοτρεφῆ
> cύγκειται δ' οὗτος ὁ cτίχος ἀπὸ προκελευcματικῶν, ὁ δὲ τελευταῖος πούc ἀνάπαιcτος.

τεταμένα *Et. Gen.* (τεταμέν⁻ *Et. Gen.* A), *Anec. Par.*, *Et. Mag.* cod M μυεᵘλ/ τροφῆ *Et. Mag.* cod. M: δμοελοτρεφῆ *Anec. Par.* post μυελοτρεφῆ habent *Et. Mag.* cod. M o (δ superscr.), cod. D o (δ superscr.) δ'', om. *Et. Gen.*, *Anec Par.*

800 Macrob. *Sat.* 1. 17. 19–20 (i. 86–7 Willis)
Apollodorus in libro quarto decimo περὶ θεῶν (*FGrH* 244 F 95. 19–20) Ἥιον solem scribit: ita appellari Apollinem ἀπὸ τοῦ κατὰ τὸν κόcμον ἵεcθαι καὶ ἰέναι, quod sol per orbem impetu fertur. sed Timotheus ita:

> cύ τ' ὦ τὸν ἀεὶ πόλον †οὐράνιον†
> λαμπραῖc ἀκτῖc' Ἥλιε βάλλων,
> πέμψον ἑκαβόλον ἐχθροῖc⟨ι⟩ βέλοc
> cᾶc ἀπὸ νευρᾶc, ὦ ἰὲ Παιάν.

1 cύ τ' ἰὼ Crusius Οὐρανίων Holford-Strevens: οὐράνιοc Hordern 2 ακτιcιν NDPBVZ ναιε N: ηαιε D: ελιε P: ηλι BVZ 3 Crusius: -οιc⟨ιν⟩ G. S. Farnell: εχτροιc V εχθροιc cett.

801 Plu. *De fort. Alex.* 1. 334 B (ii. 2. 94 Nachstädt–Sieveking)
Ἀρχελάωι δὲ δοκοῦντι γλιcχροτέρωι περὶ τὰς δωρεὰς εἶναι Τιμόθεος ᾄδων ἐνεcήμαινε πολλάκιc τουτὶ τὸ κομμάτιον·

> cὺ δὲ τὸν γηγενέταν ἄργυρον αἰνεῖc
> ὁ δ' Ἀρχέλαοc οὐκ ἀμούcωc ἀντεφώνηcε· cὺ δέ γ' αἰτεῖc.

Plu. *Reg. apophth.* 177 B ἐπεὶ δὲ Τιμόθεος ὁ κιθαρωιδὸς ἐλπίcαc πλείονα λαβὼν δ' ἐλάττονα δῆλος ἦν ἐγκαλῶν αὐτῶι καί ποτ' ᾄδων τουτὶ τὸ κομμάτιον· cὺ δὲ κτλ. ἀπεcήμαινεν εἰc ἐκεῖνον, ὑπέκρουcεν ὁ Ἀρχέλαος αὐτῶι "cὺ δέ γε αἰτεῖc".

cὺ δὲ *Reg.*: cὺ δὴ *Alex.*

802 Plu. *De laude ipsius* 1. 539 C (iii. 372 Pohlenz)
ἧι καὶ τὸν Τιμόθεον ἐπὶ τῆι κατὰ Φρύνιδος νίκηι γράφοντα·

μακάριος ἦcθα, Τιμόθε᾽, ὅτε κῆρυξ
εἶπε· νικᾷι Τιμόθεος
Μιλήcιος τὸν Κάμωνος τὸν ἰωνοκάμπταν
εἰκότως δυcχεραίνομεν ὡc ἀμούcως καὶ παρανόμως ἀνακηρύττοντα τὴν ἑαυτοῦ
νίκην.

1 Τιμόθεε codd.: -θεος Hartung   ὅτε codd.: εὖτε Wil.   κῆ- C¹ΧJΘ: κά-
Hartung, Wilamowitz   3 Bergk: ὁ Μιλήcιος codd.   Κάρωνος,
Κάρβωνος codd. (Pollux 4. 66 Κάμωνος) ἰωνοκαμπ. varie corruptum (οἰωνο- J,
πιτνοκάμπτην Θ, -κάμπαν C¹ΩΝΣ, -κάμπταν (η super a scriptum) G¹)

803   Plu. Quaest. conviv. 3. 10. 3. 659 A (iv. 115 Hubert)
ὅθεν οἶμαι καὶ τὴν Ἄρτεμιν Λοχείαν καὶ Ἐλείθυιαν, οὐκ ἑτέραν ἢ τὴν cελήνην,
ὠνομάcθαι. Τιμόθεος δ᾽ ἀντικρύc φηcιν·
    διὰ κυάνεον πόλον ἄcτρων
    διά τ᾽ ὠκυτόκοιο cελάνας.

Plu. Quaest. Rom. 77. 282 CD (ii. 316 Nachstädt–Sieveking) καὶ νομίζειν
(sc. Ἥραν) ἐν ταῖc λοχείαιc καὶ ὠδῖcι βοηθεῖν, ὥcπερ καὶ τὴν cελήνην, διὰ
κυάνεον πόλον κτλ.; Macrob. Sat. 7. 16. 28 (i. 460 Willis) et hoc est quod
eleganter poeta Timotheus expressit διὰ λαμπρὸν πόλον—cελάναc.

1 κυάνεον Plu.: λαμπρὸν Macr.   κυανέου πόλου Reiske: κυανέων πόλων Turnebus,
Valkenarius

804   Stob. 1. 49 (περὶ ψυχῆc) 61 (i. 448 Wachsmuth–Hense)
τοῦ αὐτοῦ (sc. Πορφυρίου ἐκ τῶν περὶ Cτυγόc)·
πάλιν αἰνιττόμενος, ὅτι ταῖc τῶν εὐcεβῶc βεβιωκότων ψυχαῖc μετα τὴν τελευτὴν
οἰκεῖόc ἐcτιν τόπος ὁ περὶ τὴν cελήνην, ὑπεδήλωcεν εἰπών· ἀλλά c᾽ ἐc ἡλύcιον
πεδίον καὶ πείρατα γαίηc | ἀθάνατοι πέμψουcιν, ὅθι ξανθὸc Ῥαδάμανθυc (Od. 4.
563–4), Ἡλύcιον μὲν πεδίον εἰκότως προcειπὼν τὴν τῆc cελήνηc ἐπιφάνειαν ὑπὸ
ἡλίου καταλαμπομένην,
    ὅτ᾽ αὔξεται ἡλίου αὐγαῖc,
ὥc φηcι Τιμόθεος . . .

αὔξεται FP: ἀέξεται coni. Meineke   ἡλίου F: ἠελίου P¹: ἠέλ- P²: ἀλίου coni.
Meineke

*804Α Phld. De poem. col. 89. 5–18
[ὅ]ταν δὲ λέγηι Τιμό[θεος
⟨ ⟩]νον δ᾽ ὁ πλάτανο᾽c᾽ c[εμ]νόν
ἐφθεγγόμεθ᾽ [ἄρ᾽ οὐ]κέτι ταὐτό, ἀλλά τ[ινα] πτῶcιν, εἴ που, φηcίν, [ἡ] μὲν φύcει
δι᾽ αὐτὸν τ[ὸν] ἦχόν ἐcτιν ἁπλῆ, ὅτ[ι οὐ]θὲν ἔτι δεῖ{ν} προcά[γειν] ὅ φαcιν ἄλλο
γένοc, [μό]νωι δ᾽ ἀποδιδόναι τ[ού]τωι τὴν χάριν, ἀλλ[ωc] τε πά[ν]τωc καὶ τῶ[ι τὸ]
λοιπὸν ἀc[ήμ]ωι ὄν[τι].

COMMENTARY

777. THE MADNESS OF AJAX
(Dithyramb)

The story of the contest of Ajax and Odysseus for the arms of Achilles is obviously pre-Homeric, although Homer nowhere gives an extended account of it. The κρίcιc is mentioned briefly at *Od.* 11. 543 ff., but Ajax' madness and subsequent death are not included. The κρίcιc ended the sequence of events in the *Aithiopis* (cf. fr. 5 Bernabé), and begun that in the *Ilias Parva* (Arg. 1; cf. fr. 2 Bernabé): see further M. Davies, *The Epic Cycle* (Bristol, 1989), 60, 62 ff. Heubeck (on the passage in *Od.* 11) suggests that Sophocles was the first to portray Ajax as mad, but Sophocles borrowed other motifs from the Epic Cycle (Davies, 1) and there is no reason to doubt Proclus' statement that it featured in the *Little Iliad*. Davies notes that the madness is an un-Homeric theme. A feeling that the subject was not quite heroic may also account for the silence of Pindar in his two versions of the story (*N.* 7. 20–31; 8. 23–8). It is impossible to tell whether it featured in Aeschylus' Ὅπλων κρίcιc (frr. 174–8 Radt), but without the motif of insanity the story loses much of its drama, though the suicide was deferred to Θρῆιccαι, if indeed that was the next play in the trilogy. There are four fourth-century tragedies on the subject: Astydamas II's Αἴαc μαινόμενοc (*TrGF* 60 F 1a), Carcinus II's Αἴαc (*TrGF* 70 F 1a), and Theodectas' Αἴαc (*TrGF* 72 F 1).

Although most of the pictorial representations of the story date from the fifth century, a black-figure amphora by Exekias (*ABV* 145. 18), dated to c.540, appears to depict Ajax before his sword, presumably about to kill himself (*LIMC* i/1. 329). A black-figure pelike (*ABV* 338. 3), dated to c.520–490, depicts a scene with Ajax, Odysseus, and the Greek vote. The motif is better known from the classical period. Amongst others, two red-figure cups (*ARV²* 433. 71,

433. 72), painted in the style of Douris and dating to the first quarter of the fifth century, depict the Greek decision (cf. also *ARV²* 416. 7: second quarter of the fifth century, and a group of vases by the Brygos painter in *LIMC* i/1. 328), and another depicts an argument between Odysseus and Ajax on one side and the vote on the other (*ARV²* 429. 26 and p. 1653). The same scene is found on two cups by the Brygos painter (*ARV²* 369. 2; *Para* 374). It seems from this that the outlines of the story remain relatively fixed in the fifth century; it is perhaps unusual that no vase shows the madness, which is, however, found in a Hellenistic relief on a bowl from Boeotia (*LIMC* i/1. 327). The depictions cannot indicate which particular version, if any, was in the artist's mind. However, it is tempting to connect the large number of depictions with the interest in Salaminian Ajax that developed in Attica in the early fifth century (see Parker, *Religion*, 312). The nature of Timotheus' treatment is unknown. Clearly the theme of madness would have provided scope for mimetic music and language such as he favoured.

A papyrus fragment with musical notation (P. Berol. 6870) has been ascribed to this poem by Del Grande and by Bélis, '*Ajax*':

> Χ(ορός)· αὐτοφόνωι χερὶ καὶ φάcγανον ι[
> Τελαμωνιάδα τὸ⟨ν⟩ còν Αἶαν ε[
> δι' ⟨'Ο⟩δυcέα τὸν ἀλιτρὸν ο ηι[
> ἕλκεcιν ὁ ποθούμενοc[

(I print the text given by Bélis, '*Ajax*', with slight modifications; ed. pr. by Schubart, *Sitz. Berl. Akad.* 1918, 763–8.) The subject is clearly Ajax, the speaker apparently Tecmessa. The chorus-designation in the margin may not necessarily preclude a dithyramb, although convincing parallels are wanting: even the papyrus of Ba. 18 does not include speaker-designations except by paragraphos. Nevertheless, there is no real reason to connect the lines with Timotheus, and the authorship must remain uncertain. Egert Pöhlmann, *Denkmäler altgriechischer Musik* (Nuremberg, 1970), 100–3, no. 32 discusses, and rejects, an attempt at assigning the Ajax fragment to the "Οπλων κρίcιc.

778(a)–(b). ARTEMIS
(Monody; perhaps a nome?)

The main source of information about the *Artemis* is a fragment of Alexander of Aetolia, transmitted by Macrobius in his *Saturnalia*. Alexander wrote in the third century BC, and no doubt knew Timotheus' work well. According to Macrobius Alexander said that the *Artemis* was written for the rededication of the temple of Artemis at Ephesus. There does not seem to be much evidence for this in the verses quoted, but there may have been some indication of the occasion in the preceding lines. Unfortunately, the high degree of corruption in l. 4 of Alexander makes his meaning slightly unclear, but even if we read ἱερὴν . . . χιλιάδα, and take it to refer to a millennial festival (chronologically impossible, but conceivably held on the basis of spurious reckoning) there is nothing to suggest a rededication of the temple. The earliest shrine at Ephesus seems to date from *c*.700; this was destroyed by the Cimmerians in *c*.600, and the construction of the second temple was begun by Croesus only in *c*.550 and not finished until about 430. See G. L. Huxley, *The Early Ionians* (London, 1966), 27, 54.

Alexander's testimony is supplemented by an anecdote in Plutarch, which has Timotheus performing the poem in Athens in the presence of Cinesias. The four adjectives which make up the line quoted by Plutarch seem particularly appropriate for the Ephesian Artemis. Her cult had close affinities with that of Cybele, although direct recognition of the connection is made only rarely; cf. e.g. Diogenes, *TrGF* 45 = *Semele* F 1 κλύω δὲ Λυδὰc Βακτρίαc τε παρθένουc | ποταμῶι παροίκουc ῎Αλυϊ Τμωλίαν θεόν | δαφνόcκιον κατ᾽ ἄλcοc ῎Αρτεμιν cέβειν, where the goddess of Tmolus is obviously Cybele (Farnell ii. 473–4).

Macrobius explains that Alexander uses the name *Opis* here to mean Artemis: this is no doubt true, but we do not know whether Timotheus used it. Οὖπιc (Dor. ῏Ωπιc) was a cult-name for Artemis in Sparta (cf. Palaeph. *De incred.* 32) and perhaps also in Troezen, where the οὔπιγγοι were hymns sung in her honour (cf. Didym. in *Σ* A.R. 1. 972; Athen. 14.

619 B; Pollux 1. 38), but there is no further evidence that it
was also one of her names in Ephesian cult. However,
Callimachus (*H.* 3. 204) uses the name without reference
to a particular cult, and Alexander may also have used it in
this way. See Farnell ii. 487–8. As with the *Aias*, the subject
seems suited to Timotheus' musical taste; Cinesias' (Athenian) reaction has much in common with Dorion's criticisms
of the *Nauplius* (fr. 785), and those of Stratonicus of the
Birthpangs of Semele (fr. 792).

Brussich ('Artemide') assigned to this poem *PMG* adesp.
955, a highly corrupt fragment of a hymn to Artemis quoted
at Athen. 14. 636 CD:

> Ἄρτεμι σοί μέ †τι φρὴν ἐφίμερον
> ὕμνον νέναιτε ὅθεν
> αδε τις ἀλλὰ χρυσοφανια†
> κρέμβαλα χαλκοπάραια χερσίν

1 ⟨ἐφίηcιν⟩ ἐφίμερον Wilamowitz   2 ὑφαινέμεναι Bergk   θεόθεν Hiller,
Crusius   3 'α⟨ἴρε⟩ δέ τις καλὰ χρυς. *sim.*' Page

The style of this fragment certainly seems that expected of
late classical poetry, especially the adjective χαλκοπάραια,
and perhaps 3 χρυσοφάεννα (cj. Bergk), but there are no firm
reasons for the ascription: other poets of the late fifth and
fourth centuries presumably wrote hymns to Artemis, and
our knowledge about Timotheus' poem is too limited for
any judgement to be made. Bergk, on no good grounds,
assigned to this poem frr. 803 and 804.

Metre

fr. 778(*b*)   – ∪∪ – ∪∪ – ∪∪ – ∪∪ | 4da |

Four regular dactyls, as at *P.* 139, with which we might also
compare the pentameter at *P.* 130 and the dactyls at *P.* 83.
Plutarch gives a different order of words in *De aud. poet.*, but
there is little reason to prefer one over the other; it is clear that
with such a line confusion might easily arise, and there are no
metrical or verbal indications of the correct order.

It is initially unclear how to take the sequence of four words;
Cinesias' supposed barb gives no clue. Campbell and
Edmonds translate them all as adjectives, though θυιάδα is
found in the fifth century only as a substantive. But

Timotheus would probably not have made any clear distinction himself between adjectives and substantives in such a case; what is important is that they are all epithets of the same sort, a fact underlined by the homophony and rhythm. For a similar series, cf. E. *Ba.* 915 cκευὴν γυναικὸc μαινάδοc βάκχηc ἔχων, where the effect is one of 'cumulative scorn' (Dodds). The epithets clearly refer to a deranged female. The title of the work may suggest Artemis, but perhaps rather one of her worshippers is meant. This at least may be implied by μαινάδα; and the other forms are predominantly attested for human beings. But Artemis could behave in the way the line envisages, as for example in the story of Niobe. Could Cinesias' reaction also imply a certain disapproval of the way the goddess was portrayed?

θυιάδα: before Timotheus only in Aeschylus at *Sept.* 498, 836, *Suppl.* 564, and always as a substantive, but Alcm. fr. 63 mentions a class of nymphs called the Thyiades (Θυιάδεc), αἱ cυμβακχεύουcαι Διονύcωι καὶ cυνθυίουcαι, and presumably Aeschylus' 'coinage' was derived from this name, rather than being formed directly from θυίω/θύω. Sophocles calls them Thyiae at *Ant.* 1151. As an adjective, 'frantic', θυιάc is found only at Lycophron 143 τῆc πενταλέκτρου θυιάδοc Πλευρωνίαc, 505.

The MSS of Plutarch's *De aud. poet.* give the form θυάδα, also attested in the MSS at A. *Sept.* 498 θυάc (but θυιάc rightly in T (Naples, Biblioteca Nazionale II F 31)); however, θυι- is the expected form: see *P.* 65 n.

φοιβάδα: the name is conjectured by Haslam at S. *Aiax Locr.* fr. 10c. 9 Radt ἐκ δὲ φοι[βάδοc (-[βάδα Luppe: cf. J. Diggle, *Tragicorum Graecorum Fragmenta Selecta* (Oxford, 1998), 34), but otherwise restricted to Euripides, who uses it to describe Cassandra as priestess or prophetess of Phoebus at E. *Hec.* 827, and (probably) to describe a μάντιc at *IA* 1064–5 μάντιc †δ' ὁ φοῖβα† μοῦcαν εἰδώc (L), where Hermann conjectures μάντιc ὁ φοιβάδα.

Wilamowitz (107) suggested the more common φοιτάδα 'frenzied' (cf. e.g. A. *Ag.* 1273, S. *Tr.* 980 etc.), regarding prophecy as out of place amongst the other adjectives denoting madness. However, prophecy was frequently

associated with madness in antiquity; cf. esp. Pl. *Phaedr.*
244 A–245 A, where Plato distinguishes between types of
divine madness and connects prophetic madness with
Apollo (ritual madness is associated with Dionysus). The
connection is especially common for female figures, such as
the Pythia at Delphi, the Sibyl, and the priestess of Zeus at
Dodona, in all of whom oracular powers were linked with
ritual madness. In tragedy we can compare the figure of
Cassandra (e.g. in A. *Ag.*, E. *Tro.*). See E. R. Dodds, *The
Greeks and the Irrational* (Berkeley, 1951), 64–101; H. W.
Parke and D. E. W. Wormell, *The Delphic Oracle* (Oxford,
1956), i. 19–24; for tragic portrayals of madness, see
R. Padel, *In and Out of the Mind* (Princeton, 1992), esp.
72–5.

μαινάδα: used at E. *Tro.* 173 of Cassandra (again), and of
Pentheus made mad by Dionysus at *Ba.* 915 (quoted above).
If Artemis is the subject, she is not literally being described
as a 'Maenad'; the imagery of madness emphasized in θυιάδα
and φοιβάδα is simply continued here.

λυccάδα: 'raging mad'; apparently a neologism at E. *Herc.*
1024 λυccάδι μοίραι 'by (your) lot of madness' (see Bond on
the passage), and probably at *Herc.* 887 λυccάδεc ὠμοβρῶτεc
ἄδικοι Ποιναί 'mad, devouring, unjust vengeance' (cod. λύcca
δέ c' : corr. Hermann).

779. ELPENOR
(Dithyramb for boys' chorus)

Elpenor was a companion of Odysseus, who, falling asleep
on Circe's roof, fell to his death when woken by the noise of
Odysseus' departure (*Od.* 11. 552 ff.). His meeting with
Odysseus in Hades is described at *Od.* 11. 50–80, and his
burial, in accordance with his spirit's request, at 12. 8–15.
Nothing further is known about him; he otherwise appears
only as a companion of Odysseus in retellings of the *Odyssey*
(e.g. Ov. *Met.* 14. 252; Juv. 15. 22). There is therefore little
evidence for the exact content of Timotheus' poem.

Elpenor appears in a scene on four Etruscan mirrors not
obviously related to anything in Homer and showing Odys-

seus threatening Circe (presumably in order to force her to
restore his companions to human form); Elpenor is standing
to one side, his name sometimes clearly marked. The earliest
of these representations dates to the mid-fourth century at
the latest (Cambridge, Fitzwilliam Museum GR 10. 1972),
and has a slightly different scenic arrangement from the
other three. Of the remaining mirrors, two date to the end of
the fourth century: Louvre Br. 1725, R 63, found at
Tarquinia, and inscribed with the Etruscan names *Cerca*,
Uthste, and *Velparun* (Circe, Odysseus, Elpenor); and New
York MMA 09. 221. 17, from near Campiglia Marittima;
the other (discovered in 1507) is now lost, and although the
scene survives in a drawing, its date is uncertain. Although
these mirrors are all of Etruscan origin they may point to a
different version of the Circe/Odysseus story in which
Elpenor played a larger role. Alternatively, the artists
could simply be conflating elements from the Homeric
account. Two underworld scenes including Elpenor are
known from mid-fifth-century Athens (450–440). The
first, a pelike by the Lykaon painter (ARV^2 1045. 2), is
essentially Odyssean, but the second, a calyx-krater by the
Nekuia painter (so named after this vase), shows the descent
of Heracles (ARV^2 1086. 1) in a tableau of various figures
associated with the underworld, and is probably just an
artistic conflation of myths. See O. Touchefeu in *LIMC* iii/
1. 721–2.

   G. A. Gerhard, *Griechische Papyri: Urkunden und litera-
rische Texte aus der Papyrus-Sammlung der Universitätsbi-
bliothek Heidelberg* (Heidelberg, 1938), 26–38, no. 1,
assigned *PMG* adesp. 925 (P. Hibeh 693 + P. Heidelb.
178) to Timotheus' poem since it appears to deal with the
Nekuia and Odysseus' meeting with his mother. However,
the evidence to support the attribution is, as both Roberts
and Page saw, extremely unconvincing. There is a reference
to Circe at fr. (*c*). 6]Κίρκας, and the phrase τάφου cτηρίγματι
'the foundation of a tomb' in the next line might suit the
Elpenor story, but it is hard to see that a poem devoted to,
and named after, Elpenor should have been narrated by
Odysseus. Furthermore, τέκνον ὦ τέκνον at fr. (*a*). 5 is
probably to be understood as an address by Odysseus'

mother to her son, not, as Gerhard suggests, by Odysseus to Elpenor; cf. [μ]ᾶτερ ἐμά at fr. (d). 12. Nor is there much stylistic support for Gerhard's view. As Page pointed out (*Greek Literary Papyri* (London, 1942²), 396–403 at 397–8; cf. C. H. Roberts, *CQ* 53 (1939), 89–90), the fragment lacks the bold compounds and periphrases we associate with Timotheus; κρατεραυγής may be slightly unusual, but the other compounds are more regular formations (e.g. βαθύπορος, βαθύπολος, θρασύαιγις). Crönert's attribution of a piece of prose from Plu. *De comm. not.* 11. 1064 AB (p. 73 Pohlenz), ἄφες με καὶ καταφρόνησον ἀπολλυμένης ἐμοῦ καὶ διαφθειρομένης εἰς ὄνου πρόσωπον, which he analyses as iambic, is even less likely.

780–3. CYCLOPS

See in general F. Vierlinger, *Die Gestalt des Kyklops Polyphemos in der griechischen und römischen Dichtung* (diss. Vienna, 1939); G. Brenner, *Die Polyphemdichtungen des Euripides, Kratinos und Philoxenos und ihr Verhältnis zur Odyssee* (diss. Vienna, 1949).

There were several treatments of the Polyphemus story before the late fifth century. Aristias (*TrGF* 9 F 4) and Euripides wrote satyr-plays called *Cyclops* and there was a comedy by Epicharmus (frr. 81–3 Kaibel). Cratinus' *Odysses* (frr. 143–57 K.–A.), which either influenced, or was influenced by, Euripides' *Cyclops*, also dealt with the theme; see R. H. Tanner, *TAPA* 46 (1915), 170–206. This suggests that by the later fifth century the story may have been regarded as primarily comic, and that we might expect other treatments to have comic elements. Philoxenus of Cythera wrote a dithyrambic *Cyclops*, into which he introduced the story of Polyphemus' love for the sea-nymph Galatea (frr. 815–24). He was probably writing after Timotheus, but there is no firm evidence for the date of either poem, although Philoxenus' *Cyclops* clearly pre-dates 388 BC, when it was parodied by Aristophanes at *Plut.* 290–301. There were also dithyrambic Cyclops poems by Stesichorus II and possibly by Oeniades (*PMG* 840). Aristoxenus (frr. 135–6 Wehrli ap. Athen. 1. 20 A) describes a

citharodic poem by an Italiote called Oenonas in which the
Cyclops appeared speaking bad Greek (cολοικίζοντα) and
perhaps whistling or humming (τερετίζοντα).
In later literature the Cyclops theme is still primarily
humorous. There were comedies by Antiphanes (*Cyclops*,
frr. 129–31 K.–A.), Nicochares (*Galatea*, frr. 3–6 K.–A.),
and Alexis (*Galatea*, frr. 37–40 K.–A.), which all probably
depended on Philoxenus' version and dealt with Polyphemus' love for Galatea. The Galatea theme reappears at
Theocr. 6 and 11, Callim. *Ep.* 46, Hermesian. fr. 7. 69 ff.
Powell (*CA* 100 = Philox. fr. 815), Propertius 3. 2. 7–8,
Verg. *Buc.* 9. 39–43, and Ovid, *Met.* 13. 750 ff. On Alexis'
play, and for a brief discussion of the evidence from Middle
Comedy, see W. G. Arnott, *Alexis: The Fragments* (Cambridge, 1996), 139–41. P. Oxy. 4456 contains a literary
commentary which probably mentions Cyclopes and quotes
Douris: the author, and the exact subject, is unknown
(Philoxenus' dithyramb?).
   At *Poetics* 2. 1448ª11 (fr. 782), while discussing artistic
mimesis and the poetic portrayal of character, Aristotle
appears to associate Timotheus' and Philoxenus' Cyclops
poems with comedy. The basic sense of the text is fairly
clear. Homeric epic and tragedy represent men as better
than they are, while parody and comedy represent them as
worse. However, it is difficult to establish the place of the
nome and the dithyramb in this scheme, especially given the
obvious corruption of the text. The central problem is
the corruption γᾶc, which is found in codex A (Paris. gr.
1741, s. x/xi), the main manuscript on which almost all the
Renaissance manuscripts depend. Codex B (Florence, Biblioteca Riccardiana 46, s. xiv), which represents a distinct
line of transmission, has two folios missing at the start of the
text (1447ª8–1448ª29), and thus is not available for comparison.
   The apographs of A show a number of variant readings
that appear to derive from scholarly correction of some sort.
Parisinus gr. 2038 (probably to be dated before 1500) has ὡc
πέργαc ʾκαὶʾ κύκλωπαc, but πέργαc is clearly nonsensical and
the superscript καί is probably no more than a scribal
attempt to make sense of the syntax. A more developed

form of this type of conjecture is seen in the lost *codex Robortelli* (cited in 1548), which has ὡς Πέρcαc καὶ Κύκλωπαc. This seems likely to have been conjectured by a scribe or scholar who knew that the *Persae* was a nome by Timotheus. Of course it is possible that a more complete form of B existed during the Renaissance, and that some of the apographs of A were compared with it (it is clear, for instance, that some readings from B entered the group of MSS to which Parisinus gr. 2038 belongs), but in no case is there general evidence for B's version of the passage. See E. Lobel, *The Greek Manuscripts of Aristotle's Poetics* (London, 1933), 10.

It is not entirely clear whether the corruption pre-dates A, although it seems probable. Moerbeke's Latin translation (1278), which derives ultimately from the same source (Π) as A, has only *sicut kyclopas*. The Arabic translation gives a similar version of the text (trans. J. Tkatsch, *Die arabische Übersetzung der Poetik des Aristoteles und die Grundlage der Kritik des griechischen Textes* (Vienna and Leipzig, 1928–32), i. 223): *sicut adsimulat aliquis et imitatur sic Cyclopas Timotheus et Philoxenus*. ὥcπερ ends a line in A, and it is has often been supposed that a larger lacuna needs to be assumed. Castelvetro saw γᾶc as an element of the name Ἀργᾶc, hence Vahlen's ὥcπερ ⟨θεοὺc Ἀρ⟩γᾶc, Κύκλωπαc κτλ. (*Hermes*, 12 (1877), 192). According to Phaenias (fr. 10 Wehrli) Argas was a writer of some sort of obscene verse, and he was known to Plutarch (*Demosth.* 4. 847 EF; cf. Σ Aeschin. 2. 99) as a writer of particularly bad nomes. G. R. Holland, *Leipziger Studien*, 7 (1884), 175–80, seeking a reference to Oenonas (see above), conjectured ὥcπερ Κύκλωπαc Τιμόθεοc καὶ Φιλόξενοc ⟨καὶ Οἰνω⟩νᾶc, μιμήcαιτο ἄν τιc. More recently O. Musso, *Lo specchio e la sfinge: Saggi sul teatro e lo spettacolo antico e moderno* (Florence, 1998), 73 has proposed Γα⟨λατείαc ἐρῶντα⟩c, but we have no reason to think that this was also Timotheus' subject. Furthermore, there is no evidence from either the Latin or the Arabic versions that such a reference originally stood in the text, and the resulting asyndeton is unusual. Codex T of Moerbeke's translation (Toledo, Archivo y Biblioteca Capitulares 47. 10, *c*.1280) has *et Timotheus*, but this does not seem very

significant; the conjunction is lacking in O (Eton College
129, *c.*1300), and does not correspond to anything in the
Greek text; *et Timotheus et Philoxenus* would simply mean
'both Timotheus and Philoxenus'.

Whatever the solution, the genre of Timotheus' poem is
made no clearer. If ὁμοίως refers to Hegemon and Nicochares, then Aristotle might be saying that both Timotheus
and Philoxenus treated the Cyclops theme in a comic
manner. However, possibly the passage refers to the different types of mimesis, and a contrast is being made between
Timotheus' poem and that of Philoxenus. Philoxenus' poem
may be assumed to have been broadly humorous in its
intent, since there is ample evidence that it was at least
later conceived as an allegory attacking Dionysius I of
Syracuse (cf. frr. 816–19). There is less evidence for
Timotheus' treatment, since the two fragments of the
poem lack any context in which they might be satisfactorily
interpreted. The most that can be said is that the usual
version of the story in the later fifth century, as well as in
subsequent periods, was comic, and thus that it is at least
possible that Timotheus also gave it a humorous or satirical
treatment.

Metre

fr. 780   ‒ ‒ ∪ ‒ ‒ ∪ ‒ ‒ ∪ ‒ ∪ ‒ ‒ | ‒*e* | *e* | *ith* |
               ∪∪∪ ‒ ∪ ‒ ∪ ‒ ∪ ‒ × || *E* ∪ ‒ ‒ ||
               ‒ ∪ ‒ ∪ ‒ ∪∪ ‒ ∪∪ ‒ ∪ | *e* ∪ | *D* ∪ |
               ‒ ∪ ‒ ∪ ‒ ∪ ‒ ∪ ‒ ‒ | *E* ∪ ‒ ‒ |
     5   ‒ ∪ ‒ ∪ ‒ ‒ || *ith* ||

Resolution in dactylo-epitrite is rare in tragedy, and usually
confined to the first princeps of *E* (as here in l. 2) or *e*: see
West, *Metre*, 134. Ithyphallics are common at period-end, both in
drama and choral lyric (see ibid. 71 on the ithyphallic in
Simonides, and 132 in drama: 'perhaps always at period-end'),
but less so in fourth- and third-century verse (only in Ariphron fr.
813 and *SH* 521–6: see ibid. 140). They are also found at period-
end in the iambo-trochaic lyrics of the *Persae*, e.g. 63, 75, 85.

The metron ∪ ‒ ‒, found twice in this passage (2, 4), is not
attested in early dactylo-epitrite, but is allowed, if only rarely, in
drama e.g. [A.] *Pr.* 425, S. *Ant.* 597, E. *El.* 864, and then also in
later poetry, e.g. Arist. *PMG* 842. 1, 14, 21; Aristonous 2 (*Hymn.*

in Vestam), *CA* 165. 12. It seems to have been fairly common in late-fifth-century dactylo-epitrite, e.g. Telestes frr. 805(*a*). 6 (–D^3 ⌣ – –), 805(*c*). 1 (*D* ⌣ – –), 3 (*e* ⌣ – –), Ariphr. 813. 7 (*e* ⌣ – –), though the particular combination *E* ⌣ – – is not widely attested. For the acephalous start to epitrite, cf. Diggle, *Euripidea*, 25 n. 16 = *PCPS*² 15 (1969), 53.

780. 'And he poured in one ivy-wood cup teeming with the foam of the dark immortal drops, and poured in on top twenty measures, and mixed the blood of Bacchus with the fresh-flowing tears of the nymphs'.

1. ἔγχευε δ' ἕν . . . δέπας: Timotheus follows two passages of Homer closely, but with some elaboration; cf. *Od.* 9. 345 ff. καὶ τότ' ἐγὼ Κύκλωπα προσηύδων ἄγχι παραστάς, | κισσύβιον μετὰ χερσὶν ἔχων μέλανος οἴνοιο; 9. 208 ff. (of Maron) τὸν δ' ὅτε πίνοιεν μελιηδέα οἶνον ἐρυθρόν, | ἓν δέπας ἐμπλήσας ὕδατος ἀνὰ εἴκοσι μέτρα | χεῦ', ὀδμὴ δ' ἡδεῖα ἀπὸ κρητῆρος ὀδώδει, | θεσπεσίη. Apparently Odysseus is here pouring wine for the Cyclops, although the subject of ἔγχευε is left unstated and could possibly be Maron, who mixes the wine for Odysseus at *Od.* 9. 208 ff.; it is unclear how much of the Odyssean narrative was included in the poem. Homer says nothing about Odysseus' mixing the wine for Polyphemus. Here the idea could be comical: part of the humour of Euripides' satyr-play is the Cyclops' apparent familiarity with some of the habits and practices of the Athenian aristocracy, whilst remaining at heart a brutish and un-civilized beast. The ivy-wood cup conventionally belongs to Polyphemus. According to Athen. 11. 782 AB, it was the custom to put the water in the cup first, followed by the wine (cf. Hes. *Op.* 593, Xenoph. fr. eleg. 5), but here it is more significant that Timotheus follows the order and measure given in *Odyssey* 9, by which he has obviously been influenced.

ἔγχευε: the aorist outside epic is usually ἐνέχεα. Homer normally has ἐνέχευα, a result of vocalization of an original digamma (Chantraine, *Grammaire*, i. 159). The epic form here, in conjunction with the lack of the augment, clearly emphasizes the Homeric model.

μέν: the position of the enclitic is deliberately delayed; it is not a conjunction, but marks a contrast between ἕν in this clause and εἴκοϲιν in the next.

δέπαϲ: Myc. *di-pa* describes a jar of some sort (e.g. PY Ta 641, KN K 875), and δέπαϲ often refers to a vessel of considerable size, as it might be here if the vastness of the cup was a subject for comedy. It is used of the large cup of Nestor at *Il.* 11. 632 ff. (but ποτήριον is used in the 'cup of Nestor' inscription, ML 1), and of the cup of the sun at Pisander fr. 5 Bernabé, Pherecydes, *FGrH* 3 F 18a, Stesich. fr. 181. 5, Antimachus fr. eleg. 66, A. fr. 69. 3 Radt (where it is described as Ἡφαιϲτοτευχές), and seems to have been particularly common in this context, though other words are also attested, such as φιάλη (Panyassis fr. 9 Bernabé), λέβηϲ (Thelutus, *FGrH* 478 F 1, al.). See Allen on Mimn. fr. 12. At E. *Hec.* 527 Neoptolemus pours a libation to Achilles' ghost from a δέπαϲ πάγχρυϲον, where there appears to be no emphasis on size; cf. A. fr. 74. 3 Radt (cj.), and another libation is poured δεπάεϲϲιν 'from cups' in the Homeric imitation at Ar. *Pax* 1090–3, the only instance of the word in Aristophanes. Theocritus (1. 55) calls his herdsman's rustic κιϲϲύβιον a δέπαϲ, as well as a ϲκύφοϲ at 143.

κίϲϲινον: a constant feature of the tradition, cf. *Od.* 9. 346 κιϲϲύβιον, E. *Cycl.* 390–1 ϲκύφοϲ κιϲϲοῦ. The form κίϲϲινοϲ, 'of ivy', appears at Pi. *Dith.* 3. 7 (ϲτέφανοϲ) and again at e.g. E. *Alc.* 756 ποτῆρα . . . κίϲϲινον, *Ba.* 177, 702, *Andromeda* fr. 146 N², for the Homeric κιϲϲύβιον, although the latter may not originally have had anything to do with ivy at all (the etymology may be non-Greek: see Frisk s.v.; Chantraine s.v.; C. A. Mastrelli, *SIFC* 23 (1949), 97–112). Gow on Theocr. 1. 27 notes of the word, 'it seems likely that any rustic drinking-vessel could be so called', and its manifestation as a cup made of ivy-wood, or decorated with ivy leaves, may have been purely literary. In post-classical literature ivy is especially associated with large vessels. See A. M. Dale, *CR²* 2 (1952), 129–32 = *Coll. Pap.* 98–102.

μελαίναϲ: particularly appropriate here, as the adjective is not only common of wine (e.g. *Od.* 5. 265, 9. 346, E. *Alc.* 757) but can also be used of blood (e.g. A. *Eum.* 183). I take the genitives to be dependent on ἀφρῶι βρυάζον rather than on δέπας, though the latter is also possible.

2. cταγόνοc: cf. esp. E. *Cycl.* 67 οἴνου . . . cταγόνες, but again particularly apt here as the word can also refer to blood (e.g. A. *Ag.* 1122 with Fraenkel, *Ch.* 400, S. *OT* 1278, E. *Ph.* 1415, *Ba.* 767).

ἀμβρότας: 'belonging to the gods' (cf. LSJ s.v. 2), as of ἵπποι at *Il.* 16. 381 and τεύχεα at 17. 194. The adjective presumably refers to the traditional connection of wine with Dionysus, or, perhaps less probably, merely to the fact that this particular wine was given to Odysseus by Maron.

βρυάζον: 'teeming'. There is little to support Zimmermann's contention (129–30) that the word is borrowed from the phraseology of the cult of Dionysus. βρύω is said to be used in Dionysiac contexts at *Ba.* 6. 8–9 cτεφάνοις ἐθείρας | νεανίαι βρύοντες, E. *Ba.* 107 (with Dodds), Ar. *Ra.* 328 ff., Eubulus fr. 56 K.–A. κιccῶι κάρα βρύουcαν; add here perhaps Nicaenetus, *AP* 13. 29. 5–6 (*HE* 2715–16) τοιγὰρ ὑπὸ cτεφάνοις μέγας ἔβρυεν εἶχε δὲ κιccῶι | μέτωπον ὥcπερ καὶ cὺ κεκροκωμένον. But it is a common word in other environments: e.g. *Il.* 17. 56 καί τε βρύει ἄνθεϊ λευκῶι (of water driven by the wind), *Ba.* 3. 15–16, 13. 179 βρύουcα δόξαι (of Ἀρετά), A. *Suppl.* 966 ἀγαθοῖcι βρύοις, Licymnius fr. 770(a) μυρίαις παγαῖc δακρύων ἀχέων τε βρύει.

βρυάζω appears in a Dionysiac context in a late Orphic hymn (53. 10), where Dionysus is said to be κάρποιcι . . . βρυάζων; but at Ar. *Nub.* 45 βρύων μελίτταις καὶ προβάτοις καὶ cτεμφύλοις and A. *Suppl.* 877–80 †λυμαcιc ὑπρογαcυλάcκοι | περιχαμπτὰ βρυάζεις | ὃc ἐρωταῖc† ὁ μέγας | Νεῖλος ὑβρίζοντά c' ἀποτρέψειεν ἄιcτον ὕβριν (though corrupt), neither verb has an obvious connection with the cult of Dionysus.

Timotheus himself uses βρύω at *P.* 208, where the Spartan leader (see n.) is described as βρύων ἄνθεcιν ἥβας. Philodamus uses a compound adjective based on the root of Dionysiac song in his paean to Dionysus (*CA* 166. 19–20 πᾶcα δ' ὑμνοβρύης χόρευ|ε[ν Δελφῶ] ἱερὰ μάκαιρα χώρα); and for its use of song in general, cf. carm. conviv. *PMG* 917(c) ἄρτι βρύουcαν ἀοιδὰν πρωτοπαγεῖ cοφίαι διαποίκιλον ἐκφέρομεν. Simonides fr. 519 fr. 77. 5]τεβρυωνπο[ ]οιcι, probably βρύων πο[λλ]οῖcι (ed. pr.), lacks a clear context.

3. **εἴκοcιν … μέτϱ'**: 'twenty measures' (of water); the use of μέτρα without the accompanying genitive is unusual, but here is no doubt facilitated by the reference to δακρύοιcι Νυμφᾶν at 5. Wine was usually mixed with water, in varying quantities, no doubt depending on the supposed strength of the resulting mixture. A more potent wine would no doubt need to be diluted to a greater extent. The comedians provide numerous references to equally mixed wine (Cratinus fr. 196 K.–A.; Archippus fr. 2; Strattis frr. 23, 64; Philetaerus fr. 1; Alexis frr. 59, 232; Sophilus fr. 4; Timocles fr. 22; Xenarchus fr. 9), though Hermes drinks (and regrets) the same mixture at Ar. *Pl.* 1132. Hes. *Op.* 596 and Euenus fr. eleg. 2. 3 recommend three parts of water to one of wine (cf. Anaxilas fr. 23 K.–A., Cratinus fr. 195), and a mixture of three parts of water to two of wine is mentioned at Ar. *Eq.* 1187, Philetaerus fr. 15. At Ephippus fr. 11, where three parts of water to four of wine appear, the mixture is perhaps intended to be comically strong; cf. the mixture of one part of water to two of wine at Alc. fr. 346, while the reverse, two parts of water to one of wine, is already associated by Anacreon with Dionysiac behaviour (fr. 356. 3–6 τὰ μὲν δέκ' ἐγχέαc | ὕδατοc, τὰ πέντε δ' οἴνου | κυάθουc, ὡc ἀνυβρίcτωc | ἀνὰ δηῦτε βαccαρήcω). Five parts of water are mixed with two of wine at Ameipsias fr. 4, Eupolis frr. 6, 24, and Nicochares fr. 2 K.–A.

Page prints ἐνέχευ', but the echo of *Od.* 9. 209–10 (quoted above), together with the use of ἀναχείcθω at Anacr. 409, suggests that the verb should be ἀναχεύω (as in A), where the preverb has the sense 'onto', 'on top (of)'.

4. **αἷμα Βακχίου**: 'the blood of the Bacchic god', i.e. wine. For the periphrasis, cf. esp. Antiph. fr. 55. 12 K.–A. (A) Βρομιάδοc δ' ἱδρῶτα πηγῆc; (B) οἶνον εἰπὲ cυντεμών, which seems to parody the complex language of the dithyrambographers; further Thespis, *TrGF* 1 F 4 ἴδε coὶ Βρομίου {αἴθοπα} φλεγμὸν λείβω; Posidippus, *AP* 5. 134. 1 (*HE* 3054) Κεκροπί, ῥαῖνε, λάγυνε, πολύδροcον ἰκμάδα Βάκχου, Achilles Tat. 2. 2 αἷμα βότρυοc. The idea is also common in the Near East; cf. e.g. Deut. 32. 15 w°-dam-'ēnâv tišteh-hâmer (LXX 32. 14 καὶ αἷμα cταφυλῆc ἔπιον οἶνον) and see J. P.

Brown, *Israel and Hellas; Beiheft zur Zeitschrift für die alttestamentliche Wissenschaft*, 231 (Berlin and New York, 1995), 135.

Βάκχιος is adjectival, metrically shortened from the more usual form -ειος, with ellipsis of θεός *vel sim.*, but the substantival use of an adjective *via* ellipsis of the noun is common (cf. e.g. S. *Ant.* 154, E. *Cycl.* 9). Zimmermann (129–30) improbably perceives overtones of Dionysiac cult, and connects them with the traditional elements of the dithyramb, which ignores the narrative context in which these lines occur.

νεορρύτοιcιν: 'newly-flowing', before only at S. *El.* 894–5 νεορρύτους πηγὰς γάλακτος, where the point is that the offerings have been recently left at Agamemnon's grave; 'I saw on top of the mound streams of milk that had been recently poured there.' Here the emphasis is on the freshness of the water.

5. δακρύοιcι Νυμφᾶν: 'the tears of the Nymphs', i.e. water; cf. esp. Euenus fr. eleg. 2. 3 *(Βάκχος)* χαίρει κιρνάμενος δὲ τρισὶν Νύμφαισι τέταρτος; and similar periphrases at Antiphanes fr. 55. 13 K.–A. (A) λιβάδα νυμφαίαν δροσώδη; (B) παραλιπὼν ὕδωρ φάθι, where Antiphanes is parodying the style of the new dithyramb, if not Timotheus himself; *AP* 14. 71. 2 νυμφαίου νάματος.

Metre

fr. 781   `− − − ∪ ∪ − ∪ − | − ∪ ∪ − ∪ ∪ − − ||`   *gl* | *D*—||

For aeolic metra in the context of dactylo-epitrite, see Dale 178 ff., who notes their presence in Sophocles and Euripides (but not in Pindar or Bacchylides; in Simonides it is doubtful), and cf. Melanipp. fr. 762, to be analysed as *ar cr* | *e*—*D* (reading ψυχᾶς μεδέων; see my 'Notes', 289–90).

781. 'Never shall you ascend to the over-arching sky.'

The Cyclops is speaking, probably to Odysseus, though Chrysippus is not explicit. Perhaps the Cyclops' comment was only known to him as a proverb or through quotation in another text. Wilamowitz (108) understands the sense to be: 'Du bist doch ein Mensch, der leiden muß', comparing Pi. *P.* 10. 27 ὁ χάλκεος οὐρανὸς οὔ ποτ' ἀμβατὸς αὐτῶι (to which we

might add Alcm. fr. 1. 16 μή τις ἀνθρώπων ἐς ὠρανὸν ποτήςθω),
but there is no evidence that, spoken as it is by Polyphemus,
the phrase is intended to be gnomic as are the parallels from
Pindar and Alcman. The sense could simply be 'You will
never escape from this cave'. Polyphemus' sealed cave is a
feature of the Homeric story and parodied at Ar. *Vesp.*
181 ff., where Bdelycleon attempts to escape his house
Odysseus-fashion by clinging to the belly of a donkey.
The idea does not appear in Euripides' *Cyclops*, where
Odysseus needs to pass between the cave and the stage;
but Philoxenus appears to have followed the *Odyssey*; cf. fr.
824 οἴωι μ' ὁ δαίμων τέρατι ςυγκαθεῖρξεν, which Zenobius tells
us was spoken by Odysseus after being shut up in the
Cyclops' cave.

οὗτοι . . . γε: οὗτοι is common in tragedy and in Aristophanic oaths (Denniston, 543); here γε merely adds force
to the negation, as at Ar. *Eccl.* 522 οὗτοι παρὰ τοῦ μοιχοῦ γε
φήςεις, S. *El.* 772–3 Παιδ. μάτην ἄρ' ἡμεῖς, ὡς ἔοικεν, ἥκομεν. |
Κλυτ. οὗτοι μάτην γε.

ὑπεραμπέχοντ': 'which covers (us) from above'; only
here, but ἀμπέχω is used at S. *OC* 314 of a Thessalian hat
which protects (ἀμπέχει) Ismene's face from the sun, and
at E. *Hipp.* 192 ἀλλ' ὅτι τοῦ ζῆν φίλτερον ἄλλο | ςκότος
ἀμπίςχων κρύπτει νεφέλαις, where the idea of 'shading'
again seems operative. Semonides fr. 12 has ςπλάγχ'
ἀμπέχοντες αὐτίκ' ἰκτίνου δίκην, where it is often taken to
mean 'embracing' (e.g. Gerber), but the context is lacking; the idea may simply be that a kite covers the entrails
of a carcass with its shadow. It is obviously possible to
say that the sky might *cover* or *surround* the earth or its
inhabitants.

783. θῦςαι: rare in Homer, but always of burnt offerings
where it does occur (e.g. *Il.* 9. 219, *Od.* 9. 231, 14. 446, 15.
222, 260). By the fifth century the sense 'slaughter' is
common in other contexts. See J. Casabona, *Recherches sur
le vocabulaire des sacrifices en grec* (Aix-en-Provence, 1966),
69–109. Bergk, Page, and other editors attribute the verb
here to Timotheus' *Cyclops*, despite the fact that the
scholiast is not explicit, since the *Suda* (ε 336: ii. 211–12

Adler) attests that in Philoxenus' *Cyclops* (fr. 823) Polyphemus addressed Odysseus thus: ἔθυcαc, ἀντιθύcηι; and that
he (and other poets) here misunderstood *Od.* 9.
231: ἀπεκδέχονται γὰρ τὸ "ἔνθα δὲ πῦρ κείαντες ἐθύcαμεν" παρὰ τῶι
ποιητῆι εἰρῆcθαι ἐπὶ τῶν ἀρνῶν, οὐχὶ δὲ τὸ †"ἀπεθύcαμεν"†
(ἐθυμιάcαμεν cj. Bernhardy) νοεῖcθαι. But there is no need to
assume that this use was limited to a single poem, and
Timotheus has ἔθυετ' 'was being slaughtered' at *P.* 29.

784. LAERTES

The content of this poem is almost impossible to determine.
There seem to be few myths in which Laertes was the main
character. If the four 'Odysseus' poems are regarded in
some way as a unity then the poem may have dealt with
Odysseus' birth, but see pp. 12–13 above for arguments
against this theory. Laertes is later said to have played a role
in the Calydonian boar-hunt (Hygin. *Fab.* 173), and may
have been counted as an Argonaut (Apollod. *Bibl.* 1. 9. 16),
although neither of these stories is mentioned in earlier
literature. There is a relatively unilluminating fragment of
a dramatic *Laertes* by Ion of Chios (*TrGF* 19 F 14), which
seems to point to a group of myths relating to Laertes'
marriage to Anticleia, and such stories as these may also
have formed the subject for Timotheus' poem. See
H. Lamer, *RE* xii/1 (1924), s.v. Laertes 2, cols. 424–55;
O. Touchefeu-Meynier in *LIMC* vi/1. 181.

785. NAUPLIUS
(Nome?)

Nauplius was an Argonaut and the father of Palamedes,
although his role in the Argonautic myths is small (he is
named only twice in Apollonius: 1. 133 ff., 2. 896). Hegesandros (*FHG* iv. 416, if we adopt Casaubon's emendation)
refers to the presence of a storm in the narrative, no doubt
lavishly described. Although this might possibly have been
part of an *Argonautica*, it seems unlikely in view of the
insignificant role usually given to Nauplius. Hegesandros

may be more plausibly understood to refer to the storm at the Capherian rocks which wrecked the Greek fleet on its return from Troy.

According to Greek tradition Nauplius' son Palamedes was stoned to death through the machinations of Odysseus (e.g. [Apollod.] *Epit.* 6. 7 ff.) in revenge for proving Odysseus' madness to be fictitious (*Epit.* 3. 6 ff.). In retaliation, when the Greek fleet were struck by storm on their return from Troy, and some were driven to Euboea, Nauplius lit false beacons and thus induced many of the ships to wreck themselves on the Capherian rocks. The myth was apparently quite popular in the fifth century. It may already have formed part of Agias' epic *Nostoi*, although there is only a reference to the storm, and no mention of Nauplius, in the argument (*PEG* p. 94, Proclus, *Chrest.* 277 Severyns). Nauplius' marriage is, however, referred to in the extant fragments (fr. 1 Bernabé). The murder of Palamedes was the subject of a play by Euripides in 415 (frr. 578–90 N²; cf. Hygin. *fab.* 105), while Nauplius plays were written by Sophocles (frr. 425–38 Radt), and later by Philocles (*TrGF* 24 T 1), Astydamas II (*TrGF* 60 F 5), and Lycophron (*TrGF* 100 T 3). There are also references to the story at E. *Hel.* 767 ff. (see Dale ad loc.), 1126 ff. (see further Kannicht on 1126–31). We do not know to what extent any of these influenced, or may have been influenced by, Timotheus.

786-7. NIOBE

(Nome?)

See in general K. B. Stark, *Niobe und die Niobiden* (Leipzig, 1863); E. Liénard, 'Les Niobides', *Latomus*, 2 (1938), 21 ff.; R. M. Cook, *Niobe and her Children* (Cambridge, 1964).

The story of Niobe and her children is first mentioned at *Il.* 24. 602–20, and became a popular subject for the lyric poets. According to Homer, Niobe counted herself more blessed than Leto since she had six sons and six daughters, whereas Leto had only one of each. Consequently, Leto incited

Apollo and Artemis to kill the children, and Niobe was turned to stone.

In subsequent treatments the number of children varies, but not the essential elements of the story. The discussion of the myth in Ps.-Apollodorus (*Bibl.* 3. 5. 6) assigns ten boys and ten girls to Hesiod's account (fr. 183 in the *Catalogue of Women*), though Aelian (*VH* 12. 36) says that he mentioned only nineteen children. Aelian further records that Mimnermus (fr. 19) and Pindar (*Pae.* 13 test., also cited by Gellius, *NA* 20. 7) gave the total as twenty and Lasus (fr. 709) as fourteen; he also mentions ten children for Alcman's version (fr. 75), a possibly corrupt reference (for suggested emendations see A. Allen, *RhM²* 117 (1974), 358–9, M. W. Haslam, *RhM²* 119 (1976), 192; but the text is left unamended by Davies). The subject vexed other ancient writers. Gellius records that Sappho (fr. 205) mentioned eighteen children, Bacchylides twenty, and Euripides fourteen. This seems to depend on the same source as a papyrus scholion to Ba. fr. 20 D. 6, which refers to ten boys and perhaps ten girls (παῖδες δέκα τ' ἠϊθέους τε[) and also gives the number of children in Homer, Euripides, and Pindar. Fourteen seems to have been the standard number in tragedy. A scholion to E. *Ph.* 159 (where the tombs of the seven daughters are mentioned) quotes the Euripidean verses referring to fourteen children (fr. 455 N², attributed to his *Cresphontes*), and mentions that Aeschylus (*Niobe* fr. 167b Radt), Sophocles (*Niobe* fr. 446 Radt), and Aristophanes (*Νίοβος* fr. 294 K.–A.) had the same number. Fourteen children are also known to Ovid, *Met.* 6. 182–3, and Statius, *Th.* 3. 198, though he follows Homer at 6. 124–5; Theodoridas, *HE* 3582 (*AP* 16. 132) also follows Homer. See the addenda to *TrGF* iii pp. 575–6; W. S. Barrett in R. Carden, *The Papyrus Fragments of Sophocles* (Berlin and New York, 1974), 171–5. A lyric version by Telesilla (fr. 721) was known to Ps.-Apollodorus (*Bibl.* 3. 46), who cites her for the names of the two children to be saved (cf. Paus. 2. 21. 9).

Historical writers tended towards less extravagant figures. Gellius mentions sources who gave Niobe only three children (thus only one more than Leto, the bare minimum for her boast). In Hellanicus (*FGrH* 4 F 21) she has only four

sons and three daughters. Herodorus, another writer cited in
Ps.-Apollodorus, has the same number; see R. L. Fowler,
Early Greek Mythography, i: *Texts* (Oxford, 2000), 252, on
fr. 56. Pherecydes follows Homer's six of each (*FGrH* 3 F
38). Parthenius' peculiar version (*Erot. Path.* 33) does not
mention a transformation into stone, but makes Niobe leap
to her death from a rock, perhaps a rationalization of the
story (so Lightfoot ad loc.). A similar version may be
preserved on an Apulian vase dating to *c*.340 (A. D. Tren-
dall and A. Cambitoglou, *The Red-Figured Vases of Apulia*
(Oxford, 1978–82), no. 1).

Timotheus' treatment is difficult to establish. It might be
presumed on the basis of his date that he gave the number of
children as fourteen, but we cannot be certain. Wilamowitz
(81 n. 1) argued from the evidence for a meeting with
Charon that there was no metamorphosis, but it is not
clear that the two are necessarily incompatible. It is also
possible that frr. 786 and 787 are to be connected not with
Niobe's death, but with the killing of the children.

786. Machon relates the imagined death of Philoxenus of
Cythera, who acquired a posthumous reputation for gluttony. This might be an unjust inference from the *Deipnon*
ascribed to him in some passages of Athenaeus, if the poem
were in fact by another Philoxenus, from Leucas (see Intro.
n. 138), but that cannot be proved. In any case, it is hardly
by chance that in the extract from Teles this passage is cited
in the context of the 'well-contented guest' topos, for which
see Lucretius 3. 938 and his commentators.

Philoxenus imagines that he is being summoned by the
Charon from Timotheus' *Niobe*. It has been suggested (e.g.
by Nauck, Bergk) on the basis of l. 3 of Machon that a
phrase in Teles at Stob. 3. 1. 98, ἔμβα πορθμίδος ἔρυμα,
should be ascribed to Timotheus. In part this suggestion
relies on Casaubon's conjecture πορθμίδ᾽ for πορθμόν (codd.)
at l. 3. However, Gow ad loc. points out that πορθμόν is
possible, although there is some support for πορθμίδα from
parallel phrases (e.g. A. *Pers.* 379 ἐς ναῦν ἐχώρει, Ar. *Lys.*
605–6 χώρει 'ς τὴν ναῦν· ὁ Χάρων ϲε καλεῖ, E. *Hel.* 1548, all
with a similar use of χωρεῖν for embarkation). The meaning

would then be, 'he is shouting for me to come to the ferry' (the place not the boat). Despite this, Gow seems to accept the ascription to Timotheus. Although he may be correct to suggest that Machon, in the person of Philoxenus, is quoting from Timotheus' work at this point (79: 'for Machon would otherwise hardly omit the preposition after the verb of motion'), there is no firm evidence to suggest that ἔμβα πορθμίδος ἔρυμα was the original phrase. The second person singular imperative in -βα of verbs in βαίνω could be colloquial (cf. Ar. *Ach.* 262 πρόβα, *Vesp.* 979 κατάβα, *Ra.* 35 κατάβα, *Eccl.* 478, but *Ra.* 377 ἔμβα in lyric; perhaps E. *Ph.* 193 ἔcβα, *Alc.* 872 πρόβα, but *El.* 113 ἔμβα in lyric), while forms in -βηθι are epic and generally tragic, but rare in comedy (Ar. *Lys.* 873, *Eq.* 169): see Stevens 63. Although this does not necessarily indicate the source of the phrase, it may suggest that the ascription to Timotheus is unlikely. P. P. Fuentes González, *Les Diatribes de Télès* (Paris, 1998), 244–6, has recently suggested that the words, together with the preceding phrase in Teles (ὅταν {ἤ} ὥρα ᾖ: common in the paroemiographers) may simply be proverbial. The use of ἔρυμα, however, seems poetic. Its use with the genitive in a metaphorical sense is common in verse, e.g. Hes. *Op.* 536 ἔρυμα χροός (of a cloak), *Il.* 4. 137 ἔρυμα χροός (of armour), S. *Ai.* 467 ἔρυμα Τρώων (of a wall); there are several examples in Euripides (*Ba.* 55 Τμῶλον ἔρυμα Λυδίας, *Med.* 1322, *IA* 189 etc.).

For Charon's impatience, which probably also featured in Timotheus' poem, and which was apparently typical of ancient ferrymen, cf. E. *Alc.* 254–5 (esp. for the use of καλεῖ), Ar. *Ra.* 180 ff. (with Dover), *Lys.* 605–7 (with Henderson). Charon first appears in the seventh- or sixth-century epic *Minyas* (frr. 137–42 Bernabé), although artistic representations do not occur until later (c.500 BC). In the fifth century he becomes a popular subject of depiction, especially on white-ground lekythoi, which generally eschew mythological scenes except for other funereal guides such as Hermes, Thanatos, and Hypnos: see in general D. C. Kurtz, *Athenian White Lekythoi* (Oxford, 1975). On Charon in art, see further C. Sourvinou-Inwood in *LIMC* iii/1. 210–16, and *'Reading' Greek Death* (Oxford, 1995), 303–61.

787. Ascribed to Timotheus by Nauck (at N², s.v. A. *Niobe*), but attributed by Brunck to Sophocles and by Hermann to Aeschylus. The most that can be said is that it aptly fits the context provided by fr. 786; there is no further indication, linguistic or otherwise, to confirm Nauck's suggestion.

788–91. PERSAE
(Nome)

The Persian Wars were a popular literary subject not only immediately after the Greek victories but also well into the later fifth and fourth centuries. Regrettably little of this literature has survived; if it had, we should no doubt more easily discern its influence on Timotheus. Simonides wrote a lyric poem on Salamis (fr. 536), and an elegy on Artemisium (*Suda* c 439: cf. P. J. Parsons, *The Oxyrhynchus Papyri*, LIX (1992), 32; M. L. West, *ZPE* 98 (1993), 1–14); only a few fragments of the latter are extant (frr. 532–5), and little can be established about Simonides' treatment of the theme. He seems to have included some extraneous mythological narrative (fr. 534). More extensive fragments of an elegy on Plataea have been recently discovered, in which he seems to have emphasized the Panhellenic motif of Greek liberty (fr. eleg. 11. 2–8), a feature also found in Timotheus' *Persae*; see further I. C. Rutherford, *Arethusa*, 29 (1996), 167–92. There may have been an elegy on Marathon (fr. eleg. 86), where the emphasis appears to be on the Athenian achievement. In his epigrams, at least some of which were inscribed on public monuments, Simonides also dealt extensively with the Wars. Many, if not most, of these would no doubt have been known to Timotheus; their direct influence appears nevertheless to be slight. Timotheus may also have been influenced by Pindar, whose dithyramb on Artemisium salutes the Athenians as Ἑλλάδος ἔρεισμα (fr. 76); fr. 77, probably from the same poem, clearly associates the Athenian victory with the struggle for freedom, ὅθι παῖδες Ἀθαναίων ἐβάλοντο φαεννάν | κρηπῖδ' ἐλευθερίας; cf. also fr. 78

κλῦθ᾽ Ἀλαλά, Πολέμου θύγατερ, | ἐγχέων προοίμιον, ἇι θύεται
| ἄνδρες ὑπὲρ πόλιος τὸν ἱρόθυτον θάνατον.

The most obvious influence on Timotheus is Aeschylus'
Persae; verbal and phraseological reminiscences of the play
occur throughout the poem. In this way, Timotheus may
directly align himself with the 'mythic' interpretation of
events given by Aeschylus, and he too concentrates on the
Persian version of events. Aeschylus' *Persae* was first performed in 472, but Timotheus may have had access to a
written text (the verbal similarities are often remarkably
close); he may even have seen a performance of the play,
since a number of Aeschylus' plays were revived after his
death (cf. e.g. Ar. *Ach.* 9–11, *Ra.* 868–9; in particular
Dionysus at Ar. *Ra.* 1028–9 perhaps claims to have wit-
nessed a performance of *Persae*, though the force of this
passage is disputed). Both poets, in contrast to Simonides,
appear to concentrate on the sufferings of the Persians rather
than on the glory of the Athenian victory. In Timotheus
especially the victory celebrations are passed over in a
remarkably cursory manner (196–201), although there may
have been a greater emphasis on the Athenians or on the
Greeks in general in the first part of the poem. We may also
compare Aeschylus' model, the *Phoenissae* of Phrynichus,
perhaps produced in 476: see E. O'Neill, *CP* 37 (1942), 425–
7; Hall, *Barbarian*, 63–4. This was set in Susa (cf. *TrGF* 3 F
8 ~ A. *Pers.* 1 ff.), and with its chorus of Phoenician women
probably offered an Oriental perception of events. Phrynichus also dealt with the events leading up to the Wars in his
Sack of Miletus (*TrGF* 3 F 4b).

This play may have been performed during Themistocles'
archonship in 492; the other two were produced shortly after
the Persian defeat, but the subject was equally prominent in
Timotheus' own lifetime. He was no doubt familiar with
Herodotus' version of Salamis, and with his interpretation
of Greek history as a series of conflicts between Greece and
Asia. There is some late evidence that Herodotus publicly
recited his work, or portions of it, in Athens (Diyllus, *FGrH*
73 F 3; Syncellus, p. 297. 14–15 Mosshammer), though its
reliability is dubious. Nevertheless, his prose history was
clearly known to Thucydides, and Aristophanes describes a

medley of battles during the Persian Wars at *Vesp.* 1079–88
(produced in early 422), where his language owes something
to Herodotean descriptions (cf. MacDowell ad loc.). Choerilus of Samos' hexametrical *Persica*, dated to the last part of
the fifth century, dealt with Xerxes' invasion (*SH* 314–23),
but its scope is unclear; Timotheus may intentionally allude
to it by opening his poem with a hexameter (see fr. 788 n.).
There are several Hellenistic fragments apparently dealing
with such themes (e.g. *SH* 904, 928–35, 937, 950), and a
Perseis is attested for Musaeus of Ephesus (*SH* 560), though
its exact content is unknown. The fourth century was,
however, clearly a fruitful time, especially for Athenian
interest in the Wars: the political difficulties experienced
by Athens in their resistance to Macedon seem to have
encouraged the production of a number of forged decrees
purporting to date from the fifth century which relate to
various points in the Greek struggle against Asia; see
C. Habicht, *Hermes*, 89 (1961), 1–35.

   Contemporary with Timotheus we find a more general
literary penchant for Oriental characters; the Phrygian slave
in Euripides' *Orestes* (produced in 408) is an obvious case;
the chorus of Phoenician women gratuitously introduced
into Euripides' *Phoenissae* (*c*.409; see Mastronarde's edn.,
pp. 11–14) parodied by Strattis (frr. 46–53 K.–A.) and
perhaps Aristophanes, and the Thracian Polymestor in
Hecuba (*c*.424) are other relevant examples. The dithyram-
bographer Licymnius of Chios, mentioned at Arist. *Rhet.* 3.
12. 1413^{b}14 as a popular poet, and probably roughly
contemporary with Timotheus, wrote a *Nanis* (fr. 772).
This told the story of how Cyrus captured Sardis with the
help of Nanis, the daughter of Croesus. The erotic content is
a little reminiscent of Licymnius' other dithyrambs; in one
poem he appears to have mentioned Clio's love affair with a
mortal (fr. 768A), which produced Hymenaeus, whom
Licymnius made the beloved of Argynnus or Dionysus (fr.
768); another poem (fr. 771) told of Hypnos' love for
Endymion. The dithyrambic poet Telestes of Selinus
shows some small Oriental interest in the context of musical
invention (frr. 806, 810), while Philoxenus of Cythera wrote
a *Mysians* (fr. 826: μύθουc codd., Μυcοὺc Schneider; cf. [Plu.]

Mus. 33. 1142 F). A *Syrus* is also mentioned for Philoxenus (fr. 827 = Hsch. μεcαύχενεc: . . . ἐν τῶι Φιλοχένου Cύρωι: Bergk conjectured C⟨ατ⟩ύρωι, Berglein less convincingly Cιcύφωι or Cκίρωι).

The Structure of the Poem

Pollux (4. 66) divides the citharodic nome into seven sections: μέρη δὲ τοῦ κιθαρωιδικοῦ νόμου Τερπάνδρου κατανεί-μαντοc ἑπτά· ἀρχά, μεταρχά, κατατροπά, μετακατατροπά, ὀμφαλόc, cφραγίc, ἐπίλογοc. It is unlikely that that these divisions in fact represent an original Terpandrian arrangement of the parts of the nome, and there is no reason to believe that they formed even in the fifth century a rigid schema according to which a poem had to be written. Three of the terms are peculiar to Pollux (μεταρχά, κατατροπά, and μετακατατροπά occur only in this passage) and the others rarely have a literary meaning. We might equate the ἀρχά with the *prooimion*, although fragments are never cited as coming from the ἀρχά of a nome. Similarly, the word ἐπίλογοc, which can refer to the peroration of a speech or to the ἔκθεcιc of a play, does not seem in the same way to be a formal part of a poem. Aelius Dionysius (fr. 38 p. 102 Schwabe) cites the phrase ἀλλὰ ἄλλ' ἄναξ as ἀρχὴ ἐξωδίου (*sic*) κιθαρωιδικοῦ (cf. Hsch. α 3113: ἀλλ' ἄναξ· ἐξόδιον κιθαρωιδῶν τοῦτο), but ἐξόδιον may not there be a technical term. The exact meaning of some of Pollux' words is also unclear; we can give a reasonable sense to ἀρχά and, on the basis of the *Persae*, perhaps to cφραγίc and ἐπίλογοc, but there is no indication of the sense to be given to the other words. ὀμφαλόc should probably describe the central section of the poem; μεταρχά, κατατροπά, and μετακατατροπά look suspiciously like words invented by Pollux or another late writer in order that there should be seven parts to correspond to the seven strings of the traditional lyre. H. Koller, *Philol.* 100 (1956), 186 posits an original division of the nome into three (or four) parts: ἀρχά–ὀμφαλόc (+ cφραγίc)–ἐπίλογοc; see also B. A. van Groningen, *Mnem.*⁴ 8 (1955), 177–91. But there is still no reason to believe that these were formal terms for the parts of the nome in the fifth or fourth century.

We may contrast the division of the auletic Πυθικὸς νόμος into five formal parts, each of which had a musical and narrative significance. The final section of the *Persae* has often been divided into sphragis and epilogue, and other fragments in the corpus could belong to similar sections of poems; however, the latter are never so distinguished by the authors who quote them, and I doubt whether they were known by these names to Timotheus himself.

The extant portion of the poem follows a fairly regular structure, being divided into a series of episodes, each of which contains a narrative introduction and a speech. We must assume that the papyrus text begins *mediis rebus*.

Analysis

A. 1–201   The Victory
            1–39   General Description of the Sea-Battle
    40–85   Episode 1: The Islander
            40–71   Introduction
            72–81   Speech
            82–5   Conclusion
    86–138 Episode 2: The Persian Flight
            86–97   Introduction
            98–138   Lamentation
                     98–104   General Description
                     105–27   Speech (i): Apostrophe to Mysia
                     127–38   Speech (ii): Prayer to Cybele
    139–61 Episode 3: The Celaenaean
            139–49   Introduction
            150–61   Speech
    162–95 Episode 4: The Persian Flight and the King's Lament
            162–71   The General Flight
            171–95   The King's Lament
                     171–7   Introduction
                     178–95   The King's Speech
    196–201 The Greek Paean
B. 202–36 The Poet's Apologia
            202–5   Invocation to Apollo
            206–12   The Spartan Critics
            213–20   Response to the Spartan Critics
            221–36   The Catalogue of εὑρήματα
C. 237–40 Final Prayer to Apollo

The first episode appears to include two speeches (cf. κάλει at 50 and the extant speech at 72–81), though it is unclear how much of the lacunose passage 50–9 belongs to direct speech. The narrative sections vary in length, and are typically introduced with a temporal conjunction of some sort (thus ἔνθα at 40, ὅτε at 60, ἐπεί at 140 and 162); the amount of space devoted to each speech also varies. There is no obvious ordering of the episodes. Clearly the climax of the King's speech and his imminent flight should come last; however, one sees little artistic reason why, for example, the extended apostrophe to Mysia and the prayer to Cybele should not have preceded the drowning Islander at 40–85. The last three episodes lack a conclusion, while the first episode has a concluding passage at 82–5 after the speech; 139 could be regarded as a transitional passage between the second and third episodes, but the paragraphos after 138 suggests that 139 in fact belongs to the following section (see further ad loc.). This may be intended to suggest the increasing hopelessness of the Persian position. However, each episode repeats motifs found in earlier parts of the narrative (e.g. supplication, lamentation, the wind's hostility, etc.), which sometimes gives the impression that the sequence of events is deliberate.

There are usually clear indications of speech-openings (50 κάλει, 68 ἀπείλει, 104 ἐπανεκαλέοντ', 146 ἑλίccετ', 177 φάτο); these occur less frequently at speech-end (only φάτ' at 82 and τοιάδ' ὀδυρόμεναι at 139). A useful contrast may be made with earlier poetry. Stesichorus marks speech-end in the 'Theban fragment' (fr. 222b. 232) by ὣc φάτ[ο] after speech-end has coincided with strophe-end; a similar device is used at l. 291, and at S 88 fr. 1 col. ii. 15, S 148 fr. 1 col. i. 6 (probably). In Pindar's epinicians the practice is irregular; speech-end may be marked by a transitional gnome or generalization (e.g. O. 6. 16–18), or by closing formulae (e.g. ὣc ἔννεπεν, ὣc φάτο etc.); occasionally speech-end is marked only by strophe-end (O. 6. 62–4) or by the end of the poem (O. 4. 23), where a closing formula might be otiose (contrast, however, O. 13. 69–70). Bacchylides more frequently avoids closing formulae; I find only two examples in his epinicians where speech-end is thus marked (Ba. 3. 48

τόc' εἶπε; 5. 84 ὡc φάτο), against five instances where we find
only transitional passages (5. 93, 155, 170; 11. 106; 13. 58).
In the dithyrambs closing formulae are better attested: 17.
47 τόc' εἶπεν, 81 ὡc εἶπε; 24. 13 ταῦτ' εἶπε. At 17. 66 speech-
end coincides with strophe-end, and is followed by κλύε
(Ζεύc) at 67; at 15. 63 speech-end coincides with poem-end.
See in general Führer 46–65.

Whether this arrangement, episodes with narrative and
speeches, extended in any way to the earlier section of the
poem is unclear; frr. 789 and 790 both appear to belong to
orations. Each of the speakers in the extant section is an
Asiatic, but both the quotation fragments were probably
spoken by Greeks (perhaps both by Themistocles); the
emphasis on the Persians in the extant portion may have
been matched by a similar emphasis on the Greeks in the
first half. All the 'voices' are those of individuals, with the
exception of the generalized lamentation at 105 ff. This
variety would have been an important way for Timotheus
to exhibit his talent for musical and vocal mimesis (cf. the
use of direct speech at frr. 781, 787, 802). None of these
individuals is named: contrast the parodos of Aeschylus'
Persae with its long list of barbaric, and barbarizing, names,
and its detailed catalogue of the dead (*Pers.* 302–30).

Fragments

Fr. 788

As Plutarch implies (ἐνάρχομαι can hardly mean anything
other than 'begin'; see also A. Aloni, *Cantare glorie di eroi*
(Turin, 1998), 117–38), this was probably the opening line
of the *prooimion*. Hansen 1990 implausibly argues that the
prologue was actually *PMG* adesp. 1018 (the so-called
'Hymn to the Fates'); but the parallels between the epilogue
of the *Persae* and the Hymn to the Fates are probably due
rather to poetic conventions than to any closer connection
between the two pieces. The metre of the Hymn is dactylo-
epitrite (Korzeniewski's analysis as a mixture of aeolic and
iambic metra is unconvincing), and thus markedly different
from the iambo-trochaics that predominate in the main
body of the *Persae*, or the aeolic cola of the final invocations.

The *prooimion* might be expected to have been an invocation of some sort, although this does not seem to be reflected by the opening line. However, we do not know what followed it and it is possible that the following lines contained a hymnal element.

Metre

$$- \cup\cup - \cup\cup - - - \cup\cup - \cup\cup - - \parallel$$

A simple dactylic hexameter begins the poem. The metre was traditional in citharodic *prooimia* (cf. West, 'Stesichorus', 307–8, possibly adding Amphion's citharodic song at E. *Antiope* fr. 1023 N², of which one hexameter is cited); here it also accords with the heroic diction and the old-fashioned sentiment. Timotheus' intention may have been to create a contrast between his conventional opening and what followed; but he may also have wished to recall Choerilus' hexametrical *Persica*, the precise date of which is, however, unfortunately unknown. We shall see Timotheus elsewhere recalling other poetic genres (notably comedy and tragedy) with various effect; but possibly the reminiscence is of epic in general.

ἐλευθερίας: the defence of Greek freedom is a typical theme of poetry on the Persian Wars; cf. Pi. fr. 77 (dithyramb on Artemisium) ὅθι παῖδες Ἀθαναίων ἐβάλοντο φαεννάν | κρηπῖδ' ἐλευθερίας, Simon. fr. eleg. 11. 23–38, Antiph. Byz. *AP* 9. 294 (on Thermopylae). For the highly emotional associations of ἐλευθερία in democratic Athens, cf. esp. A. *Pers.* 402–5.

τεύχων: the application of the line to Philopoemen need not mean that an individual was the subject in the poem; I should prefer δῆμος (δᾶμος) Ἀθαναίων *vel sim.* as the subject of the verb to any of the earlier suggestions (ἀγών, Ἄρης, or Λύσανδρος Reinach; Ζεύς or Ἀπόλλων Croiset; Θεμιστοκλῆς Sitzler). With the exception of the King, there are no individual characters in the extant part of the work's body. Athens had been described as the Ἑλλάδος ἔρεισμα in Pindar's dithyramb for Athens (fr. 76); the idea that the Athenian victories in the Persian Wars were due to the whole city, rather than particular generals, was emphasized by Demosthenes in his speech against Aristocrates (23. 198).

If an individual is preferred, we may compare the praise of Pausanias in Simonides' elegy on Plataea (fr. eleg. 11. 34). **μέγαν . . . κόϲμον:** possibly a deliberate reminiscence of Simon. fr. 531. 8–9 ἀρετᾶϲ μέγαν λελοιπὼϲ | κόϲμον ἀέναόν τε κλέοϲ (of Leonidas), from Simonides' poem on Thermopylae, and another example of Timotheus' interest in his lyric past. If the subject was δῆμοϲ Ἀθαναίων, Timotheus may be deliberately creating a contrast between the emphasis on individual leaders in the 'Spartan' battles (Plataea, Thermopylae) and the 'popular' accomplishment at Salamis.

Ἑλλάδι: the poem appears generally to have been Panhellenic in sentiment rather than being restricted to purely Athenian patriotism. Such Panhellenism was generally associated with Salamis in the fifth-century Athenian tradition (see W. C. West III, *GRBS* 11 (1970), 271–82); it is not a part of the tradition about Marathon until the fourth century. A Panhellenic poem may have been felt to have greater appeal throughout the Greek world; one devoted solely or explicitly to Athenian heroism would perhaps incur disfavour from other Greek states, where, no doubt, Timotheus hoped to perform it.

Fr. 789
The exhortation may have been either Themistocles' speech before the battle (Hdt. 8. 83) or perhaps the divine shout heard at Salamis (A. *Pers.* 402 ff.; Hdt. 8. 84).

Metre

ꞏ – – – ꞏ – ᴗᴗ ᴗ – ᴗᴗ ᴗ – |

δοριμάχου: 'fighting with spears'. The use of spears is mentioned at A. *Pers.* 239–40 as a distinguishing feature of Greek warfare, especially in contrast to the Persian use of the bow; see also J. F. Lazenby, in V. D. Hanson (ed.), *Hoplites: The Classical Greek Battle Experience* (London, 1991), 87–109. Such a contrast is probably not intended here; the spear may simply have been considered characteristic of Greek modes of fighting. However, Darius praises his own skill with the spear at DNb 4–5 (p. 139 Kent) 'as a spearman I am a good spearman both afoot and on horseback'; Persian power is characterized as a spear at DNa 43–7 (p. 137 Kent) 'the spear of a Persian man has gone forth far . . . a Persian man has delivered battle far indeed from Persia'. J. M. Cook, *The Persian Empire* (London, 1983), 101–2, points out that the order in which Darius cites his achievements may be significant, and notes that he depicted himself as an archer on his royal coins; but also that that the reliefs at Susa and Persepolis show Persian soldiers armed with both bow and spear (cf. Hdt. 7. 61, who says that they were equipped with bow, spear, and dagger).

The compound is probably a Timothean innovation on existing tragic models. It only occurs otherwise at Orac. ap. Σ *Il.* 2. 543 ἄνδρες δουρίμαχοι ναίουσιν ὕδωρ καλῆς Ἀρεθούςης, and as a proper name at *SEG* 34. 281e (Corinth, 4th c. BC), but cf. the formations δορίμαργος (A. *Sept.* 687), δοριμανής (E. *Suppl.* 485), etc.

Fr. 790
Possibly from Themistocles' oration before the battle. The use of the perfect δέδοικε indicates that the line should probably belong to direct speech.

Metre

$$\cup - \cup - - - \cup - \cup - \cup - \cup$$

An iambic trimeter followed by an additional short syllable. The codices read χρυcὸν δ᾿ Ἑλλὰc, but δ(έ) disturbs the iambic metre. If we adopt Bergk's Ἑλλὰc δ(έ) then the third metron can still be scanned as *ia* with long anceps, but postponement of δέ is unusual in Timotheus, and there would be little justification for it here. It is therefore preferable to delete δέ with Farnell (*GLP*); the asyndeton is unobjectionable.

Ἄρης τύραννος: 'war is (our) lord', rather than 'Ares is a tyrant'; the speaker's point is simply that the Greeks will fight at all costs. Linguistically analogous expressions, such as Heracl. DK 31 B 53 Πόλεμος πάντων μὲν πατήρ ἐστι, πάντων δὲ βασιλεύς, καὶ τοὺς μὲν θεοὺς ἔδειξε τοὺς δὲ ἀνθρώπους, τοὺς μὲν δούλους ἐποίησε τοὺς δὲ ἐλευθέρους, Pi. fr. 169a. 1 Νόμος ὁ πάντων βασιλεύς, are therefore really quite different. There may be a faint reminiscence of A. *Suppl.* 934 ff. οὔτοι δικάζει

ταῦτα μαρτύρων ὕπο | Ἄρης, τὸ νεῖκος δ᾽ οὐκ ἐν ἀργύρου λαβῆι |
ἔλυcεν, ἀλλὰ πολλὰ γίγνεται πάρος | πεcήματ᾽ ἀνδρῶν κἀπολα-
κτιcμοὶ βίου, though there is no close similarity of situation.
The phrase later became proverbial.

τύραννος: the word is frequently used of gods, often with
a particular point; so of Zeus at [A.] *Pr.* 736, where there are
clearly political connotations. Elsewhere it may imply the
capriciousness of the god (so of Eros at E. *Hipp.* 528, fr. 136
N²; of Ares at *H. Hom.* 8. 5 ἀντιβίοιcι τύραννε). Apollo is
described by the chorus as τύραννε τᾶc ἐμᾶc φρενός at S. *Tr.*
217. In fifth-century Athens the word's connotations were
frequently, but not always, unfavourable (Ed. Fraenkel on
A. *Ag.* 828; Bond on E. *Herc.* 29); here the word seems
neutral.

χρυcόν: Bassett sees here a direct reference to the Persian
funding of Sparta during the later stages of the Peloponnesian War; more importantly, cf. Demosthenes' insistence
on the Greek immunity to bribery during the Persian Wars
(*Phil.* 3. 36–40); Ennius' Pyrrhus responds similarly to
offers of ransom for his prisoners: *nec mi aurum posco nec
mi pretium dederitis:* | *non cauponantes bellum sed bellige-
rantes* | *ferro non auro uitam cernamus utrique* (Enn. *Ann.* 6.
183–5 Skutsch).

Persian wealth was proverbial, and is a common theme in
Greek portrayals of Orientals from an early period; cf.
Archil. fr. 19. 1; A. *Pers.* 3, 9, 163–4, 250 ff., 709, 754,
826; Hdt. 5. 101. 2; E. *IA* 786–7, etc.

Fr. 790A

Dionysius quotes this line as an example of the cretic
metron. It does not seem out of place in the iambo-trochaics
of the *Persae*, and though the line does not seem to belong
with any of the fragments in column i, the ascription (first
suggested by Usener) can plausibly stand. The periphrasis
ἀπήναιcι χαλκεμβόλοιc for ships is typical of Timotheus, and
the line would fit easily into the context of the sea-battle.

Metre

  – ᴜ – – ᴜ – – ᴜ – – ᴜ – |

ἀπήναιcι: 'wagons'; for the frequent comparison of ships to carts or chariots in antiquity, see *P.* 17 n. and cf. especially E. *Med.* 1122–3 ναΐαν ἀπήνην.

χαλκεμβόλοιc: 'bronze-beaked'. A reference to the rams of the ship, which were usually made of bronze (but see *P.* 20 n.); cf. especially E. *IA* 1319 ναῶν χαλκεμβολάδων 'bronze-beaked ships' where the adjective is formed in the rarer termination -άc, -άδοc (only here). χαλκόπρωιροc is used of ships with the same effect at Pollux 2. 102.

Fr. 791

Col. i

The column is extremely fragmentary, and its contents largely obscure; none of the quotation fragments appears to correspond to anything in this part of the narrative. It is probable that battle has already been joined; there are references to the movement of ships, and possibly also to flight on the part of one fleet. For the relationship between fragments 1 and 4, see above, pp. 70–1.

1. 2. After ρ there are traces of a downstroke, consistent with the left stroke of ε, ι, κ, μ, ν, etc.

1. 3. ν[.]μφα̣[: i.e. ν[υ]μφα-; of the sea (cf. *P.* 39 Ἀμφιτρίτ]αc)?; or perhaps a compound (as at 110).

1. 4. ε̣π̣[.]υκυκλ[: i.e. ἐπ᾽ [ε]ὐκυκλ-. The adjective perhaps describes the hulls of the ships, 'rounded', with the sense the word always has in the *Iliad* (where its use is restricted to describe shields). Here, however, the meaning may coalesce with that found in the *Odyssey*, where it is always used of 'well-wheeled' carts (cf. [A.] *Pr.* 710, E. *Ion* 1391): for ships as carts, see *P.* 17 n. Both senses are found in later literature; 'circling', the meaning at Ar. *Thesm.* 968 (of dancing), appears to be an innovation (perhaps by analogy with the phrase κύκλιοc χορόc).

The case after ἐπί is uncertain here: the genitive (upon), accusative (onto), and dative (against) are equally possible.

1. 5. επ[ε]υθυ: i.e. ἐπ᾽ [ε]ὐθύ. In the papyrus the fifth letter looks like ο, but was almost certainly θ, the crossbar having been worn away over time.

4. 3.]ν̣α̣ι̣α̣ν̣.[: only a vertical stroke of the final letter is legible, possibly π, but we might just as well have ι, μ, γ, etc.

4. 4.].οcαλλα[: of the first letter only the bottom of a vertical stroke survives; perhaps -ιοc ἄλλα (ἀλλά?), or -ροc.

4. 11.]παλιμμ[: 'back-'; perhaps an indication that the Persian flight is already in progress (cf. also 86 πάλιν, 162 παλίμπορον, 173 παλιμπόρευτον).

4. 12.]μουcα[: Reinach suggests the word belongs to an invocation; we could, however, divide -]μουc ἀ[- (or ἀ[-).

2. 1.]η[: only a few traces of the right half of the letter survive; perhaps π, though η is better.

3. 3.]οιχ[: Wilamowitz could read]cτοιχο[, so perhaps 'line (of battle)'; cτοῖχοc is used of ships at A. *Pers.* 366 ἐν cτοίχοιc τρισί. Diggle suggests πρὸ]c or εἰ]c τοίχ]ουc, of the sides of a ship: see *P.* 11 n.

6. 2.]αραξει[: perhaps τ]αράξει; for the future (in speech), cf. *P.* 75 (with n.); in Greek narrative it is unimaginable.

8. 6.]λ᾽ ί νοιο: 'of flax', possibly a reference to sail-cloth (so Campbell), or to ropes (cf. 15, 74). We cannot tell whether this and]γυια at l. 8 were simple or compounded forms.

8. 8.]γυια 'limbs'; used of a ship's oars at *P.* 14 (see n.), but also literally at 23.

Underneath the α Wilamowitz saw a large dot, which he thought was simply a blot; this is no longer visible.

Coll. ii–vi

1–39. General Description of the Sea-Battle.
Wilamowitz detected similarities between the narrative at this point and Diodorus Siculus' account of the battle of Cynossema in 410 BC (D.S. 13. 45–6), and Ephorus' version of the battle of Salamis known from the summary at D.S. 11. 18 (quoted below, 5–6 n.). Diodorus' account of Cynossema begins with the start of the battle, a section of the narrative no longer extant in *Persae*:

1. D.S. 13. 45. Trireme attacks: ὁπότε γὰρ αἱ τριήρεις εἰς ἐμβολὴν ἐπιφέροιντο, τηνικαῦτα οἱ κυβερνῆται πρὸς αὐτὴν τὴν τοῦ καιροῦ ῥοπὴν ἐπέcτρεφον τὰc ναῦc πραγματικῶc ὥcτε τὰc πληγὰc γίνεcθαι κατ᾽ ἐμβολήν. οἱ μὲν οὖν ἐπιβάται θεωροῦντεc πλαγίαc τὰc ἑαυτῶν ναῦc cυνεπιφερομέναc ταῖc τῶν πολεμίων τριήρεcι, περιδεεῖc ἐγίνοντο, περὶ cφῶν ἀγωνιῶντεc· ὁπότε δ᾽ οἱ κυβερνῆται ταῖc ἐμπειρίαιc ἐκκρούcειαν τὰc ἐπιφοράc, πάλιν ἐγίνοντο περιχαρεῖc καὶ μετέωροι ταῖc ἐλπίcιν; cf. *P.*

7–13, noting especially the parallel phraseology: D.S. ὁπότε . . .
ὁπότε, P. 7 εἰ μὲν . . . 11 εἰ δὲ . . .

2. D.S. 13. 46. Missile attacks: οὐ μὴν οὐδ' οἱ τοῖc καταcτρώμαcιν
ἐπιβεβηκότεc ἄπρακτον εἶχον τὴν φιλοτιμίαν, ἀλλ' οἱ μὲν ἐκ πολλοῦ
διαcτήματοc ἐφεcτηκότεc ἐτόξευον κατὰ τὸ cυνεχὲc καὶ ταχὺ ὁ τόποc ἦν
βελῶν πλήρηc; cf. P. 21–8.

3. D.S. 13. 46. Hand-to-hand combat: οἱ δ' ἀεὶ προcιόντεc
ἐγγυτέρω τὰc λόγχαc ἠκόντιζον, οἱ μὲν ἐπὶ τοὺc ἀμυνομένουc ἐπιβάταc,
οἱ δ' ἐπ' αὐτοὺc βαλεῖν φιλοτιμούμενοι τοὺc κυβερνήταc . . .; no parallel
in Timotheus.

4. D.S. 13. 46. General summary of events: κατὰ δὲ τὰc γινομέναc
ἐλαττώcειc τῶν νικώντων ἐπαλαλαζόντων καὶ τῶν ἄλλων μετὰ βοῆc
παραβοηθούντων, κραυγὴ cύμμικτοc ἐγίνετο παρ' ὅλον τὸν τῆc ναυμαχίαc
τόπον. Cf. P. 31–4, especially comparing P. 34 with the last
sentence in Diodorus; for this phraseology, cf. also the description
of the storm at Ach. Tat. 3. 2. 8 cυμμιγὴc δὲ πάντων ἐγίνετο βοῆc . . .
πάντα θρήνων καὶ κωκυτῶν ἀνάμεcτα.

There is no reason to believe that Diodorus is directly
paraphrasing Timotheus' poem. Rather, as Wilamowitz
pointed out, both authors are depicting a typical sea-battle
and are not directly interested in the historical reality. This
view is supported by the presence of methods of warfare in
Timotheus' narrative which were first introduced in the late
fifth century (e.g. the use of flaming darts), and which would
therefore have been known to Timotheus from the sea-
battles of his own time, but would probably not have been
actual features of the battle at Salamis (see 5–6, 16, 26 nn.).

Metre

```
        _ ∪ _ _ ∪ _ _ |
 5     ] ∪ _ _ ∫
        _ ∪ ∪ _ ∪ ∪ ∪ _ ||
       † _ _ ∪ _ _ [ ] _ ∫
        ∪ ∪ ∪ _ ∪ _ _ ||
        _ [ ] _ _ ∪ ∪ ∪
10      _ ∪ ∪ _ ∪ _ _ ||
        _ _ ∪ _ ∪ _ [ |
       ] ∪ _ _ _ ∪ ∪ _ |
       ] ∪ _ _ _ ∪ ∪ ∪ _ _ ||
        _ × [ ] _ _ _ ∪ ∪ ∪ _ _ |
15      _ _ ∪ _ _ _ ∪ _ ∫
        _ _ × [ ] _ |
```

```
          – – ∪ – – – ∪ ∪∪
            – – ∪ – ∪ – [
       ] – ∪ – ∪ –
20          ∪ – ∪ – – ∪ – ||
       ∪ – ∪ ∪∪ × [ |
       ] – ∪ – ∪ – ∪ – ∪∪ |
       – ∪ – ∪ – ∪ – – |
       – × [  ] – – ∪ ∪∪ ∪ – – |
25     ∪ – ∪ – ∪ ∪∪ ∪ ∪∪ ∫
          × [  ] × ∪ ∪ ∪ ∪ ∫
          ∪∪ ∪ ∪∪ ∪ ∪∪ ∪ ∪∪ ∪ |
       – × [  ] ∪∪ ∪ |
       ∪∪ ∪ ∪∪ ∪ ∪∪ ∪ – ∪
30        – ∪ – ∪ – ∪ – × [ ||
       ∪ – ∪ – – ∪ – ∫
          ∪ ∪∪ ∪ – ∪ – ∪ –
          – ∪ – ∪ – ∪ – |
       – – ∪ – ∪ – ∪ – ∪ – – ||
35     ∪ – ∪ – ∪ – ∪ – |
       – ∪ ∪ – × [ |
       – ∪∪∪∪ ∪ – ∪ –
          ∪∪ ∪ – ∪ – ∪ – |
       – – ∪ – ∪ – – ||
```

Much is uncertain. The metre is throughout the mixture of iambo-trochaics typical of the narrative section of the poem, with frequent syncopated forms and some choriambic elements (4, 6, 36). Line 4 begins *cr tr*, and we may find occasional trochaic elements in predominantly iambic contents again at 9 (*2tr?*), 13 (πλω]cίμουc?); a more extended sequence of trochaic dimeters can probably be identified in the highly syncopated passage 27–9, ending with a dimeter and period-end at l. 30. The high level of resolution probably indicates a climax in the passage. Line 10 can be analysed as either *ch ba* or a simple aristophanean; the rhythm is common elsewhere at period-end (e.g. 185, 201). At l. 20 cιδα[ρ]⟨ϵ⟩ωι is written by Page; cιδα[ρϵ́]ωι by Wilamowitz; there is only space for one letter in the lacuna. The metre is as likely to be *ia cr* as *2ia*; I can see nothing against the contracted form.

4–39. '. . . they swept away the firwood arms with the bulging heads; and if a [. . .] [. . .]-smashing blow was inflicted on one side, all the sailors fell backwards together in that direction, but if a [. . .] on the opposite side shattered the many-banked sea-going pines, they were carried back again. And when some (ships), ripping apart the [. . .] limbs revealed the flax-bound sides, then they would capsize some by throwing (leaden?) thunderbolts onto them, and others sank . . . into the sea, stripped of their ornament by the iron helmet. Like fire the [. . .] thong-bound [. . .] was hurled from their hands and fell among their limbs, shaking their bodies . . . and covers (?) burning with fire on ox-[. . .] splints of wood; and their thronging life was slaughtered beneath the long-winged bronze-headed string-[. . . arrows]. And the emerald-haired sea was reddened in its furrows by the drops from the ships, and shouting mingled with shrieking prevailed. And together the barbarian naval army was borne back upon the fish-wreathed bosom of Amphitrite with its shining folds.'

1–13. The general sense of the passage is a description of the destruction of the enemy ships, and more particularly of their oars. This first section of the papyrus is seriously damaged, and it is only at l. 4 that the text begins to be relatively readable; nor is it quite clear what is supposed to be happening in the damaged lines. We might expect a description of the approach of the Persian (so Janssen) or Greek ships, in order to introduce the naval attack which seems to begin at l. 4 (note e.g. the verb ἐχάρα[ξ]αν).

1.]υν [ἐμ]βόλ[οιc]ι γειτ[...]c[.: 'with neighbouring rams'. Wilamowitz prints -βόλοιcι, Page -βολό[ι]cι; the second omicron and sigma are not now visible, nor can I read them in the original photographs of the papyrus. Janssen objects that ramming is first mentioned at 7 (although we find a reference to rams at 4), and reads cυνεμβολαῖcι. ξυνεμβολή is a hapax at A. *Pers.* 396 κώπης ῥοθιάδος ξυνεμ-βολῆι, where it refers to 'the action of pulling together' (Broadhead); and is conjectured by Headlam at A. *Ag.* 984 ff. †χρόνος δ' ἐπεὶ πρυμνηcίων ξυνεμβόλοις | ψαμμίας ἀκάτα† παρήβηcεν εὖθ' ὑπ' Ἴλιον | ὦρτο ναυβάτας cτρατός, where, however, Casaubon's ξὺν ἐμβολαῖς looks better.

Diggle suggests γειτ[νιῶ]c[ι; the verb is rare in poetry (Ar. *Eccl.* 327 ὁ γειτνιῶν is probably colloquial), but the suggestion provides slightly better sense than Wilamowitz's γεί-τ[ονε]c (sc. νᾶες). The 'neighbouring rams' are, of course, those on the neighbouring ships. 'Neighbour' can be used in hostile contexts in Greek; at A. *Pers.* 66 the Persian chorus describes Greece as γείτονα χώραν; Creusa at E. *Ion* 294 calls Euboea γείτων πόλιc when mentioning its war with Athens. The preceding word may be c]ύν, though the dative normally expresses instrumental or agentive meanings without a preposition; we find a different use at *P.* 238.

2-3. The scholion in the margin at this point is difficult to read, and of uncertain significance; the few surviving words that can be read clearly seem to have no bearing on the text.

2. ἐχάρα[ξ]ᾳν: 'they furrowed', probably the waves; cf. e.g. Antip. Sid. *HE* 438-9 (*AP* 10. 2. 12) Ἀκμαῖοc ῥοθίηι νηΐ δρόμοc οὐδὲ θάλαccα | πορφύρει τρομερῆι φρικὶ χαραccομένη, Nonn. *D.* 3. 46; for the imagery see also 32 n. ἄλοκα.

π..ι δὲ γε[...]λογχο[: clearly δε should be the particle rather than anything else; π.ι should therefore start the sentence. Wilamowitz suggests ποcὶ δέ (i.e. 'oars' as at *P.* 91), Danielsson ποτὶ δέ (= πρὸc δέ); it is unclear whether Timotheus would use that form of the preposition.]λογχο[should be related to λόγχη 'spear'. The words are usually connected with the phrase in l. 3 ἀμφέθ[ε]ντ' ὀδόντων cτον[α]χᾶι; ἀμφέθ[ε]ντο could mean 'put round oneself', but it is odd that it should be used in this sense of the ships. Wilamowitz suggests γε[ιcό]λογχο[ν] ὀδόντων, understanding thereby a reference to the ship's ἐπωτίδεc, which stood out from the hull shortly abaft of the ram and were designed to protect the ship from being struck (Casson 84-5). Reinach thinks of an offensive parapet with protective crenellations, probably white (and therefore to be called 'teeth'); Fraccaroli thinks the ὀδόντεc are the thole-pins. Danielsson suggests πε[ντέ]-λογχο[ν 'five-pointed', comparing δίλογχοc 'double-pointed' of ἄτη at A. *Ag.* 643. Sitzler accepts ποcὶ δέ, and proposes γε[ῖca] λογχο[ειδέων]; Edmonds translates this as 'they were shod with cornices of spearhead-like teeth', which he thinks a reference to the rams. None of this convinces; the sense of ὀδόντων may be other than 'teeth', but its metaphorical uses are generally comparable to those of ModE. (e.g. the 'teeth of a saw').

3. If we supplement cτον[α]χᾶι, the word could belong with this sentence rather than with the one that begins at 4;

but 'wailing' seems an inappropriate sort of noise for the
start of an assault, and the dative an inappropriate construction, hence perhaps ϲτον[α]χᾶι· ⟨αἱ⟩, though the connection with ὀδόντων is uncertain. Reinach suggests that
ϲτον[υ]χαί might be an equivalent to ϲτόνυχεϲ; although the
sense is attractive, it would be better to read e.g. ϲτόν[υ]χ-
⟨εϲ⟩· αἱ κτλ., where ὀδόντων depends on ϲτόνυχεϲ 'the points
of teeth'.

4. αἱ: sc. νᾶεϲ.

κυρτοῖ[ϲι] κραϲίν[: 'with bulging heads'; probably of the
rams. On κυρτόϲ see J. Diggle, *Eikasmos*, 9 (1998), 45–52. In
two of its three Homeric appearances (*Il.* 4. 426, 13. 799) it
denotes the 'curving crest' (Diggle) of a wave, cf. Moschus
fr. 1. 5, and similarly κῦμα . . . κυρτωθέν *Od.* 11. 243–4 (V.
Georg. 4. 361 *curuata unda*). The third Homeric instance (*Il.*
2. 218) refers to Thersites' humped shoulders; cf. *AP* 11.
120, and perhaps Hipponax fr. 117. 3, where it may mean
'hunchbacked': although the context is unclear, in the
preceding line we have ἡ χλαῖν[α]. [Arion], *PMG* adesp.
939. 15 uses it of the humped backs of dophins on which
Arion travels to land, where again the crested shape of a
wave may be suggested. The adjective is not found in
tragedy (though Soph. fr. 314. 201 Radt has ἐπίκυρτος)
except at E. *Ba.* 1066–7 (of the branch drawn down by
Dionysus) κυκλοῦτο δ' ὥϲτε τόξον ἢ κυρτὸϲ τροχόϲ | τόρνωι
γραφόμενοϲ περιφορὰν ἑλικοδρόμον (Reiske: ἑλκέδρομον codd.).
Having established that κυρτόϲ refers to a curve or an arc,
Diggle continues: 'And that is precisely why E. has used it
here. When the branch is pulled downwards, it begins to
curve, like Pandarus' bow, and like the outline of a wheel.
The complete circle of a wheel could not be called κυρτόϲ.'

5–6. [χε]ῖραϲ . . . ἐλα[τίνα]ϲ: 'fir-wood arms', i.e. oars; cf.
14 γυῖα, 90–1 ὀρείουϲ πόδαϲ ναόϲ, E. *Hel.* 1461 εἰλατίναϲ
πλάταϲ. Because of their buoyancy, fir- and pine-wood
were standard materials for ship-building in antiquity; cf.
Theophr. *HP* 5. 7: ἐλάτη μὲν οὖν καὶ πεύκη . . . ναυπηγήϲιμα.
τὰϲ μὲν γὰρ τριήρειϲ καὶ τὰ μακρὰ πλοῖα ἐλάτινα ποιοῦϲι διὰ
κουφότητα, τὰ δὲ ϲτρογγύλα πεύκινα διὰ τὸ ἀϲαπέϲ· ἔνιοι δὲ καὶ
τὰϲ τριήρειϲ διὰ τὸ μὴ εὐπορεῖν ἐλάτηϲ. The form ἐλάτινοϲ is not
attested earlier than Euripides (*Cyc.* 386, *Ba.* 1070, 1098),

but may well be old; epic εἰλ- appears to have been
lengthened for metrical reasons.
For χείρ in the sense 'arm', cf. Hes. *Th.* 150, *Il.* 11. 252, 5.
336, 21. 166–7, etc.; the first syllable of the genitive may be
either short or long in Timotheus (*P.* 90 χειρῶν, 165 χερῶν);
the only instance of the dative singular is *P.* 110 χερί, and the
plural is always χερσίν (23, 44); the accusative is χεῖρας at 126.

παρέϲυρον: 'swept away', in order to disable the ships,
and thus leave them open to being rammed. Janssen prefers
the aorist παρέϲυραν after the aorists ἐχάρα[ξ]αν, ἀμφέθ[ε]ντο,
but a new sentence begins at l. 4, and the imperfect is on the
whole standard for the narrative sections of the poem (see
above, pp. 51–2). παραϲύρω is common in later Greek in
descriptions of the destruction of an enemy ship's oars (e.g.
Plb. 16. 14. 4, D.S. 13. 6); the word may here have technical
overtones.
    Janssen sees a reference to the διέκπλους, a tactical
manoeuvre which involved sailing through the line of
enemy ships and destroying their oars, and which may
have been in use at the time of the Persian Wars (Morrison–Williams 137–8; J. F. Lazenby, *GRBS* 34 (1987), 169–
77). There are no references to the manoeuvre in Thucydides or Xenophon, but Diodorus describes the tactic being
used at Salamis: οἱ δὲ Ἀθηναῖοι θεωροῦντες τὴν ταραχὴν τῶν
βαρβάρων ἐπέπλεον τοῖς πολεμίοις, καὶ τὰς μὲν τοῖς ἐμβόλοις
ἔτυπτον, ὧν δὲ τοὺς ταρϲοὺς παρέϲυρον . . . διὸ καὶ πρύμναν μὲν
ἀνακρούεϲθαι κατέπαυϲαν, εἰς τοὐπίϲω δὲ πλέουϲαι προτροπάδην
ἔφευγον (D.S. 11. 18).
    7. †αδλ: Probably ἀλλ', 'furthermore', with a rare almost
purely connective rather than adversative force (*pace*
Danielsson); see Denniston 21. GOH wonders whether
ἀλλ', if correctly restored, may be an interpolation caused
by asyndeton.
    [ἐ]νθένδ[(ε): 'on one side', contrasted with 11 ἀντίτοιχος.
We do not know whether the epsilon was elided in the
papyrus or not.
    [. . . . . .]ιϲτος: Page suggests *ex. grat.* [ἀπρόϲο]ιϲτος
'irresistible', as at A. *Pers.* 90–1 ἄμαχον κῦμα θαλάϲϲης· |
ἀπρόϲοιϲτος γὰρ ὁ Περϲᾶν ϲτρατὸς ἀλκίφρων τε λαός 'a sea-wave
cannot be fought; the Persians' army and brave-hearted

people are irresistible'. Wilamowitz fails to explain how he
understands his suggested ἀπροφάς]ιϲτος, but the sense
'implacable' in LSJ (s.v. 2), with a reference to E. Ba.
1002, is unjustified: it generally refers to 'unquestioning
obedience' (Dodds ad loc., who suggests ἀπροφαϲίϲτωϲ
there), which is hardly an apt epithet for πλαγά.

9. ῥηξ[. . . .]οϲ: '[ ]-breaking'. Wilamowitz supplements
ῥηξ[ίζυγ]οϲ, with reference to the rowers' thwarts or seats,
for which ζυγόν was a technical term (cf. e.g. Il. 2. 293 νηῒ
πολυζύγωι 'a many-thwarted ship', 20. 247 and see Casson
220); if ἀλλά at l. 7 is not adversative, and if Janssen is right
to see a reference to the διέκπλουϲ, Page's suggestion
ῥηξ[ίκωπ]οϲ is more attractive.

9–10. [ἅμ'] ἀνέπι[πτον] . . . **να[ῦ]ται:** 'the sailors fell
backwards together', presumably under the force of the
blow that broke the oars; thus perhaps not a reference to
the marines (so Janssen), who were known as ἐπιβάται
(Casson 304). This word may have been felt to be somewhat
prosaic, and so avoided in poetry, but there is nothing here
to suggest marines are meant. ναῦται generally describes
rowers ([Dem.] 50. 10, 25, 32, etc.). ἐπ]ανέπι[πτον is suggested by Danielsson, but no satisfactory force can be given
to the prefix ἐπ-. We might also write πι[τνον, but -πιπτ- is
found at e.g. P. 23, 60.

11–13. We may assume from εἰ δέ that the events
described contrast with the attack at 7–10, and also that
the subject of the verb ἐφέροντο must be same as the subject
of ἀνέπι[πτον at 10 (i.e. ναῦται). Thus 11–12 must describe
something that would cause the sailors to fall back again
(thus the sense of πάλιν ἐφ.); this I take to be a blow from the
other side of the ship. ἀκτ[therefore must be a word for
'blow'. Page supplements ἀκτά 'headland', and Campbell
translates 'and if a headland opposite the ships' side snapped
. . .', but it is not immediately obvious that this is the
expected meaning, and leaves the problematic lacuna . . .]οϲ.
Page suggests the verb [ἄ]ξειεμ 'shatter', and supplies μῆχ]οϲ
(πολυκρότο[ιο πλώ]ϲιμον πεύκας), with the explanation machi-
nam pinus navalem = remum; this periphrasis strikes an odd
note, and it is doubtful whether μῆχος can have the sense
which Page wishes to give to it. The verb, however, appeals.

Wilamowitz wrote πρ]oc[άι]ξειεμ 'dash, speed against'; this is also attractive, but requires the support of his implausible ἀκτ[ίc 'ray' as an equivalent for a weapon, for which good parallels are lacking. Danielsson cites Hsch. ἀκτίc· οἰκέτου ὄνομα. παρὰ δὲ Cυρακουcίοιc ὁδηγόc. ἢ ναῦc; this, however, probably means that Ἀκτίc could be the name for a ship, as it is at e.g. *IG* ii². 1629, 645, 768, etc. Janssen tentatively suggests a compound of the type ἀκτ[-φορ]οc (or -βολ]οc), but it is hard to imagine what the first term might be: not, in this case, from ἀκτίc, which regularly forms compounds in ἀκτινο-.

There is a trace of ink in the lower right hand corner after ἀκτ-. Occasionally the lower stroke of ε extends this far to the left, but the trace may not belong to the following letter.

11. ἀντίτοιχοc: 'on the other side', not 'side to side' (Janssen); to be taken in contrast to ἐνθένδε. The compound itself is new, but τοῖχοc is common in the plural as a word for the sides of a ship; for the form we may compare compounds such as ἀντίπορος 'on the opposite coast', but which occasionally means simply 'opposite' (E. *Med.* 210 with Page).

12–13. [πο]λυκρότο[υc . . . πεύκαc: 'the many-banked pines', i.e. the ships (cf. πεύκαιcιν at 77). I prefer to take πεύκαc as an accusative plural and to supplement -ο[υc (so Diehl) as opposed to the sing. -ο[ιο (so Page), as this provides the required object for Page's [ἄ]ξειεμ. Campbell renders Page's πολυκρότο[ιο] as 'noisy'; this cannot be the meaning here. In later Greek μονόκροτοc, δίκροτοc, and τρίκροτοc are standard nautical terms used to describe a ship, either with reference to the number of banks of rowers or to their division into squads: see W. W. Tarn, *JHS* 25 (1905), 143 ff.; J. S. Morrison, *CQ* 41 (1947), 122–5. At E. *IT* 407 ff. Platnauer takes ῥοθίοιc . . . δικρότοιcι 'with double-beaten surge' to refer to the beat of the oars on each side of the ship, but the phrase more probably refers to the beat of two banks of oars. Therefore the adjective here refers to a ship with more than one bank of rowers.

13. . . .]cιμουc: Page reads πλώ]cιμον (with Schubart) to agree with his hypothetical μῆχ]οc, but there is easily space for five letters, all of which are very unclear, after the lacuna. Perhaps πλω]cίμουc 'sea-going', agreeing with πεύκαc.

πλώςιμος is a classical hapax at S. *OC* 662–3 φανήςεται |
μακρὸν τὸ δεῦρο πέλαγος οὐδὲ πλώςιμον, with the passive sense
'navigable', but adjectives in -ιμος have a known tendency to
function as either active or passive; see also *P.* 63 n.
In later Greek we find Diogenian. 6. 78 (i. 282 Leutsch–
Schneidewin) ναῦς παλαιὰ πόντωι οὐχὶ πλωςίμη, where it is a
three-termination adjective; Timotheus tends to regard
adjectives in -ιμος as two-termination (cf. *P.* 64, 112–13).

πάλιν ἐφέροντο: the subject is ναῦται as at 10.

14. αἱ δὲ . . . [δ]ιαφέρουσα[ι: 'when the ships, tearing
away . . .'; probably the Greek ships, although the change of
subject is marked only by the change of gender from ναῦται.

[...]αι.η γυῖα: Page's tentative ἀν]αιδῆ 'shameless' is unconvincing. The adjective is used of the stone of Sisyphus at
Od. 11. 598 λᾶας ἀναιδής, and the same formula is found of a
stone thrown in battle at *Il.* 4. 521–2; at *Il.* 13. 139 ἀναιδέος
. . . πέτρης has much the same force. 'The stone, anthro-
pomorphically, has no pity' (Heubeck). Pindar uses it of
hope at *N.* 11. 45–6 δέδεται γὰρ ἀναιδεῖ | ἐλπίδι γυῖα, and of
death at *O.* 10. 104–5; in both cases it means little more than
'cruel' (so glossed by W. J. Slater, *Lexicon to Pindar* (Berlin,
1969), s.v.). This sense would here be inappropriate.

Better sense is obtained by reading [ἀκρ]αινῆ 'powerless
(i.e. no longer functional) limbs'; ἀκραινές is given by Hsch.
(α 2533) as an equivalent for ἀκρατές, which is used of
paralysed limbs at *IG* iv. 951. 22 (Epidauros: 4th c. BC):
ἀνὴρ τοὺς τᾶς χηρὸς δακτύλους ἀκρατεῖς ἔχων πλὰν ἑνὸς ἀ[φ]ίκετο
ποὶ τὸν Θεὸν ἱκέτας. Page and Wilamowitz allow for four
letters in the lacuna; this may well be correct, but the
spacing is not entirely clear at this point; κ and α can both
be quite wide letters. 'Limbs' refers to the oars (cf. 5 χεῖρας,
91 πόδας ναός), the removal of which would naturally expose
the sides of the ship, rather than the hull (so Gildersleeve).
The anthropomorphic description of the ships throughout
adds to the gruesome detail of Timotheus' narrative.

15. πλ]ευρὰς λιγ[ο]ζώςτους ἔφαινον: '(they) revealed the
linen-bound sides'. The sides of Greek ships were often
strengthened with cables called ὑποζώματα (see Casson 91),
which ran from stem to stern, under the line of the gunwale.
They were made of flax or linen, and were typical of

warships in the classical period (Morrison–Williams 294–8).
Aeschylus may mention them at *Suppl.* 134–5 πλάτα μὲν οὖν
λινορραφής | τε δόμος, ἅλα στέγον δόρυ; Johansen–Whittle,
however, see an allusion to the sewing together of the planks
with flax (cf. Σ 134–5 λινορραφὴς δόμος δορός· ἡ ναῦς, παρόσον
τρυπῶντες τὰς ναῦς σπάρτοις αὐτὰς συνέρραπτον). Timotheus
shows some interest in the technical details of shipbuilding,
but usually only for poetic colour in his complicated periphrases (as here and at e.g. 20 σιδα[ρ]ῶι κράνει). A similar
compound is found at *P.* 74 πέδαι . . . λινοδέτωι, which refers,
however, to the cables used to bind ships together for
Xerxes' bridge.

πλευρά is not usual for the sides of a ship, but here is
obviously meant to suggest the rib-like bands which support
the hull.

16. τὰς μ[ὲν: sc. νῆας or νέας; we do not know what form
Timotheus used for the accusative plural; cf. 14 αἱ δέ.

16–17.]ις σκηπ[τοῖς: the accusative might be preferable
after ἐπεμβάλλοντες (so Janssen), but the iota is clearly legible
in the papyrus, which, if correct, suggests that the participle
must here be used absolutely. Janssen and Edmonds see yet
another reference to rams; but Gildersleeve is clearly correct
to see a reference to δελφῖνες, leaden weights, apparently
roughly in the shape of a dolphin, which were hung from a
ship's yard-arm and dropped or swung onto enemy vessels;
cf. Ar. *Eq.* 761–2 πρότερον σὺ | τοὺς δελφῖνας μετεωρίζου καὶ
τὴν ἄκατον παραβάλλου (with Σ: σιδηροῦν κατασκεύασμα ἢ
μολίβδινον, εἰς δελφῖνα ἐσχηματισμένον. τοῦτο δὲ ἐκ τῆς κεραίας
τοῦ ἱστοῦ αἱ ναυμαχοῦσαι ἠφίεσαν εἰς τὰς τῶν πολεμίων, καὶ
κατεδύοντο), Thuc. 7. 41. 2 (with Dover) αἱ κεραῖαι αἱ ἀπὸ
τῶν ὁλκάδων δελφινοφόροι, Pherecrates fr. 12 K.–A. ὁ δὲ δὴ
δελφίς ἐστι μολιβδοῦς, δελφινοφόρος τε κεραία | ὃς διακόψει
τοὔδαφος. They appear to have been an innovation in naval
warfare of the later fifth century (Casson 239 n. 67). Page
understands the same sense, but supplements wildly: [αἰόλας
ὕβρε]ις σκηπτ[ῶν]. I prefer simply μολυβδίνο]ις or μολιβδ- (for
the alternation between the forms, both of which were in use
in classical times, see Chantraine, s.v., with bibliography),
which provides *mol ia*.

17. ἀνε[χ]αίτιζον: 'they capsized'; cf. the sequence of

events at A. *Pers.* 417–19 Ἑλληνικαί τε νῆες οὐκ ἀφρασμόνως |
κύκλωι πέριξ ἔθεινον, ὑπτιοῦτο δὲ | cκάφη νεῶν. The verb is
properly used intransitively of a rearing horse or transitively
of a horse that throws its rider, but frequently, both
transitively and intransitively, has a more general metaphorical sense, 'upset, overturn' (cf. esp. E. *Hipp.* 1232
with Barrett). Ships are more frequently compared to
chariots or carriages in ancient literature, and Timotheus
himself may make such a comparison at fr. 790A; cf. e.g. A.
Suppl. 32 with Johansen–Whittle, [A.] *Pr.* 468, S. *Tr.* 656,
E. *Med.* 1122–3 and see Wærn, 47–8. *Od.* 4. 707–9 οὐδέ τί μιν
χρεὼ | νηῶν ὠκυπόρων ἐπιβαινέμεν, αἵ θ' ἁλὸc ἵπποι | ἀνδράcι
γίγνονται may suggest a comparison with horses, but ἵπποι
there may be nearly equivalent to 'chariots' (S. West ad
loc.).

18–19. αἱ δὲ πρα[. . . . .]αc: clearly another form
of destruction should take place in the lacuna; some ships
have been capsized after their oars have been swept away;
others must be destroyed in another way. πρα[requires a
word like πρα[νεῖc 'bottom upwards' (yielding a colon *ia ba*);
Page conjectures -έεc here, but the open orthography εε is
not otherwise attested in the papyrus or called for by the
metre. The reference is probably simply to sinking after
their prow or stern has been knocked off (19–20); the usual
word for this is καταδύω, followed by an accusative (Hdt. 8.
90. 2, Thuc. 2. 92. 3, 7. 34. 5 etc.), but δύω can also be used
for descent into water (e.g. *Il.* 6. 136 δύcεθ' ἁλὸc κατὰ κῦμα,
18. 140 δῦτε θαλάccηc εὐρέα κόλπον, 18. 145). Hence I suggest
supplementing πρα[νεῖc ἔδυνον καθ' ἅλμ]αc. I take ἅλμ]αc to be
genitive singular; for the construction cf. Hdt. 7. 235. 2 κατὰ
τῆc θαλάccηc καταδεδυκέναι (of the island of Cythera).

GOH suggests that a genitive may be desirable after
ἀπηγ⟨λ⟩αϊcμένα[ι] in the next line; if so, perhaps κορύμβ]αc,
since the whole passage is reminiscent of A. *Pers.* 410–11
(quoted below). But ἔδυνον could still stand in the lacuna in
that case.

19–20. ἀπηγ⟨λ⟩αϊcμένα[ι] cιδα[ρ]ῶι κράνει: 'stripped of
their ornaments by the iron helmet', i.e. by the ram
(instrumental dative); cf. A. *Pers.* 410–11 κἀποθραύει πάντα
Φοινίccηc νεὼc | κόρυμβ(α), where κόρυμβα probably refers to

the stern-ornament (so Broadhead). Possibly it should be
read here (see preceding n.); the verb is not otherwise
attested until well after the classical period (κομάων | τὴν
ῥαδινὴν κούρην πάμπαν ἀπαγλαΐσαι, Agath. *AP* 5. 220. 5–6).
Greek ships tended to leave the prow unadorned; Phoenician triremes 'had either a figurehead or a tutelary deity
carried somewhere in the bows' (Casson 95–6; cf. Hdt. 3. 37.
2). According to Herodotus, the Phoenicians and Syrians
provided the largest number of ships for the Persian fleet (7.
89), and the Aeschylean passage, which Timotheus is
perhaps directly recalling, describes the Phoenician ships
which were posted opposite the Athenians (cf. Hdt. 8. 85).
αἰδα[ρ]ῶι κράνει: cf. 4 κυρτοῖ[ϲι] κραϲίν. Rams were more
usually made of bronze. Both Pliny and Vitruvius provide
late evidence for the use of iron in the construction of rams,
but the practice may have originated much earlier; cf. Plin.
NH 32. 3 *heu vanitas humana, cum rostra illa aere ferroque ad
ictus armata semipedalis inhibere possit ac tenere devincta
pisciculus*, Vitr. 10. 15. 6. Casson (85 n. 40), believes this
to be a reference merely to a reinforced tip and not an
indication of the material from which the ram was made, but
it is perhaps possible that in some instances the casing,
normally of bronze, was replaced by iron.
    **21–3. ἴϲοϲ δὲ πυρὶ δαμ[. . . . .]ν ἀγκυλένδετ[ο]ϲ μεθίετο
χερϲίν:** 'like fire the [ ], thong-bound [ ] was hurled by their
hands'. Wilamowitz supplements δαμ[αϲίφωϲ] 'man-slaying';
the word is found otherwise at Simon. fr. 601 δαμαϲίφωτα (of
Hypnos) as a variation on δαμαϲίμβροτοϲ (used of weapons at
Pi. *O*. 9. 79, Ba. 13. 50–1; cf. Simon. fr. 616). Nor is there
any other compound in Greek with -φωϲ as a second term
(O. Poltera, *Le Langage de Simonide* (Berne, 1997), 422);
possibly Timotheus may be deliberately imitating Simonides, though there is no obvious poetic point in such a
reminiscence. The size of the lacuna is uncertain; the
papyrus fragment containing δαμ, which begins a line, is
not attached to the rest of col. ii. Page's δαμ[αϲτάϲ] also
provides good sense.
    The trace before ἀγκυλένδετοϲ is inconclusive; ἄκω]ν (Jur-
enka), producing *ba ia*, seems more plausible, and is more
compatible with the traces, than Wilamowitz's Ἄρη]ϲ as a

metonym for spear. The ἄκων was a light throwing-javelin (Snodgrass 78 ff.); the word is used by Timotheus at *P.* 164. For Ἄρη]ς, Janssen compares *Il.* 7. 329–30 τῶν νῦν αἷμα κελαινὸν ἔρροον ἀμφὶ Cκάμανδρον | ἐcκέδαc᾽ ὀξὺc Ἄρηc, where the adjective may simply mean 'bitter' or similar; and Alc. fr. 140. 4–5 παῖca δ᾽ †ἄρηι κεκόcμηται cτέγα | λάμπραιcιν κυνίαιcι, where ἄρηι is not certain and the sense obscure.

ἀγκυλένδετ[ο]c: 'thong-bound'; a reference to the throwing-loop, probably made of leather, which was fastened to the middle of the javelin-shaft: see Snodgrass 80, and cf. A. fr. 16 Radt ἀγκυλητά 'javelins'; E. *Ph.* 1141 καὶ πρῶτα μὲν τόξοιcι καὶ μεcαγκύλοιc; *Andr.* 1132–3 ἀλλὰ πόλλ᾽ ὁμοῦ βέλη, | οἰcτοί, μεcάγκυλ᾽; *Ba.* 1205. The thong 'enabled the thrower to give a rotary motion to the javelin, which not only helped it to keep its direction . . . but also increased its carry and its penetrating power' (E. N. Gardiner, *JHS* 27 (1907), 251).

Adjectives in -ένδετοc are generally rare; they otherwise occur mainly in texts of a Hellenistic date or later; cf. ἀνένδετοc (Philo Mech. 1. 71), ἀργυρένδετοc (*IG* ii². 161 B 79, 3rd c. BC; also Jo. Chrys.), νευρένδετοc (Manetho 5. 163 κίθαραc νευρ.), cιδηρένδετοc (*Edict. Diocl.* 15. 50), χρυcένδετοc (Philemon fr. 73 K.–A.). Hutchinson on A. *Sept.* 315 notes that adjectives formed from a verb with preverb are normally comic in the fifth century. Timotheus elsewhere happily incorporates elements from comedy, and this may be another aspect of his rejection of convention.

23. ἐν δ᾽ ἔπιπτε γυίοιc: the subject is the same as that found in l. 22. ἐν is probably a preverb rather than a preposition with the dative γυίοιc; for the tmesis, see also 180 n. and above, p. 47; and for a similar use of -πίπτω, cf. A. *Pers.* 460–1 τοξικῆc τ᾽ ἀπὸ | θώμιγγοc ἰοὶ προcπίτνοντεc ὤλλυcαν. Janssen believes that γυίοιc means 'bodies' not 'limbs', but the point is no doubt that the parts struck are those not covered by armour (another realistic detail); cf. Thuc. 3. 23. 4 ἐτόξευόν τε καὶ ἐcηκόντιζον ἐc τὰ γυμνά.

24. αἰθε[. . . . .]ωμα διακρα[δ]αίνων: Page tentatively supplements αἰθέ[ρια δούρατ᾽] and then ὠμὰ διακραδαίνων (or ὠμάδια κρ.; but ὠμάδιοc is a very rare adjective, attested in Nonnus and occasionally elsewhere as a cult-title of Dionysus); presumably he means '(the javelins) fell among their limbs, shaking the shafts (sc. of the javelins)'; but there is no parallel for ὠμός in such a context, and δούρατ' provides an odd object. διακραδαίνων, only otherwise attested at Arius Didymus in Stob. 1. 36. 2 (Diels, *Doxogr.* p. 453. 15), ought to require an object; therefore read c]ῶμα.

Wilamowitz paraphrases τρέμοντα ἔτι ὑπὸ τῆς δι' ἀέρος φορᾶς, apparently understanding αἰθε[ροφόρητον] cῶμα to refer to the spear's shaft. The adjective ('airborne') is a plausible, if unattested, formation, but it is more natural to take the noun as denoting human bodies. Janssen prefers to supplement αἰθε[ροφόρητος], but αἰθε[ροδρόμος], used in the parody of Cinesias at Ar. *Av.* 1393, is perhaps better: the darts can run through the air like birds, just as the arrows are later 'long-winged' (29). For the use of the singular cῶμα as a collective, see Kühner–Gerth i. 13–14.

25. cτερεοπαγῆ: 'hard'; the second element is redundant, not unusually for compounds.

26–8. Edmonds's restoration here is superficially attractive, [λίθια πιcc]ᾶ[ν]τα 'stones and tarred (covers)', but it is doubtful whether such artillery would have been used in a sea-battle before the Hellenistic period.

26. τά τε περίβολα πυρὶ φλεγόμεν': 'missiles (?) burning with fire'; the sense of περίβολα is uncertain. If derived from ὁ περίβολος, then possibly 'covers' (Janssen) is the sense; there is no other example of the neuter substantive, but masculine nouns sometimes produce neuter plurals, originally with a collective sense (Wackernagel, *Kl. Schr.* i. 660–1; Schwyzer i. 581, ii. 37). Such covers could presumably have been wrapped around the ends of the arrows, and set alight.

Flaming bolts appear to have been a development of the late fifth century at the earliest, and they are not mentioned by either Herodotus or Aeschylus in their accounts of Salamis. Artillery firing flaming bolts was used by Demetrius in 304 BC (D.S. 20. 96). See E. W. Marsden, *Greek and Roman Artillery: Historical Development* (Oxford, 1969), 51, 93. Smaller incendiary arrows are mentioned at Thuc. 2. 75. 5 πυρφόροις οἰcτοῖς; these are probably meant here, as artillery is attested for naval battles mainly in later times.

27. ἐν ἀποτομάcι: 'on splints of wood', i.e. arrows; cf.

Hsch. α 32 ἀποτομάδα· cχίζαν. καὶ ἀκόντιον πεντάθλου, Pollux 10. 64, for the similarly derived sense 'javelin'. The papyrus reads -εcι, more probably to be corrected to -αcι than read as a misformation for -ευcι; ἀποτομεύc 'javelin' perhaps occurs at Pollux 3. 151, but the form is corrected in the MS from -άc.

28. βουδο[: Wilamowitz suggests βουδό[ροιc 'ox-flaying', and Babr. 97. 7 has μαχαίραc βουδόρουc 'knives for flaying', while Hsch. gives a substantive βουδόρωι· μοχλῶι, ὧι βοῦc δέρουcιν; cf. also Hes. *Op.* 504 μῆνα δὲ Ληναιῶνα, κάκ' ἤματα, βουδόρα πάντα. But it is somewhat unclear how 'splints of wood' would be used for flaying oxen; Edmonds compares the 'skewer-like pegs used by tanners', presumably to stretch the hides; from Ar. *Eq.* 371 it appears the usual word was πάccαλοc. Janssen suggests βούδο[ρα, to be taken as a passive 'stripped from oxen', and agreeing with περίβολα 'covers', but περίβολα is itself of uncertain meaning, and in Timotheus adjectives are usually positioned closer to the nouns they qualify. The only other attested compound in βου-δο- is βουδόκοc 'receiving oxen' (Callim. fr. 58. 2 = *SH* 268 ἄξονται δ' οὐχ ἵππον ἀέθλιον, οὐ μὲν ἐχῖνον | βουδόκον).

A reference to a goad is expected (cf. Wilamowitz 45: 'ein Stecken, mit dem man die Ochsen prügelt'); the darts look like an ox-goad, which was usually a straight stick with a sharp spike at one end. Timotheus' periphrases are usually based on a visual similarity between otherwise unconnected objects. Perhaps, therefore, supplement e.g. *βουδό[νοιc(ι) 'ox-driving' as a possible (if unattested) formation, for which cf. Leonidas, *HE* 2318 (*AP* 6. 305. 6), Ariston, *HE* 757 (*AP* 6. 306. 2) ἐτνοδόνοc 'soup-stirring'; earlier compounds in -δονοc are usually passive (e.g. οἰcτρόδονοc, ἁλί-δονοc). The spits used as missiles at E. *Andr.* 1133–4 are ἀμφώβολοι . . . βουπόροι 'ox-piercing', because used for cooking sacrifices; the adjective again appears as an epithet for a spit at E. *Cyc.* 302, Hdt. 2. 135. 4.

......]**βίοτοc**: a connective is required at the start of the new sentence, and we expect δέ in Timotheus. This leaves space after βουδό[νοιc(ι) for only three or four letters; Page attractively supplements τῶν δὲ] βίοτοc 'their life', though this leaves little space for a noun in the lacuna after νευρε[(e.g. βέλεcι, οἰcτοῖc, sim.). A substantive agreeing with the

dative adjectives may therefore be better here. Wilamowitz's
[ὄφεcι δέ] seems too long for the lacuna and the image too
bizarre; better would be GOH's [ἰοῖc δέ].

29. ἀδιν[ό]c: possibly to be understood adverbially, 'in
great numbers' rather than as a simple adjective with βίοτοc.
For the use of an adjective as an adverb, see Schwyzer ii. 178–9.
ἔθύετ(ο): 'was being slaughtered'; for the sense of the verb
in the fifth century cf. esp. Timoth. fr. 783 n. For the
(collective) singular as a mark of the plural see Kühner–
Gerth i. 13–14.

τανυπτέροιcι: 'long-winged', the adjective of arrows only
here, and traditionally of birds in earlier epic and lyric
poetry; cf. Hes. *Th.* 523, *Od.* 5. 65, *H. Hom.* 2. 89, Alcm.
fr. 89. 6, Alc. fr. 345. 2, Ibyc. frr. 317(*a*). 3, 317(*b*), Pi. *P.* 5.
11, Ar. *Av.* 1411. 'Winged arrows', referring perhaps as
much to their flight through the air as to their feathered
shafts, are, however, common (e.g. *Il.* 5. 171 πτερόεντεc
ὀϊcτοί, 16. 773 ἰοί . . . πτερόεντεc, E. *Herc.* 368 πτανοῖc βέλεcιν
etc.); this sort of variation on a traditional formula is typical
of Timotheus' style.

30. χαλκόκραcι νευρε[: 'bronze-headed, ?'. Bronze was
the usual material for arrow-heads: see Snodgrass 81. For
the expected sense of the second word, we might compare
S. *Ph.* 290 νευροcπαδὴc ('drawn by the string') ἄτρακτοc;
Wilamowitz suggests either νευρε[πεντάτοιc or νευρε[ρύcτοιc.
The size of the lacuna is unclear, since νευρε stands at the
end of a line, and the beginning of the next line is also
seriously lacunose; the supplement of a noun for 'arrows' at
the start of the sentence avoids this problem. Wærn argues
that three adjectives would be sufficient to describe an
arrow, but Timotheus never uses a periphrasis without a
substantival element. We could just as well print -κραcιν
ευρε[, though this does not solve the problem by any means.

31. cμαραγδοχαίταc . . . πόντοc: the sea is not otherwise
considered emerald-coloured in Greek literature; the adjective here is clearly modelled on κυανοχαίτηc of Poseidon in
Homer, not necessarily with reference to the colour of the
sea. κυάνεοc originally meant simply 'dark' (E. Irwin, *Colour
Terms in Greek Poetry* (Toronto, 1974), 108 ff.), and probably has this sense in Homer, but by the fifth century its

meaning had gravitated to 'blue'; cf. Pi. fr. 52f (*Pae.* 6. 83–4) κυανοπλόκοιο ποντίας Θέτιος and Simon. fr. 567. 3–5 ἀνὰ δ' ἰχθύες ὀρθοί | κυανέου 'ξ ὕδατος ἄλλοντο καλᾶι cὺν ἀοιδᾶι, which is the first explicit use of κύανεος of the sea. At Pi. fr. 33 μάκαρες δ' ἐν Ὀλύμπωι | τηλέφαντον κυανέας χθονὸς ἄςτρον (of Delos), κυανέας χθονός is taken by Wærn (84–5) and others to be a periphrasis for 'sea'. But this might be rather surprising after χθονὸς εὐρείας in ll. 3–4, and κυανέας probably here just means 'dark'. The island of Delos, a wonder of the broad earth, stands out brightly (like a star) on the dark earth.

Elsewhere in Greek, greenness is not a typical quality of the sea; rivers can be χλωρός, perhaps 'green' (E. *Hel.* 349, *Ph.* 660–61, fr. 1069 N²), but more probably with reference to the surrounding plants than to the colour of the water (Irwin, op. cit. 46 ff.), while other liquids, mainly dew and tears, can also be χλωρός (e.g. Pi. *N.* 8. 40, S. *Tr.* 847–8; also of blood at S. *Tr.* 1056, E. *Hec.* 129), but with the sense 'fresh'. The 'hair' of the sea may here be a reference to the waves.

32. ἄλοκα: 'furrow'; cf. [Arion], *PMG* adesp. 939. 16–17 ἄλοκα Νηρείας πλακὸς | τέμνοντες, Ar. *Av.* 1400 (parody of Cinesias) αἰθέρος αὔλακα τέμνων, also Ba. 17. 4. Keil thinks the accusative of respect odd, and in the next line supplements cταλά[γμαςι χέων], which is grammatically even odder. GOH suggests ἄλοκι, and notes that Wilamowitz on E. *Her.* 1273 regards double datives as typical of the dithyramb; but after ἐφοινίccετο any dative other than an instrumental dative looks unlikely.

ναΐοιc . . . cταλά[γμαcι: 'with drops from the ships', but the adjective is infelicitous, since the blood should strictly belong to the sailors; possibly it has intruded from l. 35 νάϊος cτρατός. Its deletion would allow cμαραγδοχαίτας δὲ πόντος to be scanned as *ia tr* |; then ἄλοκ' ἐφοι- would be a cretic of the form ◡◡◡–. Van Leeuwen, however, suggests the attractive emendation δαΐοιc.

Clearly the sea should be reddened with the blood that has been shed; cf. Orac. ap. Hdt. 8. 77 αἵματι δ' Ἄρης | πόντον φοινίξει, [Theocr.] 23. 61 νᾶμα δ' ἐφοινίχθη. A comma is required after cταλά]γμαcι to give κατεῖχεν an understood object.

FRAGMENT 791. 34–8   151

34. κϱ]αυγᾶι βοὰ δὲ [υ]μμι[γ]ὴϲ κατεῖχεν: cf. A. *Pers.*
426–7 οἰμωγὴ δ' ὁμοῦ | κωκύμαϲιν κατεῖχε πελαγίαν ἅλα, D.S.
13. 46 (quoted above). If βοά means war-cry here, there
could be a contrast between the (already victorious) Greek
βοά against the Persian κραυγή.
For the postponement of δέ, unique in Timotheus, but
here the result of the close connection between κραυγᾶι and
βοά, see Denniston 187 ff.

[υ]μμι[γ]ήϲ: 'mixed with' (Wilamowitz). The dative is
common after ϲυμμιγήϲ (e.g. A. *Sept.* 741 πόνοι δόμων νέοι
παλαιοῖϲι ϲυμμιγεῖϲ κακοῖϲ, Antiph. fr. 55. 7 K.–A.), although
it stands absolutely at S. *OT* 1281 ἀλλ' ἀνδρὶ καὶ γυναικὶ
ϲυμμιγῆ κακά 'but evils are mixed for man and woman'.
However, παμμιγήϲ (Diehl) never takes the dative construction; cf. A. *Pers.* 269 βέλεα παμμιγῆ, Lycophr. 5 παμμιγῆ
βοήν. Note the repetition of a similar word at 36 ἀμμιγ[-.

35. νάϊοϲ ϲτρατὸϲ βάϱβαροϲ: 'the naval barbarian army';
cf. *P.* 86–7 Πέρϲηϲ ϲτρατὸϲ βάρβαροϲ (with n.), E. *IA* 260 ναΐου
ϲτρατοῦ, i.e. 'fleet', and the common Herodotean ναυτικὸϲ
ϲτρατόϲ.

36. ἄμμι[: the sense should be 'in confusion'. ἄμμιγα is
possible (cf. A. *Sept.* 239, S. *Tr.* 837 ff. μελαγχαίτα τ' ἄμμιγά
νιν αἰκίζει φόνια δολιόμυθα κέντρ' ἐπιζέϲαντα), or perhaps
*ἄμμιγδα (cf. ἀνάμιγδα only at S. *Tr.* 519). ἀμμίγδην is a
late formation at Nic. *Th.* 912, although the forms -δην, -δα,
and their variations, appear to have been largely interchangeable (cf. e.g. ἀμφαδόν, but ἀμφάδην at Archil. fr. 128.
4, ἀμφαδίην at e.g. *Il.* 13. 356, Thgn. 90, and see Schwyzer i.
626–7).

37. ἰχ]θυ[ο]ϲτεφέϲι: 'fish-wreathed'; cf. Timocles fr. 17. 1
K.–A. τόν τ' ἰχθυόρρουν ποταμόν, and various phrases with
ἰχθυόειϲ, e.g. *Il.* 9. 4 πόντον . . . ἰχθυόεντα, *Od.* 3. 177 ἰχθυόεντα
κέλευθα, Ar. *Th.* 324 μυχὸν ἰχθυόεντ' etc. The form ἰχθυο-
(Danielsson) is clearly correct; ἰχθυϲ- (Wilamowitz) is not
otherwise attested, and the only alternative forms to ἰχθυο-
are ἰχθυ- and ἰχθυϲι-. The epithet is especially apt here for
Amphitrite (or another sea-nymph), and contributes to the
personification of the sea (cf. -π[τύχ]οιϲ, κόλποιϲιν).

38. μαϱμαροπ[τύχ]οιϲ: 'with shining folds'; cf. *Il.* 14. 273
ἅλα μαρμαρέην, *P.* 92 μαρμαροφεγγεῖϲ (with n.). The choice of

adjective has no doubt been influenced by the use of κόλποι 'breast, bosom'. Compounds in -πτυχος more usually have a numeral as the first term; e.g. δίπτυχος, τρίπτυχος, πολύπτυχος (all Homeric, and then not until later, e.g. δεκάπτυχος at Orph. fr. 247. 21, ἑπτάπτυχος at Σ D Il. 7. 220 etc.). Wilamowitz suggested -π[τέρ]οις, but we should not expect the sea (or Amphitrite) to be 'shining-winged'. Danielsson's -π[έπλ]οις is more felicitous, but otiose in conjunction with κόλποισιν, and again less apt for the sea.

39. κόλποισιν: cf. Il. 6. 136 Θέτις δ᾽ ὑπεδέξατο κόλπωι, 18. 140 θαλάσσης εὐρέα κόλπον, 21. 125, Od. 5. 25, [A.] Pr. 837 πρὸς μέγαν κόλπον ('gulf') Ῥέας, i.e. the Adriatic. κόλποι can be used for various types of hollow; it seems primarily to describe a shape rather than any particular object (such as a dress): see Dunbar on Ar. Av. 694–5. Here we are to think both of the folds of Amphitrite's dress, and the (visually similar) folds of the waves.

Ἀμφιτρί]τας: for Amphitrite as a metonym for sea, cf. E. IT 425 ἐπ᾽ Ἀμφιτρίτας ῥοθίωι and see Breitenbach 176. Although the supplement is not certain, the periphrasis requires a determining substantive; Amphitrite is the most appropriate sea-deity given the size of the lacuna and the genitive in -ας. She was the daughter of Nereus and Doris according to Hes. Th. 243, and is the owner of the waves already at Od. 3. 91 ἐν πελάγει μετὰ κύμασιν Ἀμφιτρίτης, and 12. 60 κῦμα μέγα ῥοχθεῖ κυανώπιδος Ἀμφιτρίτης. [Arion], PMG adesp. 939. 11 makes her the mother of the Nereids (or of the dolphins: see West, 'Analyses', 5 ff. for the emendation). She is Poseidon's consort at Hes. Th. 930, but is not named in the (incomplete) catalogue of the Nereids at Il. 18. 37–53. In Attic red-figure vases (the earliest dating to c.510 BC) depicting the marriage of Peleus and Thetis, she often appears as an attendant; so in a cup from Vulci by the Euergides Painter, now in London (ARV² 89. 13), where she may be Nereus' consort, behind whom she is standing; see J. M. Barringer, *Divine Escorts: Nereids in Archaic and Classical Greek Art* (Ann Arbor, 1995).

40–71. The Islander: Introduction. At l. 40 the first individual character in the extant part of the poem is introduced. After a brief passage the text becomes too lacunose to be legible, but it seems probable that he should be identified with the drowning person at 60 ff. The description at 44 ff. in particular corresponds with the description of drowning; there thus seems good reason to combine the two passages, though much of 40–59 is unclear. There is no specific reference to identify the man at 60–85, as we should certainly expect if he were different from the one introduced at 40.

In fifth-century and later Greece it was almost proverbial that barbarians were unable to swim. According to Hdt. 8. 89. 2 one of the reasons for the scale of Persian casualties at Salamis was their inability to swim, in contrast to the Athenians (cf. 6. 44. 3); possibly this was in part due to their heavy and cumbersome clothing (cf. A. *Pers.* 277). Thucydides notes that many of the Thracian mercenaries sent back to Thrace by Athens in 413/2 could not swim, and therefore died when set upon and driven into the sea by the Thebans (7. 29–30). Other examples from later literature are collected by Hall, 'Drowning'. Timotheus again suggests the hostility of Asiatics to the sea at 79–80 παλαιομίσημα (see n.). The accuracy of the Greek view is open to some doubt; the skill of Tyrian swimmers is noted at Arrian, *Anab.* 2. 21. 6. In the Behistun inscription Darius twice refers to his success in crossing rivers; that of the Tigris in flood at DB i 86–8 (p. 118 Kent), and the raft crossing to Scythia at DB v 23–5 (p. 133 Kent). The concern to record such achievements may indicate a general unfamiliarity with sea-travel; but Xerxes, who seems to allude in a Persepolis inscription to the sack of the Acropolis at Athens (XPh 28–41; p. 151 Kent), makes no mention of his remarkable crossing of the Hellespont.

Metre

40     $- \cup - [$ $] \cup\cup\cup |$
         $- - - \cup\cup\cup$
           $- \cup - - \cup - [$
     $] \cup - [\; |$
      $\cup\cup\cup - - \cup - \int$
45        $- \cup - - \cup - \int$

$$-[\ ]-\cup\times[$$
$$]\cup-\cup-[\ |$$
$$\cup-\cup\cup\cup-\times[\ |$$
$$?$$

50     $\cup-[\ ]\cup-\cup-|$

51–9   *metr. incert.*

60     $\cup\cup\cup---\cup--|$
$$-\cup-\cup-\cup-\int$$
$$-\cup-\cup-\cup-\cup|$$
$$-\cup\cup\cup--||$$
$$\cup-\cup--\cup\cup-\int$$

65     $-\cup\cup\cup\cup\cup-\cup||$

65a $-\cup\cup---|$
$$--\cup\cup\cup-|$$
$$\cup--\cup-|$$
$$\cup\cup\cup-\cup--|$$
$$-----|$$

70     $--\cup--\cup-\int$
$$\cup-\cup-\cup--||$$

The section begins with two trochees if we read $\tau[\iota c - \times]\pi\acute{\epsilon}\delta\iota oc$, and continues with the expected iambo-trochaic rhythm. West ('Analyses', 1) notes that if 41 is *ba ia*, as Page suggests, we must assume period-end after the trochaic dimeter at 40 in order to avoid *anceps iuxta breve*, but that period-end after a trochaic dimeter is 'practically a solecism itself', at least in regular iambo-trochaic verse (see also Wilamowitz, *Verskunst*, 476). He therefore reads $\dot{\alpha}\nu\acute{\eta}\rho$ with long alpha (*sp*), then *cr ia cr*. This analysis, however, depends on reading $\dot{\alpha}\mu\epsilon\rho o\delta'\rho\acute{o}\mu o\iota o$, whereas Timotheus usually treats stop + liquid as syllable-releasing between terms of compounds. If the alpha of $\dot{\alpha}\nu\acute{\eta}\rho$ is long, we may have *sp cr* (of the form $-\cup\cup\cup$), then 2 *cr*, breaking the line $\dot{\alpha}\mu\epsilon\rho o\widehat{\delta\rho\acute{o}}|\mu o\iota o$; for this scansion (a metrical licence in the oblique cases formed with $\dot{\alpha}\nu\epsilon\rho$-, other than $\dot{\alpha}\nu\acute{\epsilon}\rho\omega\nu$, already in Homer, and thence perhaps extended to the nominative case; see Chantraine, *Grammaire*, i. 214–15), cf. Pi. *O.* 3. 12, 14. 7; *N.* 2. 3, 3. 72, 9. 15; *I.* 3/4. 88, and see Braswell on Pi. *P.* 4. 21. As an alternative possibility Holford-Strevens suggests *ex. grat.* $\tau[\iota c\ \dot{A}c\iota\alpha]\pi\acute{\epsilon}\delta\iota oc\ \kappa\tau\lambda.$, which would produce $\overset{\smile\smile}{}cr$ *ia ia ba*, with period-end after $\chi\acute{\omega}\rho\alpha c$.

At 60 (presumably period-beginning) we again find a trochaic dimeter leading into an iambo-trochaic sequence; the period ends with an ithyphallic (63), common at period-end in Timotheus as in Euripides. If we read $\ddot{\alpha}\phi\rho\iota\zeta\epsilon\nu$ with Sitzler at 61 (see n.), we can analyse the line as *2tr* instead of *lk*, the second of the form $-\cup--$ as

in 60; this would leave unaltered the scansion of 62. The sequence
of dochmiacs at 65a–69 is unexpected; normally they are restricted
to tragedy, often in association with iambics, as here (Wilamowitz,
Verskunst, 404); there are several Aristophanic examples, some of
which are paratragic, though not all (Parker, *Songs*, 67). Outside
drama, isolated dochmiac-shaped cola can be identified in Pindar,
but never in sequence; however, they form an important part of
the metre of the so-called *Fragmentum Grenfellianum* (*CA* 177–9).
The latter is likely to be a piece of quasi-dramatic monody, and
thus to share characteristics with both Attic drama and the nome.
I see no reason to doubt the presence of dochmiacs in Timotheus;
we have seen before his desire to incorporate metrical and linguistic influences from a variety of genres; cf. also isolated
dochmiacs (or dochmiac-shaped cola) at 76, 105, 123. In tragedy
always and usually elsewhere dochmiacs have a highly emotional
tone. They are particularly noticeable in the Phrygian's aria at E.
Or. 1369 ff. (e.g. 1381 ff.) and form the basis for Polymestor's aria
at E. *Hec.* 1056 ff.; in Cassandra's lyrics at A. *Ag.* 1072 ff.
dochmiacs occur in conjunction with a variety of iambic metra.
The two resolved forms (65a – ◡◡ – – –, 66 – – ◡◡ ◡ –) are both
attested in tragedy. For the form of 65a, it is important to note
that drag ('admission . . . of a long syllable into a position which
by the rules of contrast ought to be short': West, *Metre*, 194) tends
to be associated with a resolved second position, and that the line
conforms to the rule that the fourth position is only lengthened
when the third and fifth positions are unresolved: see N. C.
Conomis, *Hermes*, 92 (1964), 23–50; Dale 104–19; West, *Metre*,
108 ff. δ– (hypercatalectic) appears at A. fr. 204c. 3 ~ 12 Radt
(◡ ◡◡ ◡◡ ◡ – –), and possibly *Ag.* 1103, 1123 (West, *Metre*, 111).
Line 69 is an unresolved dochmiac with double drag.

40–71. 'Then a man from the [ ] plain, a lord of the land that
it takes a day to cross . . . striking the water with his feet and
hands swam, an islander, being dashed (?) (. . .), seeking
ways of escape and decoying . . . evenly balanced . . . (. . . .).
And whenever the winds left off on one side, they attacked
on the other, and the unbacchic spray foamed and poured
into his stomach; and when the brine raged, surging up from
his mouth, he immoderately hurled insults with distorted
voice and deluded perceptions, gnashing his teeth at the sea
the destroyer of his body'.

   40. τ[ιc . . . .]πέδιος ἀνήρ: the man is later described as an islander (45), a statement which appears to contradict the sense here. Janssen suggests that although a plainsman in origin, he has become like an islander because he is now paddling a raft (cf. 44 ποcί τε χ]ερcίν τε). This is possible, but the image would be surprising even in Timotheus. The 'plain' here may therefore be a reference to the 'plains of the sea', as at 78 πεδία πλόϊμα. The χώρα which it takes a day to cross would indeed be small for a country, and while it may refer to the man's private estates (as at e.g. X. *Cyr.* 8. 4. 28, 8. 6. 4), it could equally well describe an island. With the exception of the King, the other 'characters' in the poem are given a specific national identity, and the 'islanders' of the Red Sea are mentioned at Hdt. 7. 80. 1 and 7. 95. 1 as a separate group of tribes who provided Xerxes' army with 17 ships.

Most supplements depend on the view that a real plain is meant: thus Wilamowitz's Φρυγιο]πέδιοc, which is too long for the lacuna, Sitzler's τ[ιc Πέρcηc], also too long, and Edmonds's Ἑρμο]πέδιοc. The first term may simply have indicated the breadth of the sea: Page's ἀμετρο]πέδιοc does not fit the lacuna, but MLW plausibly supplements *ex. grat.* εὐρυ]πέδιοc. Alternatively, the first term made clear the sense to be given to -πέδιοc; e.g. ὑγρο- 'the watery plain' (cf. the Homeric ὑγρὰ κέλευθα, and Ionic ἡ ὑγρή 'sea').

41. ἀμεροδρόμοιο χώραc ἄναξ: 'lord of the land which it takes a day to cross', rather than 'lord of the land of couriers' (Edmonds); ἡμεροδρόμηc is 'courier' at Hdt. 6. 105. 1, 9. 12. 1 (cf. Liv. 31. 24 *hemerodromos vocant Graeci ingens die uno cursu emetientes spatium*), but this can hardly be the sense here. The compound will not bear the sense desired by Fracarroli, 'crossed by couriers' (supposedly a reference to the Persian ἄγγαροι).

43–4. Wilamowitz tentatively suggests πλάκ' ὁ]μβρίαν ἀρ[ῶν 'ploughing the watery plain', which he understands to be a reference to swimming. Page proposes *δυcο]μβρίαν, which he presumably wants to mean 'wretched water' (tr. Campbell); the form δύcομβροc already exists as a hapax at S. *Ant.* 358 δύcομβρα . . . βέλη 'stormy missiles', perhaps with the implication of a 'cloud' of arrows. The rest of the lacuna is more easily dealt with: Wilamowitz provides the desired sense with ϲκέλεϲι, which Page improves with ποϲί τε χ]ερϲίν. It is, of course, with the hands and feet that one strikes the water if one is trying to keep afloat, or to paddle a raft.

45. ἔ]πλει: at *Od.* 5. 240 we find the verb with the sense 'floating': *(δένδρεα)* . . . αὖα πάλαι, περίκηλα, τά οἱ πλώοιεν ἐλαφρῶϲ, and the phrase αὖα πάλαι, περίκηλα is repeated at *Od.* 18. 309 of firewood. 'The poet appears still to be thinking of a raft, for ship timber was not permitted to dry out' (Hainsworth on *Od.* 5. 240); it is highly likely that we are to think of a similar sense here.

νηϲιώταϲ: see 40 n.

46. θεινόμε[νοϲ: 'being dashed', 'battered'; an effective word, cf. esp. A. *Pers.* 302–3 Ἀρτεμβάρηϲ . . . ϲτύφλουϲ παρ᾽ ἀκτὰϲ θείνεται Ϲιληνιῶν. The papyrus is particularly unclear at this point; we might also read ϲτεινόμε[νοϲ 'distressed', though there seems to be a curve at the top left hand of the traces which makes τ less likely. Page plausibly supplements [ποντίαι]ϲ θεινόμε[νοϲ ἄταιϲ], Wilamowitz [ἀνέμοι]ϲ.

47. διεξόδουϲ μ[. . . .]ν: διεξόδουϲ 'ways of escape' seems certain; Wilamowitz is no doubt right to surmise that μ[ατεύω]ν is the correct sort of verb to supplement, but the lacuna may be too short. MLW suggests μ[ετρῶ]ν, which could mean 'counting the ways of escape'; a rather remarkable activity for a drowning man? Possibly μάταν δ]ιεξόδουϲ μ[ετρῶ]ν; but μάταν might be slightly too long for the first lacuna.

48. ἰϲόρροπα: probably adverbial, 'equally'.

παλευο[: the obvious supplement is παλευό[μενοϲ; παλεύω is found at Ar. *Av.* 1083, 1087, of using a decoy bird as a trap (Dunbar ad loc.); the passive 'to be decoyed' is late (of a bird at Philostr. *Im.* 2. 33). The image may here be metaphorical. Alternatively, we could emend to ϲαλευο- 'shaken to and fro' (at e.g. [A.] *Pr.* 1081), or παλε{υ}ο- (e.g. παλέ{υ}ο[ντα?) 'wrecked, disabled'; the latter is rare, but attested at Hdt. 8. 21. 1 in an appropriate context: . . . εἰ παλήϲειε ὁ ναυτικὸϲ ϲτρατόϲ. The element παλευ- recurs at 57 διαπαλεύων, where the sense is uncertain; δια- may have the force of 'completely'.

49–59. A (sea-?) god is invoked, perhaps Poseidon (50 κάλει θ[αλάϲ]ϲιον θεόν; or κάλει θ[᾽?), who is probably also the πατήρ mentioned at 51 (or possibly, with GOH, πατέρα τ[ε Δία); the following passage presumably contains some direct speech, although since no first- or second-person verbal forms survive in the fragmentary text this cannot be confirmed. At 53 Περcᾶν seems certain. Wilamowitz suggests ἀμ]βλὺ δ' ὠ[χ]ρὸν at 55 'blunt, pale'. At 57 βάcιμον and δίοδον look as if they should be connected, 'a way through to tread on', and might be related to the ways of escape mentioned at 47; a contrast could be made with 58 δ]εcμ[ὸ]c [ἄπ]ειροc (?) 'unending imprisonment', unless we are to read ἑcμόc 'swarm, stream' with Danielsson. At 58 ναΐοιc is certain; the preceding word might be ἀμφί, or perhaps a dative in -φι, although these are not otherwise attested in Timotheus. At the end of the line, ἐ]λιχθείc is universally and rightly read; for the problematic τρυ[a form of τρύω would perhaps fit, but the sense and syntax are completely uncertain. Danielsson atractively supplements ἀμ]φὶ ναΐοιc τρύ[φεcιν ἐ]λιχθείc 'an die Schiffstrümmern angeklammert'.

60–4. Janssen suggests that Timotheus was here inspired by Empd. 31 B 100 DK = fr. 91. 10–15 Wright (of a girl playing with a clepsydra) εὖτε μὲν αὐλοῦ πορθμὸν ἐπ' εὐειδεῖ χερὶ θεῖcα | εἰc ὕδατος βάπτηιcι τέρεν δέμαc ἀργυφέοιο | †οὐδετ' ἐc† ἄγγοc δ' ὄμβροc ἐcέρχεται, ἀλλά μιν εἴργει | ἀέροc ὄγκοc ἔcωθε πεcὼν ἐπὶ τρήματα πυκνά, | εἰcόκ' ἀποcτεγάcηι πυκινὸν ῥόον· αὐτὰρ ἔπειτα | πνεύματοc ἐλλείποντοc ἐcέρχεται αἴcιμον ὕδωρ 'when she puts the mouth of the pipe against her shapely hand, and dips it into the smooth body of shining water, no liquid enters the vessel, but the mass of air pressing from inside against the close-set perforations holds it back until she releases the compressed current; but then, as the air escapes, a due amount of water enters'. But although Empedocles is at this point discussing respiration, it seems unlikely that Timotheus would have had this passage in mind; there are superficial verbal similarities (e.g. †οὐδετ' ἐc† ἄγγοc δ' ὄμβροc ἐcέρχεται), but these are not by any means extensive, and the sense required for ἄγγοc is different in each passage.

60. τᾶι . . . τᾶι (δ'): the opposition here has caused some confusion. Danielsson emends the first τᾶι to παι, presumably with the sense 'whenever the winds attacked in some place', but this is too indefinite to correspond to ταῖ in the second clause. Gargiulo argues that if we read ταῖ δ(έ), instead of Wilamowitz's ταῖδε, the second ταῖ might be resumptive (cf. *P.* 216–17); I cannot see how this fits with the two different verbs. His tentative ταί (taking up αὖραι) has little to recommend it: this form is never found in Timotheus. The sense must surely be that seen by Campbell, 'in one place . . . in another' (for which we may compare e.g. *P.* 7–11); the contrast between the two uses is sufficiently indicated by δέ, and by the change from the optative (λείποιεν) to the indicative (ἐπεισέπιπτον), which indicates the transition from subordinate to main clause (Rijksbaron 85–6).

αὖραι: most naturally understood as 'winds', rather than as the 'air above the waves' (Janssen). Wilamowitz objects to to αὖραι as the subject of ἐπεισέπιπτον, but cf. e.g. Hes. *Th.* 872 ff. αἱ δ᾽ ἄλλαι μάψ αὖραι ἐπιπνείουσι θάλασσαν· | αἳ δή τοι πίπτουσαι ἐς ἠεροειδέα πόντον, | πῆμα μέγα θνητοῖςι, κακῆι θυίουςιν ἀέλληι.

61–2. ἄφρει δ᾽ ἀβακχίωτος ὄμβρος: 'and the unbacchic spray foamed'; the papyrus' αφρωιϲδε (*fort.* αφρωι[ϲ]δε) obviously requires emendation. (1) Page proposes ἀφρῶι δ᾽ ⟨ὖ⟩ ἀβ. ὄμβρος; ὕω usually takes Ζεύς *vel sim.* as its subject, and this is true even in cases where the verb appears impersonal (e.g. at Hdt. 4. 28. 2, where the masculine participle ὕων implies a masculine subject); see Wilhelm Schulze, *Kleine Schriften*, 2nd edn. (Göttingen, 1966), 854–7. However, Apollonius has ὄμβρος . . . ὗε . . . πόντον καὶ νῆϲον of a storm (2. 1115). There are no parallels contemporary with Timotheus. (2) Wilamowitz writes ἀφρώδηϲ, and takes the verb to be ἐπεισέπιπτεν (emended from -πιπτον at 61): 'whenever the winds left off in one place, the foaming unbacchic water attacked in another'; but we have seen that there is no reason to emend ἐπεισέπιπτον. (3) Gargiulo sees connections with sympotic language; accepting Page's ἀφρῶι, he posits δ᾽ ἔ⟨ζε᾽⟩ (comparing the scribal errors at *P.* 190 τετράο⟨ρο⟩ν, 227 ν⟨ιν⟩). Sudhaus, retaining ἀφρῶι, had already proposed ⟨περιέζεςεν⟩; but the lacuna here would be surprisingly long, and we should expect an imperfect here. ἔ⟨ζε᾽⟩ has much to recommend it for the sense (cf. Theophil. fr. 2. 1–3 K.–A.), but by this date we expect contraction of the sequence εε; the disyllabic pronunciation is improbable even in verse.

Both Page and Gargiulo are correct to look for a verb; ἄφρει (Danielsson) or ἄφριζε(ν) (Sitzler) gives the right sense. ἀφρίζω is more widely attested in drama (S. *El.* 719, Alexis fr. 124. 3 K.–A.); ἄφρεον is found in poetry at e.g. *Il.* 11. 282, and seems better to explain the corruption in the papyrus. For the image, cf. also Timoth. fr. 780. 2.

62. ἀβακχίωτος ὄμβρος: the water described as ὄμβρος is probably the sea-spray; the word more normally means 'rain', 'storm'; here Gargiulo, Janssen, and others compare S. *OT* 1427–8 τὸ μήτε γῆ | μήτ᾽ ὄμβρος ἱερὸς μήτε φῶς προσδέξεται, where, however, 'ὄμβρος is not a synonym but a symbol of water generally' (Jebb). Timotheus' usage is not precisely paralleled, but cf. perhaps δρόσος, which has a wide variety of uses, and Latin *imber*, so used from Ennius, *Ann.* 516 Skutsch onwards, and in the general sense of water from v. 221. The spray 'foams' because it is thrown up by the winds as they attack. Rainwater can, of course, be drunk; the water here is unbacchic because it is, unlike wine, undrinkable.

The expression has some similarity to the phrases at e.g. S. *OT* 1214 γάμοι ἄγαμοι, E. *Or.* 319–20 ἀβάκχευτον . . . θίασον, 621 ἀνηφαίστωι πυρί, though in these cases the adjective negates an essential characteristic of the noun (see Breitenbach, 236 ff.; J. Diggle, *PCPS*² 20 (1974), 11–12 = *Euripidea*, 101–2). By contrast, it is not an essential quality of ὄμβρος that it be 'Bacchic'.

ἀβακχίωτος: for the unusual formation -ίωτος, formed on the theme βακχιο-, cf. βακχιώτης (S. *OC* 678), Βακχειώτην (*SLG* adesp. 318; perhaps in hexameters) and βακχιόω (only at S. fr. 959. 1 Radt). For Βάκχος 'wine', cf. E. *IA* 1061, *IT* 164, *Cyc.* 519–20, and see Dodds on E. *Ba.* 274–85 (Δημήτηρ 'grain', Διόνυσος 'wine') and 625–6 (Ἀχελῷος 'water'), Timoth. fr. 780. 4 n. The adjective may have been chosen here under the influence of ἄφρει; cf. ἀφρίζω of wine at e.g. Antiphanes fr. 172. 4 K.–A.; Alexis fr. 124. 3 K.–A., where Arnott's comment, 'a brief emergence of riddling language in the dithyrambic style', is unjustified; further Pi. *O.* 7. 1–2 φιάλαν . . . ἔνδον ἀμπέλου καχλάζοιϲαν δρόϲωι. The papyrus spelling -χχ- instead of -κχ was already used in the 5th/4th c., probably the result of assimilation of κ to χ (cf. also 165 ἐχ χερῶν). Threatte, i. 541 ff., cites Βάχχε (*ARV²* p. 1158), Βάχχη (*ARV²* p. 1159 ii), Βάχχιοϲ (*ABV* p. 413) as examples from Attic inscriptions; Mayser–Schmoll i/1. 186 give forms such as Βάχχοϲ, Βαχχίου as later instances from the Ptolemaic papyri.

63. τρόφιμον ἄγγοϲ: 'his alimentary vessel', i.e. his stomach, or possibly the whole alimentary tract up to the oesophagus. The description continues the imagery associated with drinking; the normal liquid which would be poured into one's stomach would, of course, be wine.

τρόφιμοϲ is a fifth-century (Euripidean) innovation, with both an active (*Tro.* 235, *Ion* 235) and a passive sense (*Ion* 684), later adopted by medical writers; see C. Arbenz, *Die Adjektive auf -ιμοϲ* (Tübingen, 1933), 51. The suffix is highly productive in the fifth century, and is remarkably prominent in Timotheus (e.g. *P.* 64, 78, 114).

64. ἀμβόλιμοϲ: 'surging up', not 'back-thrown' (so e.g. Edmonds, Janssen), which gives little sense and does not agree with the uses of the verb ἀναβάλλω; cf. similar formations based on the same verb; e.g. ἀμβολαδίϲ 'with uplifted arms', ἀμβολάδην 'bubbling up' (esp. *Il.* 21. 362 ff. ὡϲ δὲ λέβηϲ ζεῖ ἔνδον ἐπειγόμενοϲ πυρὶ πολλῶι | . . . πάντοθεν ἀμβολάδην, Hdt. 4. 181. 4, Polem. Hist. 83 ἀναβολάδην ζέοντα ὕδατα). Janssen's appeal to logic is misplaced: 'how could the drowning man speak as he does, if the waves really surged over his mouth?'; the situation is not a real one, and poetry does not work at this level. The homoioteleuton of -ιμο- here and in 63 is typical of Timotheus' style.

The sense appears to be a Timothean neologism; otherwise the word has the technical legal sense 'adjourned', in inscriptions and Hsch. (α 4206) ἀναβόλιμοι δίκαι· αἱ διὰ περίϲταϲιν εἰϲ ὑπέρθεϲιν ἐμπίπτουϲιν.

65. ϲτόματοϲ: perhaps genitive after ἀμβόλιμοϲ 'surging up from his mouth', rather than after ὑπερέθυιεν 'foamed over his mouth' (Janssen).

ὑπερέθυιεν: 'raged'; the sea seems here to be personified, though θύ(ι)ω is used in epic of rivers (*Il.* 21. 234) and the sea (Hes. *Th.* 109, 131, *Il.* 23. 230), and is thus connected with the action of water at an early stage (cf. also Alexis fr. 5 K.–A. μεστὴν ἀκράτου Θηρίκλειον ἔσπασεν | κοίλην ὑπερθύουσαν). The Homeric MSS transmit both θύω and θυίω, but the latter is probably older; cf. Hes. *Th.* 109 with West. υι- is also Ionic–Aeolic against Attic υ- (Chantraine, *Grammaire*, i. 50–1; Kühner-Blass i. 136, ii. 88; Schwyzer i. 868; K. Meisterhans, *Grammatik der attischen Inschriften* (Berlin, 1900³), 59–60; W. Schulze, *Quaestiones Epicae* (Gütersloh, 1892), 331 ff.).

65a–66. ὀξυπαραυδήτωι φωνᾶ⟨ι⟩: the second element of the compound may also have medical connotations. Danielsson persuasively compares παραλέγω 'rave', παραληρέω 'babble, talk nonsense' (also at Ar. *Eq.* 531, *Ra.* 594; cf. παράληρος 'raving, delirious'); the epic meanings of παραυδάω are clearly less appropriate here ('console, encourage' at e.g. *Od.* 15. 53, 16. 279, 18. 178; 'speak lightly of' at *Od.* 11. 488). Compounds in -αύδητος are otherwise generally rare, except for ἀναύδητος in tragedy; for compounds formed from compound verbs, see 21–2 n. Abandonment to grief was often regarded by the Greeks as characteristic of Orientals, and their formalized style of lamentation became a literary *topos*; see Hall, *Barbarian*, 83–4.

66–7. παρακόπωι . . . δόξαι φρενῶν: 'with maddened fancy of his mind'; i.e. with confused (mental) perceptions. The man is of course not literally mad; he is simply enraged and confused because he is drowning.

There may be some influence from A. *Eum.* 329 ff. παρακοπά, | παραφορὰ φρενοδαλής, | ὕμνος ἐξ Ἐρινύων | δέσμιος φρενῶν; this and E. *Ba.* 33 ὅρος δ' οἰκοῦσι παράκοποι φρενῶν could be cited as support for linking παρακόπωι with φρενῶν; cf. also *Hipp.* 238 παρακόπτει φρένας; Hp. *Epid.* 3. 17.ε´ παρακοπὴ . . . τῆς γνώμης. But here it is more natural to take φρενῶν as a genitive depending on δόξαι, and the phrase may be a simple periphrasis for φρένες.

68. κατακορής 'immoderately'; cf. Pl. *Phaedr.* 240 E εἰς δὲ μέθην ἰόντος πρὸς τῶι μὴ ἀνειστῶι ἐπαισχεῖς παρρησίαι κατακορεῖ καὶ ἀναπεπταμένης χρωμένος, Arist. *Rhet.* 3. 3. 1406ᵃ13 (of a λόγος); the meaning 'full' (cf. Campbell 'sated by it all') is confined to late authors. It is no doubt to be connected rather with the verb ἀπείλει than with γόμφους ἐμπρίων 'gnashing his teeth immoderately'.

69. γόμφους ἐμπρίων: 'gnashing his teeth'. The usual word for 'molar' is γομφίος, although it is more common in comedy (e.g. Ar. *Pax* 34, Epicharmus fr. 21 Kaibel); it may have been regarded as vulgar. Wilamowitz convincingly suggests that it is here replaced by γόμφος in order to avoid the apparent (and less poetic) diminutive. For γόμφος as 'teeth', cf. Hsch. γ 805: γόμφοι· μύλοι . . . καὶ ὀδόντες γομφίοι, Dsc. 4. 164 γομφαλγία 'toothache'. The avoidance of the 'less poetic' here may seem odd; Timotheus has no such concerns when he borrows the Celaenaean's barbarized Greek from comedy later in the poem. However, although various genres and styles contribute to the overall effect, they tend to be confined to individual sections. Thus tragedy is particularly influential in the King's flight and lamentation, no doubt to contrast with the preceding use of comic forms.

The papyrus gives γόμφοις, but we expect an accusative after ἐμπρίων as at D.S. 17. 92. 3 ὀδόντας ἐμπεπρικώς, Lucian, *Somn.* 14 (cf. Ar. *Ra.* 927 μὴ πρῖε τοὺς ὀδόντας), unless the case has been influenced by the prefix ἐν- (the sense 'bite deep into' as at D.S. 10. 17 τὸ οὖς ἐνέπρισε τοῖς ὀδοῦσι is clearly not required). The corruption is a minor one. Wilamowitz cites Opp. *H*. 5. 185–6 γένυν σκολιοῖσι χαλινοῖς ἐμπρίει, where, however, the verb is construed differently. Inama compares Lat. *infrendere dentibus* (e.g. Verg. *A*. 3. 664), but it is not clear that the two phrases are directly comparable.

70. †μιμούμενος: the whole clause here is problematic. (1) Wilamowitz takes μιμούμενος with γόμφους ἐμπρίων and paraphrases μιμεῖται γὰρ τὸν τοῖς ὀδοῦσι τὸν ἀντίπαλον ἐμπρίοντα, but it is improbable that the sentence could be construed in this way. (2) Diehl prefers the accusative θαλάς⟨ς⟩ας, 'imitating the sea', but the plural is unjustified, and it is difficult to read λυμεῶνι cώματος as an indirect object after ἐμπρίων ('gnashing his teeth at the destroyer of his body'?); in any case the phrase looks as if it were in apposition to θαλάς⟨ς⟩αι. (3) Aron takes λυμεῶνι cώματος as the object of ἀπείλει 'he immoderately threatened the sea', and thinks θαλάς⟨c⟩ας the object of μιμούμενος, but fails to explain adquately what this would mean. (4) Sudhaus also requires an object and emends both λυμεῶνι and θαλάς⟨c⟩αι to λυμεῶνα and θάλας⟨c⟩αν, which provides better syntax, but worse sense (explained as βοῶν . . . ὥσπερ ἡ θάλαττα). (5) Gildersleeve gives us the unconvincing explanation '*imitatus (regem Xerxem)*', but the King is not mentioned until 76; it would hardly be clear to an audience that this was the intended meaning. (6) Gargiulo believes that γόμφοις may allude to the nails of Xerxes' ship-bridge (cf. A. *Pers.* 71–2 πολύγομφον ὅδισμα ζυγὸν ἀμφιβαλὼν αὐχένι πόντου), and argues that this might explain the 'imitation': 'minacciava, mordendo con i denti, imitando colui che aveva maltratto il corpo del mare'; he suggests μιμούμενος λυμεῶνα cώματος θαλάς⟨c⟩ας. However, that this allusion is to be found in γόμφοις is highly improbable; and Gargiulo's parallels (Timoth. fr. 780. 1–2, 4–6, fr. 789) for the sequence of words, verb + object + objective genitive + possessive genitive, are not parallels at all.

μιμούμενος is clearly dubious. Danielsson proposes βριμού-μενος 'indignant' (corrected by Inama, 645, to βριμώμενος, from βριμάομαι; but βριμόομαι is attested at X. *Cyr.* 4. 5. 9, and explained as ἀπειλεῖ at Ael. Dion. fr. 95); more attractive is perhaps van Leeuwen's θυμούμενος 'angry', though neither of these suggestions contributes significantly to the sense of the passage. Keil ingeniously suggests λαιμοῦ μένος 'the strength of his throat', and, accepting γόμφοις, takes it as object of ἐμπρίων; but it is doubtful whether this could really be the required sense, or even physiologically plausible. μύλου μένος 'the strength of his molars' (MLW), accusative after ἐμπρίων, is slightly better, but otiose with γόμφους/-οις. Janssen proposes μιγνύμενος, 'engaged in a hand-to-hand fight', but this sense of the verb usually requires an explanatory phrase (e.g. ἐν δαΐ, ἐν παλάμηισι); since the upsilon is short, this conjecture would necessitate –∪∪––∪–, presumably, though Janssen does not say so, *ch cr* (choriambs appear elsewhere in *P.* in an iambo-trochaic context). C. Collard (*per litt.*) suggests δινούμενος.

λυμεῶνι cώματος: 'the destroyer of his body', in apposition to θαλάς⟨c⟩αι. The sea will not literally destroy his body, but the forceful personification here prepares for the Islander's abusive speech in the following lines.

The rare Attic–Ionic substantival formation in -εών may be a fifth-century innovation; cf. the forms ἀπατεών, ὀργεών, κοινεών, with Chantraine, *Formation*, 163, and W. Headlam, *CR* 15 (1901), 401–4, who argues that most (though not λυμεών) should be paroxytone.

72–81. The Islander: Speech. There are several direct parallels to Aeschylus' *Persae* in the speech. Most notably we can cite A. *Pers.* 70–1 and 747–8 ~ *P.* 72–3, both of which relate to the yoking of the Hellespont, and *Pers.* 723 ~ *P.* 77. The yoking of the Hellespont was for Aeschylus an important act of hubris closely associated with the Persian defeat; cf. A. *Pers.* 69 ff., 725, 744–6: in the last passage Darius explicitly attributes Xerxes' defeat to the act; see also B. H. Fowler, *C&M* 28 (1970), 3–10; M. Anderson, *G&R* 19 (1972), 166–7. In Aeschylus 'yoking the Hellespont' usually refers to the construction of the ship-bridge; Herodotus records another story, in which Xerxes scourged the water with whips, and cast a pair of fetters (πεδέων ζεῦγος) into it after the destruction of the first bridge (7. 35); C. Faraone, *ClAnt* 10 (1991), 165–220, provides evidence for the use of bound images to control inimical gods or demons. Simonides' elegy on Plataea (fr. 11) may also have attributed the Persian defeat to an element of divine vengeance; see M. L. West, *ZPE* 98 (1993), 7, who supplements θεῶν τεράε]cci πεποιθότεc at l. 39 and cites the good sacrificial omens mentioned by Hdt. 9. 19. 12. Other attacks on rivers are sometimes associated with hubris: at Hdt. 2. 111 the violent attack by the Egyptian king Pheros on the Nile is followed by blindness, which is only cured by propitiating the river's anger.

Timotheus, however, nowhere offers a direct explanation of the Persian defeat, or suggests divine intervention in any firm way. Possibly the allusion to Aeschylus' version here should recall the idea; and the divine shout heard at Salamis (A. *Pers.* 402 ff.; Hdt. 8. 84. 2) may have been mentioned early in the poem (cf. fr. 789 n.). But there is a general absence of divine characters; the only gods mentioned in the extant portion describing the battle are

Poseidon(?), the Mountain Mother (invoked at 127 ff.), and Artemis (mentioned at 160), the latter both appearing in speeches; Amphitrite's name probably appears as a metonym at 39, and Bacchus in ἀβακχίωτος at 62. Timotheus seems to be offering a version of events which is explicitly not mythologized, and he also avoids any direct comment on the narrative.

Metre

72   — — ∪ — ∪ — ∪ — |
      — ∪ — ∪ — ∪ — |
          ∪ — ∪ — — — ∪ ∪∪ ∪ — ∪ — |
75   — ∪ ∪∪ ∪ — — ||
      ∪ ∪∪ — ∪ — |
      — — ∪ ∪∪ ∪ — ∪ —
              — — ∪ ∪∪ ∪ ∪∪ ∪ ∪∪ ∪ — — |
      — ∪ ∪ — ∪∪ ∪ — ∫
80   — ∪ — — — ∪ — ∫
      ∪∪ ∪ ∪∪ ∪ — — ||

The speech begins with pure iambics mixed with syncopated forms (73 *lk*, 75 *ith*); at 75 Sitzler suggested ἀνταράξει from ἀντί + ἀράσσω; this would also produce *ith*, but the compound is not attested elsewhere, and ἀράσσω is not found of water. Period-end at 75 is ensured by the hiatus (cf. 128, 131, 155, 156, etc.). At the beginning of the period at 76 there seems to be an isolated dochmiac, or dochmiac-shaped metron; Wilamowitz notes that it emphasizes the mention of the King. Its presence here is nevertheless slightly unusual; but the form ∪ ∪∪ — ∪ — is common, accounting for about 650 examples of the dochmiac in drama (Parker, *Songs*, 65), and there is an earlier sequence of dochmiacs at 65a–69. For the pattern of anadiplosis in the dochmiac, see J. Diggle, *CQ²* 40 (1990), 109–11 = *Euripidea*, 376–8. The isolated dochmiac leads into another iambic sequence, with a single choriamb in association with a cretic at 79.

72–81. ' "Already even before now in arrogance you had your turbulent neck yoked in a hemp-bound fetter; but now my lord, mine, will stir you up with his mountain-born pines, and enclose your navigable plains with his wandering sailors, you enraged ancient object of hate, untrustworthy darling of the swift and drenching wind." '

72. θρασεῖα: 'in arrogance'; λάβρον echoes the image. The

sea's θράcoc is probably the destruction of the first ship-
bridge over the Hellespont; θραcύc generally has an unfavourable connotation; significantly, the noun is used by
Aeschylus to describe Xerxes' actions at *Pers.* 829 ff. πρὸc
ταῦτ' ἐκεῖνον, †cωφρονεῖν κεχρημένον† | πινύcκετ' εὐλόγοιcι
νουθετήμαcιν | λῆξαι θεοβλαβοῦνθ' ὑπερκόμπωι θράcει. The
point here may be ironic; the Asiatic maintains the arrogant
and confident attitude which has, it seems, led directly to the
situation in which he finds himself. An effective contrast is
provided by the later speaker at 114 ff., who may also refer to
the ship-bridge, but who wishes it had never been built.
Timotheus frequently develops motifs in this way as the
Persian situation worsens.

καὶ πάρος: 'even before now', emphatic (pleonastic) after
ἤδη. πάρος is never used in Attic prose, but is frequent in
epic and tragedy. For the emphatic use of καί 'even', see
Denniston 317–18.

73. λάβρον: 'turbulent'; the adjective frequently describes
the turbulence of the sea; it is also used of the action of the
wind, which may also be alluded to here (the violent action
of the wind on the waves). Aeschylus uses it in the latter
sense at *Pers.* 109–11 εὐρυπόροιο θαλάccαc | πολιαινομέναc
πνεύματι λάβρωι | . . . πόντιον ἄλcοc. The derived sense
'fierce' or 'violent', used of people, is no doubt also operative.

λάβρον αὐχέν(α) is probably accusative after ἔcχεc, though
Janssen takes it as an accusative of respect after periphrastic
ἔcχεc . . . καταζευχθεῖcα (see n.). The scansion λαβ'ρ- is to be
expected; λαβρ-, the standard Attic pronunciation, appears
only occasionally even in fifth-century verse (e.g. E. *Herc.*
861, *Or.* 697).

αὐχέν': after A. *Pers.* 71 ζυγὸν ἀμφιβαλὼν αὐχένι πόντου.

ἔcχεc . . . καταζευχθεῖcα: Janssen takes this to be a
periphrastic use of ἔχω with the participle for the perfect
(i.e. expressing present result of a past action), 'you have
been yoked'. But the aorist ἔcχεc is unusual; normally an
imperfect or present would be expected. The participle
usually stands in the aorist (as here), more rarely in the
perfect (Kühner–Gerth ii. 61; W. J. Aerts, *Periphrastica*
(Amsterdam, 1965), 128 ff.); but it is very rarely passive (e.g.

Hdt. 7. 143. 1; Pl. *Crat.* 404 c), and the word-order here favours taking αὐχέν᾽ ἔςχες ἐμ πέδαι as the main clause, 'you had your neck in a fetter', with the participle used independently, καταζευχθεῖcα 'when you were yoked'.

74. πέδαι: probably after A. *Pers.* 747–8 καὶ πόρον μετερρύθμιζε καὶ πέδαις сφυρηλάτοις | περιβαλὼν πολλὴν κέλευθον ἤνυсεν πολλῶι στρατῶι, or Hdt. 7. 35. 1 δεινὰ ποιεύμενος τὸν Ἑλλήсποντον ἐκέλευсε τριηκοсίας ἐπικέсθαι μάстιγι πληγὰς καὶ κατεῖναι ἐς τὸ πέλαγος πεδέων ζεῦγος. Both passages suggest a plural is desiderated; πέδαι⟨c⟩ is possible, though λινοδέτωι would need to be emended to λινοδέτοις. The plural is otherwise standard in Aeschylus (*Cho.* 493, 982, *Eum.* 645) and Euripides (frr. 595, 670. 5 N²).

λινοδέτωι: 'bound with hemp'; cf. A. *Pers.* 70 λινοδέсμωι сχεδίαι (with reference to the yoking of the Hellespont). Herodotus states that six cables were used for the second ship-bridge, two of λευκόλινος (not white flax, which would have been too weak, but hemp) and four of papyrus (Hdt. 7. 7. 36); Timotheus may have seen these cables, which were reportedly brought to Athens as trophies after the war (Hdt. 9. 121).

λινόδετος first appears at Ar. *Nub.* 763 λινόδετον ὥσπερ μηλολόνθην; then at E. *IT* 1043 οὗ ναῦς χαλινοῖς λινοδέτοις ὁρμεῖ сέθεν 'where your ship is moored with bridles bound with hemp'. χαλινοῖς here refers not to the ship's cables but to its anchors (cf. Pi. *P.* 4. 25 with Braswell, S. *OC* 694, E. *Hec.* 539–40), of which there were two on Greek ships (Morrison–Williams 302–3): T. C. W. Stinton, *GRBS* 17 (1976), 323–8 = *Coll. Pap.* 265–70, notes that by the fifth century at least the word was a technical term, although it may have been derived from an earlier poetic metaphor.

τεόν: this form of the possessive is, in fifth-century tragedy, firmly attested only in Aeschylus (*Sept.* 105; [A.] *Pr.* 162–3) and Sophocles (*Ant.* 604); it is also conjectured in Euripides at *Med.* 1255, *Heracl.* 911, *El.* 1185 (see Page on E. *Med.* 1255). It is not common in early lyric, but belongs if anywhere to the fifth century and later: e.g. Pi. *O.* 4. 1, Simon. fr. 543. 13, and perhaps fr. 519 fr. 4. 5; Praxilla fr. 748; [Timoth.] fr. 794 τεὰ δῶρα; *PMG* adesp. 1019. 6 [5th/4th c. BC?]. The 'poet' of Ar. *Av.* 904 ff. uses the form twice, at 906–7 τεαῖc . . . ἀοιδαῖc, 938 τέαι φρενί. Later Corinna uses it at fr. 654 iii 8(?), 19, and 695(*a*). Among the lyric adespota, we find it also in the very late hymn to Pan, *PMG* adesp. 936. 17 (for the date see 198 n.); and in adesp. 1037. 3, apparently late but written in imitation of earlier dithyrambic poetry.

75. ἀναταράξει: 'will stir up', suggesting the stirring of the waters by the oars; the use of ταράccω is traditional for the stirring up of the sea (e.g. *Od*. 5. 304, Archil. fr. 105. 1–2, Solon fr. 12. 1, E. *Tro*. 88, 692). Normally it refers to the action of divine or natural powers; perhaps the verb marks the pretensions of the Great King to divine status. The form with a preverb is attested before Timotheus only at S. *Tr*. 218 ff. ἰδού μ' ἀναταράccει . . . ὁ κιccóc, where it has a metaphorical sense, perhaps partly operative here; Simon. fr. 571 has ἴcχει δέ με πορφυρέας ἁλὸς ἀμφιταραccομένας ὀρυμαγδός, referring to the surging sea around an island, where ἀμφιταράccομαι is a hapax. Timotheus here indulges in a similar variation on a standard formula. Hall, 'Drowning', 64, sees a reference to Xerxes' attempt to build a bridge from Attica to Salamis after the battle (Hdt. 8. 97), but the verb hardly seems appropriate to the construction of a bridge; there is no reason to assume so specific a threat on the Asiatic's part.

76. ἐμὸc ἄναξ ἐμόc: 'my lord'; cf. 129 ἐμὸν ἐμὸν αἰῶνα, Pratinas fr. 708. 3 ἐμὸc ἐμὸc ὁ Βρόμιοc, E. *El*. 1149 ἐμὸc ἐμὸc ἀρχέτας, *Herc*. ἐμὸc ἐμὸc ὅδε γόνοc. There is no precise parallel for repeated ἐμόc separated by its substantive, but it is not uncommon with other types of word; for some relevant Euripidean cases see e.g. *Hipp*. 826 τίνι λόγωι . . . τίνι, *Hec*. 1063 τάλαινα κόραι τάλαινα, *Suppl*. 281 οἰκτρὸν ἰήλεμον οἰκτρόν, *Or*. 1537 ἕτερον εἰc ἀγῶν' ἕτερον. Indeed, repetition of this sort is particularly associated with highly emotional passages in later Euripidean lyric (Breitenbach 214–21). Hall, *Barbarian*, 119 less plausibly sees a possible connection with 'Orientalism', noting the high occurrence of repetition in the Phrygian's aria in *Orestes*, and in the chorus of *Phoenissae*; there is little to distinguish the latter from non-Oriental choruses, while the level of anadiplosis in the Phrygian's aria may simply indicate the high emotion of the passage.

Though there are some (casual?) phonetic repetitions in Timotheus, genuine anadiplosis is comparatively rare.

ἄναξ is the usual epic and tragic word for 'king', although outside poetry in the fifth century it is restricted to cultic contexts; the word need not stress the divinity of the Persian king (thus Janssen), despite the hint in ἀναταράξει (see 75 n.). There is some evidence that it was used as a loan-word in Asiatic languages: *wa-na-k-s* occurs as a translation for Phoen. *'dn* (*'adon*) in a bilingual Cypriot inscription (*ICS* 220. 2 p. 246; the Cypriot text also in *DGE* 680). Midas is described as *vanaks* in an OPhryg. inscription (*c*.600 BC), although it is uncertain whether the word here is native to Phrygian or a Greek loan-word; see O. Haas, *Die phry- gischen Sprachdenkmäler* (Sofia, 1966), 185–9; E. Benveniste, *Le Vocabulaire des institutions indo-européennes* (Paris, 1969⁶), ii. 24.

77. πεύκαισιν ὀριγόνοισιν: 'with mountain-born pines'; πεύκαισιν probably means ships as at 13 (see also 5–6 n.). The verb might encourage us to agree with Wilamowitz and to understand 'oars', but there is no reason why the King could not stir up the water with his ships.

ὀριγόνοισιν: 'born in the mountains', since mountains are less likely to suffer the effects of agriculture, and so to provide an abundance of timber: thus the Argo is made from wood cut in the groves of Pelion (cf. E. *Med.* 1 ff., and its imitations, Ennius, *Med.* fr. 103 Jocelyn, Catull. 64. 1). We normally expect ὄρος to have a sigmatic root (ὀρεσ-: e.g. ὀρεσκῶιος) or a dative–locative stem (sg. ὀρει-, pl. ὀρεσί-: e.g. ὀρειλεχής, ὀρεσίτροφος). These formations persist well into the classical period: e.g. ὀρείκτιτος first at Pi. fr. 313; ὀρεσσίγονος first at A. fr. 168 Radt; and ὀρειγενής first at Moschion, *TrGF* 97 F 6. 5, then Nic. *Th.* 874. The metrically assured instances of ὀρι- are all fifth-century or later: E. *Ba.* 985 ὀριδρόμων, *Phaeth.* 71 Diggle οὐριβάται, Ar. *Av.* 276 ὀριβάτης (paratragic: see Dunbar ad loc.), *PMG* adesp. 924. 10 ὀρικοίτος (= Ba. fr. 66 dub.), Opp. *Cyn.* 1. 24 Ὀρίβακχος. The innovation was perhaps made by analogy with the alternative dative forms of δόρυ (and similar words): δο(υ)ρί (actually from the historic locative *δορϝί) and δόρει (the historic dative), although the latter does not occur in compounds. See also Schwyzer i. 448; Fraenkel, *Kl. Beitr.* i. 431–2.

ἐγκλήιcει: perhaps after A. *Pers.* 723 καὶ τόδ᾽ ἐξέπραξεν ὥcτε Βόcπορον κλῆιcαι μέγαν;, which also refers to the ship-bridge over the Hellespont; but the verb appears in similar contexts elsewhere, as at Thuc. 4. 8. 7 τοὺc μὲν οὖν ἔcπλουc ταῖc ναυcὶν ἀντιπρώιροιc βύζην κλήιcειν ἔμελλον, 7. 59. 3 ἔγκληιον τὸν λιμένα εὐθὺc τὸν μέγαν . . . τριήρεcι πλαγίαιc.

78. πεδία πλόϊμα: 'navigable plains', i.e. sea; cf. A. fr. 150 Radt δελφινοφόρον πόντου πεδίον διαμειψάμεναι, Ion, *TrGF* 19 F 60 ὅταν πεδίον Αἰγαῖον δράμω, E. *Ph.* 209–10 περιρρύτων | ὑπὲρ ἀκαρπίcτων πεδίων. The alliteration seems typical of Timotheus (cf. also νομάcι ναύταιc, 189 μηκέτι μέλλετε), though D. Fehling, *Die Wiederholungsfiguren und ihr Gebrauch bei den Griechen vor Gorgias* (Berlin, 1969), 78–80, casts doubt on the alleged effect of most instances of alliteration in Greek.

νο{μ}μάcι ναύταιc: 'with his wandering sailors'. The papyrus has νομμαcιναυγαιc, which Wilamowitz read as νομάcιν αὐγαῖc 'with his wandering eyes' (for this sense of αὐγαῖc cf. *h. Hom.* 4. 361, E. *Andr.* 1179–60, [E.] *Rhes.* 737). Keil takes αὐγαῖc as a metonym for 'ships', which often had eyes painted on the prow (Morrison–Williams 37 n., 93 ff.) or the ram, which could be shaped in the form of an animal's, particularly a boar's, head (cf. the phrase κυανώπιδεc νᾶεc at A. *Pers.* 559–60). Both these interpretations are far-fetched; it is easier to emend to νομάcι ναύταιc with Danielsson.

For the use of a feminine adjective in -άc with a masculine noun (perhaps here under the influence of the *a*-stem ναύτηc, but cf. E. *Or.* 837 δρομάcι βλεφάροιc), cf. E. *Or.* 269–70 (with Willink), 837, *IT* 1235, *Hel.* 1301. Danielsson correctly puts a comma, not a stop (so Wilamowitz), at the end of the line.

79. οἰcτρομανέc: 'enraged and mad'; οἶcτροc can simply mean 'frenzy'; here it no doubt refers to the sea's wild temper. At *Thesm.* 325 Aristophanes uses a similar compound when he talks of Poseidon παραλιπὼν | μυχὸν ἰχθυόεντ᾽ οἰcτροδόνητον, where the sense is no more than 'agitated', 'stirred up'.

παλαιομίcημ(α): 'ancient object of hate'; possibly a direct reference to the loss of Mardonius' fleet near Mt. Athos in 492 (Hdt. 6. 44), or perhaps to the destruction of Xerxes' first ship-bridge over the Hellespont and to the disaster at Artemisium; πάλαι can refer to a relatively recent point in time.

The papyrus has παλεο-; there is no Attic instance of ε for αι before Roman times, but the Ptolemaic papyri provide some non-Attic examples. It appears occasionally in papyri of the third and second centuries and more frequently in those of the first; in public inscriptions the earliest Attic example dates from the first century AD, and it becomes more common from c.125/150 AD (Wackernagel, *Kl. Schr.* ii. 1027–33; K. Strunk, *Glotta*, 38 (1959), 83 ff.; A. Bartoněk, *Development of the Long-Vowel System in Ancient Greek Dialects* (Prague, 1966), 107–8; Mayser–Schmoll i/1. 83–4; Threatte i. 294 ff.). Cf. also e.g. the forms Ἐνιῆνες (codd.) at *Il.* 2. 749, but Αἰν- in the papyri, and ἑώραις v.l. at S. *OT* 1264 (but read αἰ-). The form -αιο- here is further supported by μουσοπαλαιολύμας at 216 (see n.; cf. also fr. 796. 1, 5 παλαιά), and νυμφαιογόνον at 110 (Wilamowitz: πα[λ]ε[ο]νυμφαιο-).

μίσημα is a tragic word (first at A. *Sept.* 186, *Eum.* 73, then S. *El.* 289, E. *Hipp.* 407, fr. 530. 4 N²); S. *El.* 289–90 ὦ δύσθεον μίσημα, σοὶ μόνηι πατὴρ | τέθηκεν; was, according to a scholion, parodied by Aristophanes in his *Gerytades* (fr. 175 K.–A.: 408/7 BC?), but the parody may only have involved the second half of the sentence. Verbs of hating commonly form nouns with the -μα suffix, while in Sophocles in particular we frequently find -μα nouns with a contemptuous nuance; cf. also ἀγκάλισμα below (Breitenbach 28; P. T. Stevens, *CQ* 39 (1945), 103).

80–1. ἀγκάλισμα: here 'that which is embraced' rather than 'embraces'; the concrete sense 'darling', 'beloved' is generally confined to later Greek (e.g. Lycophr. 308 ὦ σκύμνε, τερπνὸν ἀγκάλισμα συγγόνων, Lucian, *Am.* 14). Before Timotheus we only find the compound ὑπαγκάλισμα, which has the same fluctuation in meaning. The idea that the sea embraces the air or land may have been influenced by E. fr. 941 N² ὁρᾶις τὸν ὑψοῦ τόνδ' ἄπειρον αἰθέρα | ⟨καὶ⟩ γῆν πέριξ ἔχονθ' ὑγραῖς ἐν ἀγκάλαις.

81. κλυcιδρομάδοc: 'drenching and speeding' (speeding because blown by the wind?); cf. Page's gloss: ἐπιτρεχούcηc ὥcτε κλύζειν, although the formation is slightly obscure. The first element is apparently formed on a root *κλυ- (cf. κλύζω?, Lat. *cluo* ap. Plin. *NH* 15. 119) with a -*ti*- suffix forming an action noun, and we find κλύcιc as a medical term for drenching (Hp. *Acut.* 11). The expected meaning is something like 'washing, surging'; the verb κλύζω is frequently used in this sense of the sea (*h. Hom.* 3. 74 ἔνθ' ἐμὲ μὲν μέγα κῦμα . . . κλύccει, *Il.* 14. 392 ἐκλύcθη δὲ θάλαccα ποτὶ κλιcίαc, *Od.* 9. 484, 541, [Hes.] *Sc.* 207 ff. etc.). Janssen compares Ar. *Thesm.* 47 ὑλοδρόμοc, and understands 'speeding over the waves', but there is no reason to suspect that κλύcιc should have the sense 'waves'; contrast the late formation κλύc-μα at e.g. Lucian, *Nav.* 8. Edmonds suggests the first element is from a nominative *κλύc, comparing accusative κλύδα at Nic. *Alex.* 170 ἀφροῖο νέην κλύδα λευκαίνουcαν 'the fresh and whitening surge' (tr. Gow–Scholfield); but the latter is a late, poetic innovation and unlikely to be relevant here.

82–5. The Islander: Conclusion. The Islander drowns in a welter of sound-effects.

Metre

85

The colarion *D* is introduced at 83, between *ia* and *lk*; *D* is not otherwise attested in Timotheus, though we find several instances of other dactylic rhythms; it is an important colarion in [Arion], *PMG* adesp. 939 (e.g. ll. 3, 7, 8, 11, 12, 13: for the analysis, see West, 'Analyses', 5–9). The predominantly iambic sequence ends with another choriamb followed by an ithyphallic.

82–5. 'He spoke in distress from his gasping and spat out a dreadful foam, belching back up from his mouth the deep-sea brine.'

82. φάτ': modelled on the epic phrase ὣc φάτο, traditionally used to end a speech; cf. φάτο opening a speech at 177. The epic formula is common at speech-end in Stesichorus (above, pp. 126–7) and is used once by Bacchylides (5. 76); Pindar uses the formula to end a speech at *P*. 3. 43, 4. 120, *I*. 8. 45.

ἄ⟨c⟩θματι: 'by his gasping'; causal dative after the participle cτρευγόμενοc. While the papyrus' αθματι is unlikely to result from a fricative pronunciation of theta, the scribe may also have had trouble with cθ in ὀπιccοπόρευτον at 182, where perhaps we should read ὀπιcθο- (see n.), and possibly also in μαχέc⟨θ⟩' (cj. Wilamowitz) at 155.

In the classical period φ, θ, χ were still aspirated stops; there is no positive evidence for spirantization either in Attic inscriptions or in the Ptolemaic papyri. The first clear evidence for the fricative pronounciation of θ dates from the first century AD, except in Laconian, where it occurs considerably earlier, in about the sixth century BC (Mayser–Schmoll i/1. 153–4; W. S. Allen, *Vox Graeca* (Cambridge, 1987³), 23; Threatte i. 469); and even in the sixth and fifth century, the combination cθ was probably not a fricative in Laconian (Colvin 170).

83–4. βλοcυρὰν δ᾽ ἐξέβαλλ᾽ ἄχναν: 'he spat out a horrible foam'; cf. *Od*. 5. 322–3 cτόματος δ᾽ ἐξέπτυcεν ἅλην | πικρήν. βλοcυρός is a rare word, largely restricted to poetry in the classical period; its original sense is disputed (see M. Leumann, *Homerische Wörter* (Basle, 1950), 141 ff.). It appears twice in Homer (*Il*. 7. 212, 15. 608), where it means 'grim', 'shaggy'; at [Hes.] *Sc*. 191 the word means little more than 'destructive', and both meanings operate in Hellenistic poetry (A.R. 2. 740, 4. 1437). See Hopkinson on Callim. *H*. 6. 52. The sense 'destructive' is apt here; the foam is destructive because it is choking him; cf. also Antiphanes, *GP* 730 (*AP* 9. 84. 2) βλοcυροῖc κύμαcι cυρόμενον 'dragged by the rough wave' and Bianor, *GP* 1718 (*AP* 9. 278. 6) ὑπὸ βλοcυροῦ χεύματοc ἐφθάνετο 'he was overtaken by the savage flood'.

84. ἐπανερευγόμενοc: 'belching back up', a vividly realistic image. In this sense Homer has only ἐρεύγομαι (e.g. *Od*. 9. 374 ὁ δ᾽ ἐρεύγετο οἰνοβαρείων, *Il*. 16. 162 ἐρευγόμενοι φόνον αἵματος). The homoioteleuton with cτρευγόμενοc may be another instance of Timotheus' insensitivity to casual phonetic repetitions; the two prefixes are also characteristic, as is

the way in which neither contributes significantly to the
sense.

85. βρύχιον ἄλμαν: 'the sea brine'; after A. *Pers.* 397
ἔπαιcαν ἅλμην βρύχιον (of rowers).

86–97. The Persian Flight: Introduction. The narrative is
resumed from 39. It is highly reminiscent of the messenger-
speech in Aeschylus' *Persae*, which also opens with the
attack of the Greek ships (408–11 εὐθὺc δὲ ναῦc ἐν νηῒ χαλκήρη
cτόλον | ἔπαιcεν· ἦρξε δ' ἐμβολῆc Ἑλληνικὴ | ναῦc, κἀποθραύει
πάντα Φοινίccηc νεὼc | κόρυμβ', ἐπ' ἄλλην δ' ἄλλοc ηὔθυνεν
δόρυ). This is followed by a description of the dead and
drowning Persians in the sea (419–20 θάλαccα δ' οὐκέτ' ἦν
ἰδεῖν | ναυαγίων πλήθουcα καὶ φόνου βροτῶν) and on the shore
(421 ἀκταὶ δὲ νεκρῶν χοιράδεc τ' ἐπλήθυον). The Persian
lamentations are briefly mentioned at 426–7 (οἰμωγὴ δ'
ὁμοῦ | κωκύμαcιν κατεῖχε πελαγίαν ἅλα). Timotheus was
clearly directly influenced by the whole passage.

Metre

```
86      ∪ – ∪ ∪∪ – ∪ ∪ – ∫
            – ∪ – – ∪∪ ∪ – – – |
        – – – – | – – – – |
        – – ∪∪ – |
90      – – – – ∪ ∪ – ∫
            – ∪ – – – ∪ ∪ – |
        – – – ∪ – ∪ ∪ – ∫
        – – – – – ∪ ∪ – |
        ∪ – ∪ – ∪ – ∪ – |
95      ∪ – ∪ – – – ∪ ∪∪ |
        ∪ – – ∪ – ∪ – ||
        – – – ∪ – ∪ ∪ – ||
```

The section begins with *ia ch* (86), if the temporal augment is
present in ἵετο; if not, we have *ia cr*. There are no indications of
which we should prefer. Lines 87–9 are slightly confusing: Saija
reads *2cr* and a molossus, but there are no other firm examples of a
cretic of the form – ∪∪∪ (though ∪∪∪ – is relatively common). I
suggest 87 should be *cr ia sp*; in 88 the spondaic rhythm may
continue, perhaps followed by an iamb if we read μακρ-; alternatively, 88 may be analysed as an anapaestic dimeter with
contraction of both bicipitia, and 89 as an anapaestic metron
with contraction of first biceps. 89 might be scanned – – ∪ – –,

reading -αυχενοπ'λουc, thus producing a baccheus, but see p. 61. If they are anapaests, cf. the less regular anapaests at fr. 800, where contraction is nevertheless still quite common (e.g. 800. 2 – – – – | – – ∪ ∪ –, 4 – ∪ ∪ – – | – ∪ ∪ – –). A sequence of wilamowitziani (or 'choriambic dimeters') begins at 90, which is of a form common in Euripides (K. Itsumi, CQ^2 32 (1982), 72); the wilamowitzianus is in any case especially associated with Euripides in tragedy. The form of 92 – – – ∪ – ∪ ∪ – is particularly frequent, and here recurs in 97; both – ∪ – – – – ∪ ∪ – (91) and – – – – – ∪ ∪ – (93) are less common.

86–97. 'The barbarian Persian army went backwards in flight, rushing along; and one line of ships, sailing the long neck [of the sea], shattered another, and from their hands [the sailors] threw down the ship's mountain feet, and from their mouths leapt the bright-shining children, as they were struck together. And the starry sea swarmed with their bodies, deprived of light (?) through drowning, and the shores were laden.'

86. πάλιν: 'backwards', rather than 'again', as there has been no indication that the Persian flight begun at 35 ff. has ceased in the meantime. There need be no reference to backing water as a symbol of retreat (so Janssen, comparing E. *Andr.* 1120 χωρεῖ δὲ πρύμναν with Stevens); the Persians may simply have turned their ships around.

86–7. Πέρcηc cτρατὸc βάρβαροc: 'the barbarian Persian army'; a somewhat unusual pairing of epithets, although neither is in itself unlikely; cf. A. *Pers.* 117 Περcικοῦ cτρατεύματος, 412 Περcικοῦ cτρατοῦ, 423 βαρβάρου cτρατεύματος. Most editors delete one or the other adjective; Janssen asserts that the two adjectives refer to two different contingents in the Persian fleet (as at A. *Pers.* 434 Πέρcαιc τε καὶ πρόπαντι βαρβάρων γένει); this is impossible with the adjectives in apposition, despite Kühner–Gerth ii. 340–2. 'Persian' coupled with 'barbarian' seems tautologous (Broadhead on A. *Pers.* 924–7: 'in this play "Persian" is occasionally used by [Aeschylus] in a comprehensive way to denote the lands and races ruled over by the Great King'), but could perhaps be emphatic; the deletion of βάρβαροc produces *ia sp* for the line.

ἐπιcπέρχων: 'rushing along'; often intransitively of the action of the winds (whose effects may thus be suggested here), as at e.g. *Od.* 5. 304–5 ἐπισπέρχουσι δ' ἄελλαι παντοίων ἀνέμων, Pi. fr. 94b. 17 ff. (*Parth.* 2) cθένει φρίccων Βορέαc ἐπιcπέρχηc'.

88. ἄλλα δ' ἄλλαν: here perhaps after A. *Pers.* 411 ἐπ' ἄλλην δ' ἄλλοc ηὔθυνεν δόρυ, but the construction is typical (e.g. *Od.* 14. 228, Archil. fr. 25. 2, Telestes fr. 808. 1–2 etc.).

cύρτιc: 'line (of ships)'; otherwise only at Hsch. cύρτιc· φθορὰ καὶ λύμη, although this meaning does not suit the context here, as ἄλλα and ἄλλαν require the same substantive (despite Sitzler 1907). We should connect the word with the root *cυρ- (cf. cύρτηc, cύρτοc, cύρω) rather than with *ser- (so Keil 106, comparing ὅρμοc, ὁρμαθόc, Lat. *series* etc.), with a -τι- suffix. The form must be old, as -τι- had become -cι- in such substantives even in Doric well before the fifth century and the original dental stop was preserved only in a few archaic words, except after c, where τ is maintained (e.g. κύcτιc); e.g. φάτιc (φάcιc in Pl., Arist.), μῆτιc, ἄμπωτιc (G. R. Vowels, *CP* 23 (1928), 34–59; Chantraine, *Formation*, 275 ff.). The sense should be related to cύρδην 'in a long trailing line' of the Babylonian army at A. *Pers.* 53; cύρω of a serpent-like line of ships at Lyc. 216–17 λεύccω πάλαι δὴ cπεῖραν ὁλκαίων κακῶν, | cύρουcαν ἅλμηι. Sudhaus improbably sees a reference to the waves, Keil to the row of oars.

Cύρτιc is also the name of the Gulf of Sidra or Khalīj Surt near the North African coast (Hdt. 2. 32. 2), well known for its dangerous shallows (cf. Σ A.R. 4. 1235–6 Cύρτιc· τόποι ἐν τῶι Ὠκεανῶι, ὅπου καταcύρονται οἱ πλέοντεc); Wilamowitz connects the two words, suggesting that the area had been given its name by Ionian sailors. However, the lack of semantic linkage makes it seem more likely that the place-name, whatever its derivation (possibly Greek, but also possibly a non-Greek loan-word), was an independent development. The area's reputation for danger will no doubt have given rise to the definition of cύρτιc given in Hesychius, with which we may compare Cic. *De Orat.* 3. 163 '*Syrtim patrimonii*', *scopulum libentius dixerim;* '*Charybdim bonorum' voraginem potius*, Verg. *A.* 1. 111 *in brevia et syrtis* ('sandbanks') *urgeret*, 146.

89. μακραυχενόπλουc: 'sailing the long neck (of the sea)';

nominative singular with cύρτιc (for the contraction, cf. 128 ἱκνοῦμαι), certainly not agreeing κατὰ cύνεcιν with ἄλλαν (so Edmonds) nor with πόδαc (Danielsson, Aron); the postponement of δέ is rare in Timotheus and awkward here. The final element is more likely to be connected with πλέω (cf. e.g. [Arion], *PMG* adesp. 939. 18 ἁλιπλόου 'sailing the sea'), rather than with ὅπλον (although cf. e.g. E. *Hel.* 693 χαλκεόπλων Δαναῶν) or ὁπλή.

Edmonds translates 'sailing with long necks', but in the context of ships αὐχήν usually refers to the steering paddle (cf. Pollux 1. 90, Polyaen. 3. 11. 14); but the 'long neck' of the sea would aptly describe the straits of Salamis and would explain why the ships were colliding.

90–1. ὀρείουc πόδαc ναόc: 'the ship's mountainly feet', i.e. oars; cf. 5–6 χεῖραc . . . ἐλατίναc, 77 πεύκαιcιν ὀριγόνοιcιν (with n.), Hsch. ο 1134 (*TrGF* adesp. F 244) ὀρείοιc ποcί· κώπαιc· ἐπεὶ ἡ ἐλάτη ὄρειοc. Probably the oars used by the rowers, rather than the steering-oars, are meant, although the removal of the steering equipment was a common means of disabling ships (Morrison–Williams 135). Not relevant here is the chief nautical sense of πούc, 'sheet' as at E. *Hec.* 939–40 ἐπεὶ νόcτιμον ναῦc ἐκίνηcεν πόδα and probably *Od.* 10. 32 (so Heubeck; 'steering-paddle' LSJ).'

91. cτόματοc: 'from their mouths'; the parallelism with χειρῶν δέ clearly indicates that the mouths of the sailors are meant, certainly not those of the ships (Wilamowitz *et al.*), although cτόμα can sometimes have a metaphorical value (cf. e.g A. *Pers.* 415 χαλκοcτόμοιc of ships). If so, the παῖδεc (cτόματοc) can only be the teeth; cf. Ion fr. eleg. 26. 6 ὀφθαλμῶν δ' ἐξέθορον πυκινοὶ παῖδεc, of the vine, where the 'eyes' appear to be the buds of the vine, and the 'children' the grapes. The teeth of the sailors have been knocked out by a blow from the oar, which easily explains cυγκρουόμενοι 'struck together'.

Diels (ap. Wilamowitz) argued that these 'teeth' were the cκαλμοί 'thole-pins', and called attention to Hsch. τράφηξ· τὸ τῆc νεώc χεῖλοc; this gives no satisfactory sense to either cτόμα or cυγκρουόμενοι. Croiset, also thinking that the cτόμα was that of the ship, believed the 'teeth' to be the figureheads of the ships, comparing A. *Pers.* 410; Privitera thinks of yet another reference to the rams. But the passage has moved beyond the destruction of the enemy ships; the most recent subject to which we can relate ϲτόματοϲ must be ναῦται (understood at 90).

92. μαρμαροφεγγεῖϲ: 'bright-shining'; only here, but cf. the (probably dithyrambic) compound at *PMG* adesp. 927. 56 ἀϲτερομαρμαροφεγγής; and that at A. *Sept.* 400–1 νύκτα . . . ἄϲτροιϲι μαρμαίρουϲαν. The element -φεγγής is common in the second position in compounds, usually with an adjective as the first term (e.g. χρυϲειοφεγγής, καλλιφεγγής, παμφεγγής); μαρμαρο- here probably indicates brightness or whiteness rather than referring directly to marble.

94. κατάϲτεροϲ: 'starry'. Mazon thinks that the sea may be starry with bodies; the conception perhaps recalls A. *Ag.* 659–60, where the sea is 'aflower' with corpses: ὁρῶμεν ἀνθοῦν πέλαγοϲ Αἰγαῖον νεκροῖϲ | ἀνδρῶν Ἀχαιῶν ναυτικοῖϲ τ' ἐρειπίοιϲ.

Cricca notes that κατάϲτεροϲ does not appear again till Greg. Naz. *Or.* 38. 24, Greg. Pisid. *Hex.* 1287 (both of a peacock's tail), Greg. Naz. *Or.* 5. 7 (of a garment), and Jo. Damasc. *Nativ. BVM* 7 (of the Virgin); these instances probably represent a new formation rather than a survival from the fifth century. It reappears in Moschopoulos (*c.*1300) on Hes. *Op.* '546' = 548.

95. λιποπνόηϲ: 'lack of breath'; only here, but cf. λιπο- ψυχία, λιποψυχεῖν (S. fr. 496 Radt), λιποθυμία, ἐκπνοή 'death'. Probably an innovation rather than a medical term (as Croiset believes), for which there are no parallels; the word suggests death by drowning and is to be connected with the phrase ϲώμαϲιν λιπ[.]ϲτερέϲιν (whatever the sense of the adjective) rather than with κατάϲτεροϲ.

λιπ[.]ϲτερέϲιν . . . ϲώμαϲιν: the papyrus has either λιπ- or possibly λιγ-. Diehl printed λιπ[α]ϲτέρεϲ⟨ϲ⟩ιν, which should mean 'having left the stars'; this is bizarre after κατάϲτεροϲ, and 'leaving the stars' is not a usual locution for dying. λιπ[ο]- may be the result of dittography after λιποπνόηϲ. Wilamowitz emended to the simple ψυχ[ο]ϲτερέϲιν, which provides the right sense: bodies deprived of life through lack of air. Page suggests the palaeographically easier αὐγ[ο]ϲτερέϲιν 'deprived of light'; 'leaving the light' is a common expression for dying. Sudhaus, less plausibly, emends to λιν[ο]cτέρεcιν 'deprived of clothes', comparing the apparent loss of clothing at *P.* 136; a connection with ἐγ λιποπνόης is hard to see. Danielsson suggests λιβ[ο]cτερέcιν, comparing ἀλίβας, which ancient grammarians derived (dubiously) from ἀ-λίβας, hence 'dry, withered' (e.g. Didym. ap. *Σ* Ar. *Ra.* 186); it is doubtful whether this interpretation existed in the fifth century, and whether it would justify, especially in the context of drowning, the formation *λιβοcτερής, which should really mean 'deprived of water'. MLW suggests αὐρ[ο]cτερέcιν 'deprived of air', which seems otiose with λιποπνόης.

96. ἐγάργαιρε: 'swarmed', 'teemed'; a rare word, chiefly found in comedy, and more usually with the genitive; cf. Cratinus fr. 321 K.–A. ἀνδρῶν ἀρίcτων πᾶca γαργαίρει πόλις, Ar. fr. 375 K.–A. ἀνδρῶν ἐπακτῶν πᾶca γαργαίρει cτοά, Sophron fr. 30 Kaibel τῶν ἀργυρωμάτων ἐγάργαιρεν ἁ οἰκία.

97. ἐβρίθοντο: 'were laden'; after A. *Pers.* 421 (above, p. 175); cf. also E. *Tro.* 89 ff. ἀκταὶ δὲ Μυκόνου Δήλιοί τε χοιράδες | Cκῦρός τε Λῆμνός θ' αἱ Καφήρειοί τ' ἄκραι | πολλῶν θανόντων cώμαθ' ἕξουcιν νεκρῶν. *Troades* was first performed in 415 BC, and may have influenced Timotheus here; Poseidon, at Athena's behest, plans to destroy the Greek fleet because of the impiety of Aias, as the Persian fleet is destroyed, perhaps because of its impiety towards the Hellespont.

98–138. The Persian Flight: Lamentation. The lamentations of the Persians who have managed to get ashore. Despite the plurals ἐπανεκαλέοντ' at 104 and ὀδυρόμενοι κατεδάκρυον at 139, there is no need to assume with Janssen that there is more than one speaker. The singular forms in the speech itself με (107), ἀμὸν cῶμα (108–9: here the possessive is equivalent to ἐμός; see n.), λιπὼν ἦλθον (116–17), ἱκνοῦμαι (128), ἐμόν (129), με (130), κείcομαι (137), clearly indicate a single speaker, albeit representative of the Persians as a whole; cf. the sense of the Homeric formula ὧδε δέ τις εἴπεcκε(ν) (e.g. *Il.* 2. 271 with Kirk, 4. 81, 22. 372, *Od.* 2. 324, 4. 769). The highly developed literary form of the speech can be seen in the incorporation of a second, internal prayer at 127 ff., and there may have been elements in the performance, such as musical or vocal variation, which distinguished the two sections: there is a marked metrical change at 127. It is unclear whether the appeal to Cybele ends at 129 or is intended to continue to the end of the speech at 138. The latter seems more likely, for there are no indications of closure, and the first person and the aeolic metre continue throughout.

Excessive lamentation is often associated with Orientals in fifth-century literature; at *Pers.* 937, 1054 Aeschylus mentions the Mariandynian and Mysian styles of mourning, and at *Ch.* 423–4 Cissian mourning. Dirges were normally performed in Greece and elsewhere by women, and there are often suggestions of effeminacy in portrayals of (male) Oriental lamentation. It is unclear whether we are to see such overtones here; although breast-beating is often specifically Oriental or female, it is also mentioned frequently in other mourning contexts (e.g. A. *Ch.* 423 ff., S. *Ai.* 631 ff.). See Alexiou 55 ff.; Hall, *Barbarian*, 83–4, 115–16. Later in the poem, the Persians again rend their clothes and disfigure their faces (166–8); the King also maltreats his body (176). Cowardice is certainly suggested.

Metre

98	– ∪ – – ∪ ∪ – |
	– ∪ – – ∪ ∪ – |
100	∪ – – ∪ – ∪ –
	∪ – ∪ – |
	– – ∪ – ∪ – – |
	– – – ∪ – – ∪ – – ||
	∪∪ ∪ [– –] ∪ ∪ – ∪ ∪∪ ∪ – |
105	∪ – – ∪ – |
	– ∪ ∪ – – ∪ – |
	– – ∪ – – ∪ – ∪ – – |
	∪∪ ∪ – ∪ ∪∪ ∪ – – |
	– ∪ – ∪ – ∪ – |
110–10a	*metr. incert.*
111	∪∪ ∪ – – – ∪ – – ||
	∪∪ ∪ ∪∪ ∪ |
	[∪ –] ∪ ∪∪ – – |
	– ∪ – ∪ – ∪ – – ||

115   – ∪ ∪∪ ∪ ∪∪ ∪ – |
       – ∪ – – ∪ – – ∪ – |
       – ∪ – ∪ – ∪ – – ∪ – |
       – ∪ – – ∪ – – ∪ – |
       – ∪ – – ∪ – – ∪ – ∫
120   – ∪ – – ∪ – ∪∪ ∪ – ||
       – ∪∪ ∪ – ∪ – ∪ – ∫
       – ∪ – ∪ – ∪ – |
       ∪ ∪∪ – ∪ –
       ∪ ∪∪ ∪ – ∪ – ∪ – – – |
125   – ∪ ∪∪ ∪ ∪∪ ∪ – |
       – – ∪ – ∪ – ∪ – ∪ – – |
       ? |
       ∪ – – ∪ ∪ – – ||
       ∪ ∪ ∪ ∪ – – ∪ ∪ – – ∪ ∪ – |
130   – ∪ ∪ – ∪ ∪ – ∪ ∪ – ∪ ∪ – ∪ ∪ |
       – ∪ ∪ ∪ – – ||
       – ∪ ∪ – ∪ ∪ – – – ∪ ∪ – – |
       – ∪ ∪ – ∪ ∪ – ∪ –
       – – – ∪ ∪ – ∪ – |
135   ∪ ∪ ∪ ∪ – – ∪ ∪ – |
       – – – ∪ ∪ – – ||
       – ∪ – ∪ ∪ – ∪ –
       – – – ∪ ∪ – ∪ – ∪ – – ||

The section starts clearly with *cr ch* in 98 and 99, and continues with simple iambics and bacchiacs to the end of the period; 103 begins with an isolated molossus. The next period also begins *cr ch*. If [γᾶν] is correct at 104, we may read *cr cr ia* (West, 'Analyses', 2), assuming synizesis in -κα[λ]έοντ'. 105 appears to be a dochmiac; while the exclamation ἰώ may be *extra metrum*, which would leave a simple cretic, it appears to count metrically at 178 and 187, and we should need to have the metrically difficult - κα[λ]έοντο· in 104. The sequence of choriambic metra continues in 106 (*ch cr*), followed by *ia ith* (107). A trochaic dimeter interrupts at 108; trochaic elements seem to continue (111) after the lacunose lines at 110–10a. Aeolic metra first appear in the poem at the mention of the Mountain Mother (Cybele) at 128 (*ph*); the series is maintained until the end of the prayer at 138. The ibycean at 133 has the same form as those at 184, 189, 194, 197. The dactylic pentameter might be compared with the tetrameter at fr. 788(*b*) and the dactylic cola at *P*. 83, 139. Hiatus marks period-end at 131 and 128; cf. 75. Correption of αι before a vowel is found at 130 ἀποίϲεται ἐν- and 137 κείϲομαι οἰκ-; of οι at 132 -φθόροι αὖρ-. Line

127 is corrupt; the conjecture λιϲϲ⟨οίμαν· ϲῶϲ⟩ον produces *mol sp cr*
(if the upsilon of χρυϲο- is short: see n.), but West suggests
('Analyses', 3) that there should be a longer gap between the
two words: see further ad loc. Lines 129 and 135 end with
choriambic metra (- ◡◡ -), but both lines begin with the rhythm
◡◡◡◡ -; this is probably to be taken as an iambic metron with
resolution of the first princeps rather than a resolved choriamb. At
131 we find the unusual colarion - ◡◡◡ - - after a dactylic
pentameter (130; cf. *5da* at 132). Possibly we could compare
E. *Ph.* 1581, where, however, Page suggests emending to ὃϲ τάδ᾽
ἐ⟨κ⟩τελευτᾶι, thus producing a simple ithyphallic rather than a
penthemimer (Diggle later preferred perhaps τάδ᾽ ὃϲ); or *IA*
1332–3, where perhaps read ἀνδράϲιν [ἀν]ευρεῖν with Dindorf (see
Diggle, *CR*² 34 (1984), 68 = *Euripidea*, 316, and *CR*² 40 (1990),
10–11 = *Euripidea*, 361; Mastronarde on *Ph.* 1581). Diggle suggests μήϲτωρι here; thus - - ◡◡ - -(?). A glyconic and a phalaecian
(extended glyconic) ends the section.

98–138. 'And others, breast-beating mourners, sitting
frozen and naked on the sea-headlands with shouts and
tear-shedding lamentation were occupied with wailing; and
at the same time they called on their fatherland: "O tree-
tressed Mysian glens, rescue me from here; now we are
being carried along by the winds; never again will my city
welcome my body . . . Ward off the warlike . . . ! Would that
my master had never built the ship which made the crossing;
for then I should not have come to ward off Greek Ares,
leaving Tmolus and the Lydian city of Sardis; as it is, where
am I to find a sweet refuge from death, from which it is hard
to escape? Conveying (me) to Ilium, that alone would be a
deliverance from woes, if I might fall at the black-leaf-robed
queenly knees of the Mountain Mother and throwing my
beautiful arms about them might pray: 'I beseech you, gold-
tressed goddess Mother, save my life, for which there is no
escape, since someone will soon destroy me with the throat-
slitting sword, or the ship-wrecking winds will dash me in
pieces with the north-east wind that freezes during the
night; for the savage wave has torn away all the well-
woven warmth from my limbs: here pitiable I shall lie, a
feast for the flesh-eating birds.' "'.'

99. γυμνοπαγεῖϲ: 'frozen and naked'; as later (134–5) the
Mysian laments that the waves have stripped him of his

clothes. The episode, narrative and speech, thus begins and
ends with the same image.

The compound appears only here; compounds with
γυμνο- as their first term rarely date from before the fifth
century, e.g. γυμνοπαιδίαι, γυμνοσοφισταί (Chantraine 241).
The image, commonly associated with shipwrecks, is
repeated at 135–6 ἀνέρρηξεν ἄπαγ | γυίων εἶδος ὑφαντόν (see
n.); cf. also the imagery of the Strasburg epode (Hippon. fr.
115. 5–9), κἂν Cαλμυδ[ησс]ῶι γυμνὸν εὐφρονε[| Θρήϊκες
ἀκρό[κ]ομοι | λάβοιεν . . . | ῥίγει πεπηγότ' αὐτόν, Antipater
Thess. GP 145–7 (AP 7. 286. 1–3) δύσμορε Νικάνωρ πολιῶι
μεμαραμμένε πόντωι, | κεῖcαι δὴ ξείνηι γυμνὸς ἐπ' ἠϊόνι | ἢ cύ γε
πρὸς πέτρηιcι, Zonas, GP 3464–71 (AP 7. 404. 1–6), Flaccus,
GP 3809–10 (AP 7. 290. 3–4), Hor. Ep. 10. 21 ff.

100–1. δακρυσταγεῖ [γ]όωι: 'with tear-shedding wailing';
Cricca refers to Methodius, Symposium, 11. 2, ed. G. N.
Bonwetsch (GSS 27; Leipzig, 1917), 136, l. 9 νόcων πόνοι
δακρυσταγεῖc, but more relevant are the comparable forms at
A. Suppl. 113 δακρυοπετῆ, 682 δακρυογόνον, and especially cf.
[A.] Pr. 399 δακρυcίcτακτον. A form of cτάζω is first used of
tears as A. Suppl. 578–9 δακρύων δ' ἀποcτάζει πένθιμον αἰδῶ,
but a connection between the two words is common in later
drama; e.g. E. Hec. 760, IA 1466; see D. Arnould, Les Rires
et les larmes dans la littérature grecque (Paris, 1990), 134, 147.

[γ]όωι: generally of lamentation, more especially of
lamentation for the dead; here, however, the grief is occa-
sioned by the fear of imminent death. See Fraenkel on A. Ag.
57. γόος, γοάω, γοάομαι, and adjectives derived from the root
are almost exclusively poetic, though γοάομαι occurs in prose
once at Xen. Cyr. 4. 6, γοώδηc once at Pl. Lg. 7. 800 D
(Arnould, op. cit. 146–7); the repetition of the root γο-,
although awkward, is not unusual for Timotheus. Keil
suggests [ῥ]όωι 'flood' as at [A.] Pr. 399 δακρυcίcτακτα . . .
ῥέος.

102. cτερνοκτύποι: Wilamowitz's emendation for the
papyrus' -κτύπωι (an error easily made under the influence
of the preceding successions of datives). The later narrative
returns to this image, with the references to self-mutilation
at 166 and 176 (the King): see nn.

γοηταί: 'mourners'; not otherwise attested, although

possibly γοητῶν νόμον 'songs of mourners' at A. *Ch.* 823, where, however, γοήτων 'of sorcerers' (M and Σ : -τῶν M^ac) is probably to be preferred for the sense; see West, *Stud. Aesch.* 255–6. Edmonds proposes βοητᾶι, but we can satisfactorily derive γοητής 'wailer' from γοάω.

103. θρηνώδει: 'mournful' (first here). Although there was no formal distinction in classical times between the γόος and the θρῆνος, the two may originally have been distinct terms, one referring to the lamentation of kinswomen, the other to the more elaborate lamentation provided by hired female mourners; see Alexiou 11 ff.

ὀδυρμῶι: 'lamentation'; the sense of ὀδύρομαι can often approach that of κλαίω or γοάω, thus especially of lamentation for the dead. For the combination of words, cf. E. *Tro.* 609 θρήνων τ' ὀδυρμοί, Pl. *Rep.* 3. 398 D.

104. [γᾶν] πατρίαν ἐπανεκα[λ]έοντ': γᾶν is probably correct, though there may be space for four letters in the lacuna. On the metre, see above, p. 182.

105. ἰώ: generally used in tragedy for strong excitement, but not uncommon in invoking aid, cf. e.g. A. *Sept.* 97 ff. ἰὼ | μάκαρες εὔεδροι, | ἀκμάζει βρετέων ἔχεσθαι (but see Hutchinson ad loc.: 'an exclamation rather than an address'), and see Fraenkel on A. *Ag.* 503. In Aeschylus and Sophocles ἰώ with the vocative always marks a proper address or apostrophe (as here); see Hutchinson on A. *Sept.* 481. There are no other examples in archaic or classical lyric, though Timotheus himself uses it three times, here and at *P.* 178 and 187, both times in association with Aeschylean reminiscences (see also next n.). Bacchylides also makes occasional use of non-lyric exclamations (e.g. φεῦ, αἰαί).

Μύσιαι . . . πτυχαί: perhaps a reminiscence of A. *Mysians* fr. 143 Radt ἰὼ Κάϊκε Μύσιαί τ' ἐπιρροαί (the opening lines of the play), spoken by the returning servant of Telephus (Ed. Fraenkel on A. *Ag.* 503). Here they evoke the speaker's desire to return to his native country.

Mysia was in the north-western region of Asia Minor, bordering Troas and Aeolis. Mysian mourning was proverbial, which may partly account for the choice of ethnicity here; cf. A. *Pers.* 1054 καὶ στέρν' ἄρασσε κἀπιβόα τὸ Μύσιον. Sardis and Tmolus, mentioned at 116–17, were both in the former kingdom of Lydia, which, together with the Greek settlements on the Ionian coast, constituted part of the satrapy of that name; Timotheus may have mentioned them simply as important governmental centres, but Herodotus (7. 74. 2) records a tradition in which the Mysians were said to have been Lydian colonists.

106. δενδροέθειραι: 'tree-tressed'; only here, but cf. E. *Hel.* 1107 ἐναύλοις ὑπὸ δενδροκόμοις, Ar. *Nub.* 279–80 ὀρέων κορυφὰς ἐπὶ δενδροκόμους, Rufinus 6. 5 Page (*AP* 5. 19) ὁ δενδροκόμης Ἐρύμανθος, also E. *Andr.* 284–5 ὑλόκομον. The connection between hair and foliage is common (e.g. *Od.* 23. 195, Cratinus fr. 328 K.–A.).

107. [ῥύ]ϲαϲθέ: the imperative with πτυχαί as the subject is slightly odd; the subject of such prayers is usually a god (e.g. A. *Sept.* 93, 302, 824); the emphasis may be on the divinity of the Mysian glens.

νῦν: 'now'; Korzeniewski suggested νῦν ⟨δέ⟩, but the asyndeton can be regarded as having a strongly emotional effect, as in prose (Denniston, p. xlv). For the use of νῦν contrasting an actual state with a potential one, see Kühner–Gerth ii. 117. Wilamowitz unnecessarily emends to ἵν(α).

ἀήταις: 'by the winds'; cf. Pl. *Crat.* 410 B οἱ γὰρ ποιηταί που τὰ πνεύματα ἀήτας καλοῦϲιν. For the gender see West on Hes. *Op.* 675. Aron oddly sees a reference to the scattering of remains by the wind, but there can be little doubt that the passage simply describes the effect of the wind's force on the fleet.

108. φερόμεθ': Page prints a comma; but a stronger pause is required between the next clause and this, which intervenes illogically after [ῥύϲ]αϲθέ μ' ἐνθέν[δε]. Danielsson and Sudhaus' φερο⟨ί⟩με[θ]α is unnecessary.

γάρ: the connection is not with the directly preceding phrase but with [ῥύϲ]αϲθέ μ' ἐνθέν[δε]. 'This looseness of structure is characteristic of Homer and Herodotus; the Attic examples are few and not remarkable' (Denniston 63). Here it emphasizes the Mysian's despair and confusion.

108–9. ἀμὸν [cῶ]μα: 'my body', i.e. 'me'. It is not quite certain whether the speaker is fearful lest his body not receive adequate burial, or lest he never return home alive.

109. δέξεται [πόλ]ιϲ: the adverb ἔτι indicates that the

subject of the verb must be something which has received
the Mysian in the past, but which will, if he dies at sea, be
unable to do so again; [κόν]ιc therefore will not do, despite
IG i³. 1179 (*CEG* i no. 10) αἰθὴρ μὲν ψυχὰc ὑπεδέξατο, cώμ[ατα
δὲ χθών. Better sense is provided by Danielsson's [πόλ]ιc; cf.
E. *Med.* 386 ff. τίc με δέξεται πόλιc; | τίc γῆν ἄcυλον καὶ δόμουc
ἐχεγγύουc | ξένοc παραcχὼν ῥύcεται τοὐμὸν δέμαc; (though of a
living person).

110–10a. These two lines are boldly supplemented by
Aron, Ebeling, Sudhaus, and others, but with no success. I
take the damaged text to be relatively legible from 111
onwards: βαθύ[τ]ερον πόντοιο χ[άcμ]α (rather than
Wilamowitz's τ[έρμ]α; MLW tentatively suggests τ[ἐλμ]α),
although there is no indication as to what is a chasm deeper
than the sea; possibly Tartarus, if we can compare Hes. *Th.*
740, E. *Ph.* 1604–5 Ταρτάρου . . . ἄβυccα χάcματα. This may of
course be the same as the ἄντρον at 110a; there has been
universal agreement that this cave should be qualified by
νυμφαιογόνον (or πα[λ]ε[ο]νυμφ. with Wilamowitz) at 110.
The first term of this adjective must be related to νυμφαία
'water-lily'; Wilamowitz, in a desperate effort to make sense
of the passage, emended it to νυμφαγόνον and assumed that
this referred to the Cave of the Nymphs; but the nymphs
simply live below the waves at e.g. Pi. *O.* 2. 28–9, Ba. 17.
97–116, E. *Tro.* 1–3, *Andr.* 1232. The whole looks as if it
ought to be a description of death by drowning; γάρ marks a
logical connection with 109. We could begin with κ[αὶ] ἐν
(for the combination, see Denniston 108 ff.); κ[εῖ]θεγ
(Danielsson, Sudhaus), or κ[ῦρ]εγ (Wilamowitz).

112–13. The phrase ἄπεχε μάχιμο[ν] looks certain: the
Mysians' god(s) (ἀπέχε⟨τε⟩: Danielsson, given the plural
address; the line would then consist of a sequence of seven
shorts, which could still be analysed as a trochee with
resolved anceps) are invoked to ward off something that is
warlike. πλόϊμον ελλαν is also certain, but it is unclear
whether we should read Ἕλλαν 'Helle' or Ἕλλαν' | Ἄ[ρη]
(Danielsson); the latter would be a little surprising, given
the same phrase at 118. Timotheus seems insensitive to
casual phonetic echoes, but this phenomenon is quite distinct from the direct repetition of a whole phrase; however,

δυσέκφευκτον is repeated at 119 and 129. Ἕλλαν 'Helle' could be supported by the apparent reference to the crossing at 115; but unless the Hellespont is to be regarded as responsible for the Persian defeat, why should the Mysian wish his gods to ward it off? After ạ[..] in l. 113 the scribe has made a lengthy deletion of about 7.5 cm; possibly the papyrus was subsequently too wet to write over the space.

114. εἴ[θε μ]ὴ . . . ἔδειμε: the passage is highly reminiscent of E. *Med.* 1 ff. εἴθ' ὤφελ' Ἀργοῦς μὴ διαπτάσθαι σκάφος | Κόλχων ἐς αἶαν κυανέας Συμπληγάδας, | μηδ' ἐν νάπαισι Πηλίου πεσεῖν ποτε | τμηθεῖσα πεύκη, κτλ. Perhaps we are to think of Medea's status as a typical Euripidean barbarian.

στέγην: literally 'cover' and so often 'house'; the sense 'deck of a ship' can be seen in the Latin borrowing *stega* (Plaut. *Bacch.* 278, *Stich.* 413).

115. [.]η.[.]: [δ]ῆτ[α] is the neatest supplement, even though the particle is not attested in epic or lyric. It is common in drama (Denniston 269), and since we are in direct speech here it would be particularly appropriate (especially if we are meant to recall tragedy as represented by the prologue of *Medea*). For its use in 'passionate negative wishes' see Denniston 276; but there seems to be no parallel for the wish's relating to the past.

τελεοπορον: we could accent either τελεοπόρον, 'which made the whole crossing', cf. Asclep. *HE* 836 (*AP* 5. 203. 5) ἦν γὰρ ἀκέντητος τελεοδρόμος, or τελεόπορον, 'of which the crossing was completed', cf. τελεόμηνος 'with full complement of months' (LSJ). The latter sense would be more appropriate to a ship than to Xerxes' ship-bridge, which is probably alluded to here (though the reference need not be so specific). Janssen unconvincingly compares A. *Pers.* 113 λαοπόρος and assumes that the phrase means 'conveying soldiers'; cf. Keil, who writes [β]ῆμ[α] τε λεωπόρον, which he regards as equivalent to λαοπόρον τε μηχανήν.

115–16. ἐμὸς [δ]εσπότης: Darius is addressed as δέσποτα δεσποτᾶν at A. *Pers.* 666, and 'Hybrias the Cretan' at *PMG* adesp. 909. 9 may describe himself as δεσπόταν ⟨ἐμὲ δεσποτᾶν⟩ (Crusius), though the supplement is far from certain; 'Hybrias' echoes closely the language of Asiatic kingship in the next line, μέγαν βασιλῆα (cf. 174 n.). The Persian king is described as ἄναξ by the Islander at 76, as δεcπότηc again by the Celaenaean at 152, and as Βαcιλεύc in narrative at 174.

116. Τμ]ῶλον: Tmolus was the centre of the Cybele cult in Asia Minor (cf. A. *Pers.* 49, E. *Ba.* 65), which may account partly for the invocation to the Mountain Mother at 124 ff.; but an invocation to Cybele would hardly be unusual in the mouth of any Asiatic (as imagined by a Greek). See further 124 n.

117. ἄcτυ Λύδιον . . . Cάρδεων: Sardis (OP *Sparda-*) was the capital of the satrapy of Lydia, conquered by Cyrus in 547/6 BC, and of Asia Minor as a whole; the name generally appears in the plural (cf. e.g. A. *Pers.* 45, 321, Hdt. 1. 7. 2, 5. 101. 1 etc.). Timotheus may been influenced by A. *Pers.* 45 ff., where both Sardis and Tmolus are again mentioned together. The Lydians would have been among the contingents of the Persian army more familiar to the Greeks; Timotheus shows some knowledge of Lydian vocalism at 160.

[λι]πὼν: a typical formula introducing the starting-point of a journey; cf. e.g. Hes. *Op.* 636, Mimn. fr. 9. 1, Pi. *P.* 4. 6–7, A. *Pers.* 961, E. *Ba.* 13.

118. ["Ε]λλαν': see fr. 788 n.

ἀπέρξων: 'to fend off', the future participle indicating purpose after a verb of motion; the use of ἀπέργω is unusual, as there is no indication that the Persian invasion was regarded by either side as an act of Persian self-defence, though Telamon expresses a similarly dubious view-point at Trag. inc. 86 Ribbeck, *praeterea ad Troiam cum misi ob defendendam Graeciam.* Danielsson conjectures Ἑλλανά τ' ἔρξων, but τε in this position is hard to defend and the sense not significantly different. Janssen translates 'shut up'; the meaning of this is no clearer, and it cannot bear the weight of meaning desired by Janssen, 'to put out of action the Greek fleet'.

Ἄρη: divine names can frequently refer to qualities or objects closely associated with the god. 'Ares' is usually an equivalent for war, but the specific sense 'army' occurs twice in Aeschylus (*Pers.* 85–6, 951), whence perhaps the usage here; more frequently in Euripides (e.g. *Andr.* 106, *IA* 237, 283, 775, *Ph.* 134, *Tro.* 560) and later literature (e.g.

Athenaeus, *Paean* 25, p. 71 Bélis, Γαλατᾶν Ἄρης, Limenius 31–2, p. 121 Bélis ὁ βάρβαρος Ἄρης etc.). See Breitenbach 176.

119. νῦν: 'as it is'; see 107 n.

πᾶι: 'by what route' as in E. *Hipp.* 877–8 πᾶι φύγω | βάρος κακῶν. A typical utterance in such moments; cf. S. *Ai.* 403 ποῖ τις οὖν φύγηι, E. *Or.* 598 ποῖ τις οὖν ἔτ᾽ ἂν φύγοι, 1376 πᾶι φύγω, *Hipp.* 672 πᾶι ποτ᾽ ἐξαλύξω τύχας, Ar. *Pl.* 438, etc. The question here is no more than rhetorical; as the Mysian's next comments make clear, there is no real hope of escape.

δυσέκφευκ[τ]ον: at 129 we find αἰῶνα δυσέκφευκτον, where the adjective means 'finding it hard to escape'; here, however, the sense should be 'a refuge from which it is hard to escape'. Adjectives in -τος fluctuate freely in meaning (Fraenkel, *Nomina Agentis*, ii. 76; Ed. Fraenkel on A. *Ag.* 12, 238; Barrett on E. *Hipp.* 677–9). But why should the Mysian wish to escape from his refuge? Possibly we should take δυσέκφευκ[τ]ον with μόρου, thus 'a refuge from inescapable death' (though the presence of γλυκεῖαν makes this awkward); enallage is rare in early lyric, but becomes more common in the fifth century (Kühner–Gerth i. 263; Breitenbach 182 ff.); see V. Bers, *Enallage and Greek Style* (Leiden, 1974). Alternatively, there may have been some interference from 129; GOH tentatively emends to δυσέκφευκ[τ]ος: 'where might I, who find it hard to escape, discover a refuge . . .?'.

εὕρηι: deliberative subjunctive, but the use of τις as the subject is rare (Kühner–Gerth i. 221).

120. μόρου καταφυγήν: 'a refuge from death'; cf. E. *Or.* 448 καταφυγὰς . . . κακῶν.

121. Ἰλιοπόρος: 'conveying to Ilium'; active -πόρος rather than -όπορος (Danielsson). Sudhaus, concerned about the absence of the Cybele cult in fifth-century Ilium, emended to ἰδιο-; more plausibly Keil suggests Ἰδαιοπόρος 'conveying to Ida'; Cybele is invoked as Ἰδαία μᾶτερ by the Phrygian at E. *Or.* 1453 ff.: see also 123, 124 nn. But Ilium, which was in Troas, may be mentioned as a well-known site close to Mysia; Troas was the starting-point for the Persian expedition, and Persians are often equated with Trojans in fifth-century literature (Willink on E. *Or.* p. xlv; West on E. *Or.* 888).

Wilamowitz assumed that the subject was the Mother,

who might appropriately convey a worshipper to Asia, but who is not mentioned until 124. It is tempting to understand καταφυγή from 120, 'that refuge conveying to Ilium might alone be . . .'; however, it is doubtful whether a καταφυγή could 'convey'. A third, and better, option is to understand the subject to be the general idea of the supplication mentioned at 122 ff., 'that alone would be a deliverance from troubles, which might convey me to Ilium, if I might fall at the knees of the Mother . . .'.

κακῶν λυαία: 'deliverance from troubles'. An abstract noun is required by the context; cf. Democr. DK 68 B 196 λήθη τῶν ἰδίων κακῶν, Pi. *N.* 10. 76, S. *Ph.* 877–8, E. *Alc.* 213–14 τίς ἂν [πῶς] πᾶι πόρος κακῶν | γένοιτο καὶ λύcιc τύχας, *Andr.* 900 πημάτων δοίηc λύcιν; E. *Or.* 213 has ὦ πότνια Λήθη τῶν κακῶν, but the personification is unusual in this context. The form λυαία is otherwise unknown, and although Λυαῖοc is an attested cult-title of Dionysus (cf. Lat. *Lyaeus*; probably to be connected with epithets such as Λύcιοc) there is no evidence that a feminine form was used as an epithet of Cybele; Cricca refers to cώτειρα, λυτηριάc of Cybele at *Orph. H.* 14. 8. The -αιοc suffix was still productive in the fifth century (cf. the new formations at Pi. *O.* 13. 69 δαμαῖοc, A. *Sept.* 292 λεχαῖοc, E. *Tro.* 188, *Ion* 1583 νηcαῖοc, Ar. fr. 754 K.–A. χορταῖοc); Danielsson suggests that the word is equivalent to λύcιc, comparing the formations ἀναγκαίη < ἀναγκαῖοc, γαληναίη < γαληναῖοc (also perhaps τροπαία < τροπαῖοc). These parallels are not exact; although -αιοc generally forms adjectives from stems in -a, λυαῖοc (and λυαία) must be formed directly from the verbal root λυ-, not from λύη. See K. Zacher, *De nominibus graecis in* -αιοc -αια -αιον (Halle, 1877), 251–2; G. Sandsjoe, *Die Adjektiva auf αιοc* (diss. Uppsala, 1918), 11; Chantraine, *Formation*, 45–6, 49. λύcιc might be read here (GOH), metrically 2 *cr* ('Ιλιοπόρος κακῶν) | 2*tr* (λύcιc . . . εἰ).

123. δυνα{c}τά: there is no need to restore δυνατά ⟨μοι⟩ (Janssen: ⟨τῶι⟩ Page, less probably), if the person can be supplied by e.g. λιcc⟨οίμαν⟩ at 127. δυναίμαν (-μην tent. Janssen), although unnecessary, would give excellent sense. For the use of the neuter plural, cf. Hdt. 1. 91. 1 τὴν πεπρωμένην μοῖραν ἀδύνατά ἐcτι ἀποφυγεῖν καὶ θεῶι.

Though there is no verb, the optative in the preceding clause suggests an optative should also be supplied here.

μελαμπεταλοχίτωνα: 'black-leaf-robed'; probably a reference to the forests of Ida, where Cybele had her cult; cf. E. *Palamedes* fr. 586 N², *Hel.* 1323–4. G. M. A. Hanfmann, *Archaeology*, 22 (1969), 264–9, believes that there may be a reference either to a real dress, or its imitation in painted sculpture, presented to the goddess, or to an image of Cybele with inlays, like the black obsidian used on the base of Pheidias' Zeus in Olympia.

The adjective here is an amalgamation of two common compounds, 'black-leaved' and 'black-clothed'; cf. Pi. *P.* 1. 27 ἐν μελαμφύλλοις . . . κορυφαῖς, A. *Pers.* 115–16 μελαγχίτων φρήν, Meleager, *HE* 3939 (*AP* 4. 1. 14) δάφνης κλῶνα μελαμπέταλον, Philip, *GP* 2661 (*AP* 9. 307. 2) κλῶνα μελαμπέταλον. But the result is an extravagant form of the type parodied by Aristophanes in his 'Euripidean' lyrics at *Ra.* 1336 μελανονεκυείμονα.

124. Ματρὸς οὐρείας: 'the Mountain Mother', to be identified with Cybele; cf. *h. Hom.* 14. 1, Pi. fr. 70b. 9 (*Dith.* 2), fr. 95. 3, Ar. *Av.* 746 Μητρὶ ὀρείαι, 873 ff., Telestes fr. 810. 2–3 Ματρὸς ὀρείας | Φρύγιον . . . νόμον, E. *Cretes* fr. 472. 13, *PMG* adesp. 1030 (of Rhea), A.R. 1. 1118–19 τὸ (i.e. a vine-tree) μὲν ἔκταμον, ὄφρα πέλοιτο | δαίμονος οὐρείης ἱερὸν βρέτας, where a scholion (on 1117–19a) notes Euphorion's explanation (fr. 125 Schneidweiler = 145 Powell) that the vine was sacred to Rhea as Mother of the Gods. There is no reason to believe with Aron that Artemis is meant, except in so far as the two could sometimes be identified, and Artemis could also be associated with mountains (as e.g. at E. *Tro.* 551 ff.).

Cybele first appears in Greece *c.*600 (cf. the form Κυβήβη at Hippon. fr. 127), and from the late fifth century becomes increasingly popular. Her cult was identified at an early stage with that of the Mother (Μήτηρ τῶν θεῶν or just Μήτηρ), who was also at times identified with Rhea, and occasionally with Aphrodite and Demeter (cf. esp. S. *Ph.* 392, E. *Hel.* 1301, Melanippides fr. 764, Telestes fr. 809). P. Derveni xviii 7–8 identifies her with both Demeter and Ge. Pindar (*P.* 3. 77 ff., fr. 95) connects her with Pan, also a mountain deity, and she is invoked as Ἰδαία μᾶτερ by the Phrygian slave at E. *Or.* 1453 ff. The extent of the Cybele cult in fifth-century Greece is uncertain, although there was a statue of her attributed to Pheidias in the Old Bouleuterion in Athens (Paus. 1. 3. 5; cf. Plin. *NH* 36. 17, who ascribes it to Pheidias' pupil Agoracritus of Paros). Her worship appears to have been quite familiar to the Greeks, and was probably introduced in the fifth century by immigrants from Asiatic Ionia. See Farnell iii. 298 ff.; Dodds on E. *Ba.* 78–9; Burkert 177 ff.; Parker, *Religion,* 159; N. Robertson in E. N. Lane (ed.), *Cybele, Attis and Related Cults. Essays in Memory of M. J. Vermaseren* (Leiden, 1996), 239–304; D. R. West, *Some Cults of Greek Goddesses and Female Daemons of Oriental Origin* (Neukirchen-Vluyn, 1995), 76–81.

125. δεcπόcυνα: 'queenly'; first attested at *h. Hom.* 2. 143–4, and as a substantive at Tyrt. 6. 2. For the adjectival use, cf. also Pi. *P.* 4. 267 (with Braswell), A. *Pers.* 587, *Ch.* 942, E. *Hec.* 99, Ar. *Th.* 41–2. δέcποινα was a common cult-title of Cybele (e.g. Ar. *Av.* 876); Timotheus may have had this epithet in mind: see A. Henrichs, *HSCP* 80 (1976), 266 ff.

πρὸc … γόνατα πεcεῖν: embracing the knees is an essential part of supplication (cf. 145), and the act is frequently associated with the use of the verb λίccομαι (cf. 127) in epic and tragedy (A. Corlu, *Recherches sur les mots relatifs à l'idée de prière* (Paris, 1966), 299; Gould, 'Hiketeia'). Given the invocation to Mysia, the image of supplication might here be blending with the custom of kissing the earth of one's native country (see also Ed. Fraenkel on A. *Ag.* 503); cf. the formulaic κύcε δὲ ζείδωρον ἄρουραν at *Od.* 5. 463 (on Odysseus' arrival in Phaeacia) and 13. 354 (on his return to Ithaca), and also *Od.* 4. 522 κύνει ἁπτόμενοc ἣν πατρίδα (of Agamemnon returning to Mycenae). There is no reference to the Persian custom of prostration (*pace* Janssen). Janssen assumes tmesis, but the separation of πρός from πεcεῖν would in that case be remarkably violent; it is more naturally taken as a preposition before γόνατα.

126. εὐωλένουc … χεῖραc: 'beautiful arms', obviously those of the suppliant; in Euripides ὠλένη is indistinguishable from χείρ, and is redundant in the compound here (cf.

E. *Hipp.* 200 with Barrett, 605 δεξιᾶς εὐωλένου). The adjective may be intended to suggest Asiatic effeminacy and vanity, especially when used by the speaker of himself.

ἀμφιβάλλων †λιccων: the Mysian needs to fling his arms around the Mother's knees and beseech her: therefore a verb of speaking is probably concealed in λιccων. Wilamowitz simply emends ἀμφιβάλλων to ἀμφέβαλλον, and writes λῦcον: however, in this case there is no indication of the start of the second prayer at 127 ff. Page suggested λίcc⟨οιτο, retaining the participle ἀμφιβάλλων, but the first-person forms at 115, 118, and 119, and in the prayer at 128 ἱκνοῦμαι, 129 ἐμόν, 130 με, 137 κείcομαι, suggest we should have a first person here also. West therefore supplements λιcc⟨οίμαν·, followed by a lacuna. The prayer itself should open with a request for help. The object is ἐμὸν αἰῶνα 'my life', and 'save' is a plausible sense to expect; for cῶc⟩ον in similar contexts, cf. E. *IT* 1082 ὦ πότνι'... cῶcόν με, 1398–400, Ar. *Vesp.* 393. Pulleyn 220 provides three literary examples of cώιζω in prayers against three epigraphic instances; but the aorist imperative is attested only in literature (*Od.* 4. 765, Ar. *Vesp.* 393). Here as elsewhere the aorist should refer to a single act of salvation (see Pulleyn 221–6).

λίccομαι sometimes implies the presence of the person supplicated (Corlu, op. cit. 293 ff.; F. Letoublon, *Lingua*, 52 (1980), 325–36); although the Great Mother is clearly not actually present here, she (or her image) is imagined to be.

127. χρυcοπλόκαμε: 'gold-tressed'; otherwise only of Leto at *h. Hom.* 3. 205, but gods frequently have golden hair; cf. χρυcοκόμας at Hes. *Th.* 947 (of Dionysus), Anacr. fr. 358. 2, E. *IA* 548 (both of Eros), Ba. 4. 2, E. *Suppl.* 975, Ar. *Av.* 217, *PMG* carm. conv. 886. 2 (all of Apollo), χρυcοέθειρ at Archil. fr. 323, χρυcεοβόcτρυχος at Philoxenus fr. 821 (of Galatea), and χρυcοχαίτης at Pi. *P.* 2. 16, Limenius 4 (both of Apollo), *Anacreont.* 43. 12 (of Eros). χρυc(ε)ο- is a common element in Euripidean compounds (Breitenbach 68). The upsilon is here short (as also at 202). Pindar has χρυcός with short upsilon (*N.* 7. 78). Loan-words (this one from Semitic, cf. Akk. *hurāṣu*) are often subject to some fluctuation in vowel-length.

128. θεὰ Μᾶτερ: cf. 124 n.

129. ἐμὸν ἐμὸν αἰῶνα: 'my life', i.e. me. West ('Analyses', 3) prefers ἀγῶνα with ἀπάλλαξ)ον as the verb at 127, 'bring my struggle to an end' (cf. E. *Heracl.* 346), but the periphrasis is supported by E. *Alc.* 337 αἰὼν οὑμός, *Ph.* 1532 còν αἰῶνα (Breitenbach 198–9). Periphrasis is in general common for personal pronouns (e.g. E. *El.* 1195, *Ion* 1475 etc.); for the anadiplosis see 76 n.

δυϲέκφευκτον: see 119 n.

ἐπεί: explains the reason for the Mysian's prayer (Rijksbaron 80–1).

130. λαιμοτόμωι: 'throat-slitting'; a favourite word of Euripides', with an active sense at *IT* 444, *El.* 459, and Ariston, *HE* 779 (*AP* 6. 306. 4); passive (λαιμότομος) at *Hec.* 208, *IA* 776, *Ion* 1054.

131. μήϲτορι ϲιδάρωι: λαιμοτόμωι μήϲτορι 'the throat-slitting deviser' may be a periphrasis for sword (Janssen), with the substantive ϲιδάρωι ('sword') in apposition, although ϲιδαρῶι could perhaps be read as an adjective 'iron'. Alternatively, μήϲτορι may have an adjectival force 'devising', although the use of substantives in -τωρ -τοροc as adjectives is not widely attested before Nonnus (e.g. *D.* 9. 51 ποδὸc ληΐϲτορι ταρϲῶι 'with plundering footsteps', 'with a robber's footsteps'; cf. Macedon. Cons. *AP* 9. 649 ληΐϲτορι χαλκῶι 'with plundering bronze'). Hsch. (μ 1269) μήϲτωρ· πολεμιϲτήc probably depends on the military image evoked by the Homeric μήϲτωρα φόβοιο, μήϲτωρεc ἀϋτῆc, of which there may be overtones here. Timotheus may here have been influenced by the Euripidean compounds δοριμήϲτωρ (*Andr.* 1016), χαλκεομήϲτωρ (*Tro.* 217). μήϲτωρ regularly has the genitive -ωροc in Homer, perhaps *metri causa* (μήϲτορα φόβοιο being metrically intractable); -οροc is the form in all compounds and in the name Μήϲτωρ -οροc; see Fraenkel, *Nomina Agentis*, i. 14 ff.

132. κατακυμοτακεῖc: 'wave-destroying (?)'. The formation here is slightly odd, and Danielsson's κατακυμοταχεῖc 'speeding over the waves' may be correct. Compounds in -τακήc generally date from after the fifth century. κυμοτακήc would mean 'melting the waves', and κατατήκω is emphatic; but tmesis in a compound adjective seems unlikely, and there is no satisfactory parallel for the use of (κατα-)τήκω in this context. The adjective might be regarded as supplementing ναυςιφθόροι, 'causing men to waste away on the waves'.

ναυςιφθόροι: 'ship-destroying'; the datival–locatival -ςι- is technically incorrect, but cf. ναυςιπομπός 'ship-wafting' at E. *Ph.* 1712 and ναυςιπόρος 'causing a ship to pass' at E. *IA* 172. Possibly the adjectival formation is based on ναυφθορία 'shipwreck' (ναύφθορος is passive, 'ship-wrecked', at E. *Hel.* 1382).

133. νυκτιπαγεῖ βορέα⟨ι⟩: 'the north-east wind which freezes during the night', see 99 n. γυμνοπαγεῖς. Boreas is noted for its freezing effects as early as Hes. *Op.* 504 ff., who mentions that it is particularly bad during winter, and concentrates on its effects in the early morning (547 ff.) rather than at night; cf. also Pi. fr. 94b. 17 ff. (*Parth.* 2) ὁπόταν τε χειμῶνος cθένει | φρίccων Βορέαc ἐπιcπέρχηιcι. For its character at night, cf. Diodorus, *GP* 2118 (*AP* 6. 245. 1–2) Καρπαθίην ὅτε νυκτὸς ἅλα cτρέψαντος ἀήτου | λαίλαπι βορραίηι κλαcθὲν ἐcεῖδε κέραc. There is probably no reference to divine influence, although Zephyrus is mentioned at Hdt. 8. 96. 2 in connection with Salamis, and Boreas was supposed to have intervened at Artemisium in response to Athenian prayers, after which a shrine was established in Athens (cf. Hdt. 7. 189). See Parker, *Religion*, 156–7.

διαρ⟨ρ⟩αίcονται: 'will destroy'; the papyrus has διαραι-, but spellings of this sort are well attested in inscriptions of the fifth and fourth centuries (Threatte i. 519–20).

134. περί: adverbial. The position of περί precludes us from taking it as a straight preposition followed by γυίων; the genitive depends on εἶδος, 'the warmth of my limbs'. The verb means 'to tear through', but γυμνοπαγεῖς at 99 indicates that actual loss of clothing is meant.

136. εἶδος ὑφαντόν: 'woven warmth', a bold (but not impossibly so) periphrasis for clothing; εἶδος is written for ἶδος (West), which is more plausible than understanding γυίων εἶδος 'shape of my limbs' as an equivalent periphrasis. The sequence of thought, however, is much the same: γυίων ἶδος can function as a term for clothes because they give warmth. The *e*-grade form of the noun is ancient (Wackernagel, *Kl. Schr.* i. 745–52), but here it could also result from a confusion between ει and ι, which is common in the later papyri (Mayser–Schmoll i/1. 66). Persian clothes were regarded as unusual in Greek eyes; cf. also 168 εὐϋφῆ and 167 n. cτολήν. Sudhaus unnecessarily conjectures ἕρκοc, citing *Il*. 5. 315 ἕρκοc βελέων of Aphrodite's robe.

137. κείcομαι: 'I shall lie'; frequently of dead bodies in poetry (cf. e.g. *Il*. 5. 467, 16. 451, 18. 338, *Od*. 3. 109, A. *Ag*. 1438, 1446, S. *Ant*. 1240, E. *Hec*. 28), but rarely in prose. Here the emphasis seems to be on the lack of burial rather than just death; the Mysian's troubles will continue even after he is dead.

οἰκτρόc: the masculine here agrees with the male speaker, rather than with the feminine predicate θοίνα.

137–8. ὀρνίθων ἔθνεcιν: 'for the tribes of the birds'; cf. *Il*. 2. 459 ὀρνίθων . . . ἔθνεα. The image is a manipulation of a traditional Homeric motif. The feasting of birds on the bodies of the dead is an epic topos (e.g. *Il*. 1. 4–5, 2. 393, 8. 379; cf. S. *Ant*. 29–30, *Ai*. 830, E. *Ph*. 1634 etc.), usually associated with the feasting of dogs, although twice birds are mentioned alone (*Il*. 11. 395, 453). On two occasions it expresses a fear: Hector to Priam at *Il*. 22. 66–75, and to Achilles at *Il*. 22. 339. See M. Faust, *Glotta*, 48 (1970), 8–31; C. Segal, *The Theme of the Mutilation of the Corpse in the Iliad* (*Mnem*. Suppl. 17; Leiden, 1971). A similar statement is found at the end of a speech at Theocr. 3. 53.

ὠμοβρῶcι: 'flesh-eating', cf. *Il*. 11. 453–4 οἰωνοὶ ὠμηcταί. ὠμοβρώc otherwise only occurs at E. *Tro*. 436, *HF* 889, and also probably at S. fr. 799. 5 Radt (cj. Brunck).

θοίνα: 'feast'; cf. A. *Suppl*. 801 ὄρνιcι δεῖπνον, S. *Ai*. 830 οἰωνοῖc . . . ἕλωρ, E. *Hec*. 1077 κυcίν τε φοινίαν δαῖτ', *Ion* 505 πτανοῖcι θοίναν. R. Renehan, *AJP* 100 (1979), 473–4, takes this passage to be earlier evidence for Zenodotus' variant δαῖτα for πᾶcι at *Il*. 1. 5 (see Leaf ad loc.; R. Pfeiffer, *The History of Classical Scholarship* (Oxford, 1968), 111–12).

139–49. The Celaenaean: Introduction. The next episode of the poem follows directly from a summary of the preceding episode at 139. The narrative is generalized throughout, a fact marked by the use of the optative at 140 (ἄγοι) and of the indefinite article τιc (cf. 130); thus it is perhaps surprising when the Oriental is given a specific ethnicity. Wilamowitz regarded the Celaenaean as a counterpart to the plainsman at 40 ff.; Hall, 'Drowning', suggests that he is in fact an amalgam of several Asiatic subgroups (cf. the references to Susa, Sardis, Ecbatana, and nn.); Gildersleeve notes: 'The Kelainite is the spokesman for reasons best known to Timotheos, but we must imagine the other captives falling in at the end.' But the man is explicitly called a Celaenaean, and it is absurd to suppose that any other captives are imagined to be speaking. Instead, Sardis, Susa, and Ecbatana, locations progressively further away, emphasize the distance which the man is willing to keep between himself and Greece. The effect is spoilt (comically?) by his last reference to Ephesus, a city not merely closer even than Sardis, but indeed one of the Greek cities of the Ionian coast. Celaenae (always pl.) was a major town in Lydia, west of the central Anatolian plateau and lying at the junction of the Marsyas and the Maeander. See Hdt. 7. 26–7; X. *An.* 1. 2. 7–9, who claims that Xerxes built a palace and citadel there on his way back from his defeat in Greece; Strabo 12. 8. 15.

Supplication scenes play a significant role in Greek battle narratives, especially in Homer. In the *Iliad* only Trojans supplicate (always unsuccessfully) their captors on the battle-field, and an offer of ransom is usually involved (cf. *Il.* 6. 45 ff., 10. 374 ff., 11. 130 ff., 20. 463 ff., 21. 72 ff.). By contrast, similar supplication scenes in the *Odyssey* usually phrase the request in terms of pleas for respect and mercy (e.g. *Od.* 22. 310 ff., 330 ff.). Neither of these elements is present in the Celaenaean's speech at 150 ff., and it is not made clear whether his supplication is to be regarded as successful or not. See Gould, 'Hiketeia'; V. Pedrick, *TAPA* 112 (1982), 125–40. The Celaenaean's supplication contains elements which suggest the barbarian's cowardliness, such as his importunate pleading and complete lack of resistance; see also 144 n. But here it also recalls the Mysian's desire to supplicate the Great Mother at 122 ff. While the Mysian's wish is unfulfilled, the Celaenaean must supplicate a Greek, not a god, and his appeal, in the end, avails nothing.

Metre

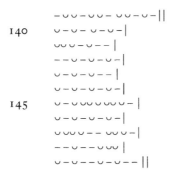

The return to the regular iambic metra after the mixed aeolic elements at 128 ff. marks the beginning of the new episode; the general regularity of the metre at this point contrasts with the abrupt periods of the Celaenaean's speech itself. The section seems to begin with a dactylic tetrameter, though this results in *anceps iuxta breve*; if period-end is assumed, as it probably should be, the line looks like an extended aeolic metron (*gl^d*), perhaps recalling the aeolics, especially glyconics, of 128–38. The paragraphos in the papyrus suggests the line belongs with this section, but it may have been misplaced. 139 belongs semantically with the preceding section. Line 140 begins the iambic sequence, which has remarkably few syncopated forms; 141 is *ith*, and at 143 we find *ia ba*, at 148 *ia cr*. Otherwise, dimeters prevail. At 145 and 147, where the Celaenaean begins his supplication and attempts to speak, the iambics are highly resolved; a degree of excitement and pace is thus achieved. The section ends with *ia ith*.

139–49. 'Thus they wept and lamented. And whenever some Greek, armed with a sword, seized and carried off an inhabitant of Celaenae rich in herds, . . . , he carried him off dragging him by the hair, and he [the Celaenaean] embracing his knees would supplicate him, weaving a Greek with an Asiatic speech, breaking the pierced seal of his mouth'.

139. τοιάδ': as a formula for introducing speeches, cf. Pi. fr. 52i. 13 (*Pae.* 8a) τοιᾶιδε κορυφᾶι cάμαινεν λόγων, E. *Ba.* 151, Theocr. 6. 4, 8. 8, 11. 18; but as a formula for closure it is only found at Theocr. [20]. 11 τοιάδε μυθίζοιca, 22. 167 ἴcκον τοιάδε πολλά. Pindar more commonly uses τοιαῦτα, twice at speech-opening (Pi. *O.* 6. 16, *P.* 8. 55), once at speech-end (*P.* 4. 94; cf. Ba. fr. 60. 21), but Führer 15–16 is wrong to say it is more common in general.

ὀδυρόμενοι κατεδάκρυον: for the language, see nn. on 100 δακρυcταγεῖ, 103 ὀδυρμῶι, where the two roots again appear together. The compound καταδακρύω is a Euripidean coinage at *Hel.* 673–4 κατεδάκρυcα καὶ βλέφαρον ὑγραίνω | δάκρυcιν, where the element κατα- has little effect on the sense, but the redundancy of the language is in any case obvious.

140. ἐπεί: at 162 the word introduces the narrative, and it is especially common in Euripides as an introduction to narrative messenger speeches; cf. e.g. *Andr.* 1085, *El.* 774, *Hel.* 1526, *Ion* 1122, *Ph.* 1090 etc. Here, although 139 is marked in the papyrus as belonging to the same section, it denotes the beginning of the Celaenaean episode.

ἄγοι: the root recurs at 144 ἄγεγ.

141. πολυβότων: 'with many herds'; a man of some wealth and power then? Nearby Cappodocia was known for its horses down to the third century AD (Herzfeld 3–5), and Persian horses were famous (Persia is regularly described as *uvaspa-* 'having good horses' in the OP inscriptions); Mysia was reputedly the first to breed horses and mules (Anacr. fr. 377). So perhaps horses, rather than cattle, are meant here, though Asia is called 'sheep-rearing' at Archil. fr. 227 ὁ δ' Ἀcίηc τὸ καρτερὸc μηλοτρόφου (of Gyges?).

πολύβοτοc may occur at A. *Sept.* 774 (πολύβοτοc αἰών) but the reading is disputed (Hutchinson prefers πολύβατοc ἀγών), and otherwise only at Dion. Hal. 1. 37 οὐδ' ἄν τιc αὐτὴν φαίη πολύκαρπον μὲν εἶναι καὶ πολύδενδρον καὶ πολύβοτον, where it does not obviously mean 'having much pasture' (LSJ). If the second term is connected with βοτόν 'grazing animal', then the sense should be 'with many herds'. It could alternatively be taken as passive 'much-grazed'; cf. A. *Suppl.* 548 μηλόβοτοc, *Od.* 4. 606 αἰγίβοτοc, although the formations are not quite analogous. Active -βοτοc is generally late (cf. Nonn. δρακοντοβότοc, λεοντοβότοc etc.; but cυβότηc -ώτηc in Hom., Arist.). Homer has πουλυβότειρα 'much-nourishing' at e.g. *Il.* 3. 89 etc.

142. ὀρφανὸν μαχᾶν: an obscure phrase, with several possible explanations:

(i) 'Away from the battle' (perhaps to be understood proleptically), and so 'cut off from his own side', but the phrase is extremely obscure. ὀρφανός with the genitive generally expresses privation, and there are several extended uses; cf. e.g. Pi. *I.* 4. 8 ὀρφανοὶ ὕβριος 'free from insolence', Herod. 3. 39 ὀρφανὴν βίου 'destitute of livelihood' (Headlam–Knox). We might compare the uses of ἀπόμαχος, but the sense 'absent from battle' is late (cf. *AP* 9. 467 tit. τίνας ἂν εἴποι λόγους ὁ Πηλεὺς ἀκούων ὅτι ἀπόμαχός ἐστιν Ἀχιλλεύς, i.e. out of the conflict) while 'disabled' does not suit the context; a better comparison would be ἀπόλεμος 'unwarlike'.

(ii) Reinach takes the phrase to mean 'unfamiliar with battles'; Croiset thinks of a non-combatant, perhaps a valet, though 155 implies that he is almost certainly a soldier. However, ὀρφανός can only with difficulty bear the sense 'unfamiliar with'.

(iii) Janssen takes μαχᾶν to mean 'of his weapons', citing Hdt. 5. 49. 3 ἥ τε μάχη αὐτῶν ἐστι τοιήδε, τόξα καὶ αἰχμὴ βραχέα, which he seems to understand as 'their weapons were these . . .'; but the sense of μάχη here is 'means of fighting'. The plural μάχαι is found only rarely, but normally in the concrete sense 'battles'.

(iv) I have thought tentatively of ὄρχαμον μαχᾶν, though ὄρχαμος in epic only appears in the formulae ὄρχαμος ἀνδρῶν and ὄρχαμε λαῶν, where its original significance is obscure (S. West on *Od.* 3. 400–1). By the fifth century, however, it was clearly taken to mean 'leader', but is still rare even in poetry. Aeschylus has ὀρχάμωι στρατοῦ in lyric at *Pers.* 129, referring to the leader of the Persian army; at fr. 451q. 9 Radt he has a possibly independent use, ὄρχαμ[οί] τ' ἐπισκο[, where Lloyd-Jones supplements ἐπίσκο[ποι. A third poetic instance is *CEG* i no. 271 (*c.*475 BC), a hexametrical inscription with]ὄρχαμε : τ [– –] at l. 4; Hiller supplements τ[όχϲο], i.e. τόξου, Raubitschek τ[έχνεϲ], though either would be odd even in the light of the Aeschylean instances. Otherwise I find ὄρχαμος only at Palladas, *AP* 11. 284. 1–2 ἐκ γῆς Λωτοφάγων μέγας ὄρχαμος ἦλθε Λυκάων | Χαλκίδος ἐκ γαίης ἀντιοχευόμενος, and (clearly Homeric) of Christ at Cometas, *AP* 15. 40. 1 ὄρχαμος ἀνδρῶν. Still, ὄρχαμος μαχᾶν could well be a Timothean periphrasis for a general; Aeschylus' 'leader of the army' is, of course, Xerxes.

(v) GOH suggests that μαχᾶν may be an error for μάχας, perhaps influenced by Κελαινᾶν in the preceding line; but, although possible, this does not make the sense of the phrase any clearer.

143. αἰδαρόκωπος: 'armed with an iron sword'. κώπη is found of a sword's hilt in Homer and later, though in earlier texts we usually find an explanatory dependent genitive; cf. *Od.* 8. 403–4 ἄορ παγχάλκεον, ὧι ἔπι κώπη | ἀργυρέη (Euryalus' sword), 11. 531 ξίφεος δ' ἐπεμαίετο κώπην, Tyrt. fr. 11. 34 ἢ ξίφεος κώπην ἢ δορύ μακρὸν ἔχων. In tragedy it can be used independently (S. *Ph.* 1254–5, E. *Hec.* 543). This explicitly iron sword is perhaps to be contrasted with the more elaborate swords occasionally mentioned in Homer (e.g. *Od.* 8. 403–4 and Achilles' sword at *Il.* 1. 219 ἐπ' ἀργυρέηι κώπηι σχέθε χεῖρα), and elsewhere (e.g. E. *Hec.* ἀμφίχρυσον φάσγανον κώπης λαβὼν). Timotheus here emphasizes the reality of the scene.

144. ἄγεγ: the imperfect is to be preferred to the present ἄγει given by the papyrus; the historic present is unusual in lyric (not in or before Pindar or Bacchylides), and not otherwise present in Timotheus. 144 is not a logical apodosis for 140–3; however, in the earlier clause the emphasis is on the participle λαβών, on which the accusatives depend.

κόμης ἐπισπάσας: 'dragging him by the hair'; for the typically Euripidean motif of hair-seizing, normally applied only to women, cf. E. *Or.* 1469, *Hel.* 116 ἐπισπάσας κόμης, *IA* 790, 1366, *Tro.* 882, *Andr.* 710, *Hec* 1166; the image also occurs at A. *Suppl.* 909 ἀποσπάσας (ἐπι- Pierson) κόμης, *Sept.* 328. Here, applied to a man, it suggests the Greek attitude towards barbarian 'effeminacy'; but the Celaenaean, in his utter helplessness, would in any case be like a woman in Greek eyes.

145. ἀμφὶ γόνασι περιπλεκείς: 'embracing his knees'; see 125 n. The verbal root is repeated at 146 ἐμπλέκων. The phrase λάβε γούνων, with variation of the verb, occurs nineteen times in the *Iliad*, and nineteen times in the *Odyssey*, always with reference to supplication (Gould, 'Hiketeia', 76 = 26). The two prepositions may suggest the

Celaenaean's desperation. The Celaenaean is allowed to perform the act so desired by the Mysian, though he must supplicate a Greek and not his god; but nevertheless, the result seems to be much the same.

146. ἐλίccετ': see 127 n.; cf. also the Homeric phrases at e.g. *Il.* 6. 45 λαβὼν ἐλλίccετο γούνων, 21. 71 ἑλὼν ἐλλίccετο γούνων, *Od.* 6. 142 γούνων λίccοιτο λαβὼν etc., on which the language here may be partly based.

147. Ἀcιάδι φωνᾶι: 'with Asian speech'; the same phrase is found in the Phrygian's aria at E. *Or.* 1395-7 ἄλινον αἴλινον ἀρχὰν θανάτου | βάρβαροι λέγουcιν, | αἰαῖ, Ἀcιάδι φωνᾶι, but in a different metrical context. A similar emphasis on barbarian speech is found in tragedy at A. *Pers.* 406 Περcίδοc γλώccηc, 635; E. *Ph.* 301 Φοίνιccαν βοάν, 679 ff. βαρβάρωι βοᾶι . . . βαρβάροιc λιταῖc, 1301 βοᾶι βαρβάρωι; *Or.* 1374, 1385, 1395-7; however, in all these cases the reference is purely conventional, and there is no attempt to distinguish the Asiatics linguistically.

διάτορον: 'pierced'; probably agreeing with cφραγῖδα and to be understood proleptically, 'breaking the seal of his mouth so that it was pierced' (cf. the passive sense at S. *OT* 1034), although it is also possible to compare the active sense 'piercing' of sound at A. *Eum.* 567-8 †εἴτ' οὖν διάτοροc† Τυρcηνικὴ | cάλπιγξ. The adjective is, of course, highly appropriate for a seal, which must be pierced or broken in order to be opened. Croiset takes διάτορον with the adjective Ἑλλάδ' (sc. φωνάν), and places a comma before cφραγῖδα.

148. cφαγῖδα . . . cτόματοc: 'the seal of his mouth', most naturally taken as a description of silence (Gildersleeve), with cτόματοc genitive of the subject; cf. Lucian, *AP* 10. 42 ἀρρήτων ἐπέων γλώccηι cφραγὶc ἐπικείcθω. | κρείccων γὰρ μύθων ἢ κτεάνων φυλακή, Christodorus, *AP* 2. 31 ὑπὸ cφρηγῖδα cιωπῆc, Nonn. *Par.* 11. 145-6, 21. 139-40, and Thgn. 421, *PMG* adesp. 960, Palladas, *AP* 11. 304. 5 for similar metaphors. Page's explanation (*quod genuinum est notat sphragis: oris sphragida corrumpit qui lingua aliena non nativa loquitur*) is fanciful. See further L. Radermacher, *WS* 50 (1933), 29-30; J. Diehl, *Sphragis: eine semasiologische Nachlese* (diss. Giessen, 1938). His mouth is 'sealed' because it is closed, and he needs to overcome his terror to speak at all.

149. Ἰάονα: usually in the plural, but for the singular cf. Pi. fr. 52b. 3 (*Pae.* 2), A. *Pers.* 950–1, Theocr. 16. 57. To Orientals Greeks were generally 'Ionian'; cf. OP *Yaunā-*, Akk. *ia-ma-nu*, Lyc. *Ijāna-*, Elam. *Yauna* (also A. *Pers.* 178, 563, 949, 950, 1011, Ar. *Ach.* 104 with *Σ*), Hebrew *Yāwān*, Syriac *Yawān*, Arabic *Yūnān*, and see J. A. Brinkman, in Robert F. Sutton, Jr. (ed.), *Daidalikon: Studies in Memory of Raymond V. Schoder* (Wauconda, Ill., 1989), 53–71. This form of the adjective may represent an attempt to reproduce Persian pronunciation (see Colvin 81–2).

In the Behistun inscription Darius (DB i 15 p. 117) simply mentions Ionia as part of his kingdom when he came to power. In a Persepolis inscription he distinguishes between 'Ionians who are of the mainland and (those) who are by the sea' (DPe p. 136 Kent); here we should probably not see a reference to mainland Greece at all, but to Ionians living in the interior of Asia (the 'countries which are across the sea' are listed next). Xerxes (XPh 23–5 p. 151) claims that he was king of the Ionians 'who dwell by the sea' and those 'who dwell across the sea'; the latter must be the Greeks on the Greek mainland; his boast is perhaps forgivable. A Greek (and Carian) community may have resided in Babylon; they were involved in transporting cedar from Babylon for the construction of Susa (DSf pp. 142–3 Kent); Greek and Sardian stone-cutters were employed on the building-works themselves. In an inscription from Naqš-i-Rustam (DNa) we find a distinction made between *Yaunā-* 'Ionians' and *Yaunā takabarā* 'petasos-wearing Ionians'; the latter are perhaps Macedonians (Herzfeld 309–10, 349). See further D. M. Lewis, *Sparta and Persia* (Leiden, 1977), 11–15, 117–18.

ἐξιχνεύων: 'tracking down'. The Celaenaean, as a foreigner, is not fully conversant with Greek; we shall not expect him to be fluent when he speaks. The word belongs to hunting terminology, but is metaphorical as early as A. *Ag.* 368 πάρεστιν τοῦτο γ' ἐξιχνεῦσαι.

150–61. The Celaenaean: Speech. The passage is intended to reproduce the sort of broken Ionian Greek spoken by Asiatics, an intention already signalled at 146–9. In an attempt to represent the actual effect of imperfect linguistic knowledge, Timotheus appears to be drawing on a tradition established in Old Comedy. Comedy frequently makes use of non-Attic dialects and non-Greek gibberish; it is not always, in the case of consistent dialect difference, intended to be comic, but here, where no other character's language is unusual, it probably had a humorous effect.

The comic example closest to Timotheus is the Scythian archer in Aristophanes' *Thesmophoriazusae*, but we may also mention the Persian Ambassador in *Acharnians* (104, 106) and at a further remove the Triballian god in *Aves*. Both of these characters speak not only barbarized Greek but also produce comic gibberish, which may in the case of the Ambassador have been intended to reproduce the actual sound of Persian in Greek ears (K. J. Dover, *Maia*, 15 (1963), 7–8; M. L. West, *CR²* 18 (1968), 5–6). Plato Com. portrayed Cleophon's mother speaking some form of barbarian language (fr. 61 K.–A. βαρβαρίζουϲα), and (fr. 183 K.–A.) attacked Hyperbolus for being unable to speak correct Attic. Hyperbolus and his mother were popular subjects for such attacks: Hermippus frr. 10, 12 K.–A. may also be referred to him. A collection of relevant passages with discussion may now be found in Colvin 287–94; see also T. Long, *Barbarians in Greek Comedy* (Carbondale and Edwardsville, Ill., 1984), 134 ff. Possibly a remote connection should also be seen with Hipponax fr. 92, in which a witch was portrayed speaking Lydian, although the words may merely have imitated Lydian sounds (West, *Studies*, 144–5).

For the use of dialect forms, cf. e.g. Aristophanes' use of Megarian, Boeotian, and Laconian (in *Lys.*, *Ach.*); Strattis' use of Macedonian and Boeotian (frr. 29, 49 K.–A.); Eubulus' use of Boeotian (fr. 11 K.–A.) etc. See Colvin 265–87; also S. Halliwell, 'The Sound of the Voice in Old Comedy', in Craik 69–79.

In later comedy the device was less widespread although still practised. An invented Indian language is used in the Charition mime, ed. I. C. Cunningham, *Herodas: Mimiambi* (Leipzig, 1987), 42–7; for alleged connections with genuine

Indian dialects, see E. Hultzsch, *Hermes*, 39 (1904), 307–11, and D. L. Page, *Greek Literary Papyri* (Cambridge, Mass. and London, 1941²), 337, although the Greek used by the Indian King at 95 ff. is not apparently marked as particularly barbarized. At Alexis fr. 146 K.–A. the medical cachet bestowed on a doctor by Doric speech is satirized (cf. Menander, *Aspis* 374 ff., 439 ff.) and at com. adesp. fr. 182 K.–A. Aetolian is used, but the context is unclear (see Long, op. cit. 150–1). At com. adesp. fr. 934 K.–A. a character boasts of the Macedonian commanders under whom he has served, all with names in -ας that make a non-Attic genitive in -α. In Posidippus fr. 30 K.–A. someone criticizes the strict Atticism of another character, which seemingly consists in finding fault with non-Attic usage in non-Athenians. Yet in New Comedy generally, surprisingly little linguistic use was made of the comic potential of slaves of foreign extraction (W. T. MacCary, *TAPA* 100 (1967), 277–94). Punic may have been included in the Hellenistic original of Plautus' *Poenulus* (C. C. Coulter, *Phil. Quart.* 13 (1934), 133–9; A. S. Gratwick, *Hermes*, 99 (1971), 25–45), but Plautus would probably have had greater knowledge of Punic than a Greek predecessor, and its use may be his own contribution.

In tragedy the possibility for realistic representation of foreign speech seems to have been lost quite early. Although there is some indication that the linguistic forms in Aeschylus' *Persae* were chosen to represent the sound of Persian speech (see C. Morenilla-Talens, *IF* 94 (1989), 158–76; and also to suggest the Ionic environment, see W. Headlam, *CR* 12 (1898), 189–93), there is little evidence for the practice after Aeschylus. See Colvin 74–87. Tragedy may have deliberately avoided the convention only after it had been adopted by comedy. However, the Phrygian's aria in Euripides' *Orestes* may, with its exuberance and exoticism, be a tragic equivalent to the barbaric Greek of the Celaenaean. See Hall, *Barbarian*, 76–8, 117–21. The evidence thus suggests that the passage in Timotheus may have had a humorous effect, despite the desperate straits in which the Celaenaean finds himself. It would also allow Timotheus to show off his talent for mimesis, an important feature of the New Music with its interest in ποικιλία.

Phonology

The phonology of the Celaenaean's speech has some Ionic colouring which distinguishes it from the rest of the poem; note αὖτις = Att. αὖθις, κῶc = Att. πῶc (*kʷ > Ion. κ, Att. π). Ἄρτιμιc is probably intended to be Asiatic (see 160 n.). However, non-Ionic is πρᾶγμα (Ion. πρῆγμα, πρῆχμα).

Morphology

(i) Verbs

At a number of points the Celaenaean clearly confuses active and middle voice. Wackernagel (*Vorlesungen über Syntax* (Basle, 1926²), i. 123) compares the form χαίρομαι in the masturbatory song of Datis the Mede at Ar. *Pax* 291 (Att. χαίρω). However, various dialects present the middle voice for verbs which were active in standard Attic. Ionic dialects in particular have a tendency to use the middle, and it is possible that χαίρομαι (the form used in modern Greek) was a legitimate dialect variant that would have had a comic reflexive sense only for speakers of Attic (Bechtel iii. 246–28; V. Bers, *Greek Poetic Syntax in the Classical Age* (New Haven and London, 1984), 111). A closer parallel is the Scythian in Ar. *Thesm.*, who generally uses voice correctly, but who produces at least one wrong active (if 1005 βούλιc stands for *βούλειc for βούλει) due to confusion about Greek voice distinctions. Elsewhere the Scythian's wrong verb-forms are so obscure that any supposed underlying meaning can only be guessed at.

The precise distinction made by the Greeks between active and medio-passive forms is not quite clear, although it was evidently operative to some extent even in later antiquity. In normal prose about three-quarters of the verbs are likely to be active in form (Y. Duhoux, *Le Verbe grec ancien: éléments de morphologie et de syntaxe grecque ancienne* (Louvain-la-Neuve, 1992), 100 ff.). The distinction between active and middle must have been a difficult one for non-native speakers, especially if their own language lacked it. Aulus Gellius, for instance, mistakenly used ἄξω and ἄξεις instead of ἄξομαι and ἄξει at 5. 11. 2–3. But nevertheless confusion about diathesis is only occasionally attested in the

Ptolemaic papyri (Schwyzer ii. 234–5; Mayser–Schmoll ii/2. 109–16, esp. 115–16 on the use of the active instead of the middle).

ἔλθω and κάθω are thought by Janssen and Friedrich to be subjunctives with a future sense (because 'the syntactic differences between the *futurum indicativi* . . . and the *coniunctivus futuralis* . . . are not clear to him'; Janssen). But we could just as meaningfully describe them as theoretical presents formed on an aorist stem. The Celaenean cannot speak Greek fluently, and the errors are the point in themselves.

(ii) Nouns

Gender appears to be confused at 160–1, although the fact that θεός is not always gender-specific obscures the issue. Aristophanes' Scythian frequently confuses genders (Friedrich 291–2).

Syntax

παρά may be used once with the dative and once with the accusative in the same line (see 158 n.). A similar use is found at Ar. *Thesm.* 1193 παρ' ἐμέ, but not in reference to a place, and elsewhere the Scythian tends to use cases correctly (Friedrich 295). The breakdown in construction at 157–61 may be a barbarism, and the high level of asyndeton could also be intended as an indication of the Celaenaean's linguistic incompetence.

Metre

```
150    ∪ – – – – – ∪ – ∪ |
       – ∪ – ∪ – – |
       – – ∪ – – ∪ – |
       – ∪ – ∪ – – |
       ∪ – ∪ – ∪∪ ∪ – ||
155    – ∪ ∪ ∪∪ – ∪ – ∪ – – ||
       – ∪ ∪ – ||
       ∪ – – – – ∪ – |
       – ∪∪ ∪ – ∪ ∪ ∪ – |
         – ∪ ∪∪ – – |
160    – ∪∪ ∪ – ∪ – ∪ – |
       ∪∪ ∪ – ∪ – – ||
```

The iambic rhythm continues; 150 appears to be *ba sp tr*, and trochaic elements may also feature at 155 if -◡◡◡◡ at the start is a trochee with resolved second princeps rather than a resolved choriamb. Saija thinks 150 'prosodiac + palimbacchiac', scanning ◡--------◡, but τί can hardly be anything but short. At 154 he finds a reizianum and a tribrach, at 155 a choriamb and enoplian, at 158 a resolved cretic + reizianum; there is little to be gained from this analysis. Although the reizianum is a common clausula in Aristophanic iambic lyric (Parker, *Songs*, 73; West, *Metre*, 104–5), there is no need to introduce it here, where an analysis in pure iambic metra is possible. *Ith* is common (151, 153), twice at period-end (155, 161). Period-end at 155 and 156 is marked by hiatus; the large number of relatively short periods is presumably intended to reflect the Celaenaean's confusion and desperate situation. The final vowel of οὐδαμά at 151 must be taken as short to allow for the elision. At 155 Wilamowitz suggests μαχέϲ⟨θ⟩', which would produce a resolved iamb (-◡◡◡-) followed by *ith*. The scansion of Cάρδι (158) is unclear: if the ending is taken as accusative, the iota must be long (acc. Cάρδιc with long -ι at Hdt. 1. 27: Cάρδι⟨c⟩ is conjectured here by Brussich), but the dative has short ε/ι (Cάρδεϲιν, Cάρδιϲι at A. *Pers.* 321, Hdt. 5. 101. 1, 5. 102. 1). Scanning it short gives *ia cr* (so above); if long, we have *ia ch*. Coῦc' in the same line appears to be an accusative; Page unjustifiably does not elide the final α of Coῦcα at 158 (West, 'Analyses', 4).

150–61. '"†I with you† how and what thing? Me no come back. This time my master brung me here to this place; but for the rest no more, sir, no more I come here again to fight. But I stay. I here not to you, I there by Sardis, by Sousa, dwelling Agbatana. Artimis, my great god, will guard me in Ephesus."'

150. †ἐγώ μοι ϲοι†: Gildersleeve's ἐγῶιμι (from ἐγὼ εἰμί) is attractive for the sense, 'how am I of concern to you?'. The crasis is found at Herod. 5. 15, where it appears to be vulgar, and can be compared to the instances of ἐγῶιμαι at Men. *Ep.* 1118, *Sam.* 298; ἐγῶιδα is found in late tragedy and comedy (E. *IT* 544, 852, *Med.* 39, *Or.* 546, *Ph.* 716; Ar. *Ach.* 904, *Vesp.* 1181, 1205, *Thesm.* 850, *Ra.* 836, *Eccl.* 797). See Stevens 59. But the syntax, with κῶc delayed to the end of the clause, is odd, although perhaps not excessively so in the mouth of an Asiatic. Aron understands the sense to be 'how can there be a contest between us?', but there is no support for the view that the reference is directly to fighting. According to Ebeling, citing Kühner–Gerth ii. 255, καί strengthens κῶc; he translates, 'How am I of any concern to you?'; again the syntax is extremely tortuous. It is most natural to take κῶc καὶ τί πρᾶγμα as 'how and what (thing)?', whatever the solution to the first half of the line is. Long- man reads επω in the papyrus, and proposes ἔπω as a barbaric equivalent of ἔψομαι, but this provides little sense for κῶc καὶ τί πρᾶγμα. Page wonders whether ἔπω might mean 'I say'; ἔπω as a verb of speaking is late (cf. Nic. *Al.* 429 ἔπουcιν, 490 ἔπουcι, *Th.* 508). Stanford pro- poses emending to an optative ἔποιμι: 'May I say something to you somehow, even a certain thing', again with an emphatic καί, although this appears somewhat too polite in the context. Janssen suggests ἔπωμαι, but there is no advantage in the subjunctive. The use of optatives and subjunctives is often one of the most difficult things for a non-native speaker of a language. cοι must presumably be an indirect object of some sort, but the sense given to μοι, if it is not emended, is less clear: it may be an ethic dative. Timotheus may have made his Celaenaean begin with a deliberate muddle, and only afterwards speak anything approximating to sense.

κῶc: 'how', regular East Ionian and common in Herodo- tus (Bechtel iii. 87–9; Buck 63). The postponement of κῶc and τί is common in tragedy as a way of emphasizing the preceding words, but may well have been colloquial (G. Thomson, *CQ* 33 (1939), 147–52).

151. αὖτιc: 'back again' (Ion., Arc.: see Buck, 105). αὖτιc is repeated at 155, and there are a number of other repetitions in the passage (e.g. 153/7 δεῦρο, 153/5 ἐνθάδε, 154/5 οὐκέτι); possibly the Celaenaean is supposed to have a very limited vocabulary (Janssen), but one would hardly expect fluent conversation from a foreigner in this situation.

οὐδάμ': 'never'; there seems little semantic difference between this and οὐκέτι at 154, which suggests that no aspectual distinction between ἔλθω and ἔρχω is intended.

ἔλθω: 'I come' = ἔρχομαι, but possibly with a future sense, 'I shall come'.

152. καὶ νῦν: 'this time' (Kühner–Gerth ii. 106–7; Denniston 317–18).

ἐμὸς δεσπότης: see 115–16 n. The emphasis is here on Xerxes' responsibility for the disaster, as in Aeschylus (e.g. *Pers.* 550–1) and the wider Greek tradition (cf. e.g. Alcaeus Mess. *HE* 34–7 = *AP* 16. 5). Colvin 56 suggests the absence of the article here, at 160, and with the place-names, is a barbarism; but Timotheus tends to omit the article even in narrative (above, pp. 50–1).

153. ἤξει: 'he brung', probably intended to be the aorist of ἄγω, but the ending is uncertain. Wilamowitz emended to ἦξε, but -ει, although a primary ending, may merely be a barbarism. ἦξα may perhaps be a legitimate if rare variant for the usual aorist ἤγαγον, but few of the alleged cases seem convincing, and it seems better to regard it as a false formation (Kühner-Blass ii. 347).

154. τὰ λοιπά: 'for the rest'; usually only in the singular in lyric (Pi. *P.* 5. 118, *N.* 7. 45) and in a large number of passages of tragic trimeters (e.g. *Alc.* 1148, *Andr.* 740, 1258, *Cyc.* 709). The plural may have been more prosaic, though Janssen quotes its use in dialogue at A. *Sept.* 66, S. *El.* 1226 (to which add E. *Ph.* 1209).

οὐκέτι: the sense cannot be 'no longer', and the usage should be classed with the idiom identified by Dawe on S. *OT* 115, with the sense 'take the further, and perhaps unexpected, step' (thus here, with reference to the future: 'For the rest, I shall not take the further step of coming back to fight again').

πάτερ: 'sir', a respectful form of address from Homer onwards; cf. e.g. *Il.* 24. 362 (with Macleod), *Od.* 7. 28, A. *Pers.* 664, 671 (both of Darius), Men. *Dysc.* 107, 171, *Ep.* 201, 231, *Sic.* 379 etc. In Menander and Homer πάτερ in this sense is used only to complete strangers; the restriction does not hold for tragedy (E. Dickey, *Greek Forms of Address* (Oxford, 1996), 78–81).

155. μαχέσ': 'to fight'; Wilamowitz's μάχεσ⟨θ⟩' avoids the barbarism, and there is at least one certain example of the scribe's difficulty with the combination cθ (82 n.). The elision of -αι may be have been felt as vulgar in the late fifth century; it is only found in epic, Lesbian lyric, Pindar, and comedy. In tragedy it is found at E. *IA* 407 cυccωφρονεῖν coι βούλομ᾽, ἀλλ᾽ οὐ cυννοcεῖν, which, if sound (perhaps βούλομαι κοὐ with Nauck; see J. Jackson, *Marginalia Scaenica*, 103), is probably not by Euripides; while at Agathon, *TrGF* 39 F 29 ἐκ τοῦ γὰρ ἐcορᾶν γίγνετ᾽ ἀνθρώποιc ἐρᾶν, we can easily emend away the elision; read either γίγνεται βροτοῖc with Nauck, or perhaps γίγνεται θνητοῖc, of which ἀνθρώποιc would be a more explicable corruption. E. fr. 1080, cited by West (*Metre*, 10) as an example, is probably spurious; *TrGF* adesp. 705b. 10 ἀλεύεται ἔνθα[- ∪ - × - ∪ -]ν is likely to be Hellenistic. See J. Diggle, *CR* 34 (1984), 67 (= *Euripidea*, 312). The further tragic examples given by M. Hose, *Hermes*, 122 (1994), 32–43, are also of doubtful value.

For the use of the infinitive after a verb of motion to express purpose, see Page on E. *Med.* 1303; to the examples there add E. *IT* 938, A. *Eum.* 488 and perhaps [E.] *Rh.* 429.

ἔρχω: 'I (shall) come'; cf. 151 n. ἔλθω.

156. κάθω: 'I sit', prob. = κάθημαι. Presumably the verb should be taken to mean 'stay, remain' in the context; '. . . but I stay (there)', cf. idiomatic ModE 'sit tight'. κάθημαι can have the sense 'do nothing', which is partly operative here: 'I shall stay at home and do nothing to cause you any more trouble.

157. μή: a negative is required rather than μέν (*Π*), which has no answering δέ. The expected negative would of course be οὐ, but the subtlety of the distinction need not have been apparent to a non-native speaker.

158. παρὰ Cάρδι: 'by Sardis' (see 117 n.); the case may be accusative (as παρὰ Coῦc᾽), and Brussich restores the correct plural form Cάρδι⟨c⟩. Alternatively, it can be read as a dative singular with short iota, though the plural is regular in standard Greek (Hdt. 1. 7, 5. 101 Cάρδιcι, A. *Pers.* 321 Cάρδεcιν). But the correct use of prepositions is notoriously difficult for foreign speakers of any language, and by this stage we can hardly expect the Celaenaean to produce correct Greek morphology or syntax. Cάρδι, then, like the following Coῦca, is not really accusative or dative, but simply an attempt to produce a recognizable Greek form.

We may expect the accusative with motion (κεῖcε), but never παρά with cities. See Gildersleeve, citing

S. Sobolewski, *De praepositionum usu Aristophaneo* (Moscow, 1890), 185: 'the fun of παρά . . . does not lie in its use with the accusative, but with the use of it at all in connection with a certain class of words'.

παρὰ Coῦc': 'by Sousa', the Persian capital on the Choaspes (modern Shūsh), whose construction by Darius, clearly regarded as a significant achievement, is commemorated in a lengthy OP inscription (DSf pp. 142 ff. Kent).

159. Ἀγβάτανα: the Persian capital of Media (modern Hamadān), usually rendered in later Greek as Ἐκβάτανα (Ar. *Eq.* 1089, *Ach.* 64 prob.), but Ἀγβ- at A. *Pers.* 16, where it possibly represents Persian pronunciation (OP *Haᵐgmatana*; Elam. *ag-ma-da-na*; Akk. *a-ga-ma-ta-nu*), Hdt. 3. 64. 4, 3. 92. 1 etc. The town was nowhere near Celaenae, but this hardly justifies Janssen's view that the man is telling lies, or his emendation Ἀγβάταν' ἀνιών. Agbatana was a stock place-name in Persian contexts (cf. the passages from Ar.).

160. Ἄρτιμιc: reflecting Asiatic phonology: ε > i in Lyd. *Artimuš*, Lyc. *Artimelin* (Gk. Ἀρτεμήλιν; also sometimes in Lyc. Greek), Pamph. Ἀρτιμιδωρίc, Ἀρτιμιδόρα (but also Ἀρτεμίδωροc etc.); perhaps cf. Herod. 2. 38 Ἀρτίμμηc with Cunningham, X. *An.* 7. 8. 25 Ἀρτίμαc. In Ionic inscriptions she is always Ἄρτεμιc. See K. Hauser, *Grammatik der griechischen Inschriften Lykiens* (diss. Zurich; Basle, 1916), 24; Bechtel iii. 130–1; J. H. Jongkees, *Mnem.*³ 6 (1938), 355–67; C. Brixhe, *Le Dialecte grec de Pamphylie* (Paris, 1976), 18–19; R. Gusmani, *Lydisches Wörterbuch* (Heidelberg, 1964–6), s.v.

On the Ephesian Artemis, whose cult was already important by the fifth century and who also had connections with Lydia, see Farnell ii. 480–2; H. Thiersch, *Artemis Ephesia*, i (1935); R. Fleischer, *Artemis von Ephesos und verwandte Kultstatuen* (Leiden, 1973); Burkert 149; D. R. West (above, 124 n.), 60–73.

ἐμόc: the language is perhaps based on a cult-phrase Ἄρτεμιc ἐμή similar to Ἀπόλλων ἐμόc at A. *Ag.* 1081, 1086 (formed after the pattern of the Homeric γαμβρὸc ἐμόc: see Wackernagel, *Kl. Schr.* ii. 973 n.), so that Ἄρτιμιc ἐμόc could be taken in apposition to μέγαc θεόc: 'my Artimis, the great god, . . .'. Alternatively, and more probably, ἐμὸς μέγας θεός may be a single phrase in apposition to Ἄρτιμις. The incorrect gender will have been facilitated by the *o*-stem θεός, if we understand (ἡ) θεός as 'goddess'. The phrase μέγας θεός is frequently used to describe Zeus (e.g. *Il.* 24. 90 etc.) and other gods (e.g. Poseidon at *h. Hom.* 22. 1, Apollo at Callim. *H.* 4. 30), but is not used of Artemis other than here. A. Henrichs, *HSCP* 80 (1976), 271 n. 44, sees a reference to Artemis' cult-title μεγάλη θεὰ Ἄρτεμις (see also B. Müller, *Μέγας θεός* (diss. Halle-Wittenberg, 1913), 331–3).

161. παϱ' Ἔφεcον: 'by Ephesus'; for the use of παρά see 158 n. Possibly intended to be a (locatival) description of Artemis, 'my great god at Ephesus' (so Wilamowitz: ὁ μέγας παρ' Ἐφέcωι θεός μου), but the accusative could be intended to indicate movement, albeit incorrectly after φυλάξει (so Campbell: 'will guard me to Ephesus').

162–95. The Persian Flight and the King's Lament. The passage resumes the flight described at 86–7 and continues with a description of the lamentation of the royal entourage. A second, longer section deals with the King's orders for withdrawal from the scene of battle (173–95). The King's speech moves away from the florid and exuberant language used earlier in the poem. We find fewer obscure compounds and less exotic imagery. There appear to be more direct reminiscences of tragic speeches (and once a direct quotation); again Timotheus attempts to incorporate elements of a wide variety of genres; he has just been imitating comedy in the Celaenaean's speech, now he imitates tragedy. Several phrases are borrowed directly from Aeschylus (e.g. 168, 178, 180, 181, 187). The audience's ability to identify the exact source of these reminiscences is uncertain; but they would no doubt have been able to identify the change in style from the preceding section and to recognize the tragic influences. There may also have been a change in musical style to mark the difference.

Metre

162   – ◡ – ◡ – ◡ – ◡ ∫
        – ◡ – ◡◡◡ – ‖

```
        – ∪ ∪∪ – – ∪ – ∪
165       – ∪ – ∪ – ∪ – – |
        – ∪ ∪∪ ∪ – ∪ – ∪ |
        – ∪ – ∪ – ∪ – – ∫
          – ∪ – ∪ – ∪ – |
        – ∪ – – – ∪ ∪∪ ∪ |
170     – – – †∪ – ∪ – |
        ∪ – ∪ – ∪ ∪∪ ∪ – ∪ – ∪ – |
        ∪ – ∪ – ∪ – ∪ – ∪ – ∪ – ||
        ∪∪ ∪ – ∪ – ∪ – |
        ∪ – ∪ ∪∪ – – ∪ – |
175     – – ∪ – ∪ – ∪ – |
        ∪∪ ∪ – – – ∪ – ∪ |
        ∪∪ ∪ – – – – ∪ – ||
        ∪ – ∪ – ∪ – ∪ – |
        – ∪ – ∪ – ∪ – – ∪ ∪ – |
180        ∪∪ ∪ – ∪ – ∪ ∪ – ∫
          – ∪ – ∪ ∪ – – |
        – – – ∪ – ∪ ∪ – ∫
          – ∪ – – – ∪ – |
          – ∪ ∪ – ∪ ∪ – ∪ – |
185     – ∪ ∪ – – ∪ ∪ – ∪ – – ||
        – – – ∪ ∪ – – ||
        ∪ – ∪ – ∪ – ∪ – ||
        – ∪ – ∪ – ∪ – ||
        – ∪ ∪ – ∪ ∪ – ∪ – |
190     – ∪ ∪ – – – ∪ ∪ – ∫
          – ∪ – – ∪ ∪ – ∪ – ∫
          – – ∪ ∪ – – |
        – ∪ ∪ – – – |
        – ∪ ∪ – ∪ ∪ – ∪ – |
195     ∪ – ∪ – – ∪ – – ||
```

The section begins with iambo-trochaics: 162–3 can be analysed
as either 3 *tr cr* (dividing as above) or as *ith* | *2ia*. The next four
lines are all trochaic dimeters (164–7), as is 169, with an intervening ithyphallic (168). At 165 the papyrus' ἔρριπτον would
disturb the trochaic metre, and I have accordingly accepted
ἔριπτον, while πρόcωπ' ὄνυξι at 166 gives *2tr* as at 164–5 and 167.
If we were to read πρόcωπον ὄνυξι (with the papyrus), we are left
with – ∪ ∪ ∪ ∪ – ∪ ∪ – ∪, which defies reasonable analysis. The asyndeton at 167 is unusual for Timotheus, but the supplements ⟨δέ⟩ or
⟨καί⟩ both disrupt the trochaic metre. As in prose, it may indicate
the beginning of the climax of the narrative (i.e. the King's

speech). Saija introduces reiziana at 166 (*cr* + *r*) and 167 (*cr* + *r*): see the metrical note on 150–61. After the iambic trimeters 171–2, the next period begins and ends with *lk* (173, 177), interrupted by two iambic dimeters (174–5) and a trochaic dimeter (176) after intervening word-end; for dramatic instances of this transition, see L. P. E. Parker, 'Trochee to Iamb, Iamb to Trochee', in Craik 331–48 (337–48). At 177 Maas reads τύχαιϲ rather than τύχαιϲιν (*Π*); the latter would give *2tr*, but it seems preferable to end the period as it began. A pair of trochees would, however, not be impossible; the transition from trochee to iamb is also permitted (though rarely) with intervening word-end, though it results in placing anceps beside anceps; see Parker, art. cit. 332–7.

The next period begins with an iambic dimeter (178), followed by *ia ch*; the choriamb introduces a series of aeolic metra (180 ff.), absent since the end of the prayer to the Great Mother at 139. The first of these (180) is a wilamowitzianus of the form ∪∪∪ – ∪ – ∪∪ –, attested for Euripides at *Hel.* 1304/1322, 1305/1323, *Or.* 807/819, 808/820, 809/821, *IA* 216, 551/566, 552/567, 793 (K. Itsumi, *CQ*² 32 (1982), 73). Another wilamowitzianus appears at 182, this one of the form – – – ∪ – ∪∪ –, again common in Euripides (Itsumi, loc. cit. 72). Pause is heavily marked by hiatus at 185; it adds weight to the dramatic statement at 186. This is a period in itself (*ph*), and is followed by a series of other short periods (187, 188); 187 is an iambic dimeter, though *cr ia* may be read if the papyrus' ὤ rather than Page's ἰώ is accepted. There are fewer syncopated iambics from 162 onwards; they are, however, not excluded, as shown by *ba* at 185 and *sp* at 193. Line 188 is another lekythion, and the next period begins with an ibycean (189). Page sees in 190 a dactylic pentameter (ζεύγνυτε–ἵππων); a wilamowitzianus of the form – ∪∪ – – – ∪∪ – can be identified if we divide ζεύγνυτε–ἵπ-|; the form is attested for Euripides at *Or.* 840 (?), 841, *IA* 574, 576 (Itsumi, loc. cit. 73). If this is accepted, 191 rather than *gl* (ὄχημ' – ὀλ-|) becomes – ∪ – – ∪∪ – ∪ –, which also looks aeolic. The aeolic metra continue to 194, with the intrusion of *ch sp* at 193; the period ends with *ia tr*.

162–95. 'And when they had made their backwards-moving, swift-moving flight, straightaway they threw down their double-mouthed javelins from their hands, and their faces were torn by their nails; they ripped their well-woven Persian garb about their breasts, and a high-pitched Asiatic lament was tuned to the many-[. . .] wailing (?). And all the King's entourage clamoured, looking in fear on the coming suffering; and the King, when he saw his assorted army rushing in flight, maltreated his body, falling to his knees, and said, tossing in misfortune: "O ruin of my house, and burning Greek ships that destroyed the multitudinous youth of young men! The ships will not carry them away, backward-travelling, but the blazing strength of the fire will burn them with its savage body, and lamentable suffering shall befall the Persian land. O you heavy fate that brought me to Greece! But go, delay no more; yoke my four-horsed chariot, and you others carry my countless wealth to the wagons; burn the tents, and let them have no benefit from our wealth.'''

162. ἐπεί: see 140 n.

παλίμπορον: 'backward-moving', cf. 86 φυγᾶι δὲ πάλιν (with n.). Timotheus typically repeats the root at 163 ταχύπορον, 173 παλινπόρευτον, 182 ὀπισσοπόρευτον.

162–3. φυγὴν ἔθεντο: periphrastic for ἔφυγον (Kühner–Gerth i. 322–3).

ταχύπορον: 'swiftly moving'; first at A. *Ag.* 486, also E. *El.* 451, *Hel.* 1272, but not normally joined with an abstract noun.

164. ἀμφιστόμους: 'mouthed on both sides', i.e. double-edged, as in Hom. ἀμφίγυον ἔγχος (e.g. *Il.* 13. 147, 14. 26, 15. 386, 712 etc.), S. fr. 152 Radt διχόστομος, E. *Hel.* 983, *Or.* 1303 δίστομος. There may be some influence from ἀμφίτομος 'cutting on both sides', at e.g. E. *El.* 164 ξίφεσι . . . ἀμφιτόμοις. At S. *OC* 473 we find λαβὰς ἀμφιστόμους 'cups with handles on either side' (Jebb).

ἄκοντας: see 22 n.

166. δρύπτετο: 'were torn': generally of mourning. For the excessive grief of Orientals in fifth-century literature, see above, p. 181. But lamentation of this sort is also attested for Greek characters in tragedy: see Denniston on E. *El.* 146–9.

πρόςωπ' ὄνυξι: the papyrus has πρόσωπον ὄνυξι, which Wilamowitz emends into ὄνυχι, but there can be little doubt that the plural ὄνυξ 'nails' is correct; cf. *Od.* 2. 153 δρυψαμένω δ' ὀνύχεσσι παρειάς; one is in any case unlikely to rend one's face with a single nail. The only question is whether πρόςωπα should be read for πρόςωπον; either would, of course, be suitable as the subject of a singular verb. However, πρόcωπον ὄνυξι is metrically awkward, and if the elided vowel of πρόcωπ' ὄνυξι was lacking in the scribe's *Vorlage*, the dittography ΠΡΟϹΩΠΟΝΟΝΥΞΙ is easily explained.

167. Περcίδα cτολήν: 'Persian robe'. Xerxes refers to his torn robes as his cτολή at A. *Pers.* 1019, and the same word is used at 199 Ξέρξηc, πέπλουc ῥήγνυcιν ἀμφὶ cώματι, 468–70, etc. Persian kings regularly wear a long robe (similar to the female πέπλοc) on Persian monuments; this was the royal κάνδυc which Alexander later adopted instead of the chlamys (Herzfeld 362). It was an oblong piece of cloth with a hole in the centre for the head, and fell to the ground. Timotheus seems to be thinking of this here, perhaps inappropriately, though Aeschylus imagines the Persian elders to be similarly clothed (A. *Pers.* 1060: Hall ad loc. cites a Persian servant from a Persepolis relief, now in Boston [31. 372] who seems to wear a 'remarkably luxurious' robe). The Persian garb familiar from Greek vase-paintings is trousers with a short χιτών, described at Hdt. 7. 61 and ostensibly Median in origin. See A. S. F. Gow, *JHS* 48 (1928), 142 ff.; W. Raeck, *Zum Barbarenbild in der Kunst Athens im 6. und 5. Jahrhundert v. Chr.* (diss. Bonn, 1981), 101–63.

An emphasis on Asiatic clothing, which differed significantly from Greek attire, is typical in works about Orientals (cf. e.g. A. *Pers.* 182 πέπλοιcι Περcικοῖc, 660–1, 1060, E. *Or.* 1370, Hecataeus, *FGrH* 1 F 284 (cf. Ar. fr. 532 K.–A.), 287, Antiphanes, *Anteia* fr. 38 K.–A., *Scythians* fr. 199 K.–A.). cτολή is sometimes used for robes in tragedy (e.g. S. *OC* 1357), and also often as a general word for 'clothing'.

168. ἔρεικον: 'ripped'; an unusual word, possibly used here after Xerxes' address to the chorus at A. *Pers.* 1060 πέπλον δ' ἔρεικε κολπίαν ἀκμᾶι χερῶν. The tearing of robes is also a typical sign of excessive Oriental grief, and the verb is particularly common in such contexts: thus Sappho's lament for Adonis includes the injunction κατερείκεcθε (fr. 140a); Aeschylus uses it again in the *Persae* at 537–40 of the mourning of the Persian women; and Herodotus has it at 3. 66. 1 Πέρcαι δὲ ὡc τὸν βαcιλέα (Cambyses) εἶδον ἀνα-

κλαύcαντα, πάντεc τά τε ἐcθῆτοc ἐχόμενα εἶχον, ταῦτα κατηρεί-
κοντο καὶ οἰμωγῆι ἀφθόνωι διεχρέωντο.

εὐϋφῆ: 'well-woven'; there may be connotations of Oriental luxury (cf. also ὑφαντόν at 136).

169. cύντονοc: 'high-pitched'. Asiatic lamentation was
characteristically regarded as high-pitched; cf. A. *Pers.*
574, 1058, *Ch.* 423–8, E. *Or.* 1384 (on which see West,
'Stesichorus', 309–11); see further Pickard-Cambridge²
31–2.

ἁρμόζετ': 'tuned'; for the musical sense cf. e.g. Ar. *Eq.*
989, Telestes fr. 806. 1–2 ἢ Φρύγα καλλιπνόων αὐλῶν ἱερῶν
βαcιλῆα, | Λυδὸν ὃc ἄρμοcε πρῶτοc etc., and related words
such as ἁρμονία.

170. †πολυcτόνωι: a substantive is needed for the sense.
Page suggests πολυ⟨γλώccωι⟩; the adjective is attested at S. *El.*
641, 798 with the sense 'loud-voiced', but if it is right here,
we might understand 'in many languages' (γλῶccα in this
sense at e.g. *Il.* 2. 804, 4. 438). Metrically, however, it is
difficult: – – – ◡ – – – ◡ – could be *sp tr cr* or *mol lk*, but
neither seems particularly plausible. More appealing is
οἰμωγὰ πολυcτόνωι ⟨γόωι⟩ (GOH) – – – ◡ – ◡ – ◡ – (*sp lk?*).

Janssen prints a comma after οἰμωγά and connects
πολυcτόνωι and φόβωι 'with fear (accompanied by) loud
wailing', comparing *Il.* 1. 445 πολύcτονα κήδεα, but the
word most naturally belongs with cύντονοc δ' ἁρμόζετ' κτλ.;
the rare postponement of δέ would be surprising.

171. Βαcιλέωc: cf. 174 n.

πανήγυριc: 'entourage' (with Campbell) rather than
'army' (Ebeling), although the word is not generally used
of royal attendants but of an assembly (especially a national
or festal one; cf. A. *Ag.* 845, Pi. *O.* 9. 96, Hdt. 2. 59. 1
etc.).

172. τὸ μέλλον ... πάθοc: for πάθοc used of the Persian
defeat, cf. A. *Pers.* 254 ὅμωc δ' ἀνάγκη πᾶν ἀναπτύξαι πάθοc.
The trimeters here and in 171 suggest influence from
tragedy; perhaps we are to think of *Pers.* 454 κακῶc τὸ μέλλον
ἱcτορῶν (of Xerxes' misunderstanding of the outcome of his
venture), and of the phrase used of Xerxes by Herodotus (8.
97. 1): Ξέρξηc δὲ ὡc ἔμαθε τὸ γεγονὸc πάθοc.

εἰcορώμενοι: the plural agreeing according to sense with the singular πανήγυρις (Kühner–Gerth i. 53; J. Humbert, *Syntaxe grecque* (Paris, 1960³), 81).

173. ὁ δὲ . . . Βαϲιλεύϲ: for the construction here, see above, p. 51.

παλινπόρευτον: 'backwards-travelling'; only here, but see 162 n. παλίμπορον, 182 ὀπιϲϲοπόρευτον.

ὡϲ ἐϲ εἶ δε{ν}: according to both Aeschylus and Herodotus (and later tradition) Xerxes set up his throne on a headland (Mt. Aegaleos) overlooking the bay of Salamis in order to observe the battle; cf. A. *Pers.* 466–7, Hdt. 8. 90. 4, Plu. *Them.* 13. 1. Herodotus (7. 212. 1) gives a similar account of his actions at Thermopylae.

174. Βαϲιλεύϲ: an appropriate title for eastern potentates; cf. e.g. Mimn. fr. 13(*a*) ὡϲ οἳ πὰρ βαϲιλῆοϲ (of Gyges), and especially A. *Pers.* 5 ἄναξ Ξέρξηϲ βαϲιλεύϲ, 24 βαϲιλῆϲ βαϲιλέωϲ ὕποχοι μεγάλου. The latter is connected with OP *xšāyaθiya xšāyaθiyānām* 'King of Kings', a title of the Great King based on Assyr. *šar šarāni* (Broadhead on A. *Pers.* 24; R. Schmitt, *Die Iranier-Namen bei Aischylos* (Vienna, 1978), 19; Johansen-Whittle on A. *Suppl.* 524 ἄναξ ἀνάκτων). In the Greek letter of Darius to Gadatas, satrap of the Ionian province, Darius begins: βαϲιλεὺϲ [βα]ϲιλέων Δαρεῖοϲ . . . (ML no. 12). But Darius is simply βαϲιλεύϲ . . . Δαρεῖοϲ at A. *Pers.* 855 (cf. 634, 918), and in OP inscriptions we frequently meet the formulaic θāti Darayavauš (Xšayāršā) xšāyaθiya 'Proclaims Darius (Xerxes) the king'. Xerxes is never mentioned by name in the extant portion of the poem, and does not appear in person until this point, although he may have played some role in the narrative leading up to the battle.

175. παμμιγῆ ϲτρατόν: 'all the contingents of his army'; cf. E. *Ba.* 1356 μιγάδα βαρβάρον ϲτρατόν, where we should read βαρβάρων with Burges, as nowhere else does Euripides attach two epithets to ϲτρατόϲ (Diggle, *Euripidea*, 481–2); hence, 'a mixed army of barbarians'. παμμιγήϲ appears before Timotheus only at A. *Pers.* 269 βέλεα παμμιγῆ 'weapons of all types'; also relevant here though is A. *Pers.* 53 πάμμεικτον ὄχλον, of the Persian army.

176. γονυπετήϲ: 'falling to his knees', first attested here or at E. *Ph.* 293 (the relative dates are uncertain), and nor-

mally, like the verb γονυπετέω, with an Oriental connotation
(G. R. Stanton, *Glotta*, 46 (1968), 2–6); cf. the account at A.
Pers. 465, 468–70 Ξέρξης δ᾽ ἀνώιμωξεν κακῶν ὁρῶν βάθος· |
ῥήξας δὲ πέπλους κἀνακωκύσας λιγύ, | πεζῶι παραγγείλας ἄφαρ
στρατεύματι | ἵης᾽ ἀκόσμωι ξὺν φυγῆι.
ἄικιζε: 'maltreated', more frequently found in the middle.
On self-mutilation and its association with barbarian characters in fifth-century literature, see 102 n., 166 n.

177. φάτο: more usually used to mark the end of a speech;
see 82 n.

κυμαίνων τύχαις{ιν}: 'tossing in his misfortunes'; perhaps
a rather bold image, but we may compare the common 'sea
of troubles' metaphor, especially at A. *Pers.* 433–4, where 'a
vast ocean of catastrophes' (κακῶν . . . πέλαγος . . . μέγα)
bursts upon the Persians 'and all the barbarian peoples'; the
passive form might have been expected, 'being tossed about
by his misfortunes'. There may be a suggestion of the fact
that the King's misfortunes result from a naval disaster; the
verb is commonly used of the swelling of the sea (e.g. *Il.* 14.
229, *Od.* 4. 425).

178. ἰὼ κατασκαφαὶ δόμων: 'O ruin of my house'; a direct
quotation of A. *Ch.* 50. δόμος had become a poetic word by
the fifth century, replaced in common usage by οἶκος, οἰκία
(see Chantraine, s.v. δόμος), and in tragedy its sense could be
extended to refer to the family. There is no need to assume
with Croiset that δόμων is out of place here, or to argue with
Janssen that the force of the phrase depends for its sense on
the passage in *Choephoroi*. The quotation calls the
audience's attention to the destructive effect of the defeat
on the royal family and their rule over Persia (cf. A. *Pers.*
584 ff.). For ἰώ, which here indicates an exclamation rather
than a true apostrophe, see 105 n.

179. σείριαι . . . νᾶες: 'burning (?) ships'. The sense of
the adjective is obscure; Aratus first uses the verb σειριάω
to mean 'scorching' at *Phaen.* 331 (see Kidd ad loc.) to
explain the derivation of the name Σείριος: the Dog-star is
said to have particularly unpleasant effects ('its heliacal
rising . . . marked the season of most intense heat and
severe fevers': West on Hes. *Op.* 417). If that is the
meaning here, it may refer back to the flaming arrows

used by the Greeks; the King also mentions the burning of the ships at 183 ff.

180. κατὰ . . . ὠλέςαθ': the compound first (also with tmesis) at A. *Pers.* 670 νεολαία γὰρ ἤδη κατὰ πᾶς' ὄλωλεν, again of the Persian youth.

μέν: answered by δέ in 182, despite the switch from second person to third, though μέν without a following δέ is sometimes emphatic (Denniston 361).

ἥλικα . . . ἥβαν νέων: an odd periphrasis, presumably equivalent to 'the young men'; cf. A. *Pers.* 669–70, on which these lines appear to be modelled; 681 ἥλικές θ' ἥβης ἐμῆς, where, however, ἥλικες is a substantive, and refers to Darius' peers, the Elders. Janssen thinks that it refers to the King's contemporaries, and Xerxes is described as a young man at A. *Pers.* 13; but there is no indication that this is the sense, and contrast A. *Pers.* 681 cited above. The combination ἥλικα . . . ἥβαν 'the equal-aged youth' looks odd, but ἥβη should nevertheless be taken abstractly (it occasionally can refer to a group of men; cf. A. *Pers.* 512, 733, 923, *Ag.* 109).

Page suggests νεῶν 'of my ships' (for which we might compare A. *Pers.* 512 ποθοῦσαν φιλτάτην ἥβην χθονός 'yearning for the beloved youth of the country'). This makes more obvious sense, but the reading is unlikely with νᾶες before and after at 179, 182; Mazon wrote Doric ναῶν, which may be right.

181. πολύανδρον: 'many'; cf. A. *Pers.* 73, 533 (both of the Persian army). A predominantly Aeschylean compound (also at A. *Ag.* 693). The adjective is perhaps odd with ἥβαν, though ἥβη can be concrete (cf. Lat. *iuventus*); however, if νέων is sound, it may be better to read πολυάνδρων 'the youth of my multitudinous young men'.

182. ὀπιccοπόρευτον: 'backwards-travelling'; see 173 n. ὀπιccο- is unusual in compounds; the normal formation is ὀπιcθ(ο)-. We might better read ὀπιcθοπόρευτον here; the scribe has miswritten cθ before (82 ἄ〈c〉θματι).

183. 〈νιν〉 ἄξουcιμ: 'will carry them'. The simplest supplement is 〈νιν〉 (i.e. ἥβαν), which provides the object required by the verb. Page proposes 〈μ' ἀπ〉άξουcιμ, but the young men referred to in the previous sentence provide a more

logical object than the King himself. Van Minnen suggests
νᾶες δ᾽ οὖ νι⟨ν⟩ (Pap. ουκι), but the metre is unclear.
πυρὸς ... μένος: cf. *Il.* 6. 182 πυρὸς μένος αἰθομένοιο.
184. αἰθαλόεμ: 'blazing'; the adjective is applied to lightning by Hesiod (*Th.* 72, 504, 707, 854) and others; cf. [A.]
Pr. 992 αἰθαλοῦcca φλόξ, E. *Ph.* 183, and *Tro.* 1104, where
Diggle, *Studies*, 71, reads αἰθαλοῦν κεραυνοφαὲς πῦρ for
Αἰγαίου κεραυνοφαὲς πῦρ. There is no other tragic instance;
elsewhere it can mean 'sooty', 'smoke-stained'.
185. cώματι: 'with its (savage) body'; for the 'body' of fire,
cf. *Il.* 11. 596 δέμας πυρὸς αἰθομένοιο, 13. 673, 18. 1.
According to Janko (on *Il.* 13. 673) δέμας is used as an
adverbial accusative (only in this formula), and the sense
evolved from 'body' to 'like', but there is no true parallel for
δέμας 'like'. Blass suggests ἀγρίωι ⟨ῥοίζωι⟩ cώματα, 'the fire
will burn their bodies with a savage rush', but the phrase
ἀγρίωι ⟨ῥοίζωι⟩ looks odd; an object can be easily understood
from ⟨νιν⟩ at 183 (rather than from νᾶες at 182 with Janssen).
187. ⟨ἰ⟩ώ: possibly ὤ (pap. χωραιω), which is also metrically possible, but the parallel with 178 makes ἰώ more
attractive, and for the tragic reminiscence, see 105 n.
βαρεῖα cυμφορά: 'heavy fate'; imitating A. *Pers.* 1044
βαρεῖά γ᾽ ἅδε cυμφορά, where the Persian elders lament
their misfortune.
189. ἀλλ᾽: introducing a command, as at E. *El.* 190, 864,
IT 1411 (Denniston 13–15).
μηκέτι μέλλετε: 'delay no longer'. Xerxes gives a similar
command at A. *Pers.* 469–70 πεζῶι παραγγείλας ἄφαρ
cτρατεύματι | ἷης᾽ ἀκόcμωι ξὺν φυγῆι, but it appears from
Herodotus (8. 113. 1) that in fact a few days passed before
his retreat. Although it seems to have been the defeat at
Salamis that caused Xerxes to decide to return to Asia, there
were still significant encounters between the Greeks and
Persians at Plataea and Mycale.
190. τετρά⟨ορ⟩ον ἵππων ὄχημ᾽: τετράορον should mean
'yoked four together' (LSJ), and in this context ὄχημα is to
be taken as 'team'; cf. E. *Alc.* 66–7 ἵππειον ὄχημα with Dale.
ἵππων is then genitive after ὄχημα, thus 'a four-yoked team of
horses'.
191. ἀνάριθμον ὄλβον: Xerxes' great wealth, and his fear

that it will be lost, are commonplaces in literature on the
Persian Wars; cf. A. *Pers.* 3, 9, 163–4, 168, 250 ff., 709,
754 ff., 826, (also 151–2 of Darius), Hdt. 7. 41. 2, 9. 80, and
especially Timoth. fr. 790, which suggests that it was a
theme of the poem.

192. φορεῖτ᾽ ἐπ᾽ ἀπήνας: 'carry on to my wagons'; cf. *Il.*
24. 275 φέροντες . . . ἐπ᾽ ἀπήνης. In epic ἀπήνη describes a
four-wheeled wagon that was not used for combat.

195. ὄνησις . . . πλούτου: 'benefit from (our) wealth';
objective genitive.

αὐτοῖσι: i.e. the Greeks. There is a clear contrast with
ἡμετέρου in the preceding line.

196–201. The Greek Paean. The Greek celebrations are
ignored by Aeschylus. In Herodotus' account, the battle is
followed by a lengthy treatment of Xerxes' return to Sardis
with the Greeks in pursuit, and he makes it clear that only
after his escape did the Greeks return to Salamis for the
spoils. Three Phoenician triremes were set apart for the gods
(8. 121), and a part of the spoils was sent to Delphi. Delphi
also received a portion of the spoils after Plataea (Hdt. 9.
81), and two statues were set up, at Olympia and the
Isthmus. We hear nothing of this from Timotheus, and he
seems to have much less formal activities in mind.

Herington believes that the citharode here may have
imitated the paean with marching dance-steps at this point
(see above, p. 31), but this argument would be more
convincing if the rhythm were here anapaestic; there is no
strong evidence to suggest that iambic or aeolic metra were
particularly associated with marching rhythms.

Metre

196   – ∪ ∪ – – – ∪ ∪ – ∪ ∪ |
　　　– ∪ ∪ – ∪ ∪ – ∪ – |
　　　　∪∪ ∪ – ∪ ∪ – ∪ – ||
　　∪ – ∪ – ∪ – ∪ –
200　　∪ – ∪ – |
　　　– ∪ ∪ – ∪ – – ||

This brief section, ending the narrative portion of the poem,
continues the metrical scheme established for the preceding part
and the King's speech. 196 could be a dactylic tetrameter,

followed by what looks like another ibycean; correption of αι in
Παιᾶν᾽ is possible but not necessary (cf. A. *Sept.* 229 with
Hutchinson ad loc.). But it is odd to find τροπαῖα and τέμενος
thus in apposition. Janssen conjectures ἁγνότατόν ⟨τε⟩ τέμενος at
197, which would produce the metrically awkward colarion
‒∪∪‒∪∪∪‒×‒. GOH suggests ⟨καὶ⟩ Διὸς ἁγνότατον τέμενος; 196
(οἳ‒cτηcάμενοι)‒∪∪‒‒‒∪∪‒ could be a wilamowitzianus, and 197
‒∪∪‒∪∪‒∪∪‒×‒, perhaps an extended glyconic with resolved
second anceps. Alternatively we could supplement ⟨ἐς⟩ (Holford-
Strevens) with period-end after 196. Blass's τέμενος ⟨κάτα⟩ is
unparalleled. Saija analyses 196 as ‒‒∪‒‒‒∪∪‒∪∪, but the
scansion δὲ τ᾽ροπ- is improbable. The period ends with a glyconic
at 198. The final period is predominantly iambic: 3ia (199–200)
followed by an aristophanean.

196–201. 'But they (the Greeks), setting up trophies to Zeus
to be a most holy place, called on Paean the healer lord, and
keeping in time stamped with the high-pounding dances of
their feet.'

196. τροπαῖα: the trophies of the Persian Wars would
originally have been wooden structures, perhaps like the
trireme dedicated to Ajax mentioned at Hdt. 8. 121. 1; by
the late fifth century they may have been replaced by stone
monuments. They were state monuments by the time of
Pausanias (1. 36. 1, 9. 2. 6); see W. C. West III, *CP* 64
(1969), 7–19, and on trophies in general Pritchett ii. 246–75.

The plural is commonly used (e.g. E. *Heracl.* 786, *Andr.*
694, Ar. *Eq.* 521, X. *An.* 3. 2. 13, Lys. 18. 3 etc.), and there
is no need to think that more than one trophy is necessarily
meant. However, multiple trophies were often set up after a
battle (e.g. Thuc. 5. 3. 4, 7. 24. 1, 7. 45. 1); after Salamis at
least two were probably established, one on Salamis itself
and one on Psyttalea (Paus. 1. 36. 1, Plu. *Arist.* 9. 324 AB).
An Athenian trophy is mentioned at *Vit. Soph.* 3 (*TrGF* iv
p. 31): μετὰ τὴν ἐν Cαλαμῖνι ναυμαχίαν Ἀθηναίων περὶ τρόπαιον
ὄντων κτλ.; each city may have had its own, but the *Vita* is
not a completely reliable source.

cτηcάμενοι: cf. the use of the middle also at E. *Andr.* 763,
Ar. *Pl.* 453, etc.

197. τέμενος: in classical times the *temenos* was technically
the land situated around an altar and dedicated to the god.

In Homeric and Mycenaean Greek the word can refer simply to a royal estate, although possibly with religious connotations even at that stage (H. van Effenterre, *REG* 80 (1967), 17–26; Burkert 84–7 and n. 37). A trophy could be regarded as a religious object, dedicated to Zeus Tropaios. There is some evidence that sacrifices were made before them; in the second century BC the Athenians sacrificed before the trophies of Marathon and Salamis on a number of occasions (W. C. West III, *CP* 64 (1969), 16). If the text is sound (see above), the *temenos* may therefore be the area around the trophy. The usual verb for establishing a temenos is ἱδρύω.

ἀγνότατον: 'most holy', cf. Pi. *P.* 4. 204 ἁγνὸν . . . Ποcειδάωνοc . . . τέμενοc, E. *Andr.* 253. The adjective establishes a claim to reverence (W. Ferrari, *SIFC* 17 (1940), 33–53; Parker, *Miasma*, 161 ff.; Burkert 271 and n. 197).

Παιᾶν' ἐκελάδηcαν: the paean was a triumphal song to Apollo, which could be performed both before (e.g. A. *Pers.* 393, X. *Cyr.* 4. 1. 6) and after (e.g. *Il.* 22. 391, S. *Tr.* 205–21, E. *Heracl.* 694–6) a battle. Not all paeans were addressed to Apollo; cf. E. *IA* 1466–99 (of Artemis), A. *Sept.* 870, *Ch.* 149–51, E. *Alc.* 424 (all of Hades), Ariphr. fr. 813 (Hygieia); these may be secondary usages. Σ Thuc. 1. 50 associates the battle-paean with Ares. In its most simple form the paean was probably little more than the ritual cry ἰὴ Παιάν, but it could acquire more elaborate forms (e.g. Pi. fr. 52b [*Pae.* 2]; Isyllus, *CA* 133–4; Macedonicus, *CA* 138 ff. (and *SEG* 23. 126); Limenius pp. 84–129 Bélis; *PMG* adesp. 933, 934). See Burkert 145; West, *Music*, 15–16.

198. ἰήϊον ἄνακτα: 'the healer lord', a traditional title of Apollo, also used by Timotheus in his invocation at 205; cf. e.g. Pi. fr. 52b. 35, 45 (*Pae.* 2), fr. 52f. 37, 43 (*Pae.* 5), A. *Ag.* 146, S. *OT* 154, Ar. *Vesp.* 874. The adjective was probably derived originally from the ritual cry ἰή, but was later connected with Apollo's healing functions, and is thus also applied to Asclepius in *Paean Erythraeus* (*PMG* adesp. 934); ἰή is used of Pan in an epigraphic hymn (*PMG* 936), which, however, probably dates to the second century AD (so M. L. West, *CQ²* 20 (1970), 215; *Metre*, 165), rather than the fourth/third century BC as suggested by P. Maas, *Epidaur-ische Hymnen* (Halle, 1933), 130 ff.

199. cύμμετροι: 'keeping in time'; Janssen's suggestion 'keeping even with (each other; sc. ἀλλήλοις)' is unconvincing.

ἐπεκτύπεον: 'stamped', perhaps inceptive 'set about stamping'. At Telestes fr. 805(*a*). 4, where the MSS have χειροκτύπωι 'hand-clapping', Meineke conjectures χορο-κτύπωι 'stamping the choral dancing-ground', perhaps rightly; cf. Pi. fr. 156 ὁ χοροιτύπος . . . Cιληνός 'Silenus who beats time in the dance'; at *Od*. 8. 261, the young dancers around Demodocus πέπληγον δὲ χορὸν θεῖον ποσίν, 'struck with their feet the holy dancing-ground'. At S. fr. 277 Radt we find ξανθὰ δ' Ἀφροδιcία λάταξ | πᾶcιν ἐπεκτύπει δόμοις; ἐπεκτύπει is Nauck's conjecture for ἐπεκύπτει, and must mean 'rang throughout', 'rang over', thus giving to the preverb more force than it has in Timotheus. Ar. *Eccl*. 483 τοῖν ποδοῖν ἐπικτυπῶν βάδιζε also refers to a type of noisy, stamping gait. For the somewhat different use at *Av*. 780 πᾶc δ' ἐπεκτύπηc' Ὄλυμπος, see Dunbar ad loc. Polyb. 30. 22. 9 again uses it of a chorus.

201. ὑψικρότοις: probably 'high-pounding', not 'loftily resounding' as LSJ. ὑψι- does not mean 'high' in a musical sense, for which ὀξυ- would be expected (West, *Stud. Aesch.* 255). Thus the Homeric epithet for Zeus ὑψιβρεμέτης should mean 'thundering from on high', and the name of the frog Ὑψιβόας at *Batr*. 202, translated in LSJ as 'high-shouter', should be taken in the same way; it is perhaps a parody of the epithet ὑψιβρεμέτας. The legs could be lifted high in Greek dances. *H. Hom*. 3. 516 speaks of Apollo playing the lyre whilst dancing, καλὰ καὶ ὕψι βιβάς, and followed by the Cretans ῥήccοντες . . . | . . . καὶ ἰηπαιήον' ἄειδον; possibly a style of dance involving leaping or prancing was particularly associated with paeans or joyful celebration. It would be particularly apt for processional dances. Pi. fr. 52 n. 99–100 (*Pae*. 2) refers to a 'swift-footed chorus', ἰcτάμεναι χορὸν [ταχύ]ποδα παρθένοι; this would again suit a processional. The 'victory dance' of Philocleon in the style of Phrynichus at the end of Aristophanes' *Wasps* (1492) involves kicking one leg skywards (οὐρανίαν). At *Vesp*. 1516–37 high kicks are also associated with the modern style of the sons of Carcinus. In the chorus's dance at the end of *Eccl.*, 1165 ὑπανακινεῖν implies the raising of one leg (cf. 1180 αἴρεϲθ᾽ ἄνω); the style is there connected with Crete. Cassandra's 'wedding-dance' at E. *Tro.* 325 involves high kicks, no doubt in ironic imitation of the normal style of joyful dance. For the evidence from vase-paintings, see T. B. L. Webster, *The Greek Chorus* (London, 1970), 1–45.

χορείαιc: 'dances', perhaps 'songs and dances'. The earliest attested use is Pratinas fr. 708. 16 ⟨ἄκου᾽⟩ ἄκουε τὰν ἐμὰν Δώριον χορείαν; Pratinas probably belongs to the early fifth century (but see Seaford, 'Hyporchema'). Here an aural element is clearly implied. Pratinas' dance also involves energetic movement of the hands and feet: 14 ἅδε coι δεξιᾶc καὶ ποδὸc διαρριφά. At E. *Ph.* 1265 οὐκ ἐν χορείαιc οὐδὲ παρθενεύμαcι (deleted with 1266–9 by Ed. Fraenkel, *Zu den Phoenissen des Euripides* (SBAW 1963/1; Munich, 1963), 67–71), the connotations are uncertain; perhaps simply 'choral dances', though song may also be meant. The paean was traditionally associated with both song and dance (*Il.* 1. 472–3).

202–36. The Poet's Apologia. Timotheus invokes Apollo's assistance (202–5) against his Spartan critics, who attack him for his musical innovations (206–20). He then explains (221–36) his inheritance of the musical tradition of Orpheus and Terpander. Timotheus was much given to musical self-justification and self-promotion; in fr. 796 he states that his new songs are better than the old ones, likening the development to Zeus' displacement of Cronos; in fr. 802 he celebrates a victory over Phrynis. Much has been made of these passages, and following Pollux' terminology they are often called *sphragides*; but there is no further evidence that the term had meaning for Timotheus, or any other ancient author. Theognis 19–26 speaks of putting a cφρηγίc on his words, and it is often assumed that his purpose is to set a mark of authorship on his poems; but it is not clear that this is Theognis' point (West, *Studies*, 149–50), and it is unlikely to have been Timotheus'. Certainly the passage does not justify the view that all first-person poetic statements should be described as *sphragides*.

Alcman occasionally speaks of his musical innovation; in fr. 39 he claims to have invented a type of song based on the cry of partridges, and in fr. 40 states he knows ὀρνίχων νόμως | πάντων. Where these appeared in the poems is uncertain; the chorus of the Louvre Partheneion (fr. 1) reverts to the subject of their own song towards the end (96–101). Bacchylides also sometimes refers to his own music at the end of his epinicians; at the end of poem 3, he emphasizes that his song will bring praise both to Hieron and himself (92–8); at the end of poem 5 he briefly invokes Calliope and quotes Hesiod to much the same effect. But in neither passage is he concerned to defend himself against attack. There are numerous similar examples in Pindar, though at *O*. 2. 86 ff. (whoever the two crows are) and *N*. 3. 80–2 (?) he decries his rivals. Perhaps closer to Timotheus, though later, is Corinna's explanation of her poetic purpose at fr. 655 fr. 1. She states that Terpsichore summons her to sing her stories for the Tanagran women, and that the city rejoices in her song; at a regrettably fragmentary point there seems to be some reference to falsehood (fr. 1. 7 ψευδ[). Probably, however, this passage belonged to the start of the poem. Corinna's other poetic statements—her criticism of Myrtis for contending with Pindar, fr. 664(*a*), and her programmatic words at fr. 664(*b*)—are of uncertain location. Also from the fourth or third century, we may at a distance compare the extended concluding prayer of Limenius' Delphic paean (ll. 34–40, p. 126 Bélis). Outside lyric, the closest parallel may be Aristophanes' defensive parabases, but we should not think that Timotheus was here deliberately imitating comedy.

The Spartans have criticized Timotheus, because he 'dishonours the older Muse'; he claims that he 'keeps off neither young man nor old nor my peer from my songs', and that he only fends off corrupters of the old Muse. The evidence connecting Timotheus with disturbances at the Spartan Carneia is collected above, pp. 7–9, and could be used to explain the sequence of thought in this passage, though its authenticity is very uncertain. However the traditions developed, they fit well with some elements in Timotheus' statement. The Spartans, and more particularly the ephors, have perhaps attempted to prevent Timotheus performing his new songs; the language at 206–7 could therefore be largely ironic, since we are unlikely to think that after beginning with genuinely complimentary language he would lambast his enemies with the phrase 'burning with smoky blame'. At 215 τῶνδ' . . . ὕμνων can hardly refer to anything other than the νέοιϲ ὕμνοιϲ of 211–12; the implication of 216–20 must therefore be that Timotheus keeps away from his own songs only performers in the old style (see 216 n.). The thought is slightly illogical, but may be: 'the Spartans prevent me from performing; by contrast, *I* do not prevent anyone from listening to my poems; I merely upset the old-fashioned performers'. Janssen thinks the sense is: 'Some people criticize my oeuvre; everybody is allowed to interfere, merely the dabblers are kept at a distance'; but δέ at 213 implies a strong contrast between the Spartan criticism and the statements at 213–20.

There follows in 221–36 a catalogue of εὑρήματα, through which Timotheus traces his poetic relationship to Orpheus and Terpander. It is somewhat similar to Aristophanes' list of his comic predecessors and their treatment at the hands of the Athenian public at *Eq.* 507–46. Pherecrates' comic catalogue of the New Poets (fr. 155 K.–A.) also culminates in Timotheus; his musical innovations are described in terms of a physical (and sexual) assault on Music personified. It is, however, unlikely that there is any direct connection between the two. Other poets of the New Music were interested in the history of musical invention; Melanippides' *Marsyas* (fr. 758) dealt with the invention of the pipes; Telestes responded in humorous fashion to this version in his *Argo* (fr. 805). Telestes mentions the invention of the Lydian mode by Olympus (fr. 806), and that of the Phrygian mode (fr. 810); the first of these at least was not the main subject of his poem, an *Asclepius*. Perhaps they belonged to concluding sections similar to the one here, or to the introduction. In fr. 808 he describes the playing of a five-stringed lyre; cf. *CQ*² 50 (2000), 298–300. Euripides describes the invention of the tympanon in lyric at *Ba.*

120–34. At. *Ra.* 1030–6 Aristophanes makes Aeschylus give an account of the πρῶτος εὑρετής of various genres (Orpheus, Musaeus, Hesiod, Homer); earlier Euripides has described in comic fashion the history of tragedy (907 ff.). But this interest was not confined to the fifth century; Hermes' discovery of the lyre is recounted at *h. Hom.* 4. 25 ff., 40 ff.; Pindar refers to Terpander's invention of the barbitos (fr. 125), and to the invention of the Ionian mode (fr. 140b. 4), the auletic art (*P.* 12. 6, 20 ff.) and the dithyramb (*O.* 13. 18; cf. Hdt. 1. 23). The popularity of the catalogue form in the fifth century seems to be a development reflecting the systematization of knowledge under the influence of the sophists. In the later scholarly tradition catalogues of musical innovators form an essential part of music history, and [Plu.] *Mus.* 3. 1131 F–5. 1132 F deals with the claims various individuals have to be regarded as the inventor of the citharodic and auletic nomes. See in general A. Kleingünther, Πρῶτος εὑρετής (*Philol.* Supplbd. 26; Leipzig, 1933).

Metre

202   – – ∪ – ∪ ∪∪ ∪ – ∫
      – – – ∪ ∪ – – ||
      ∪ – – ∪ ∪ – ∪ – ∫
205   – ∪ – ∪ ∪ – – |
      ∪ – – ∪ ∪ – ∪ – ∫
      – – – ∪ ∪ – ∪ – |
      ∪ – – ∪ ∪ – – |
      ∪ – – ∪ ∪ – ∪ – |
210   ∪ – – ∪ ∪ – – ||
      ∪∪ ∪ – ∪ ∪ – ∪ – |
      – – – ∪ ∪ – – ||
      ∪ – – ∪ ∪ – ∪ – ∫
      ∪ ∪ ∪ ∪ – ∪ – – |
215   – – – ∪ ∪ – – |
      – ∪ – ∪ ∪ – ∪ – ∫
      – – – ∪ ∪ – – |
      – – – ∪ ∪ – – |
      – – – ∪ ∪ – ∪ – ∫
220   – – – ∪ ∪ – – |
      – – – ∪ ∪ – ∪ – ∫

$$- \cup - \cup \cup - - \;||$$
$$\cup - - \; \cup \cup - \langle \cup - \rangle$$
$$?$$

225
$$- - - \cup \cup - \cup -|$$
$$- \cup - \cup \cup - -|$$
$$- - - \cup \cup - \cup -\int$$
$$- - - \cup \cup - -|$$
$$- \cup - \; \cup \cup - \cup -|$$

230
$$- - - \cup \cup - \cup -|$$
$$\cup \; \cup\cup - \cup \cup - -|$$
$$- - - \cup \cup - \cup -\int$$
$$- - - \cup \cup - -|$$
$$- - - \cup \cup - \cup -|$$

235
$$- - - \cup - \cup \cup - -|$$
$$- - - \cup \cup - \cup - -|$$

Page takes 202 to be an iambic dimeter; Wilamowitz suggests χρυϲο-rather than χρυϲεο-, which would produce $- - \cup \cup \cup \cup \cup -$ or $- - - \cup \cup \cup \cup -$ if the upsilon of χρυϲ- is treated as long; perhaps the latter may be a wilamowitzianus if the first princeps can admit resolution. It is followed by a long sequence of (frequently dove-tailed) pherecrateans and glyconics; we once find glyconics in succession (206–7), once pherecrateans (217–18). A similar sequence of aeolic metra is found in the concluding prayer section of Limenius' Delphic Paean (p. 126 Bélis), where glyconics mixed with choriambic metra similarly divide the section from the rest of the poem. In Aristonoos' Delphic Paean (*CA* 162–4) we find a mixture of glyconic, iamb and choriamb. At 214 we find either an isolated aristophanean or *ia ba*; either is a little surprising, but it is impossible to produce an aeolic metron even by reading γερα⟨ι⟩όν. Aristophaneans are found as a final clausula among aeolics at *P.* 185, and among iambics at 201 (where they might also be described as *ia ba*).

The sequence of glyconics and pherecrateans continues in the catalogue of εὑρήματα, but with less frequent dove-tailing (only the first pair, 221–2, 227–8, and 232–3, are dove-tailed), and ends with a pair of hipponacteans (the first anaclastic) which lead into the mixture of aeolic metra in the epilogue (below, 237–40). At 223–4 the text is uncertain, but 223 should be *gl*; the first syllable of υἱός may be either short or long (West, *Metre*, 12). Line 235 is an anaclastic hipponactean as printed: GOH suggests writing δωδεκα-, which could be an anaclastic hagesichorean ($- - - - \cup \cup - -$).

202–36. 'You who foster the new-fashioned Muse with the golden lyre, come as ally to my songs, healer Paean; for Sparta's great leader, well-born (and) ancient, the people teeming with the flowers of youth, drives me about and hounds me, blazing with fiery blame, because I dishonour the older Muse with my new songs. But I keep neither young man nor old nor my peer away from my songs; it is the old-fashioned corrupters of the Muse, these I keep off, destroyers of song, who screech with the cries of loud-voiced heralds. Orpheus, the son of Calliope . . . (from?) Pieria, first begot the [lyre] with its intricate music. Then after him Terpander yoked music on ten notes; Aeolian Lesbos bore that glorious man in Antissa. And now Timotheus renews the cithara with eleven-stringed metres and rhythms, opening the many-songed chambered treasury of the Muses; it is Miletus that nurtured him, the city of a twelve-walled people, first among the Achaeans.'

202. ἀλλ': traditionally beginning a prayer (Denniston 16; Pulleyn 132–3), and here perhaps calling attention to the hymnic nature of the section; cf. Limenius 36 ἀλλ' ὦ Φοῖβε, Ael. Dion. fr. 38 (p. 102 Schwabe), who cites the (probably corrupt) phrase ἀλλὰ ἀλλ' ἄναξ as ἀρχὴ ἐξῳδίου (*sic*) κιθαρῳδικοῦ, Hsch. a 113: ἀλλ' ἄναξ· ἐξόδιον κιθαρῳδῶν τοῦτο.

χρυςεοκίθαριν: only here, but Ar. *Thesm.* 315–16 invokes Apollo as χρυςολύρα | Δῆλον ὃς ἔχεις ἱεράν, and Pi. *P.* 1. 1–2 addresses the χρυςέα φόρμιγξ, Ἀπόλλωνος καὶ ἰοπλοκάμων | ςύνδικον Μοιςᾶν κτέανον (cf. [Hes.] *Sc.* 201 ff.; *Orph. H.* 34. 3). Simonides fr. 511(a). 5–6 refers to χρυςοφ[όρ]μι[γξ] | Ἀπόλλων ἑκαταβόλο[ς], apparently in an epinician. The imagery is therefore wholly traditional. The *Suda* (χ 556, s.v. χρυςάορον, iv. 830 Adler) mentions the form χρυςοκίθαρος, perhaps a corruption from -κίθαρις, although κίθαρις (used by Timotheus at *P.* 231) is the more archaic word, and κιθάρα, from which the *Suda*'s adjective may be derived, is a fifth-century innovation (probably by analogy with λύρα); cf. also Hsch. χρυςάωρ.

Compounds of the type χρυςεο- + noun occur first in the fifth century; cf. A. *Pers.* χρυςεοςτόλμους δόμους; Ba. 9. 100 χ]ρυςεοςκάπτρ[, 17. 106 χρυςεόπλοκοι. Ibycus fr. 282(a). 40

has . . .]α χρυς'ε΄όςτροφ[ος] Ὕλλις, where the epsilon has been added by the first hand in the papyrus, but χρυς{ε}όςτροφος should be read. Philoxenus of Cythera has χρυςεοβόςτρυχε Γαλάτεια at fr. 821, where Bergk suggested χρυςο-, but cf. E. *Ph.* 191 χρυςεοβόςτρυχον ὦ Διὸς ἔρνος Ἄρτεμι. Among the probably fifth-century dithyrambic fragments in *PMG* adesp. 929(*c*). 3 has χρυςεόδοντι τριαίναι. Aristot. *Rhet.* 3. 8. 1409ᵃ12 quotes the openings of two hymns to Apollo, one of which begins χρυςεοκόμα Ἕκατε παῖ Διός (*PMG* adesp. 950(*b*)). Homer already has the adjectival formation χαλκεο- beside χαλκο- (χαλκεοθωρήκων *Il.* 4. 448, χαλκεόφωνος *Il.* 5. 785) to avoid -◡- (Chantraine, *Grammaire*, i. 95). For the length of the upsilon, see 127 n.

ἀέξων: 'fostering'; cf. Pi. *O.* 6. 105 ἐμῶν δ᾽ ὕμνων ἄεξ᾽ εὐτερπὲς ἄνθος, and perhaps *Dith.* 1. 14 (fr. 70a) ἀέ]ξετ᾽ ἔτι, Μοῖςαι, θάλος ἀοιδᾶν. Variation between ἀέξω and αὔξω/ αὐξάνω is common; Euripides has only the one case of the first, and more frequently uses αὔξω or αὐξάνω, while Timotheus has αὔξεται of the waxing moon at fr. 804.

203. νεοτευχῆ: 'newly-made', here with the sense 'innovative', a key word for the argument. Timotheus regards his music as a craft; *Il.* 5. 193–4 has δίφροι καλοὶ πρωτοπαγεῖς νεοτευχέες, Theocr. 1. 28 νεοτευχέc of the herdsman's κιccύβιον, both of which refer to physical craftsmanship, while at *Il.* 21. 592 νεοτεύκτου καccιτέροιο, the variant has the same force. Poetic novelty is a standard theme in Greek literature (cf. *Od.* 1. 351–2; Alcm. frr. 14, 39; Pi. *O.* 3. 4–6, 9. 47–9, fr. 70b (*Dith.* 2)); Ar. *Nub.* 561, *Pax* 749–50 etc.), and was an obsession not merely of Timotheus', but of the poets of the New Music in general; cf. *P.* 211–12, fr. 796; Ar. *Av.* 1377 (in a parody of Cinesias) ἀφόβωι φρενὶ cώματί τε νέαν ἐφέπων, 1384–6 ὑπὸ cοῦ πτερωθεὶς βούλομαι μετάρcιος | ἀναπτόμενος ἐκ τῶν νεφελῶν καινὰς λαβεῖν | ἀεροδονήτους καὶ νιφοβόλους ἀναβολάς; E. *Tro.* 511 ff. ἀμφί μοι, Ἴλιον, ὦ | Μοῦcα, καινῶν ὕμνων | ἆιcον cὺν δακρύοιc ὠιδὰν ἐπικήδειον.

204. ἔλθ᾽: a fairly typical opening for a cletic hymn, as at *P.* 238 (Pulleyn 136–44).

ἐπίκουρος: Simonides, in his elegy for Plataea (fr. eleg. 11), uses the same word to the Muse in his hymn to Achilles (20–1): αὐτὰρ ἐγώ[| κικλήιcκω] c᾽ ἐπίκουρον ἐμοί, π[ολυώνυμ]ε

Μοῦca; E. *Or*. 1299–1300 has ὦ Διός ἀέναον κράτος, | ἔλθ᾽ ἐπίκουρος ἐμοῖς φίλοιςι πάντως, described by Willink as 'formulaic'; Pindar describes the opposite relationship at *O*. 13. 69–70 *Μοίcαις* . . . ἔβαν ἐπίκουρος. The image may be martial, as may *cύμμαχος* at Sa. fr. 1. 28; but Pi. *O*. 1. 110–11 speaks simply of a ἐπίκουρον . . . ὁδὸν λόγων. Despite the similarity of theme, there is no reason to believe that the Simonidean passage is here deliberately recalled as I. C. Rutherford, *Arethusa*, 29 (1996), 182, believes. The word is first applied to a god at *Il*. 21. 431, where Aphrodite assists Ares in battle; more importantly, ἐπικούριος was a cult-title of Apollo (Paus. 8. 30. 4, 8. 41. 7), possibly reflecting his apotropaic functions. In tragedy the term is generally used of human rescuers (e.g. E. *Or*. 211, *El*. 138, *IA* 1241, *Ba*. 1367).

ὕμνοις{ιν}: 'songs' (plural also at 212, 215), hardly a reference just to the *Persae*, as Janssen believes, but to Timotheus' work in general, as at Pi. *O*. 6. 105, where Pindar prays to Poseidon to make the 'flower of his songs' flourish (quoted above, p. 234).

205. ἰήϊε Παιάν: see 198 n. Apollo, as the citharode's patron god, was traditionally associated with the nome (above, pp. 28–9).

206–7. ὁ . . . εὐγενέτας μακραίων Cπάρτας μέγας ἀγεμών: this is most naturally read as a single phrase in apposition to λαός at 209, and should refer to the Spartiates as a whole rather than simply to the aristocracy; Janssen takes the latter view, and improbably sees ὁ γὰρ εὐγενέτας . . . λαός as in apposition to μακραίων Cπάρτας μέγας ἀγεμών. μέγας ἀγεμών may be intended to be reminiscent of the more common μέγας Βαςιλεύς of the Persian King.

Bassett thinks that ἀγεμών may suggest the Spartan hegemony over Greece after 403 BC, which would explain the apparently complimentary language ('well-born', 'teeming with the flowers of youth'), but it seems unlikely that Cπάρτας . . . ἀγεμών can mean anything other than 'ruler of Sparta', and the compliments may be ironic. That Sparta was culturally deprived was at least a common Athenian opinion (cf. Pl. *Hipp. Mai*. 283 B ff.; *Lg*. 2. 660 B: hence also the portrayal of Tyrtaeus and Alcman as Athenian and

Lydian respectively); their supposed backwardness and musical conservatism would be aptly satirized by the traditional phrase βρύων ἄνθεϲιν ἥβαϲ and the epithet μακραίων. Sparta had had a flourishing musical tradition in the archaic period, and welcomed many foreign poets, such as Terpander (see further 225 n.), who was reputed to be the first victor at the Carneia, the important musical festival of Apollo which could still attract competitors from all Greece throughout the fifth century. The Cretan Thaletas or Thales of Gortyn composed music for the Spartans, allegedly in order to deliver them of a plague ([Plu.] *Mus.* 42. 1146 B); he may also have written paeans (*Mus.* 10. 1134 D). According to Paus. 1. 14. 4 the Spartans commissioned Polymnestus of Colophon to write a poem in his honour. Ps.-Plutarch (*Mus.* 9. 1134 BC) also associates the 'second organization' of music at Sparta with Thaletas and Polymnestus, together with Xenodamus of Cythera, Xenocritus of Locri, and Sacadas of Argos, connecting their activities with what appear to be religious festivals (the Gymnopaidiai at Sparta; the Apodeixis in Arcadia; and the Endymatia at Argos); Sosibius, *FGrH* 595 F 5 mentions choral performances at the festival to commemorate the victory at Thyrea in 546, at which three choruses of naked boys, men, and old men sing songs by Thaletas and Alcman, and the paeans of Dionysodotus. An echo of this arrangement may be found at *PMG* carm. pop. 870, a lyric dialogue between three Spartan choruses. For some possibly Spartan paeans among the adespota, cf. *PMG* adesp. 867, 858. Alcman's poetry was clearly still performed in Sparta in the fifth century and later, and Spartan lyric of that sort was well enough known in Athens to be parodied by Aristophanes at *Lys.* 1296–1315. Athenaeus (14. 632 F–633 A) also reports the devotion of the Spartans to music and poetry, quoting Pratinas fr. 709 Λάκων ὁ τέττιξ εὔτυκοϲ εἰϲ χορόν, and noting that lyric poets were not only common among them but that 'even now' (καὶ νῦν) they preserve their ancient songs: τηροῦϲιν . . . τὰϲ ἀρχαίαϲ ᾠδὰϲ ἐπιμελῶϲ πολυμαθεῖϲ τε εἰϲ ταύταϲ εἰϲὶ καὶ ἀκριβεῖϲ. He goes on to quote two fragments of Laconian song (*PMG* adesp. 954).

The general absence of named Spartan poets in the

literary record is therefore slightly unexpected in the light of the popularity of poetry in Sparta and its apparent importance as a musical centre at least in the archaic and classical periods. Possibly local poets, especially given the isolationist attitude of the Spartans in general, did not feel the need to travel in order to make their name, though they clearly welcomed non-Spartan performers at the Carneia and presumably at other festivals. Their own musical fashions, in the fifth century, may have nevertheless seemed old-fashioned to the Athenians.

206. μ': according to Wackernagel's Law (*Kl. Schr.* i. 1–103; Ed. Fraenkel, *Kl. Beitr.* i. 73–139), enclitics naturally position themselves after the first significant element in a sentence in Indo-European. Hence, here με intervenes between the article (possibly in any case pronominal as at 173) and the nominal phrase.

εὐγενέτας: a variant for εὐγενής; cf. γηγενέτας at Timoth. fr. 801. It appears in Euripidean lyric at *Andr.* 771, *Ion* 1060, *Ph.* 1510.

μακραίων: rare outside Sophocles, though cf. also A. fr. 350. 1–2 Radt τὰς ἐμὰς εὐπαιδίας | νόcων τ' ἀπείρους καὶ μακραίωνας βίου. In Sophocles it seems to mean 'long-lived' at *OT* 1099, *OC* 152; but at *Ant.* 987 Μοῖραι μακραίωνες, the sense is simply 'ancient'. The latter seems to be the point here, though Wilamowitz connected it with εὐγενέτας and thought the whole meant 'of ancient nobility'.

208. βρύων: see fr. 780. 2 n.

ἄνθεcιν ἥβας: a conventional phrase in archaic and classical literature; cf. e.g. Hes. *Th.* 988; *Il.* 13. 484; Mimn. frr. 1. 4, 2. 3; Tyrt. fr. 10. 28; Solon fr. 25. 1; Simon. fr. eleg. 8. 6; Thgn. 1007–8, 1070; Pi. *P.* 4. 158; A. *Eum.* 663 etc. The whole phrase has the sense 'in their prime', 'in their full strength'.

209. ἐπιφλέγων: at 206 μ' is the object of δονεῖ, and ἐπιφλέγων here is probably intransitive (as at Pi. *P.* 11. 45), rather than transitive with an implied object (so LSJ). We find a metaphorical sense as early as A. *Pers.* 395 cάλπιγξ δ' ἀϋτῆι πάντ' ἐκεῖν' ἐπέφλεγεν 'a trumpet set them all ablaze with its sound', Pi. *O.* 9. 21–2 πόλιν μαλεραῖc ἐπιφλέγων ἀοιδαῖc 'illuminating the city with fierce blaze of song';

there is no need to understand with Janssen a literal sense 'burning (me) down'. We should expect αἴθοπι μώμωι at 210 to be dependent on the participle, 'burning with fiery blame' rather than on ἐλᾶι, 'drives (me) with fiery blame', but delayed τε is unthinkable here. ἐλᾶι τε has in fact been added almost as an afterthought, thereby disrupting the natural sequence; this is all the easier because the dative in fact coheres, in some measure, with the two main verbs as well as with the participle.

210. αἴθοπι: the adjective continues the imagery suggested by ἐπιφλέγων; it usually qualifies wine, smoke, or bronze in epic, and its general sense can be compared with αἴθων, with which αἴθοψ seems largely interchangeable (despite the arguments of K. J. McKay, *Mnem.*[4] 12 (1959), 198–203). See West on Hes. *Op.* 363 αἴθοπα λιμόν.

μώμωι: μῶμος does not appear to have any associations with literature until the fifth century and later; Pindar always refers not to μῶμος but to poetic ψόγος and athletic φθόνος. Philip, *GP* 3033 (*AP* 11. 321. 1) describes γραμματικοί as the Μώμου Cτυγίου τέκνα; Callimachus presents Μῶμος as the personification of literary envy at *H.* 2. 113, fr. 393.

211. παλαιοτέραν: 'older'; cf. Timoth. fr. 796. 1, 5 Μοῦcα παλαιά. The comparative form παλαίτερος is more common, but παλαιότερος appears at Tyrt. 10. 19, 22; 12. 42; Pi. *N.* 6. 53; Thgn. 936 (also superlative παλαιότατος at Pl. *Ti.* 83 A etc.), and is the more ancient form: see O. Szemerényi, *Syncope in Greek and Indo-European and the Indo-European Accent* (Naples, 1964), 253. The adjective can be derogatory (as at S. *OT* 290 κωφὰ καὶ παλαί᾽ ἔπη, and possibly also the other instances in Timotheus), but is not necessarily so here. The direct contrast with the following νέοις is strongly effective.

νέοις ὕμνοις: see 203 n.

212. Μοῦcαν ἀτιμῶ: cf. Ar. *Nub.* 972 τὰς Μούcας ἀφανίζων (of Phrynis), Pherecr. 155 K.–A., where Music (Μουcική) is portrayed as having been raped by Timotheus and other poets of the New Music. The phrase here is probably echoed in the forged Laconian Decree against Timotheus (Boethius, *Mus.* 1. 1, p. 182 Friedlein): ἐπειδὴ Τιμόθεορ ὁ

Μιλήςιορ παραγενόμενορ ἐττὰν ἀμετέραν πόλιν τὰμ παλαιὰν μῶάν
ἀτιμάϲδη.

213. δ': 'by contrast'.

214. γεραόν: 'old', usually written γεραιόϲ, but correption
is common in Euripides (*Med.* 134, *Hipp.* 170, *Hec.* 64,
Suppl. 43, *Herc.* 115, 446, 901, *Ph.* 1718) and γεραόν is
written by Dindorf at S. *OC* 200 for the MSS' γεραιόν. See
Denniston on E. *El.* 497.

ἰϲήβαν: 'peers', modelled on ἰϲῆλιξ. Whatever arbitrary
date between *c.*415 and 396 is chosen for the first performance of the poem, Timotheus would then have been roughly
middle-aged.

215. εἴργω . . . ἑκα⟨ϲ⟩: 'I keep at a distance'; cf. 217
ἀπερύκω. There may be a reminiscence of the vocabulary of
cult ritual; cf. e.g. *Il.* 23. 72, E. *IT* 381–4 ἥτιϲ βροτῶν μὲν ἤν
τιϲ ἅψηται φόνου, | ἢ καὶ λοχείαϲ ἢ νεκροῦ θίγηι χεροῖν, | βωμῶν
ἀπείργει κτλ., Isoc. 4. 157, Callim. *H.* 2. 2 ἑκὰϲ ἑκὰϲ ὅϲτιϲ
ἀλιτρόϲ, Verg. *Aen.* 6. 258 *procul o, procul este, profani*;
further Hor. *Od.* 3. 1 *odi profanum vulgus et arceo*, and see
Parker, *Miasma*, 37 n. 17.

216. τοὺϲ {ο}δὲ . . . τούτουϲ δ': the shortness of the
interval at which δέ recurs, here the result of beginning
the sentence with the object and using a resumptive pronoun, is somewhat unusual, but see Denniston 185 for
further examples.

μουϲοπαλαιολύμαϲ: 'ancient (old-fashioned) corrupters of
the Muse', not 'corrupters of the old Muse' (so Campbell;
Edmonds *sim.*); -παλαιο- is more naturally taken with -λύμαϲ
than with μουϲο-, despite the temptation to compare fr. 796.
Compounds in -λύμηϲ are generally restricted to comedy:
Ar. *Pax* 813 ἰχθυολύμηϲ 'destroyer of fish', com. adesp. fr.
591 K.–A. δικολύμηϲ, which LSJ translate as 'one who
destroys by lawsuits (?)', but despite the absence of a context
it is better to regard δικο- as objective, 'one who destroys the
law'. There may be a direct reference to particular performers or poets in these lines. There was competition
between the poets of the New Music themselves (cf.
Timoth. frr. 778(*b*), 802), but also attacks from other musicians; cf. Dorion's criticism of Timoth. fr. 785, Stratonicus' attack on fr. 792; Telestes, long after Melanippides'

death, seems to have felt the need to disparage (in humorous style) his *Marsyas*.

217. ἀπερύκω: 'fend off'; see 215 n.

218. λωβητῆρας: 'destroyers'. The same root appears at Ar. *Ra*. 93 λωβηταὶ τέχνης (of bad poets), and Antiphanes, *GP* 775 (*AP* 11. 322. 5) ποιητῶν λῶβαι (of grammarians), although there is no indication that the word (or related words) had a specific technical meaning in artistic contexts.

219. κηρύκων: 'heralds'; in an Athenian context probably referring to the crier at Assemblies (e.g. Ar. *Ach.* 42 ff., Andoc. 1. 36, X. *HG* 2. 4. 20), whose profession naturally required a loud voice; for competitions between heralds, in which the loudest and clearest was the victor, cf. Pollux 4. 91, Dem. 19. 338, and the competitive cries at *PMG* carm. pop. 863, 865.

λιγυμακροφώνων: 'shrill, loud-voiced'. The second term -μακρο- should mean 'loud' rather than 'far' (so Campbell); cf. Ar. *Thesm.* 211–12 τοῦτον μὲν μακρὰ κλάειν κέλευ'. There seems to have been a new fashion for quiet singing in the late fifth century (cf. E. *Herc.* 1042 ff., *Or.* 136 ff., S. *Ph.* 843 ff.), and Demosthenes criticizes excessive loudness in the actors Simycas and Socrates at 18. 262 (Pickard-Cambridge, *Festivals* 167 ff.; West, *Music*, 44). λιγυ- is not normally a negative term; possibly there has been influence from the epithet λιγύφθογγος, common of heralds in Homer (e.g. *Il.* 2. 50, 442, 9. 10, 23. 39, *Od.* 2. 6); the emphasis, however, may be on μακρο-.

220. τείνοντας: 'straining', though there is no implication of difficulty in singing. At A. *Pers.* 575 τεῖνε δὲ δυσβάϋκτον βοᾶτιν τάλαιναν αὐδάν 'stretch out your miserable voice in an agonizing howl' (Hall), it is used of Persian lamentation (cf. cύντονος at 169 above), and Broadhead takes the verb to refer to the intensity of the cry. At E. *Med.* 201 τί μάτην τείνουcι βοήν; Page understands 'sing loudly'. Here the participle therefore recalls the connotations of κηρύκων λιγυμακροφώνων; cf. also the related words τόνος 'pitch' and ἐντείνω 'put into verse'.

ἰυγ{γ}άς: cf. Hsch. (ι 1107) ἰυγή· φωνή, κραυγή, βοή, and elsewhere largely poetic; e.g. Orac. ap. Hdt. 9. 43. 2, S. *Ph.* 752, Nic. *Th.* 400.

221 ff. The papyrus gives the corrupt -μουϲοϲορινϲυν-
τεκνωϲεννιοϲκαλλιοπα | πιεριαϲενι. The subject of the verb
should clearly be Orpheus; Wilamowitz rightly saw his
name in ορινϲ, then emending -μουϲοϲ into -μουϲον and
supplementing ⟨χέλ⟩υν as the object of the verb. Despite
other early attempts to find a supplement (Reinach, κροῦϲιν;
Blass ὔ⟨μ⟩ν⟨ουϲ⟩), ⟨χέλ⟩υν has been universally accepted. The
corruption is not readily explained, and χέλυν is not altogether comfortable as the object of τεκνόω; GOH suggests
perhaps ⟨τέχν⟩ην (τέχναν), which might suit and in which τέχν
might have been omitted before ἐτέκνωϲεν. Καλλιοπα should
be genitive Καλλιόπα⟨ϲ⟩ after υἱόϲ, which leaves ⟨◡ -⟩ to
complete *gl* for the line. In the next line, Wilamowitz
emends to Πιερίαϲ ἔπι, Danielsson Πιερία⟨ι⟩ϲ ἔνι; there is no
example of a postposition in Timotheus. Page's Πιερίαθεν,
which looks like the end of a pherecratean, appeals; but this
is odd after the verb, unless a participle is supplemented in
the lacuna. MLW supplements e.g. ⟨κόραϲ | Διὸϲ⟩.

221. πρῶτοϲ: 'first', a typical opening in this context (cf.
e.g. Pi. fr. 125. 2; Telestes frr. 806. 2, 810. 1).

ποικιλόμουϲον: 'of intricate music'. Compounds in ποι-
κιλο- are common in descriptions of music or musical
instruments (cf. Hes. *Op.* 203 with West, Pi. *O.* 3. 8, 4. 3,
N. 4. 14, Nonn. *D.* 2. 510), and the word primarily suggests
artistic elaboration (see Page on Sa. 1. 1); as a technical term
for a literary or musical style ποικιλία ('variation') dates to the
late fifth or early fourth century (cf. Pl. *Lg.* 7. 812 D, Isoc. 5.
27, Dion. Hal. *Comp.* 11, etc.). The concept seems to have
been essential to Timotheus' own view of his innovations.

The papyrus has -οϲ, but we might more reasonably
expect the adjective, as a simple *bahuvrīhi*, to be applied to
the lyre than to Orpheus himself; assimilation of an ending
to that of the words that surround it (πρῶτοϲ, Ὀρφεύϲ) is a
common type of scribal error.

Ὀρφεύϲ: Orpheus appears first in the sixth century (not
in Homer or Hesiod) as a shamanistic figure whose music
was possessed of magical powers (cf. e.g. A. *Ag.* 1629–30,
E. *Alc.* 357–62, *IA* 1211–15); he is often connected with
Apollo, either as his worshipper (A. *TrGF* p. 138, Pi. *P.* 4.
177) or later as his son. He is mentioned by Plato (*Ion* 533

BC) as the chief practitioner of citharody (together with Phemius, Olympus, and Thamyras as representatives of rhapsodes, auletes, and citharists respectively; cf. his appearance as a culture-hero, together with Olympus, Amphion, and Marsyas at *Lg.* 3. 677 D); [Plu.] *Mus.* 5. 1132 F credits him with the invention of citharody. See I. M. Linforth, *The Arts of Orpheus* (Berkeley and Los Angeles, 1941), 1–38, and on the existence of works attributed to Orpheus in classical Athens, see M. L. West, *The Orphic Poems* (Oxford, 1983), 20 ff.; F. Wehrli, *Eleusis und die orphische Dichtung Athens in vorhellenistischer Zeit* (Berlin and New York, 1974).

223. Καλλιόπα⟨c: Orpheus was the son of Calliope according to Pl. *R.* 2. 364 E, A.R. 1. 32 ff., Paus. 9. 30. 4, Conon, *Fab.* 45. Such genealogies were not uncommon for mythical singers; [Hesiod] makes Linus the son of Ourania and explicitly associates him with citharody (fr. 305. 1 ff.). Calliope acquired considerable importance at an early stage. Hesiod (*Th.* 79–80) calls her the most excellent of the Muses and connected her with both kingship and poetry; cf. Alcm. fr. 27, Stesich. fr. 240, Pi. *O.* 10. 14, Ba. 5. 176–9, 19. 12–14.

225. Τέρπανδρος: Terpander was widely credited with the invention of the nome; cf. *Suda* s.v. *Τέρπανδρος, Marm. Par. Ep.* 34 (p. 12 Jacoby), [Plu.] *Mus.* 4. 1132 DE, Pollux 4. 66. According to tradition he set Sparta's laws to music (Clem. Alex. *Strom.* 1. 16. 78. 5; Ael. *VH* 12. 50; *Suda* μ 701, iii. 370 Adler), possibly the result of later confusion about the meaning of νόμος. According to another tradition he also suffered at the hands of the ephors at the Carneia, where, however, he was also regarded as the first victor (Hellanicus, *FGrH* 4 F 85a). Like Timotheus he was associated with the addition of strings to the cithara ([Plu.] *Mus.* 30. 1141 C; *Suda* τ 354, iv. 527 Adler). According to Alexander Polyhistor (*FGrH* 273 F 77) he imitated the music of Orpheus in his nomes.

ἐπὶ τῶι: 'after him'.

225–6. δέκα ... ἐν ὠιδαῖς: 'on ten notes' is possible, although the tradition is unanimous in ascribing only seven strings to Terpander's lyre (cf. e.g. Terpander fr. 4 Gostoli,

Strabo 13. 2. 4, [Plu.] *Mus.* 30. 1141 c, Plin. *NH* 7. 204),
which apparently had three added to the traditional four. If
Timotheus took seven as the basic number and assumed
Terpander added three, he may have thought (or wished us
to think) Terpander used a ten-string lyre (see West, *Music*,
362 n. 22); for ὠιδή as a possible equivalent of χορδή, cf.
perhaps the phrase τετραοίδιος νόμος 'song played on four
notes', and see L. Deubner, *Ath. Mitt.* 54 (1929), 200. 'On
ten songs' is harder to understand; [Plu.] refers to seven
citharodic nomes established in the time of Terpander (*Mus.*
4. 1132 D), but ten is not a traditional number (Pollux 4. 65
names eight, the *Suda* s.v. ὄρθιος νόμος seven). The problem
can be avoided by reading ἐπὶ τῶιδε κατηῦξε (so Aron) but
the sense is weak and the form κατηῦξε seriously disrupts the
metre.

226. ζεῦξε: 'yoked' (so Wilamowitz for the papyrus' τευξε;
the error is a simple one), a slightly unusual word in the
context, but it may refer to the ζυγόν 'crossbar' of the
phorminx (*Il.* 9. 187) to which the strings were attached.
Lucian (*DDeor.* 7. 4, *DMar.* 1. 4) uses the phrase ζυγόω
κιθάραν to describe the process of putting these crossbars on
the cithara; cf. also Diogenes, *TrGF* 45 F 1. 8–9, where
ἀντιζύγοις may mean 'counter-strung'.

227. Λέϲβος . . . Αἰολία: 'Aeolian Lesbos'; for the
construction, cf. Hes. *Op.* 636 Κύμην Αἰολίδα, Hdt. 7. 194.
1, Thuc. 3. 31. 1, etc.

Ἀντίϲϲαι: 'in Antissa' (locatival dative), traditionally the
place of Terpander's birth (cf. e.g. *Suda* τ 354, Steph. Byz.
s.v. Ἄντιϲϲα, Clem. Alex. *Strom.* 1. 16. 78. 5, [Plu.] *Mus.* 30.
1141 C). The *Suda* also mentions Arne and Cyme as possible
birth-places, while Diodorus (8. 28, ap. Tzetz. *Chil.* 1.
388 ff.) names Methymna, perhaps through confusion with
Arion.

228. γείνατο: for the idea, cf. Pi. *O.* 5. 4 πόλιν λαοτρόφον, *I.*
1. 1, E. *Ph.* 996, *FGE* anon. 124a, etc. See also *P.* 235
θρέψας'.

229–30. μέτροις ῥυθμοῖς τ᾿: 'The difference between
μέτρον and ῥυθμός is best explained by saying that an iambic
tetrameter and a trochaic tetrameter differ ῥυθμῶι but not
μέτρωι, whereas an iambic trimeter and an iambic tetrameter

differ μέτρωι but not ῥυθμῶι' (Dover on Ar. *Nub.* 638).
Dionysius of Halicarnassus notes the innovations in rhythm
developed by the New Poets: καὶ τοῖς ῥυθμοῖς κατὰ πολλὴν
ἄδειαν ἐνεξουςιάζοντες διετέλουν, οἵ γε δὴ κατὰ Φιλόξενον καὶ
Τιμόθεον καὶ Τελέςτην (*Comp.* 19). Aristoxenus defines ῥυθμός
as the particular arrangement of χρόνοι, i.e. the division of
syllables into feet and the division of each foot into arsis and
thesis (*Rhythm.* 2 with Pearson, see also ibid., pp. xxxiv f.;
cf. Psellus, *Prol.* 3). See further West, *Music*, 129–53.

230. ἐνδεκακρουμάτοις: 'eleven-stringed'. κροῦμα describes the sound produced by striking a stringed instrument; thus here the sense 'with eleven notes'; the adjective
seems to refer to both nouns. Pindar has ἐπτακτύπου φόρ-
μιγγος (*P.* 2. 70–1) 'a phorminx with seven notes', i.e. with
seven strings (cf. *N.* 5. 23 φόρμιγγ' . . . ἐπτάγλωccον,
Terpander fr. 4. 2 Gostoli ἐπτατόνωι φόρμιγγι, E. *Alc.*
446). An eleven-stringed lyre is mentioned at Ion fr. eleg.
32. See West, *Studies*, 173–4 and *ZPE* 92 (1992), 23–8. A
dozen strings are ascribed to Timotheus at Pherecrates fr.
155. 24–5 K.–A., while according to the *Suda* he added the
tenth and eleventh strings; Pausanias (3. 12. 10) makes him
add the eighth to eleventh strings, Nicomachus (4; *Mus. Scr.
Gr.* p. 274 Jan) just the eleventh. Plin. *NH* 7. 204 gives the
ninth string to Timotheus, 'Censorinus', p. 76, ll. 8–9
Sallmann the seventh and ninth. Other lists abound; Simonides is named for the eighth, Phrynis for the eighth and
ninth, Theophrastus of Pieria also for the ninth, Histiaeus of
Colophon for the tenth; cf. Procl. *Chrest.* ap. Phot. *Bibl.*
320ᵇ8–11, Plu. *Prof. virt.* 13 (West, *Music*, 62–4).

231. κίθαριν: the more archaic form of the word, and
therefore perhaps chosen here to emphasize Timotheus'
debt to the past, though it remained in use in poetry (e.g.
Alc. fr. 41. 15; Pi. *P.* 5. 65; E. *Hyps.* fr. 1.iii. 10, p. 27 Bond,
where it is used of Orpheus' cithara; Ar. *Nub.* 1357–8,
Thesm. 124; Callim. *H.* 2. 19). For the development of the
variant κιθάρα, see 202 n. The technical distinction between
the λύρα and κιθάρα can only be dated to Plato (*R.* 3. 399 D),
but is common afterwards (e.g. Arist. *Pol.* 8. 1341ᵃ19, 40;
Aristox. fr. 102; Anaxilas fr. 15 K.–A. etc.); it may of course
have existed before.

ἐξανατέλλει: 'causes to spring up', a rare word; cf. the transitive uses at Teleclides fr. 47 K.–A. μόνον ἐκ κεφαλῆc ἑνδεκακλίνου θόρυβον πολὺν ἐξανατέλλειν, and A.R. 4. 142 (also intransitive at Emped. DK 31 B 61. 2, 62. 4, Mosch. 2. 58). But the idea and language appears also at Sen. *Ep.* 40. 11 *Cicero quoque noster, a quo Romana eloquentia exiluit* etc., almost certainly independently.

The word recalls ἐτέκνωcεν of Orpheus' activity at 222; Timotheus can make the lyre spring up anew, just as Orpheus (perhaps) brought it up in Pieria. As when Terpander yokes the Muse, both objects are almost personifications of (citharodic) music.

232. θηcαυρόν: cf. Hes. *Op.* 719–20 γλώccηc τοι θηcαυρὸc ἐν ἀνθρώποιcιν ἄριcτοc | φειδωλῆc, Pi. *P.* 6. 7–8 ἑτοῖμοc ὕμνων θηcαυρόc. οἴξαc implies that here the word means 'treasury'; but θαλαμευτόν suggests that this sense blends with 'treasure'.

πολύυμνον: the adjective here may mean either 'much sung of', the usual sense, or 'with many songs'; the latter would be an innovation.

233. θαλαμευτό[[c]]ν: 'hidden in a store-room', only here (but cf. θαλαμεύω, θαλάμευμα).

234. νιν: for the position of νιν here, see 206 n.

235. θρέψαc': 'nurturing'; forms of τρέφω are sometimes applied to countries with a similar force, cf. e.g. Hes. *Th.* 479–80, Pi. *I.* 8. 40, *N.* 10. 13, E. *Hel.* 88. See C. Moussy, *Recherches sur τρέφω et les verbes grecs signifiant « nourrir »* (Paris, 1969), 37 ff.

δυωδεκατειχέοc: 'twelve-walled' (but cf. ἑπτατειχεῖc used of the exits of Thebes, presumably 'seven-gated', A. *Sept.* 284 εἰc ἑπτατειχεῖc ἐξόδουc, where ἑπτα- really belongs with the noun; see Hutchinson ad loc.). Perhaps with reference to the Ionian confederation of twelve cities (cf. Hdt 1. 141–6, 7. 95 οἱ δυωδεκαπόλιεc Ἴωνεc), of which Miletus was a member. Although the confederation may not have been in existence in the later fifth century, it is possible that its memory was strongly preserved and had a deep emotional content. Alternatively, δυωδεκα- may merely be equivalent to 'many', like ModE 'dozen'; cf. δωδεκαμήχανοc of a prostitute at Ar. *Ra.* 1327, where the sense is presumably 'having many tricks' rather than having exactly twelve.

236. πρωτέος: 'first'; although the sense is clear enough, the form of the word is obscure. I take it as genitive singular of *πρωτεύς agreeing with λαοῦ, probably created as a back-formation from πρωτεύω; cf. perhaps Doric πρατεύς, a Pythagorean term for the first principle (Pythag. ap. Syrian. *in Metaph.* 10. 4), and the proper name Πρωτεύς, though of uncertain derivation. The adjective πρῶτε(ι)ος is late and usually has three terminations. Croiset emends to πρώ-τευς⟨εν⟩, with ἅ as the subject: 'Miletus which is first among the Achaeans'.

237–40. Final Prayer to Apollo. A short prayer is a common feature at the end of hymns, especially paeans; cf. Isyllus, *CA* 134. 58–60, Macedonius, *CA* 139. 25 ff., Limenius, pp. 84–129 Bélis, Aristonoos, *CA* 164. 45 ff., 165. 14 ff., Philodamus, *CA* 166–9. 11–13, 24–6, *PMG* adesp. 937. 12–15 ἀθάναταί τε θεαὶ καὶ ςώιζετε τόνδ' Ἐπιδαύρου | ναὸν ἐν εὐνομίαι πολυάνορι Ἑλλάνων, | ἱεροκαλλίνικοι | εὐμενεῖ cὺν ὄλβωι, Callim. *H.* 1. 91 ff., 2. 113, 3. 269, 4. 325, 5. 89 ff., 6. 134 ff., etc. In view of the metrical similarity to Limenius' paean noted above, it is particularly worth comparing ll. 34–5 (pp. 126 ff. Bélis) ἀλλ' ὦ Φοῖβε, cῶιζε θεόκτιστον Παλλάδος [ἄcτυ καὶ λαὸν κλεινόν, although this comes at the start of the concluding prayer rather than at the end.

Metre

237	– ∪∪ – ∪∪ – ∪ – – |
	– – – ∪∪ – ∪ – – |
	– – ∪ – ∪∪ – – |
240	– – – – | – – ∪ – ∪∪ – ||

The hipponactean at the end of the last section (236) is followed by two more, the first (237) with double short in the second position in the base, the second with double long in the base (238). 239 is an anaclastic hagesichorean. Line 240 begins with *2sp*, which is perhaps slightly unusual, though no alternative analysis seems likely. Spondees have been noted before in the presence of aeolic metra (e.g. at 193). At the end of the line θάλλουcάν τ' εὐνομίαν (Danielsson) is possible; this would not alter the analysis (– – – – ∪∪ – can still be scanned as an anaclastic telesillean). GOH

finds the blunt close surprising, especially in the metrical context
of 202–40, and suggests that something may have dropped out of
the text, e.g. εὐνομίαν ⟨τ' ἀδελφάν⟩ (cf. Hes. *Th*. 901–2).

237–40. 'O far-shooting Paean come to this holy city with
wealth, sending to the people, that they be untroubled,
peace flourishing with good civic order'.

237. ἀλλ': see 202 n.

ἑκαταβόλε: a traditional title (cf. e.g. *h. Hom*. 3. 140),
understood in antiquity as 'far-shooting' (cf. ἐκηβόλος,
ἑκαέργος); the first term may be connected with ἑκών.

Πύθι': Apollo as cult-god at Delphi. Occasionally cult-
titles can be used in such a context with direct reference to
the festival involved (as at *h. Hom*. 3. 51, Ba. 17. 130 ff.,
Callim. *H*. 2. 72), but there is no need to believe that this is
the significance here; Croiset assumed that the first performance was at Delphi. The Pythian festival would, however, be
of special interest to a citharode; citharodic nomes (together
with the auletic nome; above, p. 31) were cultivated there
after 586.

ἀγνὰν: 'inviolable' (W. Ferrari, *SIFC* 17 (1940), 33–53),
although the more usual epithet with the sense 'holy' for
cities is ἱερός (Maehler on Ba. 18. 1); van Minnen sees a
reference to the contemporary Spartan threat, but the
adjective by itself is unlikely to convey such a connotation.

238. ἔλθοις: 'come', cf. 204 n. ἔλθ'. For the use of the
optative instead of the imperative, see Kühner–Gerth i.
229–30.

τάνδε πόλιν: unspecified as often in hymns and prayers
(e.g. *h. Hom*. 13. 3, Thgn. 757, 885–6, *PMG* adesp. 1018(b).
8–9, Philodamus *CA* 166 25, Callim. *H*. 6. 134) although
sometimes the place is actually named (e.g. *PMG* adesp.
937. 12–13).

σὺν ὄλβωι: cf. *h. Hom*. 15. 9 δίδου δ' ἀρετήν τε καὶ ὄλβον,
PMG adesp. 937, Philodamus, *CA* 166. 26 ἴθι . . . σὺν ὄλβωι
etc. A typical request, frequently paired as here with a
prayer for peace; cf. Thgn. 885 εἰρήνην καὶ πλοῦτος ἔχοι
πόλιν, Ba. fr. 4. 61–2, *PMG* adesp. 1021 etc.

239. ἀπήμονι: 'untroubled', probably proleptic, and thus
'so that they be untroubled'; cf. the same root in the

prayer at Thgn. 757–8 Ζεὺς μὲν τῆςδε πόληος ὑπειρέχοι αἰθέρι ναίων | αἰεὶ δεξιτερὴν χεῖρ᾽ ἐπ᾽ ἀπημοςύνηι, Pi. *Pae.* 9. 8–9 (fr. 52k), Callim. *H.* 1. 90–1. It was perhaps traditionally connected with the formal language of cult worship, though we find the adjective of the sea at Hes. *Op.* 670, Semon. fr. 7. 38.

240. εἰρήναν: 'peace', possibly with significant overtones at the end of the fifth century, as with the prayers for peace at e.g. Ar. *Eq.* 581 ff., *Thesm.* 352 ff.

θάλλουςαν: 'flourishing', cf. Hes. *Th.* 902 Εἰρήνην τεθαλυῖαν with West ('peace is "flourishing", because cities flourish under her rule'); at *Op.* 228 she is κουροτρόφος, because she allows youths to flourish. Peace is τάμι᾽ ἀνδράςι πλούτου 'steward of wealth for men' at Pi. *O.* 13. 7, and raised with (ὁμότροφος) Order and Justice. Happiness 'flourishes' at Pi. *P.* 7. 19–21, again because it makes men flourish: φαντί γε μάν | οὕτω κ᾽ ἀνδρὶ παρμονίμαν | θάλλοιςαν εὐδαιμονίαν τὰ καὶ τὰ φέρεςθαι.

εὐνομίαι: the papyrus has an accusative εὐνομίαν; peace is perhaps more likely to be 'flourishing' than 'good civic order', hence Danielsson's θάλλουςαν ⟨τ᾽⟩ εὐνομίαν is less attractive than Wilamowitz's dative εὐνομίαι. For the dative after θάλλω, cf. Hes. *Op.* 236 θάλλουςιν δ᾽ ἀγαθοῖςι διαμπερές, Pi. *O.* 9. 16 (πόλις) θάλλει . . . ἀρεταῖςιν. Peace and εὐνομία are frequently associated; cf. e.g. Hes. *Th.* 902, Pi. *O.* 13. 7–8, Ba. 13. 186 ff., *PMG* adesp. 1018(*b*). 6–7. εὐνομία can describe the behaviour of the citizens rather than the formal laws of the state (A. Andrews, *CQ* 32 (1938), 89–109). *Eunomia* is of course strongly (but not exclusively) associated with Spartan civic ideology: Tyrtaeus' poem, or collection of poems, on the Spartan constitution was called the Εὐνομία at least by the fifth century. It is perhaps possible that there are Laconian overtones here, recalling the Spartan criticism at 206 ff. Bassett sees a pun on νόμος 'song'. However, there is no evidence that the final lines of the poem are still concerned with Timotheus' musical defence.

792. THE BIRTHPANGS OF SEMELE
(Dithyramb)

On Dionysiac themes in dithyrambic poetry, see above, pp. 18–20. There is a group of *Semele* tragedies, which presumably also dealt with the birth of Dionysus. The earliest appears to be the *Semele* or *Hydrophoroi* by Aeschylus (frr. 221–4 Radt); there was also a *Hydrophoroi* by Sophocles (frr. 672–4 Radt), although its exact content is uncertain. Diogenes (*TrGF* 45 F 1) also wrote a *Semele*, as did Carcinus (*TrGF* 70 F 2–3) in the fourth century.

Semele appears in the earliest time as the mother of Dionysus (Hes. *Th.* 940–2, *Il.* 14. 325, *h. Hom.* 7. 1 etc.); her death by lightning and apotheosis also appear relatively early and become the usual version of the story (e.g. Pi. *O.* 2. 24–30, E. *Ba.* 1–12; cf. D.S. 5. 52, Charax, *FGrH* 103 F 4, Aristid. 41. 3, Philostr. *Im.* 1. 14, Ach. Tat. 2. 37. 4, Nonn. *D.* 8. 409, 9. 206 etc.). However, according to another version Dionysus brought her to Olympus when he had grown up. See West on Hes. *Th.* 942. If Alcaeus of Messene (*AP* 16. 7 = *HE* 54–61) is indeed referring to Timotheus' *Semele* in his epigram for the piper Dorotheus, then it seems clear from the adjective κεραύνιον (ὠδῖνα) that Timotheus used the first version. Little else can be established about the poem. The emphasis on the birthpangs (cf. esp. the statements by Athen., Dio Chrys.) again suggests fairly lavish treatment of the theme, and strong mimetic elements, as Straton implies.

Other dithyrambs on divine births are not widely attested, but Telestes may have written a poem on the birth of Zeus: fr. 809 (Philod. *De piet.* p. 23 Gomperz, reconstructed by Wilamowitz, *Hermes* 33, 1898, 521 = *Kl. Schr.* iv. 32) . . . καὶ Τελέc[της ἐν Διὸ]c γονα⟨ὶ⟩c . . .

793. SCYLLA

(Dithyramb)

The *Scylla* was another dithyramb (cf. the references to pipers and chorus-leaders at Arist. *Poet.* 26. 1461^{b}30), dealing with the wanderings of Odysseus. Its scope is uncertain, but it may be assumed that the lament of Odysseus (presumably for his dead companions) occupied a central part of the work, given the criticisms by Aristotle and the anonymous author of the Rainer papyrus, who must be assumed to depend to a large extent on this section of the *Poetics*.

The criticism levelled at the poem by Aristotle and the author of the Rainer papyrus is concerned mainly with the characterization of Odysseus. Aristotle describes the lament of Odysseus as ἀπρεποῦς καὶ μὴ ἁρμόττοντος; he means that the portrayal of Odysseus was not suitable to his character. For a brief discussion, see S. Halliwell, *The* Poetics *of Aristotle* (London, 1987), 141, and Lucas ad loc. The argument in the Rainer papyrus is slightly less clear, but the point seems essentially the same. Aristotle's criticism at *Poet.* 26. 1461^{b}30 is aimed at fourth-century performers of the work and, as such, is probably of little relevance here, but for the mimetic quality of the later dithyramb, cf. e.g. [Arist.] *Probl.* 19. 15 and see above, pp. 38–9. The *Scylla* usually attributed to Stesichorus I of Himera (*PMG* 220) might actually have been written by Stesichorus II, and thus be contemporary with Timotheus' poem (see M. L. West, *CQ*^{2} 20 (1970), 206): the precise contents of this work, however, are also unknown.

I have excluded fr. 794 as spurious (cf. my 'Notes', 290–1). Aristotle, giving an example of the *prooimion* of a dithyramb in the *Rhetoric* (3. 14. 1415^{a}11, p. 183 Kassel), cites the line:

διὰ cὲ καὶ τεὰ δῶρα †ειτα cκύλλα†

εἶτα A: εἴτε β (εἴ τι Vat. gr. 23, s. xiii exeunt.) cκύλλα A: cκῦλα β

The reading Cκύλλα, on which alone the ascription to Timotheus rests, is highly doubtful. Although cκύλλα is the reading given by the earliest MS, A (cod. Paris. gr.

1741), the majority of codices have cκῦλα. This is also the reading behind the anonymous Greek commentary on the *Rhetoric* (CAG 21. 2, p. 230 Rabe): οἷον· ἦλθον εἰc cὲ διὰ cὲ καὶ τὰ τεὰ καὶ τὰ cὰ δῶρα καὶ εὐεργετήματα καὶ τὰ cκῦλα, ὦ θεὲ Διόνυcε, although the commentator probably had no knowledge of the poem beyond the line quoted by Aristotle. Moreover, it is hard to see exactly what the 'gifts of Scylla' might be, and on these grounds alone the reading of A might be doubted. However, cκῦλα is also difficult to understand; cκῦλα are technically the arms taken from a slain warrior's body as spoils, and although these might be dedicated to a god, it is not clear how they belong in an invocation. It might rather be suspected that cκῦλα represents a later attempt to make sense of the original corruption, although it is not clear whether it originates with the commentary or the commentary took it from the MSS. Since Cκυλλίταc was a rare epithet for Dionysus, attested only at *SIG* 1025. 58, 63 (Cos, 4th/3rd c. BC), as god of the cκυλλίc (given by Hsch. s.v. as a variant for κληματίc 'vine-branch'), it is perhaps possible that some form of this name should be read. If ' Cκυλλῖτα is read, the corrupt εἶτα might be explained as a correction (with the common orthography ει for ι), originally written above the line and later inserted into the quotation in the wrong place. There thus seems little reason to accept the reading of A, and, once it has been rejected, little reason to assign the fragment to Timotheus.

795. PHINEIDAI

Phineus was a Thracian king who married Cleopatra, the daughter of Boreas and Oreithyia (S. *Ant.* 966–87; *Phineus A+B* frr. 704–5 Radt); later, according to varying accounts, he married Idaia, the daughter of Dardanus (Apollod. *Bibl.* 3. 15. 3), or Eidothea, the sister of Cadmos (S. *Tympanistae* fr. 645 Radt), or Eurytia (Ascl. Trag. *FGrH* 12 F 31). He proceeded either to blind (so S. fr. 704 Radt, D.S. 4. 44. 4, Orph. *Arg.* 671–6), or to let his new wife blind (S. *Ant.*, *Tympanistae*), his sons by Cleopatra. It seems probable that Timotheus' poem dealt with the story of the blinding. Aeschylus wrote a *Phineus* (frr. 258–60 Radt), which appears to have used the myth as its subject, and Sophocles wrote two plays with that title (frr. 704–17a Radt), as well as dealing with the same story in the *Tympanistae*. A tragic Φινεῖδαι appears among the adespota (*TrGF* adesp. F 10a), and Timocles (fr. 6. 8–13 K.–A.) mentions the 'sons of Phineus' as a typical, or at least appropriate, subject for tragedy. No other lyric version is attested, and the exact treatment of the story in the plays is uncertain.

796–804. INCERTI LOCI

796. Presumably from the conclusion to a nome or the dithyrambic equivalent; see *P.* 202–36 n., and esp. 211–12, 229–33. The style is remarkably simple for Timotheus, which may indicate that such sections were often slightly more informal in style.

Metre

– – – ∪ ∪ – ∪ ‖		*2io* ‖
– ∪ † ∪ ? ?– – ‖		? ‖
∪ ∪ – – ∪ ∪ – – |		*2io* |
∪ ∪ – – ∪ ∪ – – |		*2io* |
5 ∪ ∪ – – ∪ ∪ – – |		*2io* |

The last three lines are regular ionics, but more problems are caused by the first two lines. Bowra, followed by G. Zuntz, *Drei Kapitel zur griechischen Metrik*, Sitzb. Österr. Akk. 443 (1984), 83 ('ein "schwerer" Ioniker und Periodenende'), retains the reading of the MSS ἀείδω in the first line and suggests that it should be read as an ionic of the type – ∪ – – ∪ ∪ – –. The metron – ∪ – – as a variation of the standard ionic ∪ ∪ – – only occurs in dramatic lyric in a dimeter of the type ∪ ∪ – ∪ | – ∪ – – (see Dale 121), but greater freedom was allowed in non-dramatic lyric, at least in the fourth century: West, *Metre*, 143, cites as an example Isyllus (*CA* 134. 48–9) Φοῖβος ἐμ Μά|λου δόμοις παρθενίαν ὥραν ἔλυσε(ν) to be analysed as – ∪ – – – ∪ – – | ∪ ∪ – – – ∪ – –. Farnell (*GLP*) preferred to read ἄιδω and to scan the line as a pherecratean followed by period-end.

The second line is more problematic. If Bergk's μάλα is accepted (καινὰ γὰρ μάλα κρείccω = – ∪ – ∪ ∪ – –), we can treat the line as a pherecratean, but the conjecture is somewhat unsatisfying and the unexpected metre worrying. Zuntz reads καινὰ γὰρ ἀμὰ κρείccω as *ch ba*, 'ein Form des Dimeters, die uns bald und viel unter Ionikern begegnen wird'. This solution has the advantage of maintaining the predominantly ionic rhythm, but the emendation ἀμά (Wilamowitz) is uncertain.

'I do not sing the ancient songs (?); for (my) new ones are better. A young Zeus rules, and it is long ago that Cronus was ruler. Away with the ancient Muse!'

3. νέοc: Conomis emends to νέον, and suggests, calling attention to the opposition with the adverbial phrase τὸ πάλαι in l. 4, that it might be used here as an adverb, equivalent to νεωcτί 'just now'. However, there is no obvious objection to the adjective as it stands (with the sense 'young'), and the contrast is clearly between the young Zeus and the old Muse; the parallels adduced by Conomis ([A.] *Pr.* 34–5 Διὸc γὰρ δυcπαραίτητοι φρένεc· ἅπαc δὲ τραχὺc ὅcτιc ἂν νέον κρατῆι, 955 νέον νέοι κρατεῖτε) are hardly relevant.

5. Μοῦcα παλαιά: 'the ancient Muse'; cf. *P.* 211–12 παλαιοτέραν . . . Μοῦcαν (with n.).

797. Athenaeus' interpretation of the φιάλη Ἄρεωc as the 'cup of Nestor' is clearly incorrect in the context, where the required sense is 'shield'. The same error, again with reference to Anaxandrides, is repeated at Athen. 11. 502 B.

798. Another example of the riddling periphrasis typical of Timotheus' style. In the absence of any contradictory information, Anaxandrides' interpretation of the phrase (χύτρα, i.e. 'pot') can be assumed to be correct.

πυρικτίτωι: 'fire-made'; a neologism, but readily comprehensible. πυρι- can be taken either as an instrumental dative, 'made by the fire', or as a locative, 'in the fire' (the second element, from κτίζω, allows for either interpretation). Cf. Pi. *N.* 10. 35 γαίαι καυθείcαι πυρί 'in earth baked by fire', i.e. in a vase, Critias fr. eleg. 3. 12–13 τὸν δὲ τροχὸν γαίαc τε καμίνου τ' ἔκγονον . . . κλεινότατον κέραμον, χρήcιμον οἰκονόμον, and see W. Schulze, *Quaestiones epicae* (Gütersloh, 1892), 503.

cτέγαι: 'cover' (Kock); the MSS have -κτίτοιcι γᾶc, and it is tempting, given the parallel phrases in Pindar and Critias, to read a form of γῆ. However, the plural -κτίτοιcι γα⟨ί⟩c

COMMENTARY

(Dobree), which could be supported on palaeographical grounds, is hard to defend, while a singular does not account for the dative plural ending of the transmitted -οιcι as satisfactorily as Kock's cτέγαι.

799. The precise sense of the fragment is obscure, although it was apparently customary to strew marjoram beneath a corpse (cf. Ar. *Eccl.* 1030 ὑποcτόρεcαί νυν πρῶτα τῆc ὀριγάνου with Ussher; so also olive-branches, cf. Callim. *Ia.* 4. 38 ff. with Pfeiffer; A. Kerkhecker, *Callimachus' Book of Iambi* (Oxford, 1999), 95 n. 60); this practice may be referred to here.

Metre

$$\cup\cup\cup\cup \mid \cup\cup\cup\cup \mid \cup\cup\cup\cup\cup- \mid \qquad\qquad 2an \mid$$

The first metron is completely resolved, with word-end marking the end of each of the individual components. The second metron is resolved in the first princeps; the absence of resolution in the final princeps may indicate period-end, where resolution is not permitted. Lyric anapaests are common in Greek drama in astrophic songs, and are often marked by greater freedom of resolution (Dale 51). However, sequences of proceleusmatics (resolved anapaests) are particularly common in comedy; cf. Ar. fr. 718 K.–A. τίc ὄρεα βαθύκομα τάδ' ἐπέcυτο βροτῶν, also *Av.* 328, *Lys.* 481–2 ~ 545–6. (without the final metron ∪∪–). In tragedy the only possible example is E. *IT* 232 ἔτι βρέφοc, ἔτι νέον, ἔτι θάλοc, which Diggle takes as an iambic dimeter (*Studies*, 96; cf. *Euripidea*, 315 = *CR* 34² (1984), 68). Proceleusmatics are said to have been typical of the entry of satyr-choruses (Aphthonius *GL* 6. 99. 19) and also occur in the 'hyporcheme' of Pratinas (*TrGF* 4 F 3; more probably from a satyr-play, cf. Seaford, 'Hyporchema').

ὀρίγανα: 'marjoram'. Often written ὀρεί-, the iota is usually treated as long, but must be short here as 'Origen' says. Loan-words often admit some variation in scansion; see Frisk s.v. (the etymology is uncertain). The neuter form -γανον is the most common (e.g. also Epicharmus fr. 94 Kaibel, Ar. *Ra.* 603, Ameipsias fr. 36 K.–A.), but a masculine -γανοc is also attested (e.g. Ion fr. eleg. 5, Anaxandr. fr. 50 K.–A.) as well as a feminine ἡ ὀρίγανοc (e.g. Plato Com. fr. 169 K.–A.). See also the discussion at Athen. 2. 68 B.

μυελοτρεφῆ: LSJ translate 'marrow-breeding', but adjec-

tives in -τρεφής are always passive in meaning (so e.g. *Od.* 4.
442 ἁλιοτρεφής 'reared in the sea', *Il.* 15. 625, 11. 256
ἀνεμοτρεφής 'fed, reared by the wind', etc.; see Chantraine,
s.v. τρέφω), and thus 'marrow-bred', 'nourished on marrow'
should be meant here (so rightly Wilamowitz). The exact
sense is, however, obscure. μυελός can refer to human
marrow, and if the image here is of a human body laid out
for burial, it might at a stretch be possible to regard the
marjoram strewn beneath it as 'fed on marrow'. We might
also be tempted to take μυελο- to refer to the marrow of the
plant, which gives it nourishment, but there are no close
parallels for the usage (although μυελός is not restricted to
literal meanings: cf. E. *Hipp.* 255 with Barrett).

The upsilon is always short in Attic, but long υ is found in
Homer, perhaps *metri causa*, as in the case of μυελόεντα (*Od.*
9. 293, at line-end), from which the long vowel may have
been extended to the other cases of μυελός.

800. The identification of the sun with Apollo is first found
explicitly in extant literature in Euripides' *Phaethon* (225
Diggle), and thus appears to be a fifth-century innovation. It
is possible, however, that it pre-dates Euripides. There may
be evidence for the identification at A. *Suppl.* 213–14 Χο.
καλοῦμεν αὐγὰς ἡλίου cωτηρίους. | Δα. ἁγνόν γ᾿ Ἀπόλλω, φυγάδ᾿
ἀπ᾿ οὐρανοῦ θεόν, if Page's γ᾿ is correct for cod. τ᾿. See further
Diggle on E. *Phaethon* 225 (p. 147); Johansen–Whittle on A.
Suppl. 213–14.

Parmenides (T 213 Coxon) and Empedocles (DK 31 A 3)
also appear in a rationalizing spirit to have equated the sun
with Apollo. The fragment may be from a paean, given the
closing invocation ἰὲ Παιάν, and in this case the ἐχθροί would
presumably be those of the host city. The language and
imagery are highly traditional, which may also point to some
sort of ritualistic or cultic work. Edmonds ascribes the
fragment to the *Persae*.

Metre

∪ – ∪∪ – ∪∪ – ∪∪ – |	∪ – ∪∪ – *an* |
– – – – – ∪∪ – – |	2*an* |
– ∪∪ – ∪∪ – – ∪∪ – |	2*an* |
– ∪∪ – – – ∪∪ – – ||	2*an* ||

In order to maintain the anapaestic metre it is necessary to read ἐχθροῖϲ⟨ι⟩ (l. 3) with Crusius. Resolution and contraction are common, both − − and − ∪ ∪ being frequently substituted for the basic metron ∪ ∪ −. The first line has the irregular beginning ∪ − ∪ ∪ −. See West, *Metre*, 125, for ionics beginning ∪ − − in late fifth-century lyric; a similar licence may have been allowed in anapaestic metra (see West, *Metre*, 139, 172, who compares the Berlin Paean, *GDK* 52). Alternatively, there may be some corruption or omission in l. 1. The acatalectic ending ∪ ∪ − (and thus its variant − −) is normally found only in lyric passages (e.g. E. *Hec.* 196, 215, Ar. *Ra.* 376). Melic anapaests are generally restricted to monodies in tragedy, and are particularly common in Euripides. See West, *Metre*, 121–2.

'And you, O heavenly Sun, who strike with your shining rays the eternal vault, send on (our) enemies a far-shot arrow from your string, ō iē Paiān!'

1. τὸν . . . πόλον †οὐράνιον†: this cannot mean 'the heavenly vault' (as Campbell has it) despite [A.] *Pr.* 429 οὐράνιόν . . . πόλον, E. fr. 839. 11 N², Limenius 8 (p. 93 Bélis = *CA* 149. 7) πᾶϲ δὲ . . . πόλοϲ οὐράνιοϲ: we should need τὸν πόλον τὸν οὐράνιον or τὸν οὐράνιον πόλον, neither of which can be restored here. Perhaps οὐράνιοϲ, used of the Sun (nominative for vocative is not unknown); the adjective would be appropriate. Holford-Strevens suggests Οὐρανίων, as a singular of Οὐρανίωνεϲ. Helios is the grandson of Ouranos in Hes. *Th.* 134–5, 371–2. Artemis and Apollo are the most glittering of the Οὐρανίωνεϲ at Th. 918–19. We may have here a conflation of ideas. For πόλοϲ of the sky, cf. fr. 803.

ἀεί: here functioning almost as an adjective; E. *Ph.* 1521 has τὸν ἀεὶ χρόνον 'for ever', 'all my time', and the same phrase occurs at *Or.* 207 ἐϲ τὸν αἰὲν . . . χρόνον 'for eternity', S. *Ai.* 342–3 τὸν εἰϲαεὶ | . . . χρόνον 'for ever' (adverbial). At Timocreon fr. 731. 3 διὰ ϲὲ γὰρ πάντ' αἰὲν ἀνθρώποιϲ κακά, it is possible we should see a similar force; thus not 'thanks to you (Wealth) men have all evils always' (Campbell), but perhaps 'all lasting evils'. At S. *OC* 1700–1 ὦ τὸν ἀεὶ κατὰ | γᾶϲ ϲκότον εἰμένοϲ, the sense must be 'the eternal darkness beneath the earth' (cf. Jebb ad loc.).

2. λαμπραῖϲ ἀκτῖϲ': 'with bright rays', instrumental

dative. A traditional combination, cf. e.g. *h. Hom.* 31. 10–11 (hymn to Helios) λαμπραὶ . . . ἀκτῖνες, and very common of the sun and stars in general (cf. e.g. Hes. *Th.* 19, 371, *Il.* 1. 605). The elision of datives plural like ἀκτῖcι is normally restricted to Homer and Hesiod (West, *Metre*, 10), but the metre here forbids the form ἀκτῖcιν. Timotheus may have been deliberately imitating the epic usage for stylistic reasons.

Ἥλιε: the earliest MSS (NP) are confused on the reading here, although it is clear that ηλιε should be the form behind them. However, it is uncertain whether we should restore ἄλιε with most editors (Bergk, Diehl, all following Schneidewin), on the assumption that such (originally Doric) quotations would be Atticized during the transmission of the text. I have preferred to print the form given in the MSS. ἠλίου is found at fr. 804, although again in quotation.

βάλλων: for the use of the verb in this context, cf. e.g. *Od.* 5. 479 ἠέλιος φαέθων ἀκτῖcιν ἔβαλλεν, E. *Suppl.* 650–1, *Tro.* 1069, and for the sun's rays as arrows, *Herc.* 1090 and of the moon at *Ion* 1155; see Diggle on E. *Phaethon* 3.

4. ἰὲ: ἴε 'shoot' (so Bergk, Page) is implied by Macrobius' discussion, since he is refuting the derivations from ἵεcθαι, ἰέναι. However, it is doubtful whether this is a genuine form of the imperative; the standard formation would be ἵει (e.g. *Il.* 21. 338, E. *El.* 593), and although -ιε is found in the codd. at Thgn. 1240 ξύνιε (from ξυνίημι), this is probably to be restored as ξυνίει with Buttmann. The ancient derivation of the ritual cry ἰέ from ἵημι is first attested in Hellenistic times; cf. e.g. Callim. *H.* 2. 97–104, who derives the cry from ἵει *(βέλος)*, with reference to Apollo's slaying of the serpent Pytho at Delphi; A.R. 2. 712; Douris, *FGrH* 76 F 79.

ἰέ frequently alternates with ἰή (from which it is probably derived) as an invocation of Apollo (cf. e.g. Pi. *Pae.* 2, 4 (frr. 52b, 52d); *PMG* carm. pop. 867, adesp. 934; Isyllus, *CA* 133. 37, 61, 58; Macedonius, *CA* 139. 19, 22, 30, 140. 32 etc.; for a full list see L. Käppel, *Paian: Studien zur Geschichte einer Gattung* (Berlin and New York, 1992), 66–7).

801. Plutarch's anecdote may suggest an encomium to Archelaus, but there is no guarantee that this is so. It is hard to imagine a plausible encomiastic context for the line, and it may have belonged instead to a narrative poem; the ancient desire for biographical detail, and tendency to read such details into the text, may have encouraged the invention of the story.

Metre

$$\cup\cup--\cup\cup--\cup\cup--\mid \qquad\qquad 3io\mid$$

τόν: oddly specific, but we can only guess at reasons for the article.

γηγενέταν: 'earth-born', a variant for γηγενής (as εὐγενέτας for εὐγενής at *P*. 206), and probably first in Euripides at *Ion* 1466, *Ph.* 128 γίγαντι γηγενέται. The idea that metals are born from the earth is found at e.g. *Il.* 2. 857 ἐξ Ἀλύβης ὅθι τ' ἀργύρου ἐςτὶ γενέθλη, [Hes.] fr. 287, [A.] *Pr.* 301 etc. See West on Hes. *Th.* 161.

802. Perhaps from the conclusion of a nome (so Wilamowitz 65); see *P*. 202–36 n. The use of Timotheus' own name, in the vocative in the first verse, and in the nominative (as part of the herald's speech) in the second, is reminiscent of the use of the third person in the sphragis of the *Persae* (cf. *P*. 229 ff.). The phrasing, νικᾶι X (nom.) Y (acc.), may have been a formulaic way of announcing a victory, but parallels are wanting.

Metre

$$\cup\cup\cup-\cup-\cup\cup\cup--\mid \qquad\qquad 2ia\ ba\mid$$
$$-\cup---\cup\cup-\mid \qquad\qquad gl\ (\text{'cho. dim.'})\mid$$
$$--\cup--\cup--\cup\cup-\cup--\mid \qquad\qquad ia\ cr\ ch\ ba\mid$$

Wilamowitz (65 n. 2) assumed a lacuna at the beginning of the fragment, and analysed the first line as *2ia cr* (or *ba*) *ba*, reading Τιμόθεος with Hartung and substituting εὖτε. This form is not, however, attested for Timotheus, and therefore the MSS reading ὅτε is probably to be preferred. However, if Τιμόθεε as given by the MSS is elided with ὅτε (for elision of final epsilon, see West, *Metre*, 10), the first line easily admits analysis. The herald's proclamation of victory is also referred to in Euripides' epinician for Alcibiades (*PMG* 755, where Alcibiades is said to κάρυκι βοὰν παραδοῦναι by his victory).

1. **μακάριοc**: 'blessed, an object of admiration'; generally of mortals (μάκαρ is usually the equivalent adjective when referring to gods), and here with the connotation 'successful (because of achievement)' as at e.g. E. *Herc.* 1291, *Ba.* 1242, [E.] *Rh.* 196. In Attic Greek of the fifth century it occurs only in Euripides and Aristophanes. See C. de Heer, *μάκαρ–εὐδαίμων–ὄλβιοc–εὐτυχής* (Amsterdam, 1969), 56 ff., 83 ff.; M. McDonald, *Terms for Happiness in Euripides* (Göttingen, 1978), 276.

3. **Μιλήcιοc**: cf. the reference to his native city also in the sphragis at *P.* 234–6. An ethnic might be expected in a herald's announcement. More complicated ways of denoting origin abound in epinicians, often appearing at the first mention of the victor: cf. e.g. Pi. *O.* 1. 11–13, 2. 5–6, 3. 2–3, 4. 10–12, 5. 3–4, Ba. 2. 3–5, 3. 1–4. The victor obviously brought honour to his city by his victory, but it is possible that this emphasis on naming honorand and home-state together at the start of a poem also reflects public victory announcements.

τὸν Κάμωνοc:'the son of Camon', Phrynis, whose father's name is given as Camon by Pollux 4. 66. Adler's edition of the *Suda*, φ 761 (iv. 766) gives it as Canops, but Camon would there be a better correction of the MSS reading κάρβωνοc. Phrynis was perhaps so well known that a patronymic would have been sufficient to identify him in the context, though in an actual announcement we should expect to hear his name. See West, *Music*, 360–1.

ἰωνοκάμπταν: 'the Ionian-bender'. The first term can only be objective, 'one who bends Ionian melodies' (so West, *Music*, 361 n. 20; 182), not 'one who bends in the Ionian mode', which would require ἰαcτι-. Ionian melodies are indecent ones (Ar. *Thesm.* 163, *Eccl.* 883; Hor. *Carm.* 3. 6. 21); Phrynis is twisting and turning and bending over backwards in his music in an Ionian manner. He was accused of making music more effeminate (above, p. 34). That he was in fact an Aeolian from Mytilene (cf. Σ Ar. *Nub.* 969 ff.; Procl. *Chrest.* ap. Phot. *Bibl.* 320ᵇ8) is neither here nor there: at *Thesm.* 161–3 the three who ἐμιτροφόρουν τε καὶ διεκλῶντ' in the effeminate Ionian manner (Ἰωνικῶc) are the Ionian Anacreon, the Aeolian Alcaeus, and the Dorian Ibycus.

Phrynis' καμπαί are mentioned by Aristophanes at *Nub.*
969 ff.: εἰ δέ τις αὐτῶν βωμολοχεύcαιτ' ἢ κάμψειέν τινα καμπὴν |
οἵας οἱ νῦν, τὰς κατὰ Φρῦνιν ταύτας τὰς δυσκολοκάμπτους, |
ἐπετρίβετο τυπτόμενος πολλὰς ὡς τὰς Μούσας ἀφανίζων, and
Pherecrates (155. 26 K.–A.) uses the phrase ἐξαρμονίους
καμπάς, probably of Timotheus' own musical innovations.
A similar phrase is used of Agathon, another poet associated
with musical innovation (Ar. *Thesm.* 53). For the musical
sense of the word, see West, *Music*, 356 (and n. 2): 'They
[i.e. καμπαί] are associated with departure from the *harmonia*, the proper attunement, and it seems likely that they are
the same as what are later called *metabolai*, i.e. modulations'.

803. Artemis was not a moon goddess until the fifth century,
and her connection with child-birth probably developed at
about the same time (Farnell ii. 456–60). Despite the subject
there is little reason to believe with Bergk that the fragment
should be ascribed to the *Artemis*: the Ephesian Artemis
does not seem to have been particularly closely identified
with Artemis Locheia or Eileithyia. Wilamowitz (114)
correctly comments: 'Mit dem Artemishymnus hat das
nichts zu tun; es heißt nur "durch die Nacht bei Voll-
mond"'.

Metre

ᴗᴗ–ᴗᴗ–ᴗᴗ– – ‖   2anʌ ‖
ᴗᴗ–ᴗᴗ–ᴗᴗ– – ‖   2anʌ ‖

Two regular paroemiacs; the paroemiac is a well-established unit
in Greek metrics. It may have developed as a marching rhythm
(West, *Metre*, 53), but is unlikely to have been so here, unless we
are to imagine the fragment as coming from a prosodion.

1. κυάνεον πόλον ἄστρων: 'the dark vault of the stars'; for
the use of πόλος in this sense, see fr. 800. 1 n., and cf. esp. E.
Or. 1685 λαμπρῶν ἄστρων πόλον, which is probably responsible for the substitution of λαμπρὸν in Macrobius. The
accusative after διά, in the sense 'through', is restricted to
poetry (e.g. Homer, Hesiod, Pindar, and tragic lyric): see
Kühner–Gerth i. 483–4.
2. ὠκυτόκοιο: a fifth-century neologism, perhaps from
medical writing. As a substantive, τὸ ὠκύτοκον 'swift, easy

birth' at Hdt. 4. 35, but also τὰ ὠκυτόκια, drugs or charms to promote this, at Ar. *Thesm.* 504 and in medical writers (e.g. Hp. *Gynaec.* 1. 77). However, the active ὠκυτόκος is also adjectival at S. *OC* 689 ὠκυτόκος *(*sc. ὁ Κηφιсός*)* πεδίων ἐπινίсεται, 'giving an early reward to the cultivator's labour' (Jebb) or 'giving quick increase' (LSJ).

сελάναс: the genitive could stand after πόλον, thus 'through the vault of the stars, and through [that] of the moon', or an accusative could be missing from the start of the next line. διά with the genitive is common, but 'through the moon . . .' is in any case nonsensical.

804. For the whole phrase, cf. Mimn. fr. 2. 2 ὅτ᾽ αἶψ᾽ αὐγῆιс αὔξεται ἠελίου, which Timotheus may well be directly imitating (although Mimnermus is speaking of leaves, φύλλα, and a quite different sense should be given to the line). The view that the moon was illumined by the sun, rather than possessed of its own light, appears to originate with Parmenides (fr. 14 Coxon, and esp. fr. 15 αἰεὶ παπταίνουсα πρὸс αὐγὰс ἠελίοιο of the moon; cf. T 70–1 Coxon), or possibly Empedocles (cf. fr. 38 Wright ὡс αὐγὴ τύψαса сεληναίηс κύκλον εὐρύν). The same view is later found in Anaxagoras (DK 59 A 76). Aetius (2. 28. 5) attributes the theory to Thales, but this seems unlikely to be correct. See further T. Heath, *Aristarchus of Samos* (Oxford, 1913), 78 ff.; D. O'Brien, *JHS* 88 (1968), 93–127; W. K. C. Guthrie, *A History of Greek Philosophy* (Cambridge, 1962–81), i. 93 ff., ii. 303–4. Bergk assigns the fragment to the *Artemis*, while Meineke connects it with fr. 803 and suggests inserting a line between the two, e.g. [φάος αἰθέριον, πυρόεντος]. Both suggestions are purely speculative.

αὔξεται: see *P.* 202 n.

804A. This new fragment is quoted in Philodemus, *On Poems* by Pausimachus (who mentions Timotheus as a good poet at col. 83. 21). The precise sense of the line is unclear. I quote Janko in his new edition (290 n. 2): 'A. H. Griffiths suggests that this new fr. is from a lost scene early in his *Persae*, where Xerxes reverenced a noble plane-tree near Callatebus on his way to the Hellespont (Hdt. 7. 31) . . . The unreliable Ptolemy Hephaestionis says he sat under a golden plane-tree to view the battle of Salamis (Phot. *Bibl.* cod. 190, 148^b8 Bekker).' I doubt whether the *Persae* was long enough to include Xerxes' journey to the Hellespont, and there is no mention of Ptolemy's plane-tree in the extant portions.

⟨ ⟩]νον: Janko suggests ⟨cεμ⟩νόν. If this is correct, then neither the instance here nor c[εμ]νόν later can agree with πλάτανος; it cannot be the plane-tree that is holy, but something outside the quotation. The line is clearly incomplete, and may in any case be corrupt.

πλάτανος: elsewhere the word is always feminine, so the use of the masculine here 'must be metrically motivated' (Janko). With Janko's supplements, the line scans ‒‒◡◡◡‒‒‒. But such metrical motivations could be considered unusual given the licence shown by Timotheus in *Persae*.

INDEX LOCORUM

GENERAL INDEX

CPSIA information can be obtained
at www.ICGtesting.com
Printed in the USA
LVOW11*1433130117
520894LV00007B/45/P